nds Obygder,

seu

TA GRONLANDIÆ.

*tu hoc Gronlandiæ veteres Sualbarda app. llabant, quavis latus vel marginem
*igi um spectat, totus hic tractus montibus abundat editissimis perpetua nive tectis
ore autem glacies continuè adhæret.

Insula
Johannis M

MARE CRONIUM vel GLA

Kolbeins ey

Ægirsland

Ægirsey

POLARIS

ARC

Grimsey

Horn

Westfirdin

IS LAN DIA

Nordlendinga Fior

Dunger

Sund lendinga

Aus fird nga

Fiordungur

Hekla

Thingvöllur

Ingolshofde

Geirfugla Sker

Grindavik

Westmanöy

Portland

Urbium aqvarum	
Nomenclatura	
Antiqva	Moderna
Akurkus castrum	Agerhus
Baghus castrum	Baghus
Biorgvin urbs	Bergen
Duney Insula	Dünöe
Fiarda fielki	Fiordelan
Folliar fiordur	Oslofiorden
Gaulardalur	Guledalen
Gaudölafielki	Guledals la
Gudbrandsdalur	Gudbrands
Halogaland	Helligland
Halägiu fielki	Halleland
Ikorna Sund	Eckersund
Lidandis næs	Lindesnes
Malströnd Insula	Mönkran
Naumdala filki	Numedal
Nidarös urbs	Trondhien

Hanc Insulam Hispani
Anno 1613 o: viam habuerunt.

Fareyar
vulgo
Faro

CEANUS DEUCALEDO

NIUS

Hiatland

Forhill

Orkneyar

Petlands Fiordur

Woven into the Earth

For Ib

Woven into the Earth

Textiles from Norse Greenland

By Else Østergård

Aarhus University Press

WOVEN INTO THE EARTH

Copyright: Else Østergård and Aarhus University Press 2004

2nd edition 2009

Cover: Jørgen Sparre

Photo: Hans Kapel, Herjolfsnæs

Map (p. 14) Copyright: Kort- og Matrikelstyrelsen (A.39-03)

Graphic design: Jørgen Sparre

Typeface: Sabon

Paper: Arctic Volume

Printed in Denmark by Narayana Press, Gylling.

ISBN 978 87 7288 935 1

The book is published with the financial support of:

The Beckett-Fonden

The Research Council for the Humanities

Folketingets Grønlandsfond

Engineer Ernst B. Sund's Fond

Landsdommer V. Gieses Legat

Lillian and Dan Fink's Fond

Letterstedtska Föreningen

VELUX FONDEN

AARHUS UNIVERSITY PRESS

Langelandsgade 177

8200 Aarhus N

Denmark

Fax (+45) 8942 5380

www.unipress.dk

73 Lime Walk

Headington, Oxford OX3 7AD

United Kingdom

Fax (+ 44) 1865 750 079

Box 511

Oakville, Conn. 06779

USA

Fax (+ 1) 860 945 9468

Preface

In 1921, in agreement with the Commission for the Management of Geological and Geographical Research in Greenland, the National Museum in Copenhagen undertook the task of conducting archaeological research into Norse settlements in Greenland. One of the Museum's younger curators, Poul Nørlund, left the very same summer for Ikigaat, which should, according to written sources, be identical to the Norse settlers' *Herjolfsnæs*. The place was not chosen by chance. Already from the beginning of the 1830s the remains of wooden coffins, garments, small wooden crosses and skeleton parts had been found at regular intervals along the coast at Ikigaat. The finds had emanated from the churchyard, the south side of which was well on the way to being engulfed by the fjord.

The results of Poul Nørlund's archaeological excavations at Ikigaat were to resound throughout the world. The unique finds of well-preserved garment parts from the Middle Ages, which Nørlund and his colleagues had excavated from the churchyard under very difficult working conditions, were the reason for all this attention. Instead of being buried in coffins, many dead were wrapped in cast-off clothes. This enabled garments for adults and children, hoods and skullcaps, liripipe hoods and stockings, hitherto known only from West European medieval depictions, to be brought to Denmark, and the well-preserved garments belong today to the National Museum's most treasured possessions.

With remarkable speed Nørlund had the Herjolfsnæs garment finds published in 'Meddelelser om Grønland'. Each individual garment part was documented according to its appearance after final restoration. Dating was undertaken on the basis of contemporary picture accounts. To this very day – more than 80 years after they were found – the Herjolfsnæs garments and Poul Nørlund's publication are still frequently referred to in the archaeological literature, and it is precisely for this reason that this new book on the Herjolfsnæs garments was considered necessary.

Much has happened with methods of preservation and examination of textiles during the foregoing 80 years. The book not only uncovers new technical conquests, meaning that we are presented with detailed information on the raw materials and how they were dealt with from the first phase in the production process, where the wool was collected, through to the point where a garment could be sewn from the woven piece of cloth. Continuous preservation and day-to-day contact with the garments has revealed some hitherto unnoticed and refined details in both the weaving and sewing techniques of the Norse women. One cannot help being truly amazed by their ability, especially when one considers the conditions under which they worked.

Cloth was produced from Greenlandic materials and in Norse Greenlandic tradition, but the cut of the garments also shows quite clearly that they were not without outside influence. In a wonderful way the Herjolfsnæs garments reflect that although Norse Greenlanders lived so far away the place was described by some as the 'End of the Earth', the Norse settlers considered themselves to be part of medieval Western Europe. In the same way the garments are also an important monument to Western European medieval dress culture.

Jette Arneborg
SILA – The National Museum's Center for Greenlandic Research
March 2004

Author's Preface

In 1994 the National Museums of Copenhagen and Nuuk worked out a research programme entitled 'Man, Culture and Environment in Ancient Greenland', which aimed at throwing light on developments in arctic hunter cultures as well as in the Norse peasant culture: their mutual relations and their changing resource basis. The programme was to cover the long time-span from the earliest Stone Age culture, through the Eskimo Thule culture, to the Norse peasant culture in the southern part of West Greenland. It was an interdisciplinary project, which included not only archaeology and the natural sciences, but also history – especially Norse.

Climatic changes that had a considerable impact on resources changed the pattern of new immigration and settlement. Analyses of old as well as new finds that emerged during the project's development from 1995 and onwards were of great importance. Examinations of textiles established connections to the North American continent and to Europe, in that they revealed not only the origin of the materials and techniques, but also the influence of new ideas.

Examinations of Norse textiles have provided exiting as well as unexpected results.

The project was predominantly financed by the Danish Research Council, although financial support to the other scientists from Iceland and Canada, as well as England and USA who participated in the project was provided by funds raised in their own countries.

This book is the result of many years' examination of the textiles from the archaeological excavations in Greenland. The find of the clothing at the Herjolfsnæs church ruins in 1921 meant that all later excavations were eagerly awaited in the hope that yet another such spectacular find was possible. However, many of the textile fragments and tools which actually emerged also deserve attention, as they provide an excellent supplementation to the clothing and add to our knowledge and understanding of the Norse Greenlanders skills and craftsmanship.

In my work I have enjoyed the support and good will of many people. I especially wish to express gratitude to my advisor Jette Arneborg Ph.D., M.A., who was most helpful when I was in doubt about certain aspects of Norse life, and to the weaver Anna Nørgård, who patiently listened and provided good advice in questions of textile technology and who, through reconstruction, verified my measurements of the costumes.

Thanks to my colleague Irene Skals, who so skilfully translated my registration of stitch types into useful drawings. I am indebted also to textile engineer Joy Boutrup for her assistance in drawing up schemes and translating Penelope Walton Rogers' chapter into Danish.

My colleagues from the Conservation Department's textile workshop deserve thanks for their enduring patience throughout many years of work. This gratitude is also extended to textile and costume scientist Elsa E. Gudjonsson, M.A., Dr. Phil. h.c., in Iceland.

I also owe my sincere thanks to my colleagues at Greenland's National Museum and Archives in Nuuk, the Museums in Nanortalik, Narsaq, Qaqortoq and SILA, the Greenland Research Center at the National Museum in Copenhagen.

A special thanks to archaeologist Penelope Walton Rogers, leader of Textile Research in York, England, for inspiring cooperation throughout many years. Penelope's analyses of Norse wool and her revelation of the original colours of costumes were always awaited with great anticipation. I am deeply indebted to her also for invaluable help with the English technical terms. The results are now at hand in this book.

For financial support to the research programme and the production and publishing of Woven into the Earth, I wish to thank the following:

Augustinus Fonden
Beckett-Fonden
Dronning Margrethe II's Arkæologiske Fond
Folketingets Grønlandsfond
Illum-Fonden
Knud Højgaards Fond
Kulturfonden Danmark-Grønland
Kulturministeriets Forskningsfond
Lillian og Dan Finks Fond
Manufakturhandlerforeningen i København
The Danish Research Council for the Humanities
The National Museum of Denmark
The Royal Greenland Foundation
The State Antiquary, National Museum of Denmark
Stiftelsen Agnes Geijers fond för nordisk textilforskning
Torben og Alice Frimodts Fond
VELUX FONDEN

Else Østergård
June 2004

Contents

Introduction

Like a giant deep-freeze, the Greenland soil has preserved a unique cultural heritage, locked in the permafrost for centuries; for short periods, however, the topsoil thawed so much that crowberry and dwarf willow could grow. The roots of these plants grew like thin strands through the coffins and costumes and in 1924 this prompted Poul Nørlund to write that they had literally 'stitched' the finds to the soil.[1]

They came to a country that was green. They called it Greenland. This is the beautiful account in the *Grænlendinga saga* of how Greenland got its name.[2] That was in the Viking Age, at the end of the 900s. Tempting green expanses in the southwestern part of Greenland encouraged exiled Icelanders to go ashore. Iceland had been colonized a century earlier by Norwegians who had to flee from their homeland because of hostilities.

After a few decades Iceland had become overpopulated and the tillable land had been exhausted, with famine as the result. Some of the adventurous and discontented men sailed out, therefore, to find new pastures.

In Greenland they found what they were looking for. They 'took land', the so-called landnáma, and founded the Norse settlements – the Eastern Settlement, the Western Settlement and later the Middle Settlement. Their descendants, later called the Norse Greenlanders, lived there for just under five hundred years.

The best known of these landnáma men is Eric the Red, who gave his name to Eiriksfjord, the present-day Tunulliarfik Fjord.

Another of the discontented men who followed Eric the Red was Herjolf Bårdson. But unlike the others, who settled the inner fjords, Herjolf chose to place his farm in the outermost part of the fjord with its magnificent view of the sea. He gave the farm on the headland or 'ness' his own name. The location of Herjolfsnæs (Ø111),[3] the present-day Ikigaat, was to prove well chosen, since over the next few centuries the settlement became a port-of-call for seafarers from many lands.[4]

The King's Mirror, a didactic Norwegian work from the thirteenth century, says: 'Few are the people in that land, for only little of it is so ice-free that it is habitable, but the people are Christian and they have churches and priests'.[5]

In other medieval documents and in the saga literature too we can read about the Norse Greenlanders. Archaeological excavations can confirm that many of the events of the sagas did happen. A topographical account from the 1300s tells us that in the settlements there were some 300 farms, two monasteries/convents and 16 churches, including a cathedral at the bishop's seat, Gardar (Ø47).[6] Later much has been written about the Norse Greenlanders, while they themselves left many runic

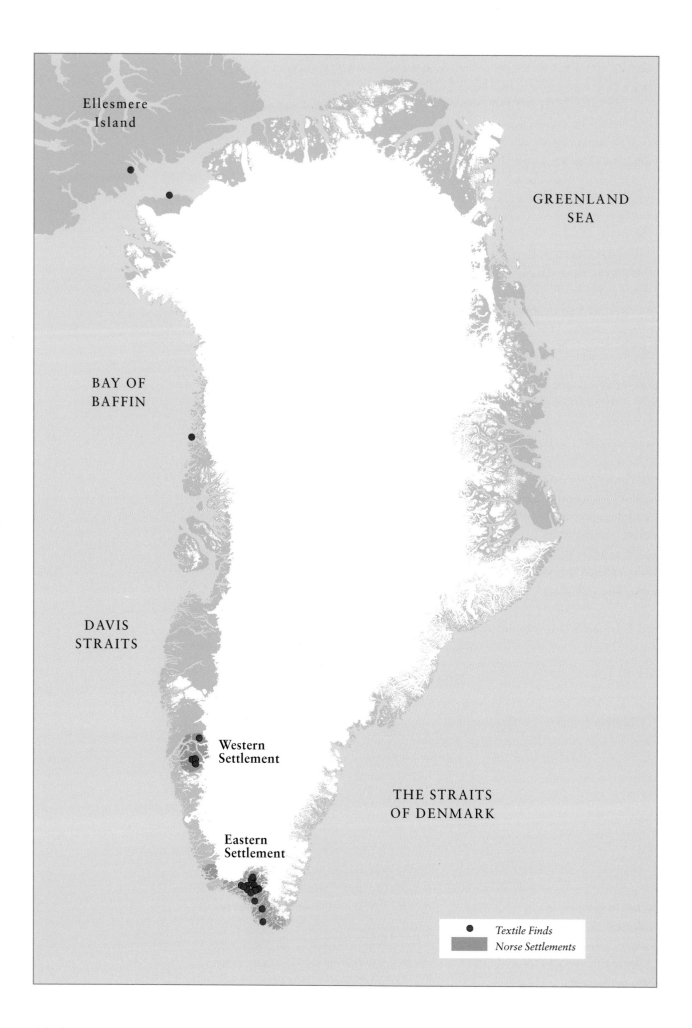

Ellesmere
Island

GREENLAND
SEA

BAY OF
BAFFIN

DAVIS
STRAITS

Western
Settlement

THE STRAITS
OF DENMARK

Eastern
Settlement

●   *Textile Finds*

   Norse Settlements

and rune-like inscriptions, carved on grave crosses, sticks and textile-working implements.

The deterioration of the living conditions of the Norse Greenlanders began as early as the mid-1200s, caused by the 'the Little Ice Age', which resulted in the green fields becoming fewer. A long chain reaction of famine and death for animals and humans had begun. Life-threatening epidemics and conflict with the Inuit, the immigrant Eskimos from Canada, were other threats. Many theories have been proposed to explain the disappearance of the Norse Greenlanders, and scientific evidence can explain much, but we do not know the full truth about the Norsemen's farewell to Greenland.

In these North Atlantic waters sailing ships were often blown off course and wrecked off the icy Greenlandic coasts. On their return, surviving travellers could tell fantastic stories about the dangerous voyages; in fact it was colourful accounts such as these that had sent Eric the Red to explore Greenland in 981.

For centuries the many historical statements about the life of the Norse Greenlanders and perhaps especially about their mysterious disappearance in the 1400s have continued to fascinate people of all nationalities. For people in Bergen, the Norwegian gateway to Greenland, and in their home country of Iceland, however, the Norse population of Greenland remained a living tradition for several hundred years.

When the Norwegian pastor Hans Egede went to Greenland in 1721 it was to seek out 'our old Norwegian Christians', descendants of the Norse Greenlanders. It was the fear that any who were left had become heathens that prompted him to travel there. He found no Norsemen, but he founded the first colony on the west coast of Greenland and called it Godthaab (Good Hope). Later he was given the name 'the Apostle of Greenland'.

Over the next few centuries voyages to Greenland became more frequent, but true archaeological investigations in the Norse settlements, conducted by people sent out from Denmark, only began in the nineteenth century.

< Fig. 1.
Kalaallit nunaat is the Green-
landic name for Greenland.
It means our land, the land that
belongs to the people who call
themselves kalaallit.

*Istprøven eller Ingeit
og Sletten med Ruinerne af det gamle Herjolfsnæs i Grønland,
ved H. Rink. September 1853.*

*Fig. 2.
Herjolfsnæs in 1853, drawn by
the geologist and Greenland
researcher, Hinrich Johannes
Rink (1819-1893). Fourteen
years earlier the first Herjolfsnæs
garment had been found on the
strand below the church ruins.*

Finds of Norse Textiles in Greenland

The first known textile find is from 1839, when the trading clerk Ove Kielsen, in a letter to the Royal Nordic Society for Ancient Manuscripts in Copenhagen, writes that a boat and some pieces of clothing had appeared after the sea had washed away a large part of the coast below the Herjolfsnæs church ruin. Kielsen thought that the garment was a jacket and that it had belonged to a drowned sailor.[1]

Over the next few decades the National Museum in Copenhagen occasionally received reports that human bones, coffin remains and small crosses and pieces of clothing had been found on the coast at Herjolfsnæs.

In 1920 what had now become many reports from Greenland prompted the Commission for Geological and Geographical Investigations in Greenland, in collaboration with the National Museum, to resume excavations at the Herjolfsnæs church ruin, before the ruin and churchyard completely disappeared into the sea.

Poul Nørlund, the later director of the National Museum, was appointed as leader of the excavation and in May 1921 he travelled to Greenland. Because of the frost, the digging work could only begin in July. After a few days' work the first coffin and a wooden cross saw the light, and on 11th July the first garment was pulled out of the mud.[2] This began what was to be the biggest event in the study of ancient textiles in Europe in the twentieth century: the find of the Herjolfsnæs costumes. In all, some 70 pieces of textile were dug up, including body garments, hoods, caps and stockings; everyday clothing from the Middle Ages, which had been used for the last time as grave clothes and shrouds for want of coffins.

After Poul Nørlund's great costume find, many archaeologists, not surprisingly, expected to find other textiles in excavations of Norse ruins. So far, there have been only a few fragments, although many textile-working implements have emerged.

At the bishop's seat of Gardar (Ø47), present-day Igaliku, near Sandnæs (V51) and at the farm (V52a) in Austmannadalen, finds include many textile-working implements, but very few textile fragments. At the *Landnáma* Farm (Ø17a) at Narsaq, textile fragments in various colours as well as textile-working implements have been dug up. Remains of Norse clothing have also appeared from excavations of Inuit settlements up along the west coast of Greenland and on Ellesmere Island (see The Textile Finds from Greenland – Overview, pp. 32-35).

The latest major investigation in Greenland is the excavation of 'The Farm Beneath the Sand', or 'Gården Under Sandet', also called GUS (64V2-III-555), which began in 1991. For this excavation we can thank two alert Greenlandic caribou hunters who, on a trip up the Ameralla fjord, east of Nuuk and close to the inland ice, saw some large pieces of wood sticking out of the sand bank. Since Greenland is a country with few trees, the sight of large pieces of wood is not an everyday occurrence. Large tree trunks normally come as driftwood from the rivers in Siberia to the east or from the Mackenzie River in northern Canada. The caribou hunters reported their find to the Greenland National Museum and Archives in Nuuk, which then, in

Fig. 3.

The 'Farm Beneath the Sand' in Vesterbygden (Western settlement) was excavated through six summers from 1992 to 1997, with a digging season of four weeks each year. In the end, the archaeologists had to abandon the task. The river inundated the ruins.

collaboration with the National Museum in Copenhagen, initiated a dig that was to prove both difficult and costly. The farm lay buried below one and a half metres of sand, and with the ice-cold meltwater from the nearby glacier pouring past, the task was hard going and not without risk.

The digging went on for six summers. Every summer, when the archaeologists returned, the abandoned excavation field had silted up again, and much precious time was spent shovelling the sand away. But the meltwater too created problems, and after the excavation of the sixth summer it had to be abandoned.[3] The river now overflowed the ruins of the large farm complex, where the oldest building was a longhouse from the eleventh century.

Fortunately the archaeologists – despite the difficult working conditions – had been able to wrench from the Greenlandic soil a large quantity of everyday utility objects and important archaeological facts about building construction, which add new pieces to the large puzzle of the lives of the Norse settlers in Greenland. The first room that was excavated at GUS was given the name Room I (Room XIII on the excavation plans) with the addition 'the Weaving Room', and it was soon to prove the most interesting room from the point of view of textile history. This was the location of the large pieces of wood that had attracted the attention of the caribou hunters, and which turned out to be parts of a warp-weighted loom.[4] And when the rooms beside this were excavated, one could see that the floor level of the weaving room was about half a metre below that of the other rooms. The fact that the floor of the weaving room was sunken like this probably means that there was a need for greater room height for the sake of the loom. In the weaving room many loom weights, various textile implements and several hundred textile fragments were also found.

1. Exhibitions of Norse textiles

After the costumes from Herjolfsnæs had come to Copenhagen in 1921 they were cleaned and described. They were also repaired so that they could be exhibited. Nørlund wrote a few years later: 'Pressed together in a murky corner cabinet of the National Museum there is now a display of the old costumes that form the most valuable part of the find from Herjolfsnæs …'.[5]

Although the costumes were not given a very prominent place in the museum displays, they were still something that people came from far and near to see. Here one could recognize everyday clothes from the Middle Ages, of the kind seen in the murals of the Danish churches, but unparalleled anywhere else in Europe. Pictures and drawings of the Herjolfsnæs costumes were used as illustrations in innumerable publications about medieval clothing. This has meant that over the years very many people – 'ordinary' people as well as experts – have wanted more (and more specific) information about the Norse clothing.

My own fascination with the clothes began when the National Museum in Copenhagen was preparing the exhibition 'Clothes Make the Man', which was held in 1971 at the Museum's department in Brede. The Museum's textile conservation department was also deeply involved and in that connection there were thoughts of moving some of the Herjolfsnæs costumes to Brede, but this idea was abandoned since it was feared that the changeable climate in the then relatively primitive exhibition rooms in Brede might damage the textiles. The conservators were thus asked to create reconstructions, which could be shown instead of the original costumes. The close contact with the costumes – quite literally – meant that I discovered in them a kind of textile processing that I had not seen before. I wondered how people could still have the energy to make such fine products, living as they did in such primitive conditions in a very harsh climate.

Ten years later I was again to work with the costumes, this time in connection with the rebuilding of the Danish Middle Ages Department at the National Museum. The costumes were taken out of the old display cases and sent to Brede. By that time they had been exhibited for more than fifty years, and this had caused visible damage. The effects of both daylight and artificial light had caused an acceleration in the decomposition of the wool fibres.

New display cases with limited light access were made, and after conservation some of the costumes could again be exhibited. However, it had been necessary to shorten the length of the exhibition, as many of the costumes could not withstand the strain of hanging for a longer term on the exhibition dummies. On the other hand, for the purpose of major special exhibitions, they can be shown in a new, less damaging way.

2. Exhibitions in Greenland

With the development of the museums in Greenland came a wish to illustrate the various cultures of the country, including the Norse one, by showing some costumes from the Norse period. Over the years a number of costumes have therefore been made for exhibition use. In 1984 collaboration began between the Danish and Greenlandic National Museums. The aim was to return parts of the Danish National Museum's Greenland collection to Greenland with a view to research and making a presentation of Greenland's past. A large Inuit collection has already been moved back, and the Norse objects will soon follow. Since the original costumes can hardly survive being displayed, either in Denmark or in Greenland, it has been decided that reconstructions are to be made. So that these reconstructions can be as authentic as possible, a number of requirements have been laid down which state that the original material must be investigated as thoroughly as is possible today. This means that colours and fibres are analysed, seams are examined and cuts measured, and against the background of the results of these investigations new costumes will be reconstructed.

3. Results of earlier analyses of Norse textiles

In the 1920s Poul Nørlund used the great costume find from Herjolfsnæs for costume studies. He dated the depopulation of the Eastern Settlement to the latter half of the fifteenth century on the basis of the so-called 'Burgundian cap' (D10612). For the first time it was now possible to show real costumes completely corresponding to those known from illustrations of the Middle Ages.

The Herjolfsnæs costumes also became important reference material for textile finds in Europe. The three Danish medieval costumes from Kragelund, Moselund and Rønbjerg, as well as the Swedish costume from Bocksten, and the northern Norwegian costume from Skjoldehamn were all dated in the mid-twentieth century on the basis of the costumes from Herjolfsnæs.[6] On the other hand Nørlund had less to say about the technology – the weaving of the cloth and the making of the clothing.

Finds of textile fragments in recent years, especially from Narsaq (Ø17a) and from the Farm Beneath the Sand (64V2-III-555) can now add to our knowledge of the clothing of the Middle Ages and the textile tradition of the Norse Greenlanders. With better investigative methods, including radiocarbon dating, much new information has emerged, not only about the Herjolfsnæs costumes, but also about the inventiveness of the Norse settlers in the use of Greenlandic raw materials.

With an overview of all Greenlandic textile finds from the Norse period we can draw conclusions about the textile knowledge that the Norse Greenlanders kept alive for centuries despite the difficult external circumstances.

4. Man, Culture and Environment in Ancient Greenland

In 1995 a Danish-Greenlandic research programme, Man, Culture and Environment in Ancient Greenland, began as an interdisciplinary project with participants from several countries. An attempt is being made with this project to elucidate the interrelations between Greenland's various cultures, and against this background to explain the cultural and social changes in the Eskimo and European communities in Greenland.

A natural part of this research project is the study of the clothing of the Norse Greenlanders, with which I have the pleasure to work.

With the clothes of the Norse settlers we have the chance to obtain a close, detailed knowledge of the women's craft skills. Clothing is close to the body. It carries an impression and bears many secrets about the life conditions of the user.

It is my hope that the reader will be able to share my enthusiasm for the Norse Greenlanders and at the same time learn many new facts about their sewing and weaving; perhaps also to reflect on the Norsewomen's living conditions or position in society, since these aspects could be expressed in such textile skills.

The Excavations

In Greenland more than 400 farms of varying sizes and 21 churches have been registered; of these, about twenty farms and eight churches have been excavated. The oldest excavated church is the small so-called 'Tjodhilde's Church' from the eleventh century. It was built at Eric the Red's farm Brattahlid and named after his wife. Two of the churches probably belonged to a convent and a monastery.

A large Norse farm would have a related church, as at Brattahlid. The Greenlandic churches were not large in comparison with other churches in the North Atlantic area, and the furnishings would have been modest. The few carved wooden crucifixes and some of the furniture in the farms show that people mastered the art of carving in wood or in the local soapstone (steatite), but it is not possible to see from which workshop or environment outside Greenland the inspiration came. Of church furnishings only a few fragments have been found.

1. Herjolfsnæs (Ø111)

Herjolfsnæs, the present-day Ikigaat in the south-westernmost part of Greenland, lies in a very beautiful area surrounded by high, steep mountains. It was the Inuit who called Herjolfsnæs Ikigaat, 'the place that was destroyed by fire'. Herjolfsnæs Church is mentioned in the *Flatey Book* as the first of twelve churches in the Norse Eastern Settlement. *Guðmundar saga biskups Arasonar* speaks of a burial at the church as early as the twelfth century,[1] and from the mid-fourteenth century the Norwegian Ivar Baardson says that Herjolfsnæs was a 'well known harbour for Norwegians and other traders'. When Herjolfsnæs was abandoned we do not know, but there are radiocarbon dates leading up to the mid-fifteenth century. There is also dating for the clothing.

The churchyard rediscovered

The churchyard was rediscovered in 1830, when the missionary De Fries found a tombstone with a carved majuscule inscription saying that Hroar Kolgrimsson was buried there. The stone had been used as a door lintel in an Eskimo hut. A few years later, when Ove Kielsen visited Herjolfsnæs, he found – besides the so-called sailor's jacket (D5674) – parts of a tombstone, also in granite and with an inscription that could be dated to the thirteenth century. What was thought to be a boat turned out to be planks from a coffin.

In 1839 Kielsen returned, and the next year, with the help of 24 men, he excavated the church ruin and turned over the churchyard without finding anything but a wooden cross and a skull with fair hair, which confirmed that the burial site was Norse; but beyond this Kielsen's excavation was not a success.

Later the Greenland researcher H.J. Rink dug at the churchyard and could afterwards write: 'The coffins are still partly preserved, as are the old burial clothes of vaðmál, some of which could be taken out intact'.[2] Other fragments of clothing that were collected, which the finder thought were the remains of a monk's cowl, were sent in to the National Museum in 1860.

Twenty years later Commander Gustav Holm dug at the churchyard and found skeletons buried in clothing.

The next textile find was from 1900, when the district medical officer Gustav Meldorf from Julianehåb had been blown ashore at Herjolfsnæs while on an official voyage. He noticed that in the collapsing banks by the church ruin one could see some human bones and 'some coarsely woven cloth of a dark brown colour project-ing but stuck in the sand'.[3] Because of the strong wind he had to extend his visit by 24 hours and he made use of the involuntary stay to dig in the banks. For want of tools, his digging equipment was a boat hook. Along with a couple of Greenlanders he suc-ceeded, at great risk of being buried by collapsing sand, in getting most of a body with its 'surrounding clothing' out. The body was partly enclosed in a coffin. Unfor-tunately his two helpers pulled so eagerly at the clothing that it fell apart, and the boat hook also did some damage.

Back in Copenhagen Meldorf rinsed the clothes thoroughly in cold water. In a report to the National Museum he said that he sometimes took the clothing out to put the fragments together. In doing this he was helped by the later famous museum man, Christian Axel Jensen. One can imagine the two men busying themselves enthu-siastically with the textile jigsaw puzzle and, by partly ignoring the proper course of the threads and the inside and outside of the fragments, getting an almost whole upper part and most of an item of clothing out of the many fragments (D8080 and D8081) and the hood (No. 75). Meldorf thought he had found a sleeveless kirtle and a hood of reddish-brown vaðmál as well as a dark brown smock with sleeves.

The excavation in 1921

Poul Nørlund's excavation at Herjolfsnæs in 1921 was launched as a result of the many reports of finds at the churchyard. Nørlund came to Herjolfsnæs in May.

Snow and ice still covered the plain by the fjord, and almost two months were to pass before the soil had thawed enough so that the dig could begin. As helpers he had five male Greenlanders and a female cook. Later the digging team was augmented with a couple of men. The greatest help came, however, from the unpredictable Greenland weather. The frost still bound the soil and, although the men dug as deep as possible, they only reached a depth of a few spits so that this excavation was about to suffer the same fate as Kielsen's. In the meantime the meltwater from the thawed soil and from the mountains behind became such a hindrance that ditches had to be dug to get rid of the water from the area of excavation. It was during this ditch-dig-ging that the men got so far into the subsoil that in the mud they could glimpse the uppermost burials in the churchyard soil. The frozen soil thawed slowly. They tried to put warm water into the excavation, but fearing they might destroy the finds they abandoned this approach. In time, the sun provided so much warmth that the soil thawed for a longer period each day. Gradually they were able to uncover the burials, and now in quick succession there emerged costumes, wooden coffins and wooden crosses. But it was difficult to get the costumes up, because they were heavy with soil and water and could by no means hold their own weight. By carefully rolling out sackcloth underneath them, they were able to lift up each item of clothing.

While the excavation was taking place, there was a great gathering of Green-landers who lived around the site and who had themselves found pieces of clothing below the churchyard. One of those interested was a woman who was able to tell

Nørlund that she had once taken some of the fragments home with her and had sewn clothes with them for her children, but they proved not to have been strong enough.

On 27th August it became necessary to stop the excavation, as transport away from Greenland had to take place before the ice once again became tightly packed around Herjolfsnæs. Because of bad weather and the lack of a ship connection, Nørlund himself only got back to Denmark at the end of November after a dangerous voyage of 26 long days. In *Buried Norsemen at Herjolfsnes* and in *Nordbobygderne ved Verdens Ende* ('The Norsemen at the End of the World') Poul Nørlund described the excavation and the costumes – accounts that still captivate their readers.

Placing of the graves

The burials were mainly concentrated in three areas: the western and the northern part of the churchyard, and a small area south-east of the church ruin. The burials were close-packed, often one on top of the other in three or four layers. The finds from the southern part were the poorest preserved despite the fact that they lay relatively deep. (See matrix pp. 152-153)

Of the church ruins in Greenland, Herjolfsnæs is the third largest with an area of 86 m². Like other Norse churches it was built in connection with a large farm. How large the churchyard was we do not know, since by the end of the 1830s the sea had already taken most of it. Eighty years later, when Nørlund came, the coastline had withdrawn a further twelve metres.

In the remaining part of the churchyard Nørlund found 110-120 burials, and there were traces of even more in the uppermost layers, although these were in such poor condition that nothing could be saved.

Fig. 4.
Drawing from Poul Nørlund's publication Buried Norsemen at Herjolfsnes *from 1924 that shows the location of the graves in the churchyard. The sea had taken its toll at that time, having completely eroded the southerly part.*

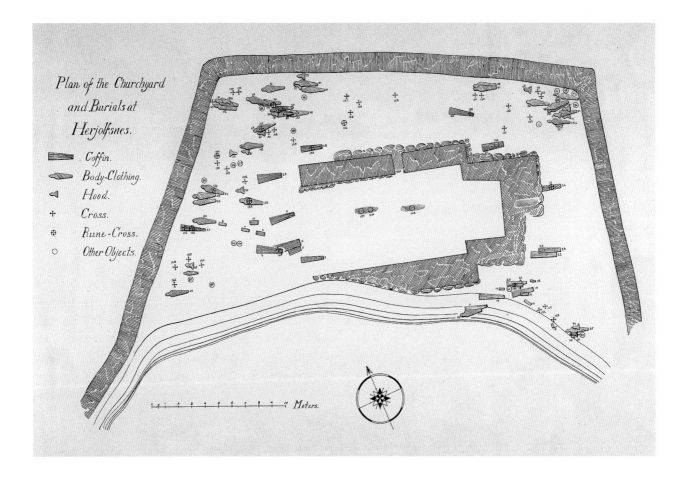

Fig. 5.

In Herjolfsnæs churchyard the dead were wrapped and buried in garments made of vaðmál. With this burial the button garment (D10594) served as burial clothes. The garment had first been cut into smaller pieces, and the sleeves were torn off and wrapped around the feet.

The excavation showed that the deceased had been buried either in a wooden coffin, in shrouds which were made from old clothing, stockings and hoods, or in a complete garment. Only in two cases had the deceased been laid in the grave in both garment and coffin; this was the child's burial with the garment D10592 and the burial with the costume pieces D8080 and D8081, which Meldorf excavated.

In a country where large trees are only known in the form of driftwood, wooden coffins for burials were probably a status symbol. The driftwood was first and foremost used to build houses and churches. If wood could not be obtained for a coffin, a burial in a costume was the next best thing.

Most of the coffins were found closely packed up against the church wall and in the narrow area that was still left of the south-facing churchyard. In all periods burial under the dripping eaves of the church or in a sunny place was most popular.

The difference between burial in a wooden coffin and in a garment, and the placing in the churchyard, was underscored by the wooden crosses found: the most poorly carved were found with the garments in the humbler northern part, and the more carefully worked crosses were found in the coffins by the church wall or in the southern part of the churchyard.

Garments used as grave clothing and shrouds

In the burials where the deceased had not been given a cross in their graves, the sleeves of the garments were laid crosswise over the chest. One of the garments (D10581) had burst at the waist because it had been pulled over the deceased. Other garments had been cut up at the back so they could be used more easily as burial clothing. In a couple of cases slits had been cut in the garments so they could be laced to the body.[4]

In his description of the Herjolfsnæs costumes, Nørlund mentioned that in a few cases remains of coarse flax-like material were stuck to the skeletons, for example under the breastbone (sternum) in Burial 65, from which the hood D10596 was taken up.[5] He further writes that the skull of Burial 79 was 'partly covered from the back of the neck to the root of the nose'.[6] On the skull was the hood D10607. Finally a few threads of hemp were found together with the costume D10581.

The hood D10596 has a shoulder cape, which means that it reaches down a good way in front of the breastbone. The much damaged hood lay beneath a costume (D10580), which in turn lay beneath another costume (No. 47). The latter costume could not be taken up from the excavation, as it was too decomposed.[7]

The small, short hood D10607 was found, along with a mixture of various rags, lying below the costume D10587.

Nørlund writes that most of this costume covered a heap of rags and skeletal parts, and that the bottom of the costume was wound around a skull. Inside the hood lay some tufts of fair hair.[8] It will be evident that several burials not only lay one on top of another, but also became intermixed.

Whether the coarse flax-like material that was registered belonged to one burial or another, or whether it remained in its original place, is impossible to say. The possibility exists that a hood was lined or that there was an underhood, as was the case with the hat D10612. However, Nørlund does not think that the costumes were lined, although the few hide and flax-like remains mentioned might suggest lining.[9] No remains of lining were found in the investigations in 1997-99 either.

The Herjolfsnæs garments sent to Denmark

In August 1921 Nørlund had to stop the excavation, since the departure of the last ship for Denmark was imminent.

Fig. 6.
The hood (D10601) after being brought to the National Museum in 1921. The sacking that was used when it was excavated still lies under the hood.

Fig. 7.
The hood (D10597) after it was
brought to the National Museum
in 1921. This large hood, with
the liripipe wound around it,
was found with skeleton parts
(lower leg and ankle) inside. The
hood had been wrapped around
the legs of the dead person.

Twelve large wooden crates were constructed and the many small rivers near Herjolfsnæs supplied the ideal packing – a moss that was perfect for protecting the costumes. It could be peeled off in large sheets and it was available in unlimited quantities. Three months later the wet, muddy costumes were in the National Museum in Copenhagen, where Nørlund could number and describe them.

The total number saved was 23 more or less intact costumes, three of which are children's costumes; 16 hoods, of which one is fragmentary; four caps, including a tall hat; and one pair and four single stockings.

For several years after the find of the Herjolfsnæs costumes a story was going the rounds that an ancient Viking had been found frozen in an iceberg. In a reply to a Canadian Nørlund had to deny the story as late as 1925.

Find circumstances

The preservation conditions at the Herjolfsnæs churchyard are complex. The soil had preserved many textiles, but few skeletal parts. In Greenland it is not only the soil conditions that help to preserve cultural objects. Other factors are quite crucial, first and foremost the cold and freezing. We must assume that the churchyard soil was consecrated for burial shortly after the Norse settlers came to Herjolfsnæs, and that the first deaths and subsequent burials took place as early as the end of the tenth century. Of these oldest burials nothing has been preserved. At the time the climate was relatively mild and the churchyard sand and gravel probably wore down coffins, clothes and skeletons. Only with the change in the climate in the course of the thirteenth century, when the cold and thus the permafrost became established, did the soil become 'preservative'. Nørlund could record that in many cases coffin and clothes were found while the skeleton had completely decomposed. In some of the burials both coffins and clothes were so grown through by innumerable plant roots that they almost had to be cut out of the ground. These burials must necessarily have lain relatively close to the surface, but in layers that were later encapsulated in the permafrost. In these layers lay the best-preserved costumes. The matrix on pp. 152-153 shows how the costumes lay in relation to one another. Some were only 30 cm from the original surface, others 130 cm below it. Those that were at a depth of 55 cm were as a rule poorly preserved. Nørlund thought that the season in which the burials took place also had an effect on the preservation of the textiles.

On the other hand it was not a particular season that had the effect that many of the clothes had been coloured red. The first time the reddish-brown *vaðmál* was mentioned was in 1840, when H.J. Rink reported on the grave clothes found in the churchyard.[10]

Several attempts were made to identify a red dye in the Herjolfsnæs costumes in connection with this publication. An analysis of some muddy pebbles collected from a stream by the churchyard in 1999 may have solved the mystery. The red colour may be due either to deliberate dyeing with ochre or an iron compound from the soil. But since none of the archaeologists mentioned that the churchyard soil contained ochre, the latter explanation was not so likely.

But within the churchyard area the circumstances varied too, since costumes found at almost the same depth could be preserved or had sometimes almost disappeared. All these different factors made traditional archaeological dating of the costumes very difficult. Nørlund concluded that a dating of the costumes by 'burial depth' was not possible.

Conservation of the garments

As mentioned, the Herjolfsnæs costumes came to the National Museum in Copenhagen at the end of 1921. The moss with which they had been packed had kept the costumes suitably wet. Of the conservation process Nørlund writes:

'In itself it was very simple. First the clothes and the supporting sackcloth were wet through with water. They were left there for a few days so that the various foreign substances like root fibres that had become entangled among the threads and deposits from the decomposed bodies that had stuck to the clothes could be dissolved. After a final rinse the clothes were slowly dried, then subjected to a kind of healing massage. The clothes were laid on a table and worked with the fingertips to remove all foreign particles. This was the most important part of the conservation work and also the most troublesome. When this had been done the material had regained its old elasticity and – to a surprising extent – its original strength. A supporting material was glued to the worst-preserved places, then the clothes were treated with Beticol.[11] The conservation work as such was now over, and there only remained the careful restoration of the costumes to their original form. Tears and bad areas had to be repaired; seams that had come apart had to be sewn again; and almost all the costume fragments that were suitable for exhibition had to be sewn to a lining before they could be hung on dummies. However, this was not only a matter of manual work. Several costumes had been cut up so they could be used as grave clothes, some had only been preserved through the centuries in a much decayed state; and often, after rinsing and conservation, what we had in front of us was nothing but a heap of loose rags which had to be put in the right relationship to one another'.[12]

Exhibitions

After the conservation and the restoration had been concluded in 1922, the costumes were shown for the first time in an exhibition. In an invitation to the press Nørlund wrote: 'On 12th February 1923 a temporary exhibition of the Norse costumes and other objects excavated at Ikigait in South Greenland will open'. The costumes were displayed in the same room as medieval bishops' vestments. Later the costumes were incorporated in the National Museum's permanent exhibition.

In an expansion of the museum in 1938 the clothes were moved and re-displayed. Thirty years later the costumes were moved over to new dummies, which were put in display cases. When the exhibition at the museum in Brede – 'Clothes Make the Man' – was being prepared in 1971, there were thoughts of moving some of the Norse costumes to the National Museum's department in Brede near Lyngby, north of Copenhagen. This idea was abandoned, however, since it was clear that the costumes would

Fig. 8.
From the National Museum's exhibition in 1997, 'Margrete I. Nordens Frue og Husbond. Kalmarunionen' (Margrete I. The North's Wife and Husband. The Kalmar Union). The garments are spread out and exhibited on a tilted structure. Hoods and caps are placed on 'dummies' that completely support the textiles.

not tolerate exhibition in climatic conditions that were substantially poorer than at the National Museum in Copenhagen. So, for the exhibition in Brede, reconstructions were made instead.

In the 1980s, in connection with a rebuilding of the medieval department, the costumes were reconserved. This meant first and foremost that new wool lining, dyed in the colour of the original costume, was sewn under the costumes. Before this the old lining and the many unsightly darns from the 1920s were removed.[13] In this reconservation process miscolouring was observed in the seams and at the worn edges of some of the costumes, especially the short-sleeved costume (D10581); the fibres appeared 'withered' and pale. A similar appearance has been observed on well-preserved British textiles found in cess-pits. It is likely that the faded edges were due to chemical attack, where the threads, after tearing or cutting, leave the ends of the fibres vulnerable.[14]

The many years of display have caused the costumes to deteriorate. In particular, light has had a disintegrating effect on the fibres. For the new display in 1980 subdued lighting was therefore installed in the display cases, and only a few original textiles have been exhibited, among other things the small child's costume with sleeves, a cap and some hoods. The others are reconstructions. Most of the Herjolfsnæs finds lie in a dark, air-conditioned store with a constant temperature of 14°C.

Only on special occasions and for short periods are a few original costumes shown, as happened in the 'Margrete I' exhibition shown in 1996-97 at the National Museum in Copenhagen, at Kalmar Castle in Sweden, at Tavastehus in Finland and at Akershus in Oslo. In addition Norse costumes have been included in the exhibitions 'The Colourful Middle Ages' at the National Museum in Copenhagen in 1999 and at 'Vikings: The North Atlantic Saga' in the USA in 2000-2003.

2. Brattahlid (Ø29a), Qassiarsuk

In 1932, in an excavation of Eric the Red's farm and church at Brattahlid, which like Herjolfsnæs was in the Eastern Settlement, 155 burials were registered in the churchyard. The excavation was headed by Poul Nørlund and the Swedish archaeologist Mårten Stenberger. Only a few of the deceased had been laid in coffins. The others had probably been wrapped in grave clothes, but almost nothing of these was preserved.[15] According to the old Icelandic Christian law of the twelfth century a corpse must not be buried naked. It was to be buried in grave clothes, but it was mentioned that a coffin was desirable. The Norse Greenlanders followed this tradition and like other Christians buried their dead lying on their backs with their heads pointing west.

At Brattahlid the skeletons were relatively well preserved, and Nørlund could note that the men had been buried south of the church, the women to the north and the children to the east of the church. There were however a few exceptions to this rule, since a couple of women lay in the southern part of the churchyard, and a few men had penetrated into the north side.[16]

3. Sandnæs (V51), Kilaarsafik.

This is the name of the largest Norse farm in the Western Settlement. Here too there were farms at Austmannadalen, Niaquusat and Nipaatsoq, which were so-called centralized farm types, that is, with rooms with different functions built together. All the farms were located by the Ameralla fjord. The Sandnæs farm had a church which the occupants of the other farms presumably used. The excavation of the farms in the Western Settlement began in 1930 and continued at intervals of years throughout the thirties. In 1976-77 and in the 1980s the digs were resumed. From the farms we have well preserved objects, including many textile implements of bone, soapstone and wood, but there are also textile fragments among the finds.[17] In addition a rare crucifix carved in driftwood was found at the churchyard of Sandnæs.

4. The *Landnáma* Farm (Ø17a) at Narsaq

The *Landnáma* Farm is the archaeologists' name for this excavation in the Norse Eastern Settlement, which began in 1954, continued in 1958 and was concluded in 1962 under the leadership of C.L. Vebæk, who until his death in 1994 devoted his life to research on the Norse Greenlanders.[18] Although it was only possible to excavate the dwelling, this was a very important part of the complex, since the residential building turned out to be a longhouse, and this dated the farm to the landnáma or pioneering period around the year 1000. This was later confirmed by radiocarbon dating.

The farm was rich in finds including objects of wood and soapstone with carved runes. But there were also textile fragments, which are very interesting viewed in the context of the other Norse weaves. The textiles consist of 25 numbered items, of which the pile weave D5/1992.9, the tvistur textile D5/1992.10 and the 'embroidered' fragment D5/1992.8 are among the most interesting. In addition the weaves from Ø17a differ from most other Norse textiles in having a higher number of warp threads per centimetre and a weft more loosely spun than normal for Norse textiles; and the finds include many dyed textiles.[19]

5. The Farm Beneath the Sand (64V2-III-555) in the Western Settlement

The Farm Beneath the Sand is the name of a farm that was excavated in the Western Settlement close to the inland ice in the years 1992-97. In everyday speech it is abbreviated to GUS ('Gården Under Sandet'). As mentioned earlier, the farm was discovered in 1990 by two caribou hunters who, on seeing some large pieces of wood sticking out of the slopes by the Ameralla fjord, knew that inland wood of this size was unusual. They examined the wood more closely and could see that it had been worked, then they reported the find to the Greenland National Museum and Archives in Nuuk, which later inspected the site.

The find resulted in a large excavation with hundreds of objects being found that tell us about the everyday life of the Norse Greenlanders.

The farm is located on an outwash – a desert-like sandy plain that is intersected by several watercourses of various sizes that run down from the ice sheet and from Lake Isortuarsuk. The plain lies at an elevation of 130 metres above sea level and the gradient from the front of the glacier to the northern boundary of the plain falls about 90 metres. The meltwater that swells early in summer drains through a narrow valley, passing over two steep rapids, and falls a further 60 metres into the Naajaat Kuuat fjord.[20] It was here that the pieces of wood were exposed.

The excavation was headed by the National Museum in Nuuk in collaboration with the National Museum in Copenhagen and was conducted for four weeks every summer for six years. Since the place is far from navigable waters, all supplies and equipment had to be transported to the excavation field by helicopter. The fifteen-member excavation team included researchers from Canada, Denmark, Iceland and Greenland. The work was often laborious and time-consuming, since tons of sand had to be removed manually each summer before the archaeologists could dig in the culture layers that contained remains of buildings, animal bones and objects including many pieces of textiles. For centuries the sand had drifted in over the farm and had covered it to a depth of almost two metres. In addition the permafrost held the soil layer in an iron grip that was very difficult to loosen. On a summer's day the temperature reaches 25°C in the sun, and on a winter's day a few years ago a temperature of minus 45°C was recorded.

As the excavation progressed, a picture emerged of a building complex extending over at least 70x18 metres, with a culture layer up to 1½ metres thick. To this we must add the relatively large part of the farm, the western part, which the archaeologists could see the river had already begun to wash away. The farm was once one of the largest in the Western Settlement. A total of more than 44 rooms was registered, although they did not all exist at the same time; some were extensions or re-buildings.

The stratigraphy showed that one can distinguish at least six phases of construction. It is not yet clear how many years passed between the individual construction periods. After a summer's work, when the archaeologists had a reasonable overview of the many rooms that had been built together, the river and sand drift had wiped out most traces the next summer. It is to be hoped that future radiocarbon analyses will be of some help in clarifying this complex work.

But so far we know that the oldest part of GUS is a longhouse built by *landnáma* settlers around the year 1000.[21]

In this house fragments of linen were found. Most interesting in the textiles context is the weaving room to which the large pieces of wood had pointed. The weaving room was sunken in relation to the adjacent rooms and later turned out to be in the north-easternmost part of the farm, which matches the placing of weaving rooms in other Norse farms. The weaving room at GUS is an annexe from the thirteenth century and was probably only in use for about a century. When the pieces of wood were uncovered, it could be seen that they were parts of one or more warp-weighted looms, but there is still wood from the weaving room that has not been fully investigated, so perhaps more loom parts will emerge.

At GUS a total of 174 finds of textile fragments were registered, and this has resulted in 382 textile analyses. In addition spindle whorls and loom weights were found. From the weaving room alone the number of finds was over 800.

The preservation conditions for the textiles varied greatly. Some fragments appear to have been quite unaffected by the many hundreds of years in the soil, while others were very poorly preserved. There are no traces of the situation seen in clothes from Herjolfsnæs, where plant roots had grown through the textiles. At GUS, too, some fragments must have lain closer to the surface than others, and the permafrost did not reach all pieces at the same time. Finally, some of the pieces of clothing must already have been almost worn out when they ended up on the floor. Others may have been fragments from the cutting of a new item of clothing.

The excavation of the sixth summer was abruptly broken off when the river flooded the field and made continuation impossible.

The river which had exposed the Farm Beneath the Sand in 1990 removed it again six years later before the eyes of the excavators.

The Textile Finds from Greenland – overview

A chronological presentation of the textile finds:

1830   Ove Kielsen finds the so-called 'sailor's jacket' (D5674) at Herjolfsnæs (Ikigaat), Nanortalik Municipality. Ruin Group Ø111. Antiquity Number 59V1-0IV-502

1894   Two textile fragments handed in to the Antiquities Commission, Ancient Manuscripts Society in Copenhagen, probably after Daniel Bruun's trip to the Norse ruins in the Eastern Settlement in the 1890s. The fragments are from Tunuarmiut, Tunulliarfik, Narsaq Municipality. Ruin Group Ø20. Antiquity Number 60V2-0IV-661

1900   Gustav Meldorf excavates two costumes (D8080-D8001) and a hood (No. 75) at the Herjolfsnæs churchyard (Ikigaat), Nanortalik Municipality. Ruin Group Ø111. Antiquity Number 59V1-0IV-502

1910   Mogens Clemmensen excavates the Hvalsey Church ruin, Qaqortoq Municipality. Ruin Group Ø83. Antiquity Number 60V2-0IV-646. A few textile fragments

1921   Poul Nørlund excavates the large costume find at the Herjolfsnæs churchyard (Ikigaat), Nanortalik Municipality. Ruin Group Ø111. Antiquity Number 59V1-0IV-502

1925   Therkel Mathiassen excavates an Inuit settlement at Inussuk, Upernavik Municipality. Antiquity Number 72V1-0IV-022. One textile fragment (L4.4892) among Norse objects

1929   Poul Nørlund and Aage Roussell excavate the Gardar bishop's seat (Igaliku), Narsaq Municipality. Ruin Group Ø47. Antiquity Number 60V2-0IV-621. Only a few textile fragments, but some textile-working implements

1930-32   Poul Nørlund and Aage Roussell excavate Sandnæs (Kilaarsarfik), Nuuk Municipality. Ruin Group V51. Antiquity Number 64V2-III-511. Only a few textile fragments, but many textile-working implements

1932   Poul Nørlund and Mårten Stenberger excavate Brattahlid (Qassiarsuk), Narsaq Municipality. Ruin Group Ø29a. Antiquity Number 61V3-III-539. Only a few textile fragments, but some textile-working implements

1934   Aage Roussell continues the excavation from 1930 of Sandnæs V51. He also excavates two neighbouring farms at Ujarassuit and Umiiviarsuk. Ruin Groups 52a and 52b, Nuuk Municipality. Antiquity Numbers 64V2-0IV-515 and 64V2-III-513. Only a few textile fragments, but many textile-working implements

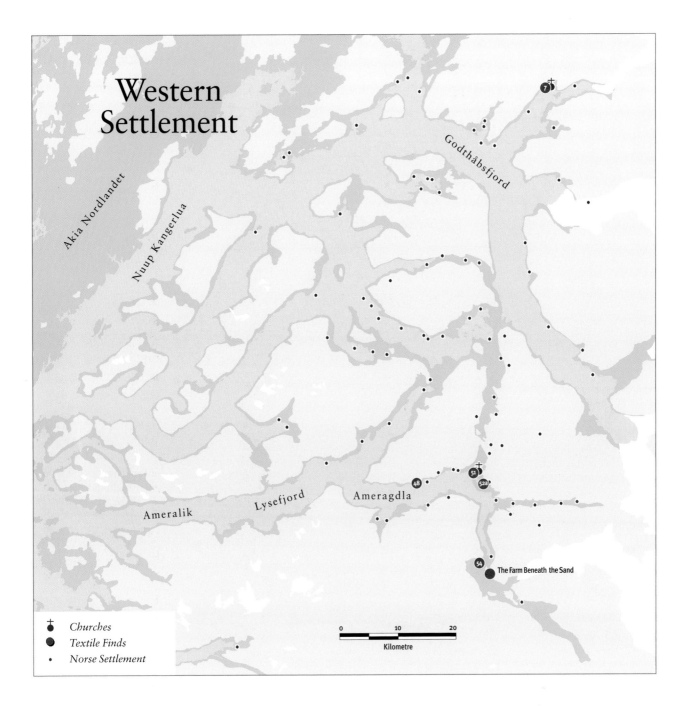

Western
Settlement

Akia Nordlandet

Nuup Kangerlua

Godthåbsfjord

Ameralik   Lysefjord   Ameragdla

The Farm Beneath the Sand

† Churches
● Textile Finds
· Norse Settlement

0   10   20
Kilometre

1935   Therkel Mathiassen excavates an Inuit settlement (Tuttutuup Isua) at
        Narsaq, Narsaq Municipality. Antiquity Number 60V1-00I-060. One
        textile fragment (L15.187) and some textile-working implements among
        Norse objects

1936   Erik Holtved excavates Inuit settlements in Inglefield Land, (House No. 6)
        Ruin Ø, North West Greenland. Antiquity Number 78V2-000-002. One
        textile fragment (L3.2591) among Norse objects

1937   Aage Roussell continues the excavation of the farms in Austmannadalen,
        Nuuk Municipality. Ruin Group V52a. Antiquity Number V64V2-III-
        513. Some textile fragments and textile-working implements

1939   Christen Leif Vebæk excavates three farms in Vatnahverfi, including
        Enoch's Ruins, Narsaq Municipality. Ruin Group Ø64a, Ø64c, Ø78a.

Fig. 9a.

Vesterbygden (Western settle-
ment). Textile finds are mar-
ked on the map of excavated
Norse settlements in
Greenland.

7   Ujarassuit (Anavik)
48 Niaquusat
51 Kilaarsarfik (Sandnæs)
52a Umiiviarsuk
54 Nipaatsoq

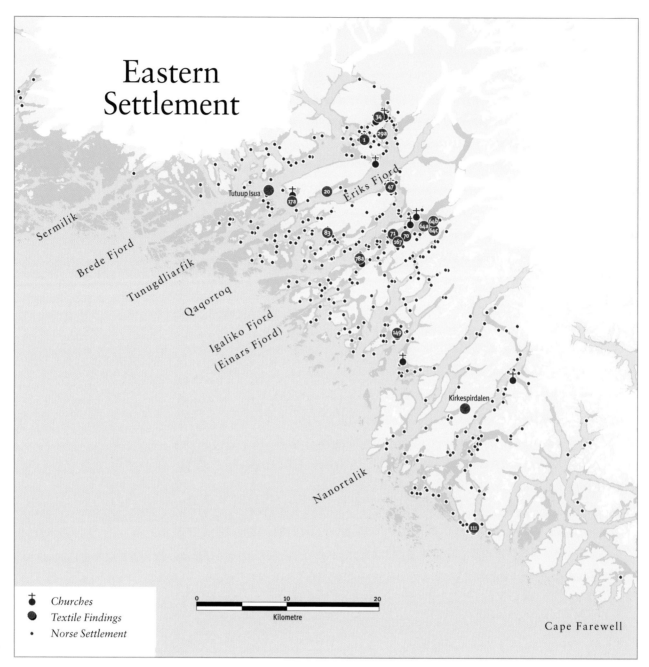

Eastern
Settlement

Sermilik

Brede Fjord

Tunugdliarfik

Qaqortoq

Igaliko Fjord
(Einars Fjord)

Tutuup Isua

Eriks Fjord

Kirkespirdalen

Nanortalik

Cape Farewell

✝ Churches
● Textile Findings
• Norse Settlement

0   10   20
Kilometre

Fig. 9b. Østerbygden (Eastern
settlement). Textile finds are
marked on the map of excavated Norse settlements in
Greenland.

1 Nunataq
17a Narsaq
20 Tunuarmiut
29a Brattahlid (Qassiarsuk)
34 Qorlortup Itinnera
47 Gardar (Igaliku)
64a-c Vatnahverfi (Enochs Ruin)
70 Vatnahverfi
71 Vatnahverfi (Russip Kuua)
78a Vatnahverfi
83 Hvalsø (Qaqortoq)
111 Herjolfsnæs (Ikigaat)
149 Narsarsuaq
167 Vatnahverfi (Abel's Farm)

Antiquity Numbers 60V2-0IV-539 and -540, -586. A few textile fragments and implements

1943   Christen Leif Vebæk excavates an inland settlement at Vatnahverfi, Nar-
        saq Municipality. Ruin Group Ø70. Antiquity Number 60V2-0IV-607.
        Textile-working implements

1945-46 Christen Leif Vebæk excavates Narsarsuaq, a farm by the Uunartoq fjord,
        Nanortalik Municipality. Ruin Group Ø149. Antiquity Number 60V2-
        0IV-504. A few textile-working implements

1949   Christen Leif Vebæk continues the excavation of the inland settlement at
        Vatnahverfi, Russip Kuua, Narsaq Municipality. Ruin Group Ø71.
        Antiquity Number 60V2-0IV-602. A few textile fragments and some tex-
        tile-working implements

1950   Christen Leif Vebæk concludes the excavation of the inland settlement at Vatnahverfi, Abel's Farm, Qaqortoq Municipality. Ruin Group Ø167. Antiquity Number 60V2-0IV-603. A few textile fragments and textile-working implements

1954   Christen Leif Vebæk excavates the *Landnáma* Farm in Narsaq, Narsaq Municipality. Ruin Group Ø17a. Antiquity Number 60V1-00I-518. Textile fragments and implements. The excavation continues in 1958 and in 1962

1971   Svend Erik Albrethsen conducts a trial excavation of a churchyard by a newly found church ruin at Nunataq. Ruin Group Ø1. Antiquity Number 61V3-III-545. So far one textile fragment has been found

1976-77 Jørgen Meldgaard excavates the farm at Niaquusat and Nipaatsoq, Nuuk Municipality. Ruin Groups V48 and V54. Antiquity Numbers 64V2-III-507 and -502. A few textile fragments and implements

1977   Peter Schledermann excavates a house ruin on Skraeling Island, Buchanan Bay, Ellesmere Island, N.W.T., Canada, Site SfFk-4-1234. In the house ruin two textile fragments were found among Norse objects

1982   Hans Kapel and Jette Arneborg excavate Ujarassuit, Anavik, Nuuk Municipality. Ruin Group V7. Antiquity Number 64V2-0IV-515. A few textile fragments

1984   Claus Andreasen and Jette Arneborg excavate a midden at Sandnæs (Kilaarsarfik), Nuuk Municipality. Ruin Group V51. Antiquity Number 64V2-III-511. Some textile fragments

1990   Rie Oldenburg receives textile fragments from the sheep-farmer Karl Kleist, found at Qorlortup Itinnera, Narsaq Municipality. Ruin Group Ø34. Antiquity Number 61V3-III-525.

1992-97 Jette Arneborg and Joel Berglund excavate The Farm Beneath the Sand, called GUS, Nuuk Municipality. Antiquity Number 64V2-III-555. Many textile fragments and many textile-working implements

1997-98 Georg Nyegaard and Jette Arneborg excavate Ruin Group Ø34 in Narsaq Municipality. Antiquity Number 61V3-III-525. A few textile fragments, accessories and textile-working implements

1998   Maria Hinnerson Berglund and Joel Berglund investigate a rock shelter in Kirkespirdalen, between the fjords Tasermiut and Saqqaa, Nanortalik Municipality. Antiquity Number 60V2-0II-574. One textile fragment

Fig. 10.

Abraham's sacrifice. Page from the illuminated Icelandic manuscript Stjórn AM 227 fol. f. 23v., dated to
c. 1350. A ram and a goat can be seen in the left margin. In the Farm Beneath the Sand, the skeleton and
pelt of a goat were found and dated to the same decade as that illustrated in the manuscript.

The source of raw materials

1. Sheep and goats

Aboard the ships of the *landnáma* settlers on the voyage to Greenland were sheep and goats. The farm animals that had been necessary in Iceland to get food on the table and clothes on the body were just as indispensable in the new country. In *Grágás,* the oldest Icelandic collection of laws, there are valuations of the animals by age and quality and there are detailed rules for both sheep and goat breeding. In each of the groups a sheep is equal in value to a goat. The conversion value given is that six goats with their kids are equal to one cow of normal size (and six times as much fodder was calculated for a cow as for a goat).[1] That sheep and goats were widespread in the Nordic countries can be seen from many old place-names.

Sheep are hardy animals; and goats can find food in even more difficult conditions. The goat was important not only as a milch animal but also a supplier of hair and skin. Goat hair was used like wool for weaving and the skins were used –among other things – for the production of parchment, in Icelandic called bókfell (book-hide). Most Icelandic sagas, however, are written on vellum parchment.[2] In *The King's Mirror* goat skin is mentioned among the export goods that came from Greenland, and *Gudmundar saga biskups Arasonar* says that a man travelled with a pack-horse 'loaded with goat-goods'. As well as skin, the load included goat's-horn.[3]

The author of *The King's Mirror* further says that in Greenland 'there are large, good farms, for people there have many cattle and sheep and they make much butter and much cheese there'.[4]

When the Norse settlers sailed south west to Greenland to find new, better pastures for their cattle, they took with them the sheep they had farmed in Iceland (see pp. 79-92). These sheep belonged to the Northern Short-tail breed group, which is noted for its hardiness. They can survive on sparse vegetation and have a double-coated fleece, which protects them from rough weather. Descendants of this stock are to be found in present-day breeds such as the Orkney on Ronaldsay, the Norwegian Spaelsau and the Goth on Lilla Karls' off South-West Gotland. The dark brown sheep of Lille Dimon, the smallest of the Faroe Islands, died out a century ago, but they probably belonged to the same group.[5] Northern Short-tails can be horned, hornless, or horned in the rams only, but the Greenland animals seem to have been mainly goat-horned.[6] Sheep of this stock have a wide colour range, including grey, brown, black and roan fleeces and this use of natural wool colours can be seen in Norse clothing.

The Northern Short-tail probably originated in the European Iron Age. Another very old sheep race is named after the Island of Soay, west of the Hebrides. The word is Norse, meaning 'Sheep Island', and the Soay breed which now survives on St Kilda is likely to be a relic of the Bronze Age sheep which were already present when the Norse colonised the Scottish Islands. Fær (sheep, pl.) has given the Faroe Islands their name[7] and similar 'sheep islands' with distinctive names are known from the whole North Atlantic area.

Fig. 11.

Icelandic sheep as shown in an unidentified book from the 1800s. On leaving Iceland, the landnáma settlers had the same breed of sheep with them. Sheep – like goats – were indispensable for the Norse Greenlanders.

In excavations of Norse farms in Greenland bone remains from sheep and goats are common. However, the two animals are so similar in build that only a few specific bones (including the skulls and the cores of the horns) can be used to determine the species. A find of an intact animal is an exception, but at the Farm Beneath the Sand (64V2-III-555) the archaeologists were lucky. They found a three-year-old she-goat lying inside one of the houses. It was also possible to see that it had died when the roof fell in.

In the excavations bones are almost always found as the remains of meals, split so the marrow could be taken out, and the skulls were crushed, as the brain was probably eaten or used in connection with the tanning of skins. The horns too had been removed, as they could find uses as household utensils.

The bone analyses show that a Norse sheep was the size of a large dog, that is with a shoulder height of c. 65 cm, varying from 55 to 70 cm. In the coldest part of the winter it might be necessary to keep the sheep in special stalls, but they would be outside for the rest of the year. Stone-walled sheepfolds of various sizes are thought to have had different functions. Close to the farm there would be a milking fold, and to obtain the highest possible milk yield the lambs would be removed from the ewe. Some smaller folds on steeply sloping terrain near running water have been interpreted as washing folds.

The bone finds confirm the information from *The King's Mirror*. Another more tangible proof of the use of sheep and goats is the many textiles that appear as soon as the archaeologists dig in Norse ruins. Wool clothes were just as important to the Norse Greenlanders as butter and cheese.

2. Sheep-farming and the use of the sheep

In *Landnámabók* we read that the Norwegian Viking *Hrafna-Flóki* sailed to Iceland with farm animals and his household to settle, but he forgot to gather hay. The next winter was very harsh, and all his animals died. Then Flóki fled back to Norway and gave the island the grim name Iceland.[8] Learning from this, the *landnáma* settlers, as soon as they came to Greenland, gathered the necessary hay as winter fodder for the animals, since their own life depended on the survival of the sheep in particular. At the end of the 1970s, at Niaqussat (V48) in the Western Settlement, a midden by a Norse site was investigated. The soil was sieved with a fine-meshed sieve and a count of the bones showed among other things that out of several thousand bones only two were from fish. The explanation could be that fish were used as animal fodder.[9] However, new isotope analyses of animal bones from Norse excavations have shown that there are very few traces of marine food in the sheep and goat bones, whereas the pig and dog bones have large quantities of marine food.[10]

Expertise in sheep-farming was of course something that the *landnáma* people brought with them, since the life of the animals in Greenland did not differ greatly from their life in Iceland, and the Icelandic traditions were probably continued. A description of the Icelandic people from the earliest settlement until the twentieth century is the history of their struggle to survive by exploiting the resources of the country as well as possible.[11] This account, which is based on a study of old Icelandic tales and more recent investigations, very probably also gives us a picture of life on the Norse farms in Greenland. The annual cycle of the animals followed the four seasons. In the autumn the sheep were herded back to the farms so that the necessary number of animals could be selected for slaughter. Several factors were crucial to the selection – the amount of hay available, the number of rams, ewes and lambs necessary for the next year's breeding. Wool, meat and milk products like cheese, curds and whey were the most important items in the household economy.[12] Sheep's milk contained three times as much Vitamin C as cow's milk and would have been an important supplement to a diet which would have been monotonous and poor in vitamins in the winter.

3. Everything was used

Nothing from the sheep went to waste.[13] The blood was made into black pudding, the offal was boiled, smoked, salted or dried and the fat from the offal was rendered down. Udders and testicles too were boiled and preserved in sour whey. In other cases the scrotum was cut away and cleaned inside, the wool was removed from the outside, then the scrotum was filled with hay and hung out to dry. When it was dry it was softened manually and used as a small storage bag. Guts and stomach became other useful containers. Head and feet were scraped, cleaned and boiled, but the legs were boiled separately. After cooling, the fat was skimmed off and used to bind the undercoat when very thin threads were to be spun.[14] Various smaller bones from the legs and feet of the sheep could be used in the knucklebones game, known in the Nordic countries as far back as the Iron Age. Similarly the metatarsal bones could be used as reels for storing wool yarn and the tibia could become flutes. In the same way the horns of the animals had innumerable uses, especially as drinking-horns and eating implements.

In the course of the winter the wool was processed. If it was from sheep that had died, as much of the wool as possible was taken off and used in the normal way, but clothes made of wool from dead sheep did not last more than a few years.[15] And if the

| Grass ▼ |
| IN LIFE |
| ▼ Blood |
| Milk |
| Wool |
| Dung |
| |
| AFTER DEATH |
| ▼ Meat |
| Fat |
| Bone |
| Skin |
| Gut |
| Horn |

Fig. 12.
Schematic presentation of sheep products and their application.

winter had been long and the hay had run out, the result could be that the ewes had no milk for milking. But a few days before lambing, the sheep would be milked again, and the raw milk would be prepared as a special dish. This meal was often the first one freshly made after a whole winter of salted, smoked, soured or dried food. It might be necessary to slaughter the lambs as soon as they were born to save the ewes if they did not have the strength to suckle the lambs.

Once the sheep were turned out to grass again, the shed would be mucked out. The manure would be cut into regular squares and laid out to dry. Then it would be split and used as fuel. These 'turfs' were the most important source of heat on many farms.[16]

4. Disease among the sheep

Sheep can be attacked by various mites and parasites which can, in the worst case, kill the animals but which in other cases can almost destroy the wool. From Scotland we have information that scab was combated with a mixture of tar and whale oil. The mixture had to be spread on the animal as close to the body as possible. This layer also protected the sheep from severe cold. After such treatment there could be a loss of wool of more than 50%.[17] In the manure layer at the Farm Beneath the Sand (64V2-III-555) the same mites and parasites were found as those feared today by sheep farmers.[18] There were also finds of both sheep and goat ked, both carriers of disease. It is thus not inconceivable that the Norse Greenlanders knew of methods like the Scottish one for preventing the spread of disease among the sheep.

5. Consumption of wool

We hear from Iceland in the eighteenth century that a human being needs at least five kilograms of wool for clothing a year.[19] In northern Norway a Sámi family in the mid-seventeenth century had an average of five sheep. We do not know how many children there were in the family.[20] Another Norwegian source says that if there were more children in a family than there were sheep, the wool was mixed with goat-hair, 'fell wool' (wool from dead animals), or other materials.[21]

In order to estimate how much wool a Norse Greenlander family needed, a garment, a hood and a pair of stockings from Herjolfsnæs were weighed. The items selected had in common that they had not been restored or supported with lining. The almost complete medium-large costume D5674 weighs 1000 g, the hood D10607 weighs 120 g and the stocking D10613 weighs 150 g. Since the textiles have dried out over the years, it is realistic to assume that they weighed somewhat more when new, and the amount of raw wool that would have been necessary to produce the clothes would have weighed almost twice as much before it was sorted and made ready for spinning. There would also have been some wastage during the weaving. Each person must as a minimum have worn two layers of clothing, an outer and inner costume, breeches or long hose, perhaps both, and a hood. In addition a cloak, pile-woven or of sheepskin, would have been necessary. Altogether these clothes would have weighed 8-10 kg. The cloak and the costumes would have been so hard-wearing that they could last several years, so the weight of these items of clothing was not the same as the consumption of wool per year. All the same the Icelandic specification of five kilograms of wool per person per year is a low estimate, since one must suppose that this was raw wool. A calculation of the wool consumption can, for example, be set up as follows.

An average family of five people would have to use at least 25 kg of wool for clothing a year. Since a sheep yielded 1½ to 2 kg of raw wool, this meant that one needed 25-30 sheep to have enough usable wool. To this consumption we must add the amount of wool or sheepskins that would be necessary for bedclothes and other items in the home. In addition an average family would have had at least as many servants or farm workers who would also need clothing. Clothes and food were their wages. Furthermore one must allow for wool for sails, tents, packing *vaðmál* – and shrouds. A cautious estimate is therefore that for such a household it was necessary to own 80-100 sheep to get enough wool and skins; but was it possible to get fodder for that number of sheep?

On the basis of recent Icelandic experiments and estimates of plant production and fodder needs in vegetation conditions like those of Greenland, it has been possible to calculate how many sheep are likely to have been fed on the pastures of a medium-sized Norse farm in an area with a radius of 1 km. A sheep, according to these calculations, had an annual fodder requirement of 700 kg of hay, which had to be fetched from 5.8 hectares of grassland or from 17.0 hectares of scrub heath.[22]

The many sheep that were necessary for the above-mentioned household could not, according to this information, have survived on the areas specified here. The sheep were therefore either forced to wander far around to find food, or the household must have managed with less consumption of wool.

Processing of the Raw Wool

1. The wool

Primitive sheep have preserved their natural hair-shedding ability, so in the early summer the wool will fall off by itself in large patches. Since at that time of the year the sheep were outdoors, they were probably gathered in small folds while the wool was plucked or sheared from them. Every year some 1½-2 kg of wool could be collected from each sheep, most from the rams and least from the ewes.

The naturally shed wool and the pulled wool do not have as many hairs as the sheared wool, since some of the hairs that are not fully grown when they are shed remain on the animal. When the sheep are shorn on the other hand, all the hair is cut off to a certain distance from the animal's skin, and there will thus be many different hair lengths along with the wool.

At the Farm Beneath the Sand (64V2-III-555) the archaeologists were fortunate enough to find raw wool or wool staples, which are the locks into which the covering on the sheep naturally falls. Such wool staples have their fibre ends intact, and on these one can see among other things whether the wool was pulled or shorn from the sheep (See pp. 79-92). They also show whether the wool was from a lamb or an adult

Fig. 13.

Coiled basket in willow root(?) (1950x1571), from the Farm Beneath the Sand. The original height was c. 30 mm and the diameter c. 60 mm. On the next page the basket can be seen from the side.

sheep. The raw wool can also reveal whether the sheep had suffered from starvation or had been ill.[1] The fibre analyses show that the Norse Greenlanders both pulled and sheared the wool from the sheep. In the Faroe Islands, Iceland, and the Shetland Islands, pulling off the wool (sometimes called 'rooing') was practised until well into the twentieth century.

A find from Sandnæs (V51) confirms that the sheep were shorn there. In the excavation, a wooden case with no lid was found (D10680) for a pair of shears of the bow type known from the Viking Age, especially from finds in Norwegian women's graves.[2] A 200 mm long pair of iron bow scissors, only half of which is preserved, was found at Abel's Farm (Ø167) in Vatnahverfi (D24/1991.152).[3] A wooden case for sheep shears was found at Bryggen in Bergen and can be dated to the end of the twelfth century, but here too the shears were missing.[4] On the other hand we have both case and shears from the Viking fortress Fyrkat near Hobro, Denmark. The case for the shears is made of poplar wood, and the 180 mm long shears are made of tin-plated iron. These fine shears probably lay in a chest along with cruder iron shears.[5]

As will be evident, the Norse settlers also had a special case for their wool shears, since shears were rare and therefore something one took care of.

2. Washing and sorting the wool

For the Norse Greenlanders the wool from the sheep was the most important raw material for spinning, but since newly gathered wool contains many impurities from the field or shed and from the sheep itself, it has to be washed before it can be spun. The sheep could also be washed before the wool was taken off it. For this kind of washing, urine had been collected from the people on the farm throughout the winter. The stored urine was alkaline and when heated became a detergent that was also

useful for removing the oily smell.[6] Until well into the twentieth century people in the Nordic countries used fermented urine for washing and dyeing. Before spinning, the wool was sorted. The best wool is on the neck of the sheep, on its sides and to some extent on its back, while the poorest wool is on the belly and the legs.

From the Icelandic *Búalög*, ('Peasant Law') – a set of regulations that lists standard rates for domestic and foreign goods as well as for the performance of different work and services, which can be found in numerous versions from the 1400s onwards – it is evident that in Iceland, as in other places, the wool was treated in various ways before spinning. Among other things it was loosened and picked apart with the hands, partly to remove dirt, partly to arrange the fibres alongside one another.

3. Combing

Another kind of sorting involved combing the hairs from the underwool, and for this special woolcombs were used. In the excavation of Sandnæs (V51) Aage Roussell found two thin wooden boards measuring 141 x 45 mm and 115 x 30 mm respectively (D11734.326). In the boards there are small holes with remains of wooden pegs. Roussell thought they were cards or perhaps brushes.[7] We must reject the possibility that they are cards, since these only came to the North at the end of the Middle Ages. *Grettis saga* mentions an *ullkambr* or wool comb. This is probably the same as a *togkambar (tog* = hair), a name occurring in 1767 in an Icelandic inventory.[8] This *kambar* has a wooden handle with an iron head and one row of iron teeth. Similar woolcombs with only one row of teeth have been found in a woman's grave from the Viking Age on the Orkney Islands. And from the Shetland Islands there are woolcombs with iron teeth set in a horn handle.[9]

Both in Iceland and the Faroe Islands the wool was sorted into three grades. The hairs were carefully combed away with *tog* combs so they could later be used as a thread of the type used for sewing on buttons. The finest underwool became a very soft yarn used for special purposes. In addition there was a medium grade consisting of both underwool and hair. This wool was used for coarser weaves.[10]

Well into the twentieth century, wool was also combed in Denmark. Combing makes the hairs run parallel, and they can then be spun into a very smooth, strong thread.

The Norse Greenlanders both sorted and combed, as can be seen from the preserved textiles. The hairs were used for the warp and the underwool for the weft, but it is also likely that there were threads that were a mixture, corresponding to the Faroese medium grade.

From fine hairs which must be specially selected and combed, sewing thread and thread for sewing/weaving the incredibly beautiful borders were made.

The prepared wool must have been stored in something until it could be spun. At the Farm Beneath the Sand (64V2-III-555) a lid was found with a diameter of 120 mm, made with withies (x1909), as well as a wickerwork fragment (x2706) of 85 x 50 mm and a small basket (x1571) with a diameter of 60 mm. The Norse Greenlanders may thus easily have had larger coiled baskets – and these could have been used to store wool, spun or unspun.

The Production of Thread

1. Spinning

Spinning is a process whereby fibres are stretched and twisted into thread. For millennia this process involved the use of a spindle and a weight known as a whorl. At one end of the spindle a notch known as a heck can be cut to fasten the thread in while new fibre material is being drawn out and spun into thread. The spindle may also be pointed and without a heck or may be furnished with a hook, and the whorl can be placed at the top or the bottom of the spindle. The spun thread is wound around the spindle, and when it is full the thread is unwound from it.

Only a few archaeological finds show the placing of the whorl on the spindle. At Juellinge on the Danish island of Lolland an incomplete spindle has been found with a whorl of glass at the bottom, and has been dated to the first century AD.[1]

In the Oseberg Queen's Grave from the Viking Age a 293 mm long spindle was found with a spherical whorl of stone at the top, and at Bryggen in Bergen, among the many spinning implements from the Middle Ages, two spindles with the weights at the bottom were found.[2]

In Greenland no spindles have been found with whorls still on them, but it is highly likely that both spinning methods, with a top-whorl or bottom-whorl spindle, were practised by the Norse women. The material, experience, and the desired thread quality would have been crucial to the choice of the placing of the weight. The relationship between the length of the spindle and the shape and weight of the whorl are important for the spinning speed and for how much the thread was spun.[3] But the spindle and the whorl do not reveal whether the thread was S-spun or Z-spun. On the whole it is very doubtful whether it is always possible from the preserved implements and the finished product to reason one's way to the human being's – in this case the spinner's – way of working (see Sections 3 and 4 below).

2. The spindle

In Norse mythology the goddess Frigg was the patroness of domestic and female work, symbolized by the spindle, and she has given her name to the constellation 'Frigg's Spindle' or 'Frøyja's Spinning-Wheel' (the 'belt' of Orion). In Christian iconography Eve can often be seen with a spindle, on which she spins thread for clothes to cover her naked body after the Expulsion from Paradise. Whether the Norse Greenlanders had a similar symbolic language or iconography we do not know, but it is certain that the spinning of thread was a very important part of their everyday life. It is thought that it took five to ten times as long to spin the necessary thread as to do the actual weaving. An experiment has shown that you have to spin 3000 metres of thread one millimetre thick to weave a piece of cloth one by one-and-a-half metres with 10/10 threads per cm. This does not include the figures for binding up or other wastage.[4]

Fig. 14.

Schematic presentation of the spinning and twining of a cable. The terms S-spun and Z-spun describe the direction of the spinning and twining. A thread is respectively Z- and S-spun when the fibres follow the oblique line in the letter Z and the letter S. In describing a weave, the two thread systems are separated with a slash (/) so that Z/S means that the warp is Z-spun and the weft is S-spun. The same applies to the twisted threads. A number indicates how many threads are used. Drawing shows Z-spun threads twisted in S (2Z1S) and thereafter Z-twisted again (4Z2S1Z).

Fig. 15.

The spinning of thread. The spindle is held and rotated with the right hand, while the left hand pulls the material to be spun (wool or linen) out of the distaff. At the same time, the diligent wife – as here – looks after her many children. Fresco in Kirkerup Church, Roskilde, from c. 1300.

3. Top-whorl spindle

For spinning with the top-whorl spindle one starts the spindle rotating by rolling it down one's leg or hip with the palm of the hand. Once the spindle is in motion, one lets go and allows the spindle to rotate freely in the air and on down towards a supporting underlay – for example a floor or a pot. The free hand stretches out the fibres from the prepared material and at the same time controls the supply of the fibre out into the spindle so that the thread will be spun evenly. The result of this will be S-spun thread if the spinner is right-handed. If on the other hand the spindle is set in motion by being rolled up the thigh, the thread will be Z-spun. If the spinner is left-handed and rolls the spindle up the left leg or hip, the thread will be Z-spun, and will be S-spun if one rolls the spindle down the hip. To obtain a tightly spun thread, one has to rotate the spindle for a long time before winding the spun thread.

Fig. 16.
Olaus Magnus, (titular) Arch-
bishop of Uppsala, had a
drawing made of a Norse
spinning woman with spin-
ning material attached to her
head with a band. To give
light, she is seen here holding
a lit stick (torch) in the mouth.
Drawing from 1555.

4. Bottom-whorl spindle

If the whorl is placed at the bottom of the spindle, the spindle is set in motion with a flick of the fingers. From then on the spinning process is the same as with the top-whorl spindle, but with the important difference that the thread is Z-spun if the spinner 'flicks to the right'. By contrast, the thread is S-spun if one 'flicks to the left'.

The result is the same whichever hand is used, but a left-handed person is more likely to flick to the left and a right-handed to the right.

5. Spinning without a whorl

Thread can also be spun on a spindle without using a spindle whorl, and a heck is not necessary. To spin without a heck one fastens the thread with a loop around the spindle. In Lapland and in Karelia in the twentieth century most spinning was done on spindles without whorls. At the beginning of the spinning one could put a weight at the bottom, but as soon as some thread had been spun, and the weight on the spindle had increased, the separate weight was removed. The length of the spindle was 200-500 mm.[5]

In Greece, as late as 1979, spinning was done on a spindle stick without a weight. To prevent the thread sliding off the stick the spinner would put a piece of dried fruit at the bottom of the spindle to stop the thread. While the spinning was being done the stick was held in the hand, where it was kept rotating with the fingertips.[6] Such spinning-sticks may also have been furnished with a weight of material that has now disappeared. In Scotland this could be a potato.

Finally, there are spinning-hooks and twining-hooks that are used without any kind of weight. Such a 'hook' may be formed from a split branch, or it may be a stick (spindle) through which a cross-stick has been stuck.[7] To spin without a weight one rotates the spinning-hook in one's hand. Such hooks have been known from eastern Finland to the Orkney Islands and are thought to have been used in Scandinavia in the Bronze Age. The Sámi (Lapps) at Lofoten and the fishermen and hunters in western Norway used hooks to make fishing lines from horse hair. The implements have been used in as late as our own time, and the names given to them indicate their special use. In western Norway the si-krog was a tool for spinning or twining animal hairs into lines, but thicker cords *(kordeller* or 'strands') were used to make ropes. The word si means threads wound with calf-hair, and *krog* means hook. *Baat-si* ('boat si') meant a thick thread of calf-hair used for caulking, and *si-tvare* was the

tarred draining-plug in a ship. From other parts of the world we know the cross-shaped spinning-hook as a tool for spinning human hair.[8]

A thickening on the spindle, often elliptical, may replace a spindle whorl, and the spinning method would then have been as with a top-whorl or bottom-whorl spindle, depending on where the thickening was on the spindle.

From the Hjortspringkobbel bog on the Als peninsula we have a two-thousand-year-old spindle with a thickening at the bottom.[9]

Spindles with a thickening up towards the top end are known from the Oseberg find and from Bryggen in Bergen. The thickening can also be in the middle of the spindle, as can be seen on two short spindles (155 mm) with pointed ends from the Viking village of Elisenhof on the Eider. One is of wood with a heck, while the other

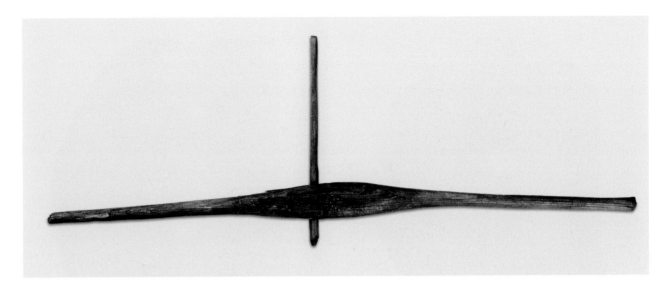

Fig. 18.

Spinning and twining hook (1950x941) of wood, found in the Farm Beneath the Sand. The long, thick, and formed stick measures 460 mm, while the short, thin stick measures 160 mm. The spindle is shown lying in a horizontal position.

is of bone and without a heck.[10] A 296 mm long wooden spindle with a 10 mm thickening in the middle of the spindle has been found in Ribe and dated to the Viking Age. One end of the spindle has been broken off. At the other end there is a small bored hole which may have been for attaching a hook.[11]

6. The distaff

On many medieval pictures one can see the spinning Eve or the Virgin Mary with the spindle in her right hand and the spinning material attached to a long stick, a distaff, which was stuck in under the left arm or fastened to a belt. The distaff could also be attached to a stick on the bench on which Eve can often be seen sitting. In Olaus Magnus' account of the Nordic peoples, published in Rome in 1555, a woman is shown with her spinning material attached to her own head by a ribbon.[12] The spinner undoubtedly went back and forth to do other work while she was spinning. In the Faroe Islands we have a record from the nineteenth century saying that a *fjeldstav* (walking-staff) was also used as a distaff.[13]

No recognizable distaffs have been found among the many worked wooden sticks from Greenland.

7. Norse spindles

In the Norse ruins a couple of hundred spindle whorls have been found as well as a number of spindles. Fewer spindles have been preserved, mainly because they were made of wood and were thus less durable than the whorls, which were made of soapstone. Among the many spindles, a total of sixteen from Sandnæs (V51) and from Umiiviarsuk (V52a), there are two complete ones. They are smooth and carefully formed with a thickening up towards one end. The longest spindle (D11878.327) measures 431 mm, of which 8 mm form a carved 'ledge' at the top (weight: 30 g). Another spindle (D12395.328) is 408 mm long, to which can be added a 15 mm long iron hook which is at the top end (weight: 22 g). A 'ledge' can also be seen on a third spindle (D12395.335). Its present-day length is 240 mm, but since one end has been broken off, the spindle was once longer. An incomplete spindle (D12397.336), 143 mm long, has the remains of an iron spike at the thickest point, but it does not penetrate right through the spindle. None of the spindles has marks from weights. Among

Fig. 19.

Form (D11166) of soapstone for the moulding of spindle whorls, found at the Bishop's seat in Gardar. An inscription with Gothic majuscules can be seen around the funnel-shaped hole. Measurement: 100x40 mm.

the Norse spindles there are also very short ones similar to the two spindles from Elisenhof.[14]

From the large rich Norse farms in the Western Settlement we also have some very rare spinning or twining hooks. Two were found at the farm Austmannadalen 5 (V53d) and three are from the Farm Beneath the Sand (64V2-III-555). The best-preserved twining hook (D12809.351) consists of a 310 mm long stick, which tapers towards the top end, and has an almost square profile. A 278 mm long flat cross-stick belonging to it is also preserved. In the find list the long stick (the spindle) was measured at 438 mm. It has two holes at right angles to each other about 20 mm apart. How far the two holes were from the ends of the spindles can only be seen on a photograph, since when examined in 1999 the spindle had broken off at the bottom hole. When the spindle was registered, only one cross-stick was mentioned, and today the cross-stick is broken in two. The other spinning or twining hook (D12809.350) consists of a 443 mm long stick (spindle) with a flat thickening at the top, under which there is a hole. The spindle has broken off at the bottom end, and no cross-stick has been preserved.[15] In the excavation of GUS no fewer than three 'hooks' were found (x941, x1165 and x1166). The first of these is 460 mm long and the cross-stick is 160 mm long; the second is 210 mm long, but both ends are broken off. The spindle measures 30 mm at the thickest point, where there are remains of the cross-sticks. The third is 470 mm long and is split lengthwise. At the thickest point of the spindle there are traces of cross-sticks. The Norse spinning or twining hooks can be compared to finds of spinning hooks from western Finland, where a spindle 450 mm long and the cross-stick 260 mm have almost the same measurements as the Norse ones.[16]

From the Norse farm Austmannadalen 5 (V53d) we also have a spindle with a carved knob (D12809.349). The spindle is 185 mm long, of which the knob alone measures 56 mm. In the list of finds the length is said to be 230 mm.[17]

Among the Bryggen finds from Bergen there are 24 of this type, found in layers that can be dated to 1170-1400. They have been catalogued as possible spindles.[18] Some of these, as well as the Norse spindle, were probably used with the knob point-

Fig. 20.
The reverse side of the form (D11166) for the moulding of spindle whorls with 18 mm high engraved faces – probably representing Norse settlers.

ing downward, corresponding to more recent Finnish and Romanian spindles which have a similar knob and a heck at the opposite end.

8. Spindle whorls

The Norse spindle whorls are found in conical form, in hemispherical form with a narrowing at the base and in disc form. The disc-formed ones are almost identical to a Danish spindle whorl from the Bronze Age found at Høje Taastrup.[19] A few Norse whorls have a collar-like rim at the top, and one also finds a spherical form like the above-mentioned spindle whorl from Oseberg. All but a few are made of soapstone (steatite). The exceptions are spindle whorls of wood, whale bone and bone from other animals. On one of the whorls from 'Abel's Farm' (Ø167) runes have been carved which can probably be translated as 'Sigrid made' (D24/1991.30). The interpretation is uncertain, since half of the whorl is missing, but it may further have said *snáld,* a word meaning spindle whorl. A Norwegian spindle whorl has a similar name carved in runes.[20]

Other whorls are decorated with crosses on the side or the bottom. Some have vertical lines, others concentric rings, which are found on both surfaces of the disc whorls. A very large whorl from Russip Kuua (Ø71) has three times three scored concentric rings (D23/1991.51).[21] Something similar can be seen on one of the four spindle whorls found at Herjolfsnæs (Ø111) (No. 183). The whorl is incomplete, but the diameter can be measured and is almost the same.[22] The holes bored in the whorls are slightly conical, narrowest at the top, and are not always placed precisely in the centre.

The whorls illustrated measure 25-85 mm at the base and weigh 12-90 g. Whorls of over 50 g would have been for twisting or spinning cord. The large whorl from Russip Kuua (Ø71), only a little more than half of which has been preserved, weighs 455 g. Large whorls, especially the disc-shaped ones which weigh more than 400 g are interpreted as *kællingerokke* (literally 'hags' spinning wheels'), a Norwegian word used for weights for flywheels in drills.[23]

From Bryggen in Bergen 410 whorls have been registered in various materials. Of the medieval ones, 69% are of soapstone.[24]

In the ruins of the farms Ø64c and 064e, and from Ø70, Ø7l and Ø167 a total of 106 spindle whorls have been found, some as fragments. Three or four weights were probably used for other purposes than spinning textile fibres.[25]

From Sandnæs (V51) and from Umiiviarsuk (V52a) a total of 49 whorls have been preserved.[26] From Brattahlid (Ø29a) there are 44, some of which are fragmentary, and none is very finely worked.[27]

At the bishop's seat Gardar (Ø47) 25 spindle whorls were found, nine of which were in the kitchen; one was in the chancel of the church and one was in the bell tower. [28] The find-spots suggest that the women spun thread wherever they happened to be. Also six highly unusual moulds of soapstone were found at Gardar, some with runes, others with majuscules carved on the inside of the mould. One of the runic inscriptions has been interpreted as 'Idur owns me'.[29] Poul Nørlund, who excavated the bishop's seat, thought that the mould may have been for making spindle whorls of lead or bronze. So far no spindle whorls of metal have been found in the Norse ruins. The last spindle whorls to appear are from the Farm Beneath the Sand (64V2-III-555), where 27 were registered.

9. The thread

The Norse Greenlandic woman was an able spinner who spun smooth, uniform yarn. The long hairs were spun in the Z-direction with a spin of 40°-50° and with a thickness of about one millimetre. The shorter underwool was S-spun into a slightly less firm thread of 30°-40° and with almost the same thickness as the Z-spun threads. However, there are variations in the thread thickness determined by the closeness of the weave, as the analyses show (see Analysis tables).

But among the Norse textiles there are also exceptions, for example costume D10587, where the weft threads are very uneven, and it would appear that they were spun directly from the bunch. The spinner may also have been unskilled.

The thread for sewing is always Z-spun and then S-plied. It is spun so thin that as finished thread it is hardly a millimetre in diameter.

In the weaves one can rarely see threads that are kinked and this is surprising considering the high spin degree in the warp threads. We do not know whether the women spun the thread in two processes – first an ordinary spin with a later winding-over – or had a special way of treating the newly spun thread. In Norway the hard-spun warp thread was formerly wound on a stick, a *nøste*, which gave the ball of yarn a hole through it. In order to stabilize the thread the ball was laid in cold water for three days. Steaming the ball was also known. In Setesdalen in Norway this process was called *dya* (killing) the thread. The weft thread was not wound on a *nøste* stick, but wound as a looser ball. All balls of weft thread (known as 'shoot') were gathered before use in a bag and buried in warm dry sheep manure. They lay there for up to three weeks.[30] Since no balls of yarn or objects for winding-up large quantities of yarn have been found, we do not know how the spun thread was stored before being used on the loom. Small flat pieces of wood, worked to a greater or lesser degree, have been interpreted as reels for winding up sewing thread, but many larger pieces of worked wood that could easily have been used to wind up yarn have also been preserved. The spin angle of the thread, its evenness and thickness, are quite crucial to the final appearance and sewing of the woven costumes.

The Warp-Weighted Loom

1. Presentation of the warp-weighted loom

In Icelandic the warp-weighted loom is called *vefstaður,* which can be translated both as 'weaving place' and as 'stone-weight loom'.[1] The latter designation also applies to the Faroese *kliggjavevur.*[2] In Norwegian the warp-weighted loom is called an *oppstadvev,* which describes the fact that the loom 'stands up', and this name was also used in the Orkney Islands. The warp-weighted loom has been in use for centuries – in western Norway it is still known in the living tradition. It is also in use today in many museums where weaving down through the ages has been demonstrated. In a famous poem, *Darraðarljóð,* dealing with the Battle of Clontarf in Ireland in the year 1014, the warp-weighted loom plays a central role.[3] The poem is known from *Njáls saga,* written down about 1280. The poem is the weaving song of the Valkyries. The first stanza describes the loom itself, then the poem follows the course of the battle as a working process in the loom of the Valkyries. In the poem the weaving has magical power: it 'conducts' the battle. The description of the Valkyries' loom is the most complete source for the weaving terminology of the Middle Ages.[4] A more recent Icelandic poem, *Króks bragur,* from c. 1700, describes a warp-weighted loom and how it is set up.[5] Viewed in the context of new finds of parts of one or more looms from the Farm Beneath the Sand (64V2-III-555) and from Umiiviarsuk (V52a) these poems are very important for the understanding of the use of the warp-weighted loom and of the products that were made on it.

None of the preserved looms that are in museums in the Nordic countries is more than 300 years old. Two Faroese looms are the oldest. One of them is in the museum in Thorshavn, the other can be seen in the National Museum in Copenhagen.[6]

2. The warp-weighted loom in use

When the warp-weighted loom was in use it stood leaning against a wall or against a roof beam. On the uprights there could, for example, be holes for wooden sticks on which the warp could be laid up. In warping, the threads were crossed each time they passed the turning-stick, so that the shed was laid. In the Faroe Islands another warping method was used. Three simple wooden sticks called *vørpur* were stuck in the door frame and then around these the warp and the shed were laid.[7]

The top beam could be furnished with a projecting edge with holes at regular intervals – as can be seen on the long beam from GUS (x598) – intended for tucking up the warp. The warp threads on the diagonally placed loom are kept separated into front threads and back threads with the shed stick in a so-called natural shed. This system of balance is the main principle of the warp-weighted loom. At the bottom of the loom the threads were tied to the weights in two rows, so that all the warp threads were evenly weighted. In the simplest set-up, for plain weave, the back warp threads were tied forward to the heddle shaft with identical long heddles, and the shed was changed with the heddle shaft. The weaving was done from the top down

and the weft was drawn in by hand. Once the weft thread had been laid in the shed it was beaten up against the woven piece with a sword beater, but only after the weaver had changed to a new shed with the heddle shaft. To order the threads a small pointed wooden stick or bone was used – in Iceland called a *hræll*. In both the Faroes and Iceland this was one of the most important implements associated with the loom.[8]

3. Loom weights

In Greenland a very large number of weights have been found. Poul Nørlund, who headed the excavations of the Herjolfsnæs Churchyard (Ø111), of Eric the Red's farm at Brattahlid (Ø29a) and of the bishop's seat at Gardar (Ø47), writes that before they had dug for half an hour a loom weight had been found. Almost all loom weights are made of soapstone, since this material is easy to bore or cut holes in and to adapt so that the stones will have more or less the same weight. It was important to have an even weight to get a uniform weave, but inequalities in the weight could be regulated by tying different numbers of warp threads to the weights. A heavy weight would have more threads than a lighter one. Besides loom weights of soapstone, a couple of weights of granite were found at Gardar, but these were probably fishing sinkers.[9] The granite weights have no hole through them; instead they have a deep groove around them for tying. In the Faroes basalt was used for loom weights. Around the stones a ribbon was tied, and to this the warp threads were attached.[10] In three of the weights from GUS (x814, x819, x1109) the cords for tying the weights to the warp threads have been preserved. This is an unusual find, since these cords usually disappeared either in fires or because of decomposition in the ground. At Nipaatsoq (V54) weights have been found which consist of lumps or rimsherds from soapstone vessels with holes bored or cut through them. In the holes there was once a strip of sealskin (kobberem), some of which have survived.[11] In Norway too soapstone (kljåstein) was used for loom weights. In the Old Town in Oslo excavations in medieval layers have turned up weights with remains of cords. One weight has been preserved with the cord still in it.[12]

Many weights have carved crosses or runes. Some of the runes have been interpreted as spells that averted illness or helped people against all sorts of evils. Other runes are carved on objects to name the objects themselves.[13] On some weights men's names have been carved. It has been thought that when they were male names these weights must have been sinkers for fishnets. A Norwegian archaeological find of 120 weights from a limited area in Gudbrandsdalen close to the River Lågen has given rise to the interpretation that the weights did not serve just one purpose, but were used as both net sinkers and loom weights.[14] Finally, one could suggest that the

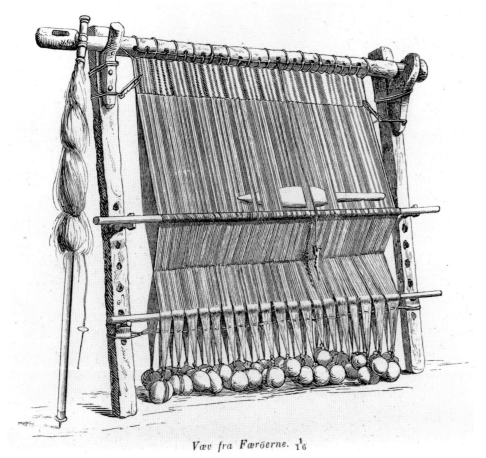

Væv fra Færöerne. $\frac{1}{16}$

Fig. 23
Loom weights with preserved cords for binding the warp threads. The weights are from the Farm Beneath the Sand (1950x814, – x1109 and –x819) and weigh respectively 680, 415 and 595 grams.

Fig. 22
An etching from 1854 of the Faroese warp-weighted loom which was named 'Worsaaes Væv' after the then Director of the National Museum. Leaning against the loom is a distaff containing spinning material. In the original introductory material the distaff is named as a walking staff. Wool could be attached to this tool, or it could be used as support for a traveller.

Fig. 24

Sword beaters and loom weights.
Two narrow wooden pieces –
possibly toy swords – and two
made of whalebone. A battle
scene is engraved on the blade of
the second-last sword (see fig.
25). The loom weights are made
of soapstone. The weight with
the double cross weighs 400 g.
The weight with two holes 420
g, the pearl-like weight 155 g,
and the weight with the chipped
edge 270 g.

weights were also used to hold down the cords of nets laid over the gathered hay –
this can still be seen in Ireland. Name-runes or owners' marks were perhaps carved
on the weights to show that they belonged to a particular farm and thus bore the
name or mark of the farmer. But it is also conceivable that the loom weights were
suitors' gifts and that it is the name of the giver that is carved. Textile-working implements are often used as suitors' gifts in other contexts.

4. Sword beaters

In Greenland sword beaters or parts of them have been found in several excavations.
They are made of whalebone or of wood. At Herjolfsnæs Churchyard, in a burial, a
beautifully worked 140 mm long wooden handle for a weaving-knife or miniature
sword beater was found (No. 189).[15] Nørlund thought that this sword beater was a
grave-gift for a woman. Similar finds of grave goods in Christian burials are known
from several places in Europe and were perhaps put in the grave to prevent haunt-
ings.[16] The preserved handle has been dated to the eleventh century. At Eric the
Red's farm in Brattahlid (Ø29a) two partly preserved blades of sword beaters have
been found, one of wood and one of bone.[17] From Sandnæs too parts of wooden
swords thought to be for weaving have been found (D11716.323, D11734.325,
D11786.324).[18] At another farm in the Western Settlement four sword beaters have
been found, two of which are of wood and measure 325 mm (handle missing) and
312 mm in length respectively. The thickness is 9-10 mm. They are very light, weigh-

Fig. 25
Drawing of an engraved battle scene.

Fig. 26
Section of sword beater (D5/1992.66), showing signs of wear and tear. The sword was used to beat the weft up into the weave. In this way, the sword hit the crossing warp threads, causing the wear marks.

ing less than 50 g. However, it is doubtful whether they were used for weaving, since the edge is almost as thick as the sword itself. They would therefore not be suitable for weaving a close-woven *vaðmál*, but they could have been used for lighter, narrower weaves that did not have to be beaten close together. They might also have been toy swords. At a large farm, Austmannadalen 5 (V53d), two sword beaters of whalebone have been found, respectively 316 mm (point missing) and 450 mm long (D12809.341 and 342). On the blade of the first, two warriors have been carved, and both can be seen to be wielding swords.[19]

At the farm Ø64c and at the *Landnáma* Farm (Ø17a) two incomplete sword beaters of whalebone have been found. From the former farm we have a 345 mm long sword with no handle (D12949.105). From Ø17a we have a 365 mm long sword – the point is missing – with a weight of 120 g (D5/1993.66). On the edge of the sword the warp threads have left clear wear-marks with almost regular cross-strokes.[20] From these farms, too, three handles of wood have been preserved which are probably from sword beaters.

In the Nordic countries sword beaters were made of whale bone, and many of these – about fifty – have been found in Norway, with a length of 60-80 cm, but there are even longer sword beaters with lengths up to one metre.[21] Sword beaters were also made of iron and are preserved in large numbers. They are of course heavier than the sword beaters made of bone and of wood. It is difficult to understand how the Norse Greenlandic women could have beaten the weft in the compact *vaðmál* together without using a heavy sword beater. So far no sword beater of iron has been found in Greenland, but it is possible that among the many whole or fragmentary iron knives there are some weavers' sword beaters.

5. Working height

The first weft thread just below the starting border was probably plucked or pulled into the warp before the top beam was laid in place at the top of the loom. After this the weaving could begin. The weaver probably had to stand on something to get a good working height and to control the motion of the threads through the weave. One may wonder how this work could be done at all in the semi-darkness up below the roof of the weaving room. The limited light of the oil lamp or the glow of the hearth were the only sources of light.

An Icelandic study of lighting types concludes that train-oil lamps provided so little light that people almost worked in the dark and when paraffin lamps became common it was seen as something quite incredible.[22] In the weaving rooms in Green-

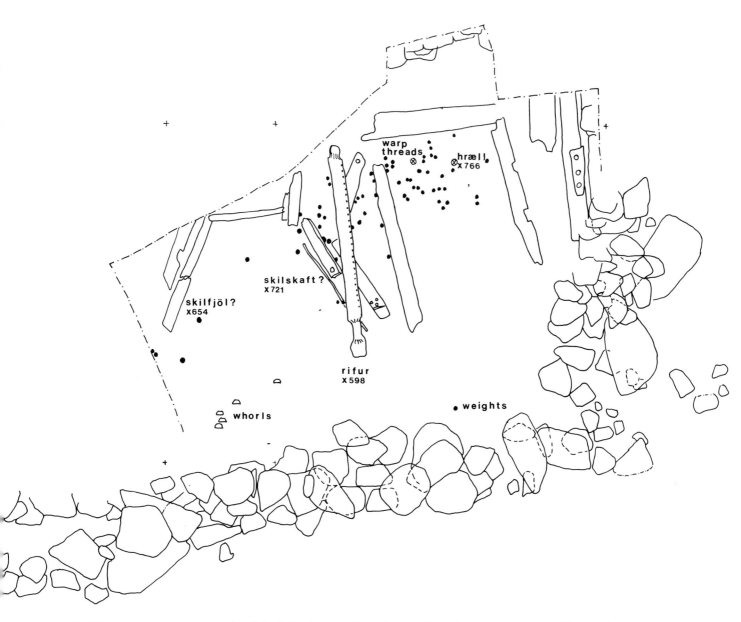

warp
threads
⊗

⊗ hræll
x 766

skilskaft ?
X 721

skilfjöl ?
x654

rifur
X 598

• weights

whorls

Fig. 27

Excavation plan of Room 1,
the so-called weaving room,
from the Farm Beneath the Sand.
The wooden implements from
one or more looms are drawn
on the plan.

land the light from the hearth must have been an indispensable supplement to the oil lamps.

Perhaps it was also necessary to stand on a stool to get plenty of power into the 'beating' for the first piece. Strength would have been necessary when the weft threads were to be as close as we can see in most Norse weaves. Icelandic women who, in the nineteenth century, were familiar with weaving on a warp-weighted loom as a living tradition said that it was necessary to beat four times with the sword beater, first in the middle then on each side of the weave. When *vaðmál* was woven, one had to beat up to twenty times to get the cloth compact.

We do not know the height of a Greenlandic warp-weighted loom, since the only two uprights found so far are not intact. In the weaving room at the Farm Beneath the Sand (64V2-III-555) a whale vertebra was found (x561) which may have been used as a weaving stool. It is 250 mm high, 380 mm wide and 320 mm long.

Two similar stools of whale vertebrae were found at farm V53d in Austmannadalen. They were not in the weaving room, but in adjacent rooms.

6. The weaving room

In the Middle Ages the women could have a special room where they prepared the wool, spun, wove and sewed. Such a weaving room was called a *dyngja*. In an excavation one recognizes that there are many textile-working implements and in particular many loom weights that lie in rows as if they had just been dropped from the loom. From the length of such a fallen row of 26 loom weights in a burnt-down house from the twelfth century in the Old Town in Oslo, it has been estimated that the width of the woven cloth was 1200 mm, if the assemblage was complete.[23] Two farms (V53c and C53d) in Austmannadalen both have a *dyngja* placed in the northern and northeastern parts of a large unified farm complex. In the weaving room in the first of these farms, opposite the middle of the back wall, there were no fewer than 63 loom weights in a heap within a square metre. In another room in the farm there were 31 weights lying in the eastern corner. The weights were made of soapstone sherds, and were much worn. Aage Roussell, who excavated the farms, wrote that a net full of the weights may have hung in this corner, or the loom may have stood there. At the other farm 98 loom weights were found with a 1600 mm long heddle rod, which has unfortunately not been preserved.[24]

In the room where the two sword beaters were found there lay no fewer than 240 soapstone sherds with holes in them. However, it is doubtful whether these were loom weights. The room had no fireplace and it is thought that it was a bedroom. A 53 cm wide door opening led out to a passage.[25] The looms at the two farms Umiiviarsuk (V52a) and Austmannadalen 5 (V52d) appear to have stood in weaving rooms close to crossbenches, since the weights were found at the end of these benches.

At GUS the first room the archaeologists excavated was in fact a *dyngja*, and it was here that the many textile-working implements were found. From a review of the find-spots of loom weights in excavations from, among other places, the Old Town in Oslo and from Scania, it is evident that they are often found on the northern side of the room in the dwelling or towards the northeast in pit-houses and it has been possible to see that a door or entrance was placed on the opposite side. The placing of the loom in relation to the door has therefore been interpreted as the result of a wish to receive any light that came in.[26] On the Greenland farms the *dyngja* was placed in the northern or northeastern part of the farms but may not have had anything to do with light, since no outside doors were found in these rooms.

7. The loom and weaving room at the Farm Beneath the Sand

One of the most important finds at the Farm Beneath the Sand (64V2-III-555) was the 1880 mm long beam of the loom (x598). It was among the large pieces of wood that revealed where the farm was buried, and which are parts of one or more warp-weighted looms. The long beam, which was placed at the top of the loom, resting on bearing uprights, is intact.[27] On the beam one can see cavities out towards the ends

Fig. 28
This 1880 mm long loom beam (1950x598) from the Farm Beneath the Sand is the only preserved medieval loom beam from the North Atlantic area. At the bottom, across the breadth of the beam, there are 34 holes for attachment of the warp threads.

Fig. 29

Section of the (fixed broad) shed rod (1950x283) from the Farm Beneath the Sand. Along both sides irregularly placed wear marks from the warp threads can be seen. The shed rod which has been broken off at the one end, is 1423 mm long, 114 mm broad, and 25 mm thick.

which meant that it could revolve on the tops of the posts. The distance between the cavities is 1600 mm. It has 34 holes for sewing the warp threads on, spread over 1400 mm measured from the first to the last hole.[28] For the weaving one must deduct some 300-400 mm on each side as 'elbow room' inside the posts. At the Icelandic National Museum a warp-weighted loom is exhibited where there are 1570 mm between the uprights, which allows a weaving width within 1270 mm.[29] In the weaving room at GUS two smaller beams of 920 mm and 1160 mm were also found (x3-x596). Since they are not terminated at the ends, the length must have been greater. In addition an incomplete upright and an incomplete shed rod with wear-marks from warp threads were found.[30] In this connection I should mention the complete shed rod (D12389.314) found at Umiiviarsuk (V52a), which like GUS was in the Western Settlement.[31] The shed rod, which measures 1682 mm in length, is 98-105 mm wide and 23 mm thick, and also has furrowed wear-marks from the warp threads on both edges at intervals of 13-20 mm. Among other weaving implements found in the weaving room at GUS were a *hræll* (x766), many loom weights and a stool.

The weaving room at the Farm Beneath the Sand (64V2-III-555) was sunken, and there was no door out to the open air. The low-lying placing may therefore not be the result of a wish for diagonally falling light. On the other hand, in the weaving room the largest fireplace registered in the farm complex was found, and this may have something to do with the light, since in a large fireplace there is room for a lot of fuel, which besides heat would also provide a good deal of light. The lack of light 'indoors' tempts one to suggest that the loom was moved outside in the summer, when there was plenty of light.

The sunken floor must thus have had another significance. Perhaps outer walls and roof construction at the farm were not high enough for the loom? The two incomplete uprights found so far cannot unfortunately document the height of the GUS loom. The Faroese loom in the National Museum in Copenhagen has 1900 mm uprights, and the loom in Thorshavn has two-metre tall uprights. In the weaving room at the farm V53d in Austmannadalen, planks were preserved from wall cladding that showed that the height of the wall was 1.65 metres.[32]

Techniques

1. 'Shaft' names

In Icelandic sources we find the designations *einskefta* and *þriskeft*, names derived from the terminology of the warp-weighted loom, which thanks to its ingenious construction (the natural shed) did not need the extra heddle shaft we know from the later treadle loom. *Vaðmál* was *þriskeft*. In Icelandic one finds the twill variant and, moreover, *hringavefnaður* (a patterned weave). For the latter of these the warp-weighted loom used four shafts.[1] *Ringvend* ('ring turn') is the Norwegian name for a twill.[2] In addition the name *tvujskefta* ('two-shaft') occurs in a Faroese description of the warp-weighted loom from the end of the eighteenth century. In modern terms these 'shaft' names *einskefta, tvujskefta* and *þriskeft* would be 'translated' as two-shaft, three-shaft (2/1 twill) and four-shaft. The new names arose when the treadle loom became widespread and partly replaced the old warp-weighted loom or was used at the same time. The Greenlandic weaves were made with *skeft* and *skefta* as a preconditon, and these old names will therefore be used in the following along with the technical weave names.

Greenlandic Textiles

1. The weaves

A Norse weave can be characterized as a weave with a strong smooth warp, closely spun from hairs and with a softer weft spun from the combed-off underwool.

This is most commonly woven as a 2/2 twill, but there are also weaves in 2/1 twill and tabby weaves. In addition there are patterned weaves which show that the weaver clearly exploited the potential of the warp-weighted loom and understood how to compensate for the limitations of the weaves by using different dyes and materials.

In the manuscripts *Búalög* and *Grágás* we find a number of names for weaves in wool: *bragðarváð, gjaldaváð, hafnarváð, munaðarváð, smáváð, vöruváð* and *pakkaváð* or Islencha. As we can see, all the names end with *váð*, which means cloth. The textile name *vaðmál* means 'cloth measure', since in the Middle Ages – and well into the nineteenth century – *vaðmál* was a measure of value and was used as a means of payment.

Bragðarváð was a fine quality that could be used to pay tithes to the church. *Smávaðmál* was also a fine weave. The word is also known from more recent times with the same meaning. A priest's salary could be paid in *vaðmál*, as is evident from an Icelandic *máldagi* (a verbal or written agreement) in which one can read that the bishop made sure that the salary of four marks, 192 alen of *vaðmál*, the value more or less of one and a half cows, had been paid to the priest.[1] In the twelfth century 72 alen of saleable *vaðmál* had the same value as a cow of a good age or as six milch ewes.[2] According to *Grágás* the *vaðmál* that was used as payment was woven as *þrískeft* (2/2 twill). Other medieval sources outside Iceland mention *vaðmál* as woven with *einskeft* (tabby weave), and since *vaðmál* is also sometimes described as fulled and sometimes as unfulled, it is not very clear what *vaðmál* actually looked like.[3] We do not know the names that the Norse Greenlanders themselves gave their various weaves, but the many garments and costume fragments from the Norse farms show that they wove several types. The uniformity of the weaves and the professional impression they make suggest that there was a standard product which must have been usable as a means of payment in the same way as the Icelandic *vaðmál*. However there is no written source that confirms that the Greenlandic *vaðmál* was used as payment or for exports. That this *vaðmál* could be used as a costly gift is evident from *the saga of Thorfinn Karlsefni*.

2. The Greenlandic vaðmál

In *Thorfinn Karlsefnis saga* (also known as 'The Saga of Eric the Red') it is said that the son of Eric the Red, Leif, gives his beloved Thorgunna a cloak of Greenlandic *vaðmál*. This *vaðmál* may be of the quality we find in, among other things, the garments from Herjolfsnæs (Ø111). The *landnáma* women took with them a weaving tradition from Iceland which they maintained in the settlements, but analyses of the weaves have shown that in time they developed their own trademark product, the Greenlandic *vaðmál,* which is characterized by having more weft threads than warp threads per centimetre. Such a close weft must have required strong warp threads to resist the many necessary blows with the sword-beater. The Greenlandic *vaðmál* is a homogeneous weave which shows that the loom was in balance, and one sees very few errors. Altogether these characteristics, as well as the special fibre composition of the thread, could be used to identify a Greenlandic weave found among archaeological textiles in countries outside Greenland. It has not yet been wholly clarified why they wove much more weft into the cloth than was ordinary practice in other places, but the reason is probably that they wanted clothes that were warmer.[4]

3. Weaving width

On the looms from the Farm Beneath the Sand (64V2-III-555) and from Umiiviarsuk (V52a), from which we have a beam and a fixed broad shed rod, cloth could be woven with a width of around 1200 mm, judging from the preserved beam and from the fixed broad shed rod from Umiiviarsuk, which has clear wear-marks from the warp threads. At GUS, besides the beam, a couple of fixed broad shed rods were also found, but they are not preserved in their full length and therefore cannot contribute any information on weaving width. And in the Greenlandic weaves no help is to be found either, since it has not been possible to find a single weave with both selvedges preserved. The widest measure registered can be seen on the costume D10579, where the middle piece measures 950 mm at the back. The second-greatest width was measured on the costume D10587, where one side – including three false seams – measures 860 mm. Both pieces are cut off diagonally from the bottom edge. Where two adjacent panels have been stitched together, the seam is made with many close stitches and it has not been possible to see whether there is a selvedge on the few millimetres that are left.

In order to maintain a given weaving width it was probably necessary to use some implement to keep the weave stretched out while the work was in progress, and at the same time to prevent it getting narrower on the way down. In a drawing of the oldest preserved warp-weighted loom, the Faroese one, one can see two short sticks or large pins *(tigler),* one in each selvedge.[5] The pins are stuck through the woven cloth, which is kept stretched out by means of cords from the pins to the uprights. (See p. 55). The pins in the drawing look like pegs, and do not look particularly efficient. The artist may not have understood the use of these 'spreaders'. The *tigler* have unfortunately disappeared from the Faroese loom, which is now at the National Museum in Copenhagen.

Grágás mentions a weaving width of two alen (1 alen = 490 mm) in connection with the pricing of *vaðmál. Búalög* says however that *vaðmál* was woven in panels of 3½ alen. If one compares the wear-marks on the fixed broad shed rods with the narrow weaving width given in *Grágás,* they do not quite match, and the 3½ alen wide measure mentioned in *Búalög* could not have been woven with the preserved 1880 mm long beam from GUS.[6]

4. Weaving length

The length of a *váð vaðmáls* (piece of *vaðmál*) is not given in the oldest sources, but may have been more or less limited by the height of the warp-weighted loom, which was probably not more than six alen.[7] However, in Iceland in the thirteenth century, according to *Grágás,* pieces were woven that were 20 alen in length. The Icelander Ólafur Olavius has illustrated in drawings of an Icelandic warp-weighted loom how

the woven piece was rolled around the top beam of the loom.[8] The reason why such long pieces were woven on the warp-weighted loom in Iceland is thought to be that Iceland exported *vaðmál* to western Europe, and in order to be competitive long pieces were necessary. How long the pieces woven by the Norse Greenlanders were we do not know. The longest pieces registered – measured on the costumes D10580 and D10583 – have a shoulder height of 1230 mm and 1280 mm respectively.

The *vaðmál* length *'hundrad alna or vaðmála'* mentioned in Icelandic sources from the earliest medieval period until the fourteenth century cannot be directly translated since the term *'hundrað'* for a long period meant 120. The measure 'one *alen'*, or ell, can also have different meanings. Originally an alen meant the length of a lower arm from the elbow to the points of the outstretched fingers.

5. Starting borders

The warp for the warp-weighted loom was prepared by weaving a starting border on a small band loom sometimes incorporating weaving tablets. The weft, which was to form the warp in the warp-weighted loom, was drawn out during warping to a certain length, probably adapted to the purpose or the length one wanted to weave, and then placed on the top beam so that the finished starting border came to look like a giant fringe. These starting borders are as a rule interpreted to mean that a weave has been made on a warp-weighted loom.

In the Greenlandic material, four such borders have been registered, the smallest of which is only preserved as a 15-20 mm long fragment. There are starting borders on the footless stocking D10616 and on the fragments D12411.8, D5/1992.9 and *No number* 0.3. The first two of these were woven in 2/2 twill. The last two are repp weaves.

Tablet-woven starting borders were formerly used by the Sámi (Lapps) in the weaving of blankets, but were later superseded by tabby-woven bands. An archaeological find of a 'sprang' stocking from Tegle in West Norway, dated to the 3rd-5th

century AD has a tablet-woven starting border that takes the living weaving tradition of the Sámi back many centuries. Among the textiles from Tegle there was also a warp showing that two balls of yarn were used for warping.[9] In Lund in Sweden tabby-woven bands were found on three fragments in 2/1 twill which can be dated to 1050-1150.[10]

In starting borders made by the Greenlanders, only one ball was used, and they were tabby woven – perhaps with tablets, since these have been found among the Norse material from Greenland. A starting border like the Greenlandic one can be seen on Överhogdal Bonaden II from Norrland in Sweden, which has been radiocarbon dated to the 10th-12th century and on the rather earlier check blanket found in Skjoldehamn Bog in northern Norway.[11]

There are also starting borders with a strong cord laid in after the warping. This method was used in Norway, in the Faroes and in Iceland.[12] A cord at the beginning of a weave can also be seen on a *refill* (wall hanging) from Hvammur Church in Iceland, radiocarbon dated to around 1450.[13] Regardless of the implement on which the starting border was woven, or whether there was a cord, it was sewn to the holes in the top beam of the warp-weighted loom. In the Faroes one could also draw a cord down through holes in the beam. At each hole the cord 'grasps' a bunch of warp threads which are thus fixed just below the beam.[14] If for some reason (lack of light?) the natural shed was spoiled by the setting-up of the warp in the loom, a new one had to be made.

On the footless stocking D10616 from Herjolfsnæs a starting border was used as termination at the top of the leg – an excellent use, because the stocking was thus given a hard-wearing edge and this saved folding and sewing.

6. Selvedges

In the Greenlandic textiles there are two different types of selvedge. In the Herjolfsnæs costumes it was possible to register a total of ten selvedges, although tight seams often hide the edges, and it can be difficult to tell which of the two types is present. There are even more in the other textile finds.

The two different types are the ordinary selvedge where one weft thread turns and is continued, and a selvedge where two weft threads turn with a crossing so that weft threads are clustered in groups of four. The selvedge with one weft thread presents as a straight edge, while the edge with the crossing weft threads is more uneven.

On the Herjolfsnæs costumes there are seven selvedges with crossing wefts; the other three have one weft. In the Norse material the crossing wefts are only found in twill weaves, but it may be a coincidence that they have not been noted on tabby weaves. It is evident from a Faroese account from the beginning of the twentieth century that the weft was wound in wedge-shaped balls of yarn (in Faroese called *vindur*) which were easy to draw through the shed on the warp-weighted loom, and that the weaver used two *vindur* alternately.[15] The Icelandic name is *vinda or snakkur*.[16] A reasonable explanation of the use of two alternating wefts in a one-colour weave is that one thus avoids streaking in the finished weave. Streaks may arise if the wool is not mixed enough before spinning for the inevitable colour shade differences to be evened out. In the same way the transition from a used-up weft thread to a new one can be highly visible if, for example, the threads are spun by two different spinners. By using two wefts one disguises these transitions.[17]

From urban excavations in Scandinavia and in northern Europe in general we have many weaves with two or more crossing wefts in the selvedges and with rein-

Fig. 33 and Fig. 34

Selvedges on the textiles in 2/2 twill. The weft threads turn one after the other, (ordinary turning), and a turning with crossing weft threads at the edge.

forced border threads. These selvedges are especially found with tabby weaves and 2/1 twill weaves, most of which are probably products from the treadle loom. Alternating wefts are known however from older times. In York for example a fragment has been found in 2/2 diamond twill from the end of the tenth century with two wefts crossing at the edge, like the Greenlandic ones.[18]

On the Danish costumes from Kragelund and Moselund, found in bogs south of Viborg, and on a fragment with a starting border from Lund, one can see similar selvedges.[19] They are all in 2/1 twill and have been dated to 1045-1150. In the cloak and stockings from Bocksten Bog in Halland, which is contemporary with the costumes from Herjolfsnæs, two wefts have also been used for a weaving width of 60-70 cm. Both are woven in 2/l twill and have been dated to the fourteenth century.[20] The weaving width or loom width apparently had no influence on the use of two wefts crossing at the edge, and we see once more that the Norse Greenlanders followed the custom that was in use in other places.

In analyses of textiles, selvedges are an important indicator, since they document which thread system is warp, and which is weft.

7. Weaving density

The analyses of the Greenlandic textiles show that many weaves have a thread number around 10/12 per cm, but with variations, since there are finer and coarser weaves (see Analysis tables).

The coarsest is a two-ply goat-hair weave with 4/3 threads per 2 cm (x608a) found at the Farm Beneath the Sand (64V2-III-555). Among the densest is a 2/1 diamond twill (21/11 threads per cm) found at Niaquusat (V48). This fragment is quite unique in Greenland and is undoubtedly an import.

In the Herjolfsnæs find, hood D10603 – with a density of 8/20-22 thr./cm, and fragments D10620 and D10621 with 14/20 and 12/15 thr./cm respectively, are some of the densest weaves. The latter is in a tabby weave, the others are in 2/2 twill. A fragment from a now unknown find-spot is a very densely woven 2/1 twill with 36/11 thr./cm. Like the above-mentioned diamond twill, this fragment probably represents an imported textile.

In the Old Icelandic law collections there are also rules for the numbers of threads in the different types of *vaðmál*. But these rules cannot be directly translated, since there is some doubt about how the rules are to be interpreted and about the correct unit of measurement.

Three pieces in tabby weave from the Farm Beneath the Sand.

Fig. 35

The fragment (1950x1607) has a dark warp and a light weft with 5/5 threads/cm.

Fig. 36

The fragment (1950x740) is an open and thin textile – probably woven for a special purpose with 6/5 threads/cm.

Fig. 37

Fragment (1950x3058) is woven from hare fur. A similar textile has never been registered before. The threads are two-plied – Z in the warp and S in the weft. There are 5/4 threads/cm.

8. Tabby weaves

In Icelandic tabby weaves are called *einskefta*. In the costumes from Herjolfsnæs there are eight items in this weave, and in the material from the Farm Beneath the Sand (64V2-III-555) there are 38 fragments. Of these, three weaves are in flax (x3103), and one fragment is woven with thread spun from the fur of the Arctic hare (x3058).

Distributed over the other Greenlandic finds there are 21 fragments in tabby weave, two of which are in flax. The weaves vary from relatively thin, open grades to thick, robust ones. They are weaves that were certainly made with a particular purpose in mind. Of the total number of weaves, 2.9% are in tabby weave, one of these in hare fur and five in flax.

9. Repp

Repp is among the tabby weaves. In repp the count of warp threads is considerably higher than that of weft threads – or vice versa – known as warp-faced or weft-faced repp. In the Greenlandic textiles – mainly from GUS – repp occurs as both warp-faced and weft-faced (x492, -x602, -x742, -x2862, -x3048). In the Herjolfsnæs find only the 'Burgundian cap' is woven in a repp, and out of 25 fragments from the farm (Ø17a) at Narsaq only one (D5/1992.7) is repp-woven.

10. Panama weaves

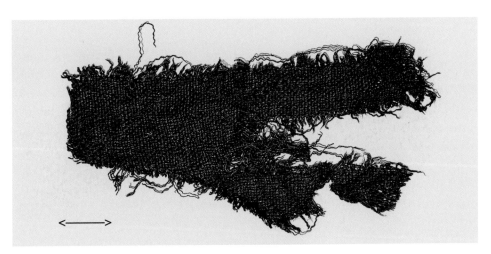

This too is a tabby weave, but with the variation that the threads run in pairs in both warp and weft. At the National Museum in Copenhagen there is an Icelandic wall hanging in black *tvistur* (panama weave) woven in wool, embroidered with a light brown wool thread. The wall hanging has been dated to c. 1450.[21] *Tvistur* is the Icelandic name, but this also covers other tabby weaves that are in balance. Also, in Norwegian wall hangings from the Middle Ages panama weaves can be found as a base for embroidery. An embroidered wall hanging from Høylandet Church in Norway, dated to the beginning of the thirteenth century, has a red-dyed panama weave in wool as its base material.[22] A panama weave from the Old Town in Oslo has two parallel Z-spun threads in both warp and weft.[23] This weave is also known as extended tabby weave. It is easy to count threads in this weave, and therefore it is well suited for embroidery. A single fragment of Greenlandic *tvistur*, which an analy-

Fig. 38

Tvistur is the Icelandic name for textiles in balanced tabby weave, and as such suitable for embroidering. Fragment (D5/1992.10) is from the Landnáma Farm. Double warp threads and single weft threads. There are 5x(2)/4 threads/cm.

sis has established as having been black, was found at the *Landnáma* farm (Ø17a) (D5/1992.10). This fragment, which has no sign of embroidery, has parallel threads running in pairs in the warp. The weft is single-threaded, but of the same thickness as two warp threads, which gives this weave an appearance like a 'real' *tvistur*.[24]

11. 2/2 twill

Vaðmálsvend is an old Norse word for a structure in twill weave. This word is still used in the Faroes, Iceland and Norway with the same meaning.[25]

The costumes from Herjolfsnæs are all sewn from cloth in twill weave (2/2), and as the right side the Norse Greenlanders used the side of the weave where the twill has a Z-twill grain. Thus the wrong side has an S-twill grain. One might think that the two sides of a 2/2 twill look the same – apart from the angle of the twill. But this is not the case. The Greenlandic *vaðmál* has a right side with an even, smooth texture, because the spinning direction of the threads and the Z-twill grain of the twill coincide, while on the wrong side they are opposite. On a number of weaves, both 2/2 and 2/1, the wrong side has a surface with diagonal 'ribs' which can be more or less prominent and which cannot be easily explained. This appearance might be due to the spin of the threads and the spinning direction in relation to the density of the weave, but since the right side has no such 'ribs', there must be another reason.

A similar feature has been observed in the medieval twill weaves from the Old Town in Oslo, where in a body of material consisting of 205 fragments (2/1 twill), diagonal 'ribs' were observed on five. These weaves all have Z-spun warp threads and S-spun weft threads with the highest thread density in the warp – unlike the Greenlandic ones. The ribs seem to have arisen because the intersections in every other diagonal line are sunken. The Norwegian textile researchers have no explanation of this rib formation. In apparently identical weaves with exactly the same combination of weave and spin there are a few with diagonal ribs all over the surface, some with ribs in parts, while most are without ribs.[26] This can be seen on both the Norwegian and the Greenlandic weaves.

Twill weaves with a relatively high number of threads (20/18 thr./cm), and Z/S spin, become common after the Roman Iron Age, but it is only from the Viking Age onwards that a coarser 2/2 twill spreads through northern Europe.[27] As a type, this common 2/2 twill with Z/S spinning always has more warp threads per cm – but not the Greenlandic *vaðmál*. In this case the opposite is true. Of the total number of weaves, 2/2 twill accounts for 82.5%.

Fig. 39
Textile in 2/2 twill, the most commonly used weave in Norse Greenland. The fragment (1950x2734) is from GUS.

Fig. 40
The characteristic diagonal structure is emphasised by the dark warp threads and the light weft. Fragment (1950x2553) is from the Farm Beneath the Sand.

12. 2/1 twill

This twill woven as *þrískeft vaðmál* was previously considered by many researchers to be unsuitable for the warp-weighted loom. It was thought that the unequal distribution of the warp threads on each of the two sides of the shed, which this weave requires, would create an imbalance in the loom and thus result in a clumsy product. But today we know that 2/l twill was – if not much used – at least absolutely possible to weave on the warp-weighted loom. Important finds in this weave from the Early Middle Ages were made in Lund and in the Old Town in Oslo in the 1970s. For the first time one could see starting borders preserved on weaves in 2/1 twill.[28] At the beginning of the twentieth century in the Faroes 2/1 twill was woven on a warp-weighted loom.[29]

Weaves in 2/1 twill were an innovation in the North in the 10th century, although in the South they appeared as early as the Roman period. They may have been produced in the first place on the two-beam vertical loom.[30] In time, however, they came to be made on the horizontal treadle loom which reached Scandinavia at the beginning of the Scandinavian Middle Ages. In Scandinavian countries, the treadle loom did not oust the warp-weighted loom, which was still used for weaving in the home, but it was used by professional weavers. The treadle loom meant that the professionals could increase production up to ninefold.[31] The two looms were used at the same time for many centuries.

In the publication of the finds from Lund, the theory was proposed that inherited methods, such as band-warping and starting borders, were transferred from the old warp-weighted loom to the treadle loom. Could the starting border on the fragment from Lund perhaps have been fastened to a beam in another type of loom, such as the two-beam vertical loom? An example of fine 2/1 diamond twill with just such a starting border has been recovered from a burial at Tavistock Abbey, Devon, UK, in a burial dated to the 14th century, long after the warp-weighted loom had ceased to be used in England.[32] However, a weave does not necessarily reveal the kind of loom used. 'That a weave can be woven on different implements does not mean that all looms are equally suited to all types of cloth,' the textile researcher Marta Hoffmann has said.[33] In analyses of small fragments it is almost impossible to distinguish the products woven professionally on the treadle loom from 'domestic' weaves done on the warp-weighted loom by able weavers.

That the Norse Greenlandic women could weave the unequal 2/1 twill is shown by the seven GUS fragments which have the typical Greenlandic *vaðmál* character (most wefts per cm) and the characteristic fibre composition (Hairy/Hairy Medium). This alone must be sufficient documentation. The fact that there are also a couple of imported weaves in 2/1 twill does not alter these facts.

On one of the Herjolfsnæs costumes an example of a 2/1 twill weave has in fact been found. It can be seen along the front edge of the costume D10594 as a very small decorative border. Originally the collar was also bordered. The decorative edge has the combination, unusual in the Greenlandic weaves, of Z/Z-spun threads, and since it is also madder-dyed this means that it was probably not woven in Greenland. Unfortunately the edge has now almost disappeared.

Fig. 41
In Greenland textiles in 2/1 twill were also woven on the warp-weighted loom. Two fragments of 2/1 twill textiles (1950x2216) from the Farm Beneath the Sand are very different. The weave on the upper fragment would seem to be a balanced tabby weave, while the fragment below is completely dominated by the weft. There are 9/13 threads/cm.

Fig. 42
Fragment (1950x2554) from the Farm Beneath the Sand is a very open textile in 2/1 twill with approximately 4/6 threads/cm.

Fig. 43
Drawing of diamond twill (KNK 985x80).

Fig. 44

Diamond twill in 2/1, dyed with madder. The 60x30 mm large fragment (KNK 985x80) was found during the excavation of a small farm in Niaquusat. It is the only diamond twill that is registered in Greenland.

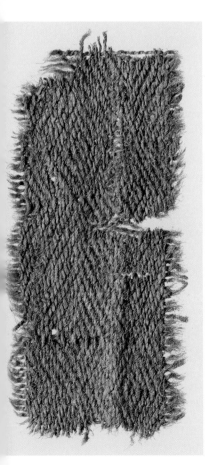

The oldest 2/l twill in Denmark was found in the Mammen grave near Viborg, and has been dated to the tenth century.[34] Later the many urban excavations have shown that 2/1 twill was in general use as early as the early post-Viking period. But outside the urban areas too there are textile finds in 2/1 twill. The contemporary costumes from Kragelund and Moselund should be mentioned here. Fragments in 2/1 twill have also been found in four medieval wrecks. It is reasonable to assume that the Danish costumes are products of the treadle loom. The fragments from the ships are woven from wool, but too small to identify anything more than the weave. Finally, a 2/l twill weave in dog-hair found in Inglefield Land in North Greenland should be mentioned. It is not possible to determine where this dog-hair weave was made until there is some material for comparison. Of the total number of weaves in Greenland 2/l twill accounts for 2.9%.

13. Diamond twill

Diamond twill is a variation of a twill weave. In Greenland one single fragment with a diamond has been found, woven in a 2/1 twill with Z/S-spun threads (21/11 thr./cm). The fragment (KNK985x80), which measures only 60x30 mm, was found in an excavation at the farm Niaquusat (V48), one of the smallest Norse farms.[35] The fragment has a faint reddish colour, and an analysis has been able to confirm that it was once dyed red with madder. Since neither the fibre, the close weave nor the madder dye is typical of the Greenlandic textiles, the fragment must be an import. The edges of the fragment are neatly cut, and one gets the feeling that it is a swatch sent to a prospective customer in Greenland. The earliest example of diamond-patterned weaves in Scandinavia is from Birka in Sweden, dated to the Viking Era.[36] In addition 2/1 diamond twill has been found in several medieval town excavations in northern Europe, from Novgorod in the east to Winchester in the west. In two English churches, St. Augustine's in Canterbury and Tavistock Abbey in Devon, fragments of similar weaves have been found in burials.[37] The fragment from Tavistock was found in the tomb of a mitred abbot, and it perhaps represents the so-called *haberget,* which was a well known weave in the Middle Ages. The fragment has Z/Z-spun threads and is more closely woven than the Greenlandic.[38] In an archaeological excavation in Leksand Church in Sweden, too, a possible *haberget* has been found, perhaps woven in the English town of Stamford, a town of Danish origin with strong trading links to Scandinavia.[39] The fine quality of the diamond-patterned weaves and the distribution of the finds suggest that it was a much-desired item. An analysis of fibres and dyes may clarify whether they are from the same production site, or whether they were made in several places. So far only the English one – and now the Greenlandic one – have been analysed in this way.

The British connection is also underscored by another find, which was made in 1976 in an excavation at the neighbouring farm of Nipaatsoq (V54), where a silver coat of arms was found only 18x14 mm in size (KNK991-109).[40] The coat of arms very likely belonged to the Scots Campbell clan, which in the Middle Ages owned a fleet that dominated the Scottish west coast.[41]

14. Diamond-patterned 2/2 twill

One of the most exciting Greenlandic weaves – from the technical point of view – is the costume item D10617 from Herjolfsnæs, which is called a stocking in Nørlund's description. This function is doubtful, however, since it has no signs of wear below the supposed heel, and with a 'leg width' of 200 mm it seems rather narrow.

But regardless of function, half of the item is woven in a 2/2-diamond twill, after which it continues in a tabby weave (or vice versa?). One could speculate that an imaginative Norsewoman had heard of patterned weaves, which she then tried to weave in a rather coarse version, but she only succeeded in one half.

We cannot know whether it was an Icelandic *hringavefnaður*, a *ringvend* or diamond twill from Niaquusat (V48) that inspired her.

15. Striped weaves

The most impressive weaving with stripes was found at the Farm Beneath the Sand (64V2-III-555), and it was undoubtedly a quite special piece even when it was on the loom. It is an original, almost black, now dark brown weaving in 2/2 twill of goat-hair with narrow stripes of fur from the Arctic hare woven in (x776). When it was newly woven, the fur of Arctic hare must have shone as whitely as the winter landscape around the farm. The stripes are still very light in colour and have not been tinged, as white wool normally is, by the soil which hid this piece for seven hundred years. Another more modest fragment (x3056) in wool has a few stripes formed by a light and a dark thread, probably wool from two sheep, one white and one brown. The stripes were later used as an effect along a fold.

Similar striping can be seen on the long stocking D10613 from Herjolfsnæs (Ø111), where light stripes are also woven in on a dark brown base. The weaving was then cut to stocking so that the stripes are flush with the top edge. Similarly, a striped weave has been 'fitted' to a hood, where the light threads in the ascending and descending direction border the hood along the neck seam. Finally I should mention

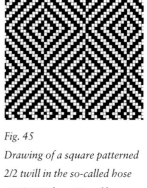

Fig. 45
Drawing of a square patterned 2/2 twill in the so-called hose (D10617) from Herjolfsnæs.

Fig. 46
Striped textile in 2/2 twill, with threads of white hare fur as weft in an originally almost black goat-hair textile with 8/10 threads/cm. The fragment (1950x776) is from the Farm Beneath the Sand.

a kind of striping on a fragment (x3091) from GUS, where thick and thin threads in the weft form the stripes. The thickest thread is two-ply. On another fragment there are stripes in the warp thread direction, formed by two-ply yarn twisted in different directions (S and Z). All striped Greenlandic weaves are in 2/2 twill.

In the Middle Ages striped weaves were much-coveted, and comparatively rare. They could be woven in two or more colours. It is perhaps interesting in this context to mention that one of the oldest striped textiles we know in Scandinavia comes from Lønne Heath on the west coast of Denmark. It has been dated to the first century AD. The 'Lønne Girl' was dressed in a blue costume with red stripes, and she had a reddish headscarf with white stripes. In the headscarf the stripes are woven alternately as close repp-woven and more open twill-woven (2/2).[42] And as we have seen, there were also a few striped weaves in Greenland.

16. Check weaves

A check weave is in principle a further development of a striped weave, since in the weft one repeats the striping in the warp and vice versa. At Sandnæs (V52) three fragments of a check weave in 2/l twill have been found (D12411.1). The largest fragment, measuring 230x155 mm, is sewn together from two smaller pieces with the warp threads at right angles to one another and with a right and wrong side on the same side. The other two fragments have similar light striping on a dark background in warp and weft. But although all four fragments are from the same weave, they cannot be joined together in one continuous piece. An analysis of the fibres shows that the wool was taken from three different animals. The warp threads are from a brown sheep which also had a few white hairs in its wool. The darkest weft is from a sheep with two brown shades, and the lightest weft is from a young lamb with white wool. The weaving is atypical of Greenlandic vaðmál, since the check fragments have most threads in the warp and fewest in the weft (9/6 thr./cm). It is not possible to tell whether this weave is Greenlandic, but since among the textiles there are a few weaves that differ from the typical Greenlandic vaðmál, this check weave may be one of them. It is evident from English wills from the fourteenth century that check weaves of combed wool that give them a smooth surface were particularly sought-after for pillows and blankets. An archaeological find from London of a checked fragment in tabby weave is an example of such domestic textiles.[43] At Skjoldehamn in northern Norway a similar check blanket was used as a winding-sheet. It measures 2600x1450 mm and is woven in 2/2 twill; the colours are apparently as in the Greenlandic weave, but the checks are rather larger.[44] Thus from the same period we have three examples of check-woven pieces in three different weaves from Greenland, London and northern Norway.

But as can often be seen in the textile context, 'new' weaves arise through repetition of the innovations of previous times. In Denmark check weaves can be traced from 2000-year-old ornamental weaves in light and dark check through a fine red and blue checked textile from the slightly later Lønne Heath find to Viking Era check weaves.

17. Pile weaves

A pile weave is an imitation of an animal fur. It consists of a base weave in which cut-off threads of a certain length or wool staples with the free ends hanging as fringes are woven in parallel with the weft threads. Among Greenlandic textiles three frag-

Fig. 47

The fragment (D12411.1) from the large farm, Sandnæs, is the only check textile that is registered in Greenland. The weave is in 2/1 twill. Top fragment displays the reverse side(?), while the other fragments display the right.

ments have been registered, all with a base in 2/2 twill and a weft that is almost twice as thick as the warp and only lightly spun (10-20°). In two of the pile weaves, the thread that forms the pile is formed from lightly spun hairs. On all fragments the pile is much worn, and one cannot see how long it originally was. The biggest pile-woven fragment (D5/1992.17) is from the eleventh century. It was found at the *Landnáma* Farm (Ø17a) and measures 170x320 mm. Warp and weft are spun from the same type of wool, so-called Hairy Medium, while the pile is Hairy, that is, hairs from which the underwool has been removed. The present-day colour is reddish-brown, but originally it was dyed reddish-mauve with *korkje*, or lichen purple.

The second-largest piece (D1/1991.15) is from Narsarsuaq (Ø149) and measures 170x115 mm. In this fragment warp, weft and pile are all spun from the same type of wool (Hairy Medium). However, there are fibre ends in both weft and pile suggesting that both were spun from white lambswool. Today the fragment is reddish, and a dye analysis has in fact established that it was originally reddish-mauve, coloured with *korkje*. The third pile weave (x3095) was found in the oldest phase of the Farm Beneath the Sand (64V2-III-555). It has been dated to the eleventh century. The fragment measures 130x140 mm and has the same wool/hair mix as the fragment from (Ø17a), that is, hair in the pile. However, in this case the hairs are from goat, not from sheep, and they are quite black. The wool in the warp threads was originally dark grey, while the weft was spun from a slightly lighter grey wool. The present-day colour is dark brown. An analysis revealed that the piled weave was originally dyed all over with tannin, whose origin it has not yet been possible to identify.

The colour/fibre determination of the pile weaves is very important if it is to be possible to point to a place of origin for these weaves. But the technical analysis is

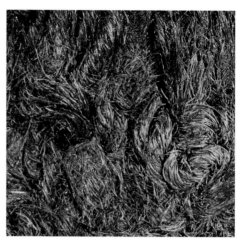

also important, since the weave and the pile knot can differ from one production site to another. One day, when all the pile weaves have been investigated, it is perhaps the knots that will be able to tell us where they were woven.

In Iceland two pile weaves with wool staples woven into a 2/2 twill have been registered, knotted in the same way as in the Greenlandic ones.[45] And from Dublin in Ireland there is an archaeological find of exactly the same pile weave with a red-coloured warp, while weft threads and pile are in the natural dark brown of the sheep's wool. On the Isle of Man and on the Hebridean island of Eigg, the graves of Viking warriors/farmers with pile-woven cloaks have been registered.[46] Swedish pile weaves found in Lund and dated to the eleventh century have wool staples woven into a 2/l twill instead of twisted threads, which gives the weave a different character.[47]

However, the most famous weaving is 'The Mantle of St. Brigid', dated to the eleventh century.[48] This piece, which is perhaps indeed a mantle, is in Bruges in Belgium, but is probably of Irish origin. The mantle is in a 'crimson' colour, which may be the same as the two *korkje*-coloured pile weaves from Greenland.

A pile-woven cloak could be used as outer clothing during the day and as a blanket at night. These cloaks were used all over Europe – perhaps in an unbroken tradition from the Bronze Age to this century, when pile-woven cloaks are still used by shepherds, for example in Portugal and Hungary. The Danish Trindhøj Cloak from the Bronze Age is the oldest known cloak, but unlike the others has a *sewn* pile.[49]

In the neighbouring Nordic countries pile weaves are known as 'shag-pile' or rya, with Swedish archaeological finds from Valsgärde and from the great trading site at Birka as examples from the seventh and tenth century respectively.[50] At Vadstena Convent, rya blankets were used as bedclothing in the fourteenth century, just as 'boat ryas' were necessary equipment for the fishermen at Lofoten in northern Nor-

way until World War II. The rya knot is tied into the weave in a slightly different way from the pile knot. The linguist Carl J.S. Marstrander interprets the Irish *ru* (rya) as meaning the same as *pill* (pile), and as a Norse word that came to Ireland with the Vikings.[51]

18. Goat-hair textiles

A small but striking group of Greenlandic weaves differs from the others in being coarser. These are goat-hair weaves of plied yarn in both warp and weft (4/3 thr./2 cm) found at GUS. These coarse weaves have been registered many times, not only in Scandinavia (Bergen, Lund, Oslo, Ribe and Trondheim), but also in other countries including England (London and York) and Germany (Lübeck), where the weaver who made haircloth was called a *Harmarker or Haardeckenmacher*.[52]

Goat-hair can also be seen used as pile (see the previous section), since the hairs are highly water-resistant and for that very reason useful for outer clothing. Finally, goat-hair is used in several of the Herjolfsnæs costumes, as the analyses have shown. Costume D10584 has warp threads of goat-hair, and cap D10608 was sewn with goat-hair thread, but since only a few of the sewing threads have been analysed, there may be more in other costumes. In the child's cap D10611, black goat hair was used as well as wool yarn in both warp and weft. The costume D10590 and the tall hat D10612 may also have been woven from goat hair. The present-day appearance of these items of clothing does not differ strikingly from those made of sheep wool. When new they may have differed more clearly. Goat hair looks so much like the hairs of the sheep that it is incredibly difficult to see the difference, so more Greenlandic textiles than those where the fibres have already been determined may be of goat hair.

Haircloth was the name given in the Middle Ages to clothes made of cattle- and goat-hair. The sagas speak of holy men and women who were to be dressed in haircloth. For example the housecarl Niels, later the patron saint of the city of Århus, is said to have worn a hair shirt under his armour. In Lund coarse hair textiles have been found in five graves dated to the eleventh century, and were probably used as shrouds. A similar custom is known from London, where a weaver wrote in his will in 1352 that he wished to be buried in a hair shirt.[53] Goat-hair clothing is also called *cilicium* (Latin: *cilix)*, referring to the idea that this cloth came from Cilicia in Anatolia. In Scandinavia it was also called *kølno-klæde*, that is 'malt-cloth' used as an underlay for malt or corn when it was to be dried in the malt kiln. Hair textiles also had other functions, as is evident from information from the beginning of the sixteenth century, when a Swedish merchant bought 100 *alen* of haircloth. It was to be used to pack 26 bales of cloth that were to be taken on an open ship to Lübeck.[54] Hair cloths (cattle and goat) were commonly used to wrap merchandise in the middle ages and are frequently recovered from ports around the North Sea.[55]

Textiles of goat hair are known from all countries where the goat lives, so perhaps it is not so surprising to find them in Greenland too.

19. Felt

In his book on the finds from Herjolfsnæs (Ø111), Nørlund also mentioned a piece of felt (D10623). Unfortunately this fragment has disappeared, and no felt has been found in later excavations in Norse ruins.

Fig. 51
Rough goat-hair textile, tabby woven with 4/3 threads per 2 cm. In both the warp and the weft the threads are Z-spun and S-plied. The fragment (1950x608a) is from the Farm Beneath the Sand. There is a selvedge on the one side.

Flax and Linen

Fig. 52

Drawing of a Norwegian 880 mm long wooden hemp and nettle breaker, to which the scutching tool from the Landnáma Farm can be compared. The Norwegian breaker is from the Nordfjord Folkemuseum in Sandane.

Fig. 53

This 260 mm long, notched wooden piece is probably one half of a breaker. An implement used in the preparation of flax tow. Landnáma Farm Ø17a. (D5/1992.65).

A textile find of microscopic size at the farm in Niaqussat (V48) in 1976-77 led to a rare discovery. Five heavy, coarse pollen grains from cultivated flax *(Linum usitatissimum L.)* were found in the midden of the farm – four in the bottom layers, the fifth in the disturbed layers that lay 40-50 cm under the surface.[1] Just ten years later at Sandnæs (V51), a farm some ten kilometres farther up the Ameralla fjord, similar finds of flax pollen were made. There too, some seeds and a piece of a 'boll' or seed capsule were found.[2] The farms in the Western Settlement had a unique location with a temperate climate and a few warm summer days with temperatures of 20-25°C. The mild climate in the Early Middle Ages probably meant that it was possible to grow flax.

Five pollen grains is not very convincing documentation, but since the flax plant is pollinated by insects it has few pollen, and it is spread poorly. Flax cultivation does not leave much pollen, as an experiment in Ireland has shown. To investigate the distribution of flax pollen, two soil samples were taken in the middle of a flax field. Out of 1034 pollen grains only three were from flax.[3] Some researchers think that flax was formerly only cultivated for the oil-bearing seeds, which have high nutrition value,[4] but in Greenland this need is unlikely to have been great, since the Norse Greenlanders ate a lot of whale meat, which is rich in calories.

The flax plant undergoes a long, labour-intensive process before it is spinnable. In Ångermanland, which lies out towards the Gulf of Bothnia, flax stalks were retted (i.e. made to decompose) by leaving them outside throughout the winter. When the snow had gone and the stalks had died, the fibres were beaten free of the decomposed

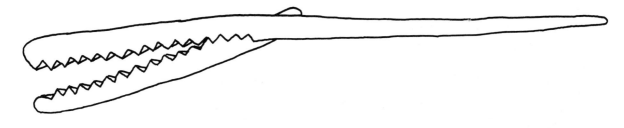

stalks with a flax beater. With a flax comb the coarsest lumps were removed and with the flax brush the fibres were brushed clean. The brush, which was made of pigs' bristles, was also used to comb the fine fibres from the coarser ones.[5] After this the flax could be spun.

One implement has been found in Greenland which may possibly be related to flax or hemp production. The find is from the excavation of the *Landnáma* Farm (Ø17a) at Narsaq, where Vebæk registered a 260 mm long piece of wood with serrated edges, which he called a 'wool card'(?).[6] In the Nordfjord Folkemuseum in Sandane in Norway there is an 880 mm long *bryde* (a beater for 'scutching' hemp and nettle), to which the piece of wood from Narsaq can be compared.[7] In excavations at Bryggen in Bergen no fewer than 33 flax combs were registered, and since this was the shipping harbour for Greenland, it is not inconceivable that there could have been flax-working implements in the cargo to Greenland.[8]

Knytlinga saga mentions bundles of unspun flax. In runic inscriptions and Eddic poems flax is also mentioned, and can thus be traced far back in time, but whether it is imported flax or a domestic product is not evident. However, it is thought that flax was cultivated as far north as Trondheim, where the coarser linens were produced. Names including the element *lin* (flax, linen) occur in many places in Scandinavia. *Línakraðalur* is however the only known place-name related to flax on Iceland, so flax is not thought to have been of any great importance there.

Fig. 54
This carbonised piece (KNK991x577) from Niaquusat was once a fine linen textile, tabby woven with Z/Z spun threads, 20/18 threads/cm.

In the northern part of Sweden and Finland, flax played an important role in the Middle Ages. Ångermanland was widely known for good grades of linen. Flax was not only cultivated there for local consumption but was also woven for sale. Linen too was used as a means of payment, for example as a duty payable to Uppsala Cathedral, the so-called *Olavsgärden*. The priest's fee for a wedding could also be paid in linen, and like *vaðmál* it was used to pay servants.[9] From the flax plant one also got linseed, which was used everywhere medicinally, and the seeds were ascribed great value as a remedy against witchcraft.[10]

1. Linen in Greenland

Eleven fragments of linen textiles have been found at three Norse farms as well as a braided flax cord at a fourth. *Bregða* is an Icelandic word which can mean interlace, tie, braid, but in Iceland a braided cord is called *krílad*.

At Gardar (Ø47) two fragments were registered (without number). On the smaller piece (measuring 100x60 mm) there are narrow folded pleats.

From Nipaatsoq (V54) comes the fragment KNK991x577, but most linen fragments are from the Farm Beneath the Sand (64V2-III-555), and are gathered under the number x3103. The braided cord D12685 was found at the farm at Hvalsey Church (Ø83).

All fragments – with the exception of the cord – are carbonised, and are preserved as black-layered flakes, which are almost impossible to investigate because the slightest touch makes the fragments crumble. Whether the carbonisation has occurred because the fragments were found in burnt layers, or because the cells in the flax thread have changed because of a slow oxidation (auto-oxidation), has not been clarified.[11] That the braided cord, which is only a couple of millimetres thick is not charred, may be due to the fact that it is sewn to a piece of *vaðmál*. In that case the wool could have had an effect on the preservation of the cord. The pleated fragment from Gardar is extremely interesting and it is therefore very regrettable that it cannot be investigated in more detail. Pleated costumes in linen are known from Viking Age women's graves, and from the clerics of the Middle Ages, when the pleated alb was an important part of priestly vestments. Since the fragment was found at Gardar, the seat of the Greenland Bishop, it is conceivable that it is part of an alb.

The linen textiles from GUS are in both fine and coarse grades. The finest is a couple of strips 140-260 mm long and 54 mm wide, each of which is sewn from two narrower strips. In addition there are two five millimetre wide *rouleau* fragments, both of which are terminated by a knot. One piece of *rouleau* runs through a sliding knot on the other, in a way that is very similar to the edging that can be seen on the so-called Viborg Shirt from around 1050.[12] On this shirt the neck opening is edged with narrow border bands that continue in two free ends, each of which runs through an sliding knot. It is not inconceivable that a Norse Greenlander owned a linen shirt that was closed at the neck in the same way as the shirt from Viborg. Among the small collection of linen textiles from GUS one can also see a thin cord from a four-thread tablet weave – so far the only find of a tablet weave in Greenland. The linens may be the remains of clothing that the *landnáma* people were wearing when they came to Greenland. They may also themselves have grown and worked the flax in the first decades when they lived at GUS. In that case this is probably only true of the coarsest linens. The finer grades were probably imported. Fine linens were three times as expensive as *vaðmál*.[13]

Fibres and Dyes in Norse Textiles

By Penelope Walton Rogers

Introduction

The raw materials used in a textile have an obvious effect on the appearance and handle of the cloth: fine fibres make soft fabrics, coarse fibres harsher ones, and the use of natural dyes has a dramatic impact on the eye. For the archaeologist, however, the identification of the raw materials can also be a useful interpretive tool. Spinners and weavers can only draw on the raw materials they have to hand and the nature of these raw materials and how they are processed can often act as a diagnostic marker for a particular culture. In this respect, the Norse textiles from Greenland are a classic case, demonstrating the usefulness of the analysis of dyes and fibres.

The campaign of analysis of Greenland textiles was initiated in 1992 by Else Østergård. The work was carried out in York by the author, using the techniques described below. During the eight years of the survey, textiles from ten Norse sites, six in the Eastern Settlement and four in the Western Settlement, were analysed. Two further textiles from Thule Inuit sites, one from Ruin Island, off the north-west coast of Greenland, and the other from Ellesmere Island, off the coast of Canada, were included in the study, along with some unprovenanced, possibly Norse, textiles held in the National Museum of Denmark. Altogether 102 textiles, one edging, one cord, one braid and five sewing threads have been studied (Table 1). The fleece-types in 204 yarn samples have been examined and tests for dye have been carried out on 115 samples.

The work has proved to be exceptionally profitable. It is now clear that the Norse on Greenland had access to a limited range of raw materials. Dyes were relatively scarce and most of the colour in the clothing derives from the natural greys, browns and blacks of wool. Black goat hair and white rabbit or hare fur were also used. More importantly for archaeology, the wool seems to be of a single type, which has been broken up and processed in an unusual way, almost certainly using a particular form of woolcomb. This last feature has proved to be so idiosyncratically 'Norse' that analysis by measurement of the fibre diameters can now be used to identify Norse textiles outside Greenland, including examples from the Canadian Arctic and Viking Age England.

Method of analysis

Fibres were examined by transmitted-light microscopy, at x100 and x400 magnification. They were viewed as whole-mount preparations and cross-sections, and, for animal fibres, casts of the cuticular scale pattern were prepared in clear varnish. For the identification of 'fleece type', fibres from a single yarn were spread out on the microscope slide and the diameters of 100 fibres were measured in a continuous sequence, at x400 magnification (see below, Fleece types). While the fibres were be-

TABLE 1

Norse textiles from Greenland included in the study of the raw materials

Eastern Settlement

Ø17a Narsaq, published	5 textiles = 10 fleece types, 8 dye analyses
Narsaq, not published	4 textiles = 9 fleece types, 5 dye analyses
Ø34	1 textile = 2 fleece types, 1 dye analysis
Ø47, Gardar (Igaliko)	1 thread = 1 fleece type, 1 dye analysis
Ø83, Hvalsø (Qaqortoq)	1 textile = 2 fleece types, 1 dye analysis
Ø111 Herjolfsnæs (42 garments)	46 textiles, 2 sewing treads, 1 border, 1 cord = 98 fleece types, 55 dye analyses
Ø149 Narsarsuaq	1 textile = 2 fleece types, 1 dye analysis
Kirkespirdalen	1 textile = 2 fleece types, 1 dye analysis
Total from the Eastern Settlement	60 textiles = 126 fleece types, 73 dye analyses

Western Settlement

V51 Sandnæs	1 linen
V54 Nipaatsoq	1 textile = 2 fleece types, 1 dye analysis
V52a Umiiviarsuk	1 textile = 3 fleece types, 2 dye analyses
GUS (Farm Beneath the Sand) published	22 textiles = 38 fleece types, 2 dye analyses
GUS, not published	11 textiles, 1 braid, 2 sewing threads = 24 fleece types, 14 dye analyses.
Total from the Western Settlement	36 textiles = 67 fleece types, 38 dye analyses

Beyond the Norse Settlements

Ruin Island, Inglefield Land	1 textile = 2 fleece types
Skraeling Island, Ellesmere Island	1 textile = 2 fleece types, 1 dye analysis.

Miscellaneous comparative material

Unprovenanced, probably Norse	4 textiles = 7 fleece types, 3 dye analyses.
Total	102 textiles = 204 fleece types, 115 dye analyses

ing measured, the presence and density of pigment granules, which indicate the original colour of the sheep's fleece, were recorded (see below, Natural pigmentation).

Dyes were analysed by extracting any organic colorants present into a series of solvent systems and using the liquid extracts first for absorption spectrophotometry (visible spectrum), and then for thin-layer chromatography (Walton and Taylor 1991). This is the first time that modern analytical techniques have been applied to the Greenland textiles, but in 1924 Poul Nørlund reported some chemical tests carried out by Bille Gram on four garments from Herjolfsnæs, Nos. 45, 50, 65 and 78, which suggested the presence of brown dyes (Nørlund 1924, 90) (Fig. 55). Tannin-based brown dyes have been identified in our own study, although not in these particular garments. In addition, Else Østergård has successfully identified indigotin (see

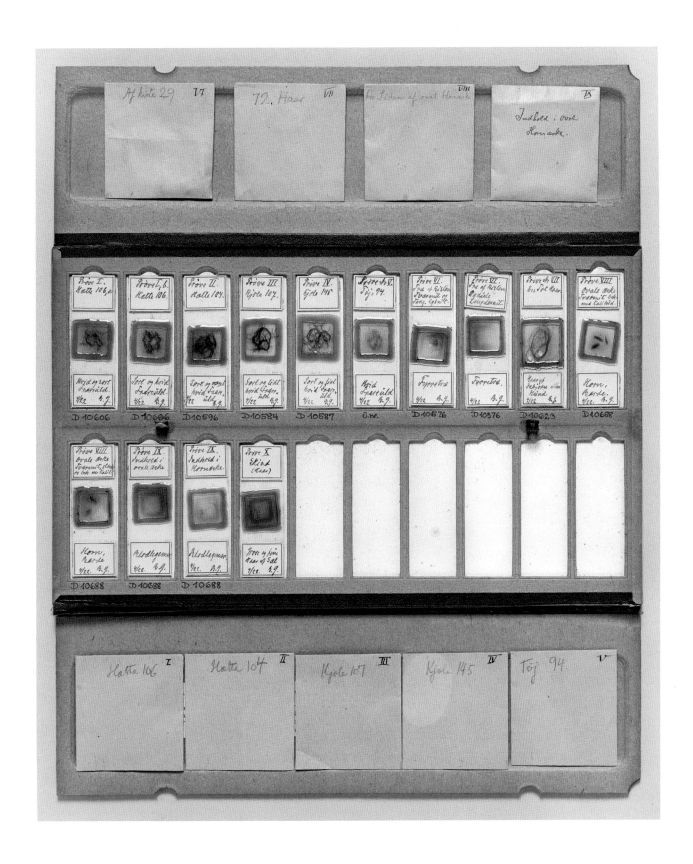

Fig. 55
Microscopy preparations in cardboard box, with samples placed under glass and in small square paper
bags. The lid is divided in two and folds in towards the middle. Folded, the box measures 345x205 mm.
In 1922 Poul Nørlund had samples of whalebone, hair, coffins, woollen threads, etc. analysed in connec-
tion with the publication of Buried Norsemen at Herjolfsnes. *Analyses were carried out by Professor J.*
Bille Gram.

below, Dyes) by a simple chemical test. Finally, where samples had a reddish tinge, which could not be explained by dye testing, the samples were exposed to a chemical test for iron compounds, devised by our research chemist, G.W. Taylor (see below, Dyes).

Plant fibres

Two textiles, one from Gardar (Ø47) and the other from Nipaatsoq (V54) had become carbonised. When mounted for microscopy, light could not penetrate these black fibres and they could be viewed only as silhouettes. Nevertheless, the smooth profiles of the fibres, with raised cross-bands and occasional 'joints', indicate that these are plant fibres, such as flax, hemp or nettle. Flax has also been identified by Else Østergård in a non-carbonised cord from Hvalsø (Ø83).

It is likely that flax was cultivated in Greenland during warm phases, as flax pollen has been identified at two sites in the western settlement (summarised in Østergård 1998, 63, and above pp. 76-78). There is also a wooden object from Narsaq (Vebæk 1993, 34, fig. 45a) which was originally identified as a wool card, but which is more probably the arm of a tool used to process flax tow (Hoffmann 1991, 58, fig. 62). Indeed, it is possible that linen textiles were worn more frequently than the archaeological record suggests. Plant fibres will not survive well in the sandy soils of sites such as GUS, especially if before burial they are left on the open ground, where they are subject to fungal attack (Jakes and Sibley 1983, 36-37). Paradoxically, charred plant fibres such as those from Gardar and Nipaatsoq have a better chance of survival, as they have lost the organic parts which make them attractive to fungi and other microorganisms (Walton 1989, 300).

Animal fibres

All animal coat fibres, when viewed at high magnification, reveal a surface pattern of overlapping scales. The arrangement of these scales, the distance between them and the shape of the scale margins (smooth, crenate or rippled) may be used to identify the species of animal from which the fibres have come. The cross-sectional shape of the fibres and the type of medulla (a medulla is the channel which sometimes runs up the middle of the fibre) are also diagnostic features.

Most of the fibres in the Greenland textiles have an irregular mosaic scale pattern, sometimes waved, with smooth, near margins. This, together with the range of fibre diameters and the oval cross-sections, indicates sheep's wool (Appleyard 1978, 26-27, 107-117). The quality of the Norse Greenland wool will be described in greater detail below (Fleece types).

Goat hair can be distinguished from sheep's wool by the presence on coarse fibres of a transitional zone in the scale pattern, where an irregular mosaic scale pattern with smooth margins runs parallel to a waved pattern with crenate margins. Goat hair has been confidently identified in three textiles from GUS, 608a, 608b, 776 and 3095 (the pile of a piled weave), and a child's cap from Herjolfsnæs, D10611 (Nørlund No. 85); and less certainly in further Herjolfsnæs garments, D10584, D10612 and a sewing yarn D10608. Goats are hardy animals which can survive on low-growing scrub in areas where there is little grass. Bones from goat have been recovered from several Norse farms, especially in the Western Settlement (McGovern 1992, 198-200), and a whole animal, with an intact white coat has been excavated at GUS.

The black goat hair textile from GUS (1950x776), had a band of white fibre woven into the weft. The identity of this fibre was something of a surprise. It had the deep chevron scale pattern, fine ladder medullas and occasional multi-serial medullas which are typical of rabbit and hare fur (Appleyard 1978, 22-23, 98-100). In the context of Greenland, the most likely source is the white Arctic hare, *Lepus arcticus*. The Arctic hare has a particularly long white coat and its bones are well represented at several sites in the Western Settlement (Degerbøl 1936, 111). Still more unexpected was the finding of another textile from GUS made entirely from plied yarns spun from the same fibre. Fur fibres are particularly difficult to spin, because they are smooth and slippy, and once spun they have a tendency to pull apart when placed under tension. Plying two yarns together helps to prevent this, but even so, such yarns can only be used for soft fabrics which are not intended to have much wear.

Since the publication of the GUS hare-fur textiles (Walton Rogers 1993), further examples of plied hare-fur yarns have been identified in three late Dorset and Thule Inuit sites on Baffin Island, namely Nunguvik, Nanook and Willows Island (author's work on behalf of Patricia Sutherland, Archaeological Survey of Canada). Patricia Sutherland informs me that there is no evidence that the Dorset and Inuit peoples practised spinning. It therefore remains a matter for conjecture, as to whether these plied hare-fur yarns were made within the Norse colonies (as the hare bones from the Western Settlement might suggest), or whether some nearby group of Dorset or Inuit peoples learned to spin from the Norse and – since they were not farmers and did not keep sheep or goats – adapted the technique to the materials they had to hand.

There is another curious fibre in a textile, radiocarbon dated to AD 1260, from the Thule Inuit site on Ruin Island, Inglefield Land, Thule district. This is a 2/1 twill made from a blend of wool and a second fibre, which, on the coarse fibres, has an irregular mosaic scale pattern with smooth distant margins, sometimes rippled, with zones of diamond petal pattern; in cross-section the fibres are mostly round-to-oval, or occasionally slightly angular on the coarse fibres. These features indicate hair from a species of Canis, a genus which includes the domestic dog, Canis familiaris, and the wolf, Canis sp. (Appleyard 1978, 8-9, 30-31, 56-57, 122-23). The wool is white and similar in quality to that found in the raw wool from GUS (see below); the dog/wolf hair is a mixture of white and pale fawn. The proportion of wool to dog/wolf hair varied from sample to sample, but it was clearly a deliberate inclusion, not a contaminant. As already noted, the Inuit were not themselves spinners, nor did they keep sheep; and yet the wool has not been processed in the traditional Norse manner (see below). This textile seems to be unique, and one of those oddities that occur at the boundaries between two cultures.

Fleece types

The quality of sheep's wool can be characterised in a number of different ways, but the method adopted here has been the measurement of the diameters of 100 fibres from each sample, as described above (Method of analysis). According to the range, mean and distribution of the measurements, the sample may be allocated to one of the seven fleece-type categories identified by Dr M.L. Ryder: Hairy, Hairy Medium, Generalised Medium, Medium, Semi-Fine, Fine/Generalised Medium and Fine (Ryder 1969, Walton Rogers 1995). Almost all of the Greenland yarn samples are either Hairy or Hairy Medium fleece type. The Hairy fleece-type is defined as having a broad range of fibre diameters, with a number of fibres over 60 microns and some over 100 microns; the mean is 30-45 microns; the distribution generally continuous. The Hairy Medium fleece-type has a similar or slightly narrower range, with fewer

TABLE 2

Textiles from Norse settlements with Hairy-Medium weft and Hairy warp

Greenland	Hairy Medium (S)	Hairy (Z)
GUS (33 textiles)	21-37 (goat 39)	33-56 (goat 54-69)
Herjolfsnæs (42 textiles)	24-38	36-56 (goat 51-61)
Other sites (8 textiles)	28-34	34-54
Total from Greenland sites (83 textiles)	21-38	33-56
Raw wool from GUS (16 specimens)	26-44	
Comparative material:		
Kirkespirdalen, Greenland	33	54
Unprovenanced (Rønbjerg)	32	47
Unprovenanced (D1451)	26	34
Outside Greenland:		
Ellesmere Island	26	47
Papa Stour, Shetland (5 textiles)	24-32	34-39
Viking Age York, England	28	41

fibres over 60 microns; a mean of 20-35; and a distribution skewed to positive. In almost every one of the Norse textiles, the Hairy fleece type appears in the Z-spun warp yarn and the Hairy Medium in the S-spun weft yarn (Fig. 56). The difference can be seen most clearly by comparing the means (average measurements) of the Z and S yarns, as shown in Table 2. The means of the Z-spun Hairy are 33-56 microns; the S-spun Hairy Medium yarns are 21-38 microns. The only textiles in which this arrangement does not appear are the obvious imports, such as the 2/1 diamond twill from Nipaatsoq (Generalised Medium in warp and weft); the three piled weaves (Hairy Medium in warp and weft, sometimes with a Hairy pile); and some of the 2/1 twills (which sometimes have a coarser weft than warp). Almost all of the 2/2 twills and tabby weaves have been made in the standard fashion.

When this combination of Hairy and Hairy Medium fleece types was first observed, it was assumed that sheep with two different qualities of wool were being farmed on Greenland and that the weavers were selecting one fleece for the warp and another for the weft (Walton Rogers 1993). Since both Hairy and Hairy Medium fleece-types are present in modern descendants of Norse sheep, this seemed a reasonable supposition. As more samples came to be analysed, however, some features emerged which suggested this might not be true. First of all, several of the Hairy fleece types had very high negative values for the Pearson co-efficient of skew. The coefficient of skew is a means of telling whether the measurements are arranged symmetrically around the mean (symmetrical distribution) or are skewed to one side. Wool taken directly from a sheep's fleece generally has values between -0.05 to +1.15. Some of the Greenland warp yarns were giving coefficients up to -0.87. In addition, it was noted that the pigment pattern in the warp nearly always resembled the pigment pattern in the weft (see Fig. 56). Given that there were many different

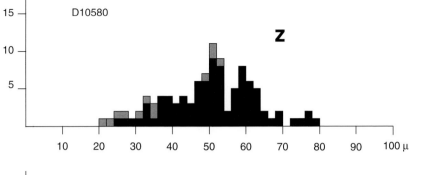

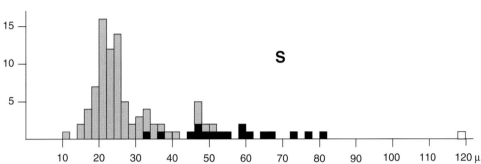

Fig. 56
Wool fleece-types in garments D10580 and D10585 from Herjolfsnæs. The histograms show the diameters of 100 fibres and the distribution of pigmented fibres. Note how the pigmentation follows the same pattern in both the warp and the weft (the Z- and S-spun threads).

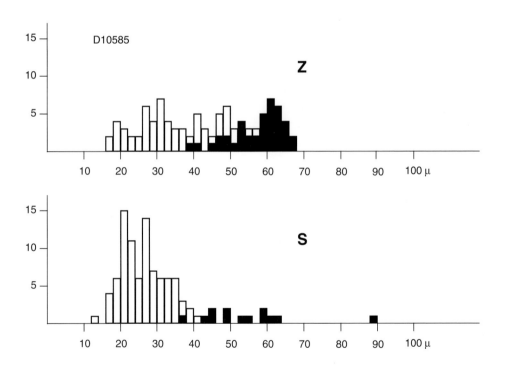

■ Dense pigmentation

▨ Moderate pigmentation

□ None pigmentation

pigment patterns in the textiles, this seemed to be significant. Finally, it was noted that the Hairy Medium wools often included 'kemp' fibres (kemp are short bristly fibres with a wide latticed medulla, found in the kinds of fleece which moult), but these were only occasionally found with the Hairy fleece types.

This raised the possibility that each textile had been made from the same fleece, but that the long hairs had been separated by some means from the short fibres, that is, the underwool and the kemp. Further support for this view was provided when 16 well-preserved examples of unprocessed sheep's fleece were found at GUS. To understand the significance of these finds, it is necessary to review briefly the evidence for sheep in the Norse colonies.

The sheep of the Norse colonies of the North Atlantic

When the Norse settlers spread out into the North Atlantic, they took with them sheep from their Scandinavian homelands. The sheep of Greenland probably arrived with colonists from the Norse settlements on Iceland. Excavated sheep bones show that there were goat-horned animals in both the Eastern and Western Settlements (Degerbøl 1936, 14-20). This original stock died out on Greenland at the end of the Norse occupation, but they survived on Iceland and on Faeroe and descendants of the broad breed-group to which they belong can be seen today in primitive breeds such as the Orkney (Scottish islands), the Shetland (developed out of the Orkney), the Romanov (Russia), the Landrace (Finland), the Gotland (the Swedish island of Gotland; the breed also known as the Swedish Landrace) and the Spaelsau (Norway). This group of breeds is known collectively as the 'European Vari-coloured Short-tail', or the 'Northern Short-tail' (Ryder 1968, 1981, 1983).

The Northern Short-tails are hardy animals, capable of living on a poor diet – the Orkney, for example will happily survive on seaweed. Their distinguishing features are a short tail, horns in the male and sometimes in the female, and a range of colours in the fleece. The fleece generally has a thick woolly undercoat combined with a substantial amount of long hairs (for this reason they are often called 'double-coated'), which allows them to survive in poor climates. Some of the breeds, such as the Orkney and the Gotland, still have an annual moult, a primitive feature not seen in most modern sheep. This means that their fleeces can be plucked in early summer (called 'rooing') as well as sheared.

The wool taken from adults of the Northern Short-tail breeds is on average 100-160 mm long (Ryder 1981, 394). The staples (staples are the locks of wool into which the fleece naturally falls) have a pointed tip and the underwool reaches only part way down the staple. Measurement of the fibre diameters reveals that they are predominantly Hairy Medium in type, with some Hairy types included (and flocks which have been deliberately improved include other types as well). The wool may be black, brown, roan, grey or white and there are frequently animals with a skimlet pattern. A skimlet fleece has black or brown hairs protruding beyond a white underwool, so that the animal appears to have a pale fleece with a dark fringe.

Raw wool from GUS

The 16 samples of raw wool from GUS have been described in detail elsewhere (Walton Rogers 1998, 68-73), but the evidence will be reviewed briefly here. The staples are pointed and mainly 60-180 mm, although there is some lambswool which is shorter (Fig. 57). Each staple has long hairs present and a short crimpy underwool

which reaches less than halfway down the staple; kemp is present in at least seven of the samples (Walton Rogers op.cit. Table 6). The fleece types are mainly Hairy Medium, with two borderline Hairy types. Four of the samples have come from cured sheepskins, but the rest have been gathered from live animals, either by plucking/rooing (three examples), or by cutting the fleece, with shears or with a knife. The root ends of rooed wool have also been noted in one of the Herjolfsnæs hats, D10612.

These GUS samples represent the wool as it was on the sheep's back. The measurements obtained from them produced means from 26 to 44 microns (Fig. 58). In other words, they were intermediate between the Z-spun and S-spun wools of the textiles and overlapped with both. Pigment patterns of the GUS fleeces matched the pigment patterns in the textiles. Six were white, two black, one dark brown, one dark grey (72% black fibres), one pale grey (16% black fibres), three brown skimlet (white with brown hairs) and two black skimlet (white with black hairs).

These samples of raw wool are exactly comparable with the fleeces of the Northern Short-tail breed group and they provide a link between the textiles and the remains of horned sheep. If, as seems likely, these 16 samples represent the kind of raw wool that the Norse spinners and weavers used to make their textiles, then that wool must have been processed in some way to separate the hairy parts of the fleece, from the shorter-fibred underwool and kemp. The most likely way that this would be achieved is by combing the wool.

Fig. 57

Raw wool staples) from the Farm-Beneath-the-Sand (GUS) left to right, x3391, x2752, x981, x2860, x1416, x1653. Length of x3391 is 150 mm. The black material at the top of x1416 and x1653 represents the remains of the sheep's skin; x2752 has been sheared; x2860 has been rooed (plucked). The original fleece colours were: x1416 and x2860 white; x1653 black; x3391 dark grey (see fig. 58); x981 black skimlet (white underwool, black hairs); x2752 brown skimlet (white underwool, brown hairs).

Woolcombing

Although no woolcombs have as yet been discovered on Greenland, many examples have been found in Viking Age Norway and in the Norse settlements of the Northern Isles of Scotland and Iceland. The typical Norse woolcomb consists of a single row of iron teeth, 100-130 mm long, set in a cylindrical wooden head, with a wooden handle (Petersen 1951, 319-324). There has been considerable confusion in European archaeological literature over these tools, first because they were originally mistaken

Fig. 58

Wool fleece-types in three raw wool staples (locks of wool) from GUS, x1543, x1386, and x3391). The histograms show the diameter of 100 fibres and the distribution of pigmented fibres. Note the different patterns in the pigmentation: x1543 is from a light grey, or 'black skimlet' fleece; x1386 is brown-skimlet, and x3391 is from a dark grey fleece.

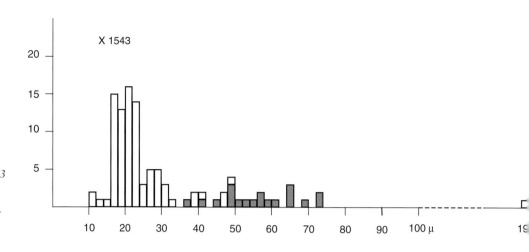

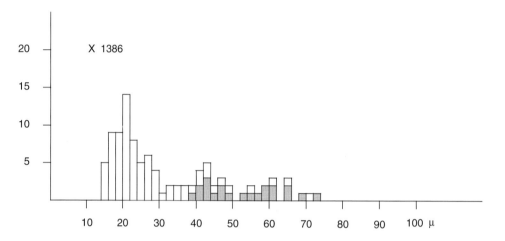

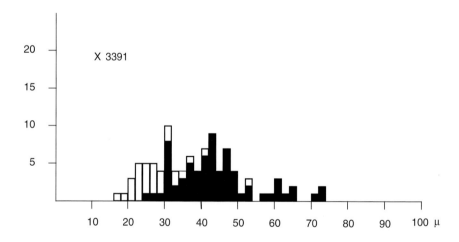

for flax heckles (ibid.), and then later because they were muddled with another form of woolcomb used in Anglo-Saxon England and on the Continent. The Anglo-Saxon woolcomb consists of a double row of teeth set in a rectangular head. They were used as a pair, held one in either hand and brushed against each other in the way that modern hand spinners used hand cards (Walton Rogers 1997, 1723; Cardon 1999, 180, fig. 56). These are different again from the heavy long-toothed iron woolcombs, with teeth 130-180 mm long, which were used with one mounted on a wooden post and the other held by both hands: these first appeared in the 12th or 13th century and are still used today in the worsted industry (Walton Rogers 1997, 1729-1731).

It is probable that the Norse form of woolcomb was the ancestor of another tool used to separate fibres, the Icelandic tog comb. These iron combs have wider gaps between the teeth than the Norse woolcombs (Guðjónsson 1979). They are held one in either hand and drawn across each other in order to separate the hair, or tog, of Icelandic double-coated sheep from the underwool, or *undankemba* (Jónasson 1974). It may be suggested that Norse woolcombs were manipulated in a similar way, to produce the effect seen in the surviving Norse textiles.

Natural fleece colours

Natural fleece colours have been mentioned several times in this work. During the analysis, the pigmentation pattern was identified by recording first the number of fibres with pigmentation in the sample and then the density of the pigment granules in those fibres. A fibre with very dense pigmentation was interpreted as black; moderate to light pigmentation was called brown (but note that the reddish brown of roan wools cannot be distinguished from other sorts of brown by this means). Where black and white fibres were combined in a single sample, this would have given an over-all grey effect. Where skimlet wools have been used, the process of dividing up the fleece has meant that the dark hairs concentrate in the warp yarn (Fig. 56). A black skimlet fleece used for a twill weave will thus produce a grey warp and a white weft, which will emphasise the line of the twill diagonal.

Less than 35% of the Greenland wools examined were white and the rest pigmented. When the Herjolfsnæs garments are divided up according to the age and sex of the wearer, there seems to be a pattern in the choice of colour. Of the six male gowns studied, four were made from dark brown or black wool (D10583/No. 41, D10584/No. 42, D10587/No. 45, D10594/No. 63) and one was a white wool coloured dark brown with a tannin dye (D10579/No. 37); only one was grey and apparently undyed (D10585.1/No. 43). The three women's dresses included two grey examples, darker in the warp than in the weft (D10580/No. 38, D10581/No. 39) and one which had a brown wool darkened with a tannin dye in the warp and a white wool in the weft (D10581/No. 39), so that all three had a marked warp-weft contrast. The three children's gowns examined were white (D10586/No. 44, D10592/No. 61) or very pale grey (D10593/No. 62). This may be tentatively summarised as dark brown-black for men, white or pale grey for children and patterned (warp-weft contrast) for women.

Dyes

The most colourful dyes were found at the early *Landnama* farm at Narsaq (Ø17a). The most common were the purple dyes derived from lichens, which were identified in seven textiles, one of which was a piled weave; the same dye was found in another piled weave from Narsarsuaq (Ø149) and, in weak concentration, in a child's hat from Herjolfsnæs, D10608. The dye had often been applied on top of grey or brown wool and, because it was encountered so frequently and in such heavy concentration at Narsaq, the possibility that it was contamination in the soil was considered. Analysis of one of the Narsaq textiles, however, showed that it had been dyed blue with woad (see below), without any trace lichen purple, although the sewing yarns of the same textile were dyed purple (Walton Rogers 1993, No. 2). The dye cannot, therefore, be a contaminant.

A wide range of lichens yield a dye of this sort, the ones available in the north being species of *Evernia, Ochrolechia, Parmelia* and *Umbilicaria* (Bolton 1960/1982 pp15-18), of which *Ochrolechia* was the most commonly exploited. It has not been possible to establish whether any of these lichens grow in Greenland, but they are so well established in the Scottish Islands and in Canada that it seems likely that they do. In Scotland, the lichens were collected from rocks and trees when they were at least five years old and prepared with stale urine (Grierson 1986 pp. 170-73, 180-82; Bolton op.cit. pp. 16-17). This lichen purple dye has also been identified in a number of textiles from Viking Dublin (Walton 1988, 56-57), although it has not yet been found in the small number of textiles analysed from Norse Shetland, or Viking Age Norway. By the 14th century, however, the dyestuff, known as *korkje* or *lacmus,* was established as a Norwegian speciality (Lunde 1975, 119).

The blue colorant indigotin was also identified in a textile from Narsaq and, as already noted, has been identified by Else Østergård in a fragment from the farm at Sandnes (V51). This colorant may be derived from either woad or indigo, but indigo from India is highly unlikely and woad, from *Isatis tinctoria* L., the more probable source. This dye has also been identified in many textiles from Viking Age burials in Norway (Walton 1988).

The red dye madder, which was so common in Anglo-Saxon England, and medieval Europe generally, was represented in the Greenland material by only two examples, one the fine 2/1 diamond twill from Nipaatsoq (V54), which is clearly an import from mainland Europe, and the other an ornamental edging on a man's dark brown gown from Herjolfsnæs, D10594. This dye, derived from roots of the plant *Rubia tinctorum* L., has not been found in any of the typically Norse textiles and it is conceivable that it only arrived in Greenland as ready-dyed yarn or textile.

The presence of a brown tannin-based dye has also been mentioned. Tannins are widely available in nature, in barks, nuts, dead leaves, peat and so on, and it was sometimes difficult to be certain that the colorant was not derived from the soil in which the textile had been buried. Only in circumstances where the colorant was present in particularly strong concentration, or where the warp was coloured and the weft was not, was it possible to be sure that dye had been deliberately applied. This tannin dye seems to have been used especially to darken grey and brown wools, presumably to give a more even colour to the yarn. It has been confidently identified in at least five of the Herjolfsnæs garments, D10579/No. 37, D10581/No. 39, D10584/No. 42, D10594/No. 63 and D10612/No. 87, and there may be others that have been missed.

Finally, an inorganic colorant, derived from iron, was identified towards the end of the study. Some textiles from Herjolfsnæs had a visible maroon tone, but all attempts to characterise the dye proved unsuccessful until a test for the presence of iron was devised by G.W.Taylor. In this test, the sample is warmed in a 7% aqueous solution of hydrochloric acid to about 50°C and a few crystals of potassium ferrocyanide are then added. If iron is present, the solution turns a vivid blue immediately. The maroon samples all gave a very strong, quick reaction; tests on samples which did not have the red tinge gave no reaction, or only a very slow and weak one. A vigorous positive reaction was found in seven garments from Herjolfsnæs, D6473/No. 59, D8081/No. 57, D10598/No. 67, D10599/No. 68, D10615/No. 90, D10617/No. 92, D10618/No. 93, and in five of these the colorant had been applied on white wool.

The source of this inorganic red colorant was unknown until Else Østergård, on a visit to Greenland, noted red pebbles in a stream at Herjolfsnæs. She took these back to Denmark, where they were analysed along with a sample of textile from the Herjolfsnæs site, 2625j, by energy dispersive spectroscopy combined with low-vacuum SEM (SEM/EDS), in the conservation department of the National Museum of Denmark. Textile and pebbles both gave evidence for the presence of iron in high concentration. It seems highly likely, therefore, that the red textiles from Herjolfsnæs were dyed in naturally iron-rich water. Of course, this also raised the possibility that the red textiles had been stained accidentally during burial, but the even nature of the colour on only some of the Herjolfsnæs garments indicates that the colour must have been deliberately applied. This use of iron as a colorant has not been recorded in medieval Europe, although ferruginous clays such as ochre were used to colour linens in pre-Dynastic Egypt and iron is believed to have been used to dye Arab sails. On present evidence, its use in medieval wool clothing seems to have been a local Greenland invention, which was probably precipitated by the lack of red dyes such as madder and the presence of iron-rich streams near at hand.

Outside the Greenland settlements

Once the raw materials of the Norse textiles had been characterised, it was possible to examine textiles which were less certainly Norse. First of all, some old items held at the National Museum of Denmark which had lost their identifying paperwork were examined: two proved to be authentically Norse (Table 2).

Work then began on more recently excavated material. A textile from a site on the outskirts of the Eastern Settlement at Kirkespirdalen was studied and it proved to have the typical Norse arrangement of a Hairy fleece-type in the warp and a Hairy Medium in the weft. This textile was one of several artefacts which allowed this site, originally thought to be an Inuit camp, to be re-identified as a Norse shieling of the medieval Norse occupation (Hinnerson Berglund 1998). In another case a textile fragment, radiocarbon dated to AD 1250, had been found in a Thule Inuit site at Skraeling Island on the east coast of Ellesmere Island in the Canadian High Arctic (Schledermann 1993). This 2/2 twill had been identified as Norse by Else Østergård and this has now been confirmed by measurement of the fibre diameters (Table 2). In the other direction, textiles from a Norse farmstead at Papa Stour in the Shetlands have also been examined (Walton Rogers 1999). This large collection of textiles ranged in date from the 12th century to the 20th century. It included a few pieces which had more in common with textiles from mainland Britain and Europe, but they were predominantly 'vaðmal'-type twills and tabby weaves comparable with the textiles from Greenland. Analysis of the wool in five of the 'vaðmal' types, showed the same arrangement of fleece-types in the warp and weft, although the Shetland examples were on average finer than the Greenland wools (Table 2). The native Shetland sheep have a finer underwool than other members of Northern Short-tail breed-group and it is possible that this breed characteristic had an early origin.

The Scandinavians were also raiding and settling in England towards the end of the Anglo-Saxon period. A piece of wool 2/2 chevron twill from 10th-century York had already been tentatively identified as Scandinavian in origin, from technical characteristics and from the association of the fragment with a nålebundet sock (Walton 1989, 324, 329, 340-41, cat. No. 1303). The wool of this textile had already been characterised as pigmented and Hairy in the warp, and white and Hairy Medium in the weft (ibid., 302-3) and this can now be more confidently called a Norse textile.

The next step in this research must be to establish the geographical and chronological boundaries of the typical Norse textile. The 10th-century York textile was clearly outside the general run of late Anglo-Saxon textiles and marks an obvious import into England. The Shetland collection proved to be a combination of Norse and medieval Scottish (or European) textile types. The study now needs to be expanded to include other Norse colonies of the North Atlantic and the Scandinavian homelands.

Conclusion

The conclusions drawn from this research may be summarised as follows. The Norse settlers brought with them the same vari-coloured sheep as were farmed in Iceland and other Norse colonies. They used the wool from these sheep to make their clothing in natural wool colours, black, brown, grey and white, and goat hair was also employed for the coarser, especially black, yarns. The earliest settlers seem to have begun by over-dyeing coloured wools with dyes, such as woad and lichen purple, which were part of their Viking Age inheritance. As the colonies on Greenland became more established, however, they turned to other local sources for their colours. A tannin-based dye was commonly applied on brown and grey wools, and iron-rich water from local streams was used to colour white wools red. In the later phases of the Norse occupation, woad and madder, which were common in medieval Europe, were used sparingly and when they occur they may represent imported textiles or yarns. By this time, the Western Settlement also seems to have been experimenting with the use of yarns made from the white fur of the Arctic hare, although the Thule Inuit may have had a hand in this. Further contact with the Inuit can be seen in the curious textile from Ruin Island, where dog or wolf hair has been blended with wool.

The original aim of this study was to look for information which would help in the authentic reconstruction of Norse garments at the National Museum of Denmark. Over the eight years of the study, however, it has become something more than this. The characterisation of the raw materials has produced clear diagnostic markers for the Norse culture, which can be used by archaeologists in future work. It is hoped that the next stage will be to expand the reach of the study to investigate how far this particular aspect of Norse culture may extend.

The Production of Garments

1. The cutting of the Herjolfsnæs garments

Before the garments could be sewn, sleeves, sides, fronts and backs had to be cut from the strong *vaðmál*. A few parts also had to be cut up the middle lengthwise – not all the way though, but only to a certain point where some of the garments had to have a division adapted to the shape of the middle gusset. Could the inspiration for this sophisticated finish have come from woodcarving work of the kind that can be seen on the door of the *Valþjófsstaður* stave church?[1] The door is from the thirteenth century and shows an Icelandic church with an entrance portal terminated above with handsome arches.[2]

Fig. 59

Section of the door of the Icelandic Valþjófsstaðaur *stave church. Perhaps the refined arched shape of this door, and other similarly superb woodwork, was the inspiration for the middle gussets in the Herjolfsnæs garments?*

In other garments a straight cut had to be made in the sides for pocket slits. The two sleeves had to be identical, with domed curves at the top and related gussets. The sleeves on the Herjolfsnæs garments are all cut from one piece except on the garment D5674, which has a two-part sleeve. A neck opening had to be cut out, oval or round, and it could be furnished with a slit down the front. Both forms required dexterity.

A hood had to have two halves, gussets and a long piece for the narrow liripipe, which was in several cases cut in a piece with the hood. Here, too, great cutting skill was necessary, especially with the attractively formed 'horn' of the hood, the upward-projecting point above the forehead, and the curved back of the neck. The cutting of the long stockings D10613 and D10614 would not have been work for beginners either. The stockings are cut diagonally across the cloth, which produced the necessary elasticity and good freedom of movement. The shorter stockings, which end below the knee, could on the other hand be cut in the lengthwise direction of the cloth. But it was not only the long stockings that were cut diagonally. So was the hood D10600, where the diagonal cut gives the hood a shape that makes it hug the head closely. But dexterity was not enough in itself. One also needed a sharp tool to cut the many parts out of the several millimetres thick *vaðmál*. The relatively frail scissors that were found at the farm Austmannadalen 5 (V53d) cannot possibly have been in use as cutting-out scissors (D12811.303).[3] They would have been better for cutting hair and trimming beards. Instead one can imagine that one of the many knives and shears that have been found was used to cut cloth.

The woven *vaðmál* – in a length unknown to us – must necessarily have been spread out on a firm underlay to be cut. But what kind of underlay? No whole table or planks from a table have been found. What have been found are doors, for example at the Farm Beneath the Sand (64V2-III-555) and at Sandnæs (V51).[4] Both doors are preserved to a height of 1280 mm. The longest garment measures 1290 mm. Perhaps a door was lifted down from its hinges and used as a table board? In medieval pictures of workshops one can often see working tables consisting of two trestles with a board laid across them.[5]

On the Herjolfsnæs garments it is clear to see that the individual parts were cut with great accuracy. The work was planned. The cutters knew which parts could be joined together and fitted so there would be as little waste as possible. All side pieces are cut with one straight-thread side and one diagonal-thread side. By reversing the cloth for every second width, they made full use of the woven cloth. Extra cut-out parts were used for the many small gussets that can be seen in sleeves and hoods. Similarly, leftover fragments of cloth were used for caps. The long working process of making clothes, from the preparation of raw materials through spinning until the finished weaving was ready, must have been taken into regard during cutting, even though time was a different dimension then than now.

The garments are constructed with a symmetrical axis in the middle at the front and back and with a mirror image of the sides at the side seams. The front and back pieces are the central parts and were probably cut first, since they are longest and would have used most cloth. The adjacent sides must have been cut then, and finally the sleeves. The cutting of the garments D10580, D10583 and D8081, which have a total of eight sides that are narrow at the top and wide at the bottom, would have been particularly demanding. It is reasonable to assume that an old unpicked garment would have been used as a pattern. Cutting so many pieces out of a twill weave would require special attention. The difficult twill weave, which is different on the right and wrong sides, had to face the same way all the way around the garment. The right side was the side where the diagonal line went from the top right-hand corner to the bottom left – a rule that would have been known and observed. On none of the garments can one see a single width or sleeve cut the wrong way or with the twill in the opposite direction. However, the gusset in the front of the hood D10596 was sewn in with the back facing out. The cutting of the Norse Greenlanders, with its consistent symmetry, is professionally done. Similar symmetry can be seen in the many garments from the contemporary man's costume from Bocksten Bog in Halland in Sweden.[6] Both the Greenlandic and Swedish garments are highly distinguishable, when compared to the tailoring carried out in the Old Town in Oslo in the Middle Ages. In that instance the researchers could note, after reviewing the many fragments – which perhaps do not provide a basis for a fair comparison – that absolute symmetry and regularity had only played a minor role, and today the sewing would be described as 'sloppy'.[7]

Several of the pieces of medieval clothing from Skjoldehamn in northern Norway also bear the marks of 'extremely poor tailoring'.[8]

2. Garment construction

In the Early Middle Ages the cutting-out of clothes was a craft associated with a good deal of mystery. Garment construction and cutting designs were new ideas. Previously, material and garment cuts with geometrical forms had been interdependent. The woven cloth was used as it was when taken out of the loom.[9] The Viborg Shirt, dated c. 1050 AD, is in principle an example of such a cut.[10] The shirt is pulled over the head, there is no shoulder seam and the sleeve is cut off straight at the top. The same cut can be seen in the male garment from Kragelund Bog (1045-1155), which is however rather sloppily cut on one long side. In the case of the shirts – and the women's shifts – weave and form were adapted to each other well into our own era. An English saying from 1546 puts it like this: 'I shall cut my cote after my cloth'.

As we have seen, the Norse Greenlanders economized with their weavings. The form was no longer the geometrical one determined by the woven cloth. Instead it was now the lines of the body that influenced the cut, which resulted in a more tightly fitting costume with an increasing width towards the bottom edge. True, this cut meant greater consumption of *vaðmál*, and it also led to a lot of sewing work to get the many breadths sewn together. One may wonder why it was so important in the Norse society to use a garment cut, which was popular in places that were far away from Greenland.

During a transitional period both types, the geometrical and the fitted, were in use, as can be illustrated by two Jutland garments. The Kragelund garment has a geometrical cut, where the added width is achieved by means of breadths set into it at the middle and the middle back, and in the side seams, and a rather primitive neck opening. The contemporary garment from Moselund, on the other hand, is cut to fit with huge armholes and domed sleeves. Further, the garment has a small, finely formed neck rounding with a short slit in front. Narrow sides give the garment width below. The new style that Moselund represents also found its way to Herjolfsnæs a couple of centuries later.

3. Comparative material

In the dating of clothing researchers often use the garments of princely and royal individuals as a basis of comparison. But since only a few original costumes are pre-

Fig. 60

Chessman from the Isle of Lewis in the Hebrides carved in walrus tooth. The figure 'the ward' or 'the rook' depicts a foot soldier dressed in a costume very much like the Greenlandic, of which the oldest dated is from the end of the 1200s. 'The ward' and 78 other chessmen are Norse crafted from the second half of the 1100s. The height is c. 90 mm.

Fig. 61

Figure of a queen carved in walrus tooth, is 84 mm in height (D 12367.278) and was found on the little island of Qeqertaq in the municipality of Sisimiut. The Thule Eskimos lived on the island during summer. Dated to 1200-1300s.

served, they use images from the tombs of prominent persons, which show the deceased full-length, carved in alabaster or in sheet metal.

In Roskilde Cathedral, for example, we can see Queen Margrete I's sarcophagus with the Queen fully-dressed in full length. And the 'golden' dress that is attributed to the same queen (1353-1412) is also in the church, but as a reconstruction. The original, re-stitched dress is on display in Uppsala Cathedral. But altarpieces, chess pieces, sculptures, illuminated manuscripts and psalters (hymn books) are also used for costume studies.

However, one finds that in the earlier part of the Middle Ages many details, such as the shape of the sleeves and the neck opening in the representations, are often hidden by a cloak or a headdress which falls down over the shoulders. The most important information will therefore be the length of the garment, and whether the wearer is a woman or a man. From the fourteenth century on, though, there are many more details in the images that can date the costumes. Many written sources, such as English documents, can supplement this with information on cutting and sewing, and this gives us much knowledge not only of the appearance of the costumes, but also of their construction.[11]

If one compares the many items of information it is often possible to find characteristic details in small archaeological textile fragments, found without any relationship to datable objects, where one can recognize sewing techniques; all this can date such fragments. In the middle of the fourteenth century, extremely large cut-out armholes were a new style in France, as can be seen on a preserved jacket that belonged to Charles de Blois (d. 1364).[12] A hundred years later one finds a similar armhole type and related sleeves on Queen Margrete I's golden dress. Even farther north this sleeve appears on the pleated garment D10590, which ended up in a grave in Herjolfsnæs Churchyard (Ø111). The pleated garments were radiocarbon dated in 1999 to 1300-1420. The material in this case is not richly wrought cloth of gold, but a warmer Greenlandic *vaðmál*.

Where and when a new style makes its appearance is hard to place and date, but that it radiates from large cultural centres and places close to the centres of power is something we know from modern times. It is also a recognized fact that it takes a number of years for a particular cut to reach the peripheral areas. But it is amazing that the art of cutting clothes was so quick in reaching the outermost periphery where Greenland has to be placed at that time.

In the thirteenth century the tailors in the major European towns joined forces and formed guilds to protect their interests and maintain better control over the cutting and sewing of garments.

From laws and regulations we can see that the tailors had to live in particular streets, which were often later given names like 'Tailor Street'. They were highly esteemed citizens who could also become mayors. One can also see that in the Nordic countries the tailors were often foreigners. In the guild regulations there are stipulations about apprenticeship periods and payment. In 1384, for example, we read how much a tailor could take for sewing 'a man's coat buttoned, hood and hose'.[13] It was thus the tailor who cut and sewed stockings. But there are no indications of how he did it. It was only in the sixteenth century that the earliest known diagrams or cutting patterns appeared. These were published in Germany and Spain,[14] and the oldest known measuring-tape of parchment is from the same period.[15]

We do not know what models or instructions the Norse Greenlanders had, but they probably got information on the 'new cuts' from some of the many travellers who came by ship to, among other landing-places, Sandhavn, which lies just north of Herjolfsnæs. Or perhaps they met the new arrivals in the church. Finally, there could be fellow-countrymen who had been abroad, and who brought drawings of costumes home with them.

4. Sewing

On the costumes from Herjolfsnæs we see seams that are almost invisible from the right side and seams that are visible and decorative as well as reinforcing. The seam allowances that can be seen on the back rarely measure more than seven millimetres in width and are always carefully terminated with tight overcast stitches, or with a tablet-woven piped edging. A cut-off edge, folded towards the wrong side, can also have a decorative element, as can be seen along the front edge of most hoods, where the tight overcasting of one or more extra (filler) threads, placed along the cut-off

Fig. 62 and Fig. 63

A turned back border (hem), with overcast stitches sewn on top of one or several (filler) threads that cover the raw edge, was prevalent in Norse Greenland. This type of needlework can be found along face openings on hoods and in neck openings; almost always seen together with one or two rows of stab stitches placed some few millimetres from the outermost edge.

97

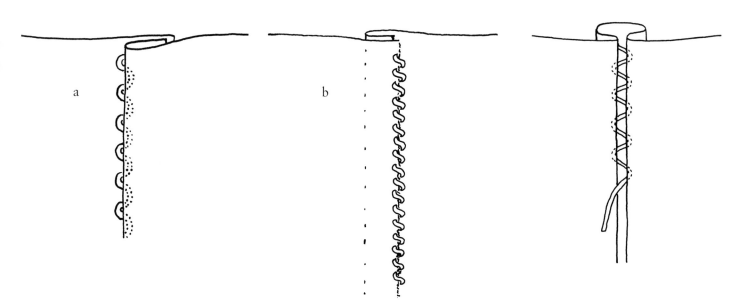

a

b

Fig. 64

Long seams were probably sewn from the right side (a) and usually with small invisible stitches, and the seam allowance was sewn down to the cloth with tight overcast stitches (b).

Fig. 65

A false seam has no function but is solely for the purpose of giving the garment symmetry, so that the number of panels is even. Right side.

edge, marks the termination of the fold. A similar edging is found around the neck openings of garments, and it is likely that this or the extra threads helped to prevent the neck edge from curling. The inlaid threads lie there, apparently unaffected by the thread from the overcasting, and could therefore be tightened so that the edge was held in against the neck.

The sewing-thread used was a specially made thread, as is evident from a few fibre analyses, and as can also be seen on the many beautiful seams. Threads were spun from sheep or goat hairs and then two-plied to a sewing thread with a diameter of less than a millimetre – always Z-spun and S-twisted. The thread may have been treated afterwards with wax, which has made it look thinner while achieving a reinforcing effect. The length of the stitch is from one and a half to five millimetres, always adapted to the position where it was used and how visible the seam was to be.

Among 'invisible' seams belongs all sewing of main garment parts, of sleeves, pieces of hoods, and gussets inserted in garments and hoods. Many of the seams may have been done from the front, where one piece with a fold along the cut-off edge has been laid in over the adjacent piece. In these seams a hem stitch has been used. The seam allowance on the back is fastened in one piece to one side with tight overcast stitching down to the cloth. On some garments, among others on the item D8081, the seam allowance has tablet-woven piped edging.

A few long costume seams consist of a so-called 'false seam'. That is, the garment's panel has been cut in double size, but for the sake of the symmetry of the garment the panel has been divided in two by a false seam. In Iceland garments with many panels were produced with the help of false seams, among other things, and called *fjolgeirungr*.

On the garment (D10584) the seams are done in such a way that the seam allowances face one another in twos, which means that the panels fall into deep, soft folds. With the side seams and the seams for gussets in the middle, the seam edges face inward in the garment. When the costume was excavated Poul Nørlund noted that the wide skirt was neatly laid in pleats.[16] The use of two different edgings on seam edges, as can be seen in this garment, meant that the thick *vaðmál* in the skirt folded in a particular way, which gave the garment a soft drape when it was in use.

Gussets in sleeves and hoods are inserted so that they 'lie under' the cloth. Some shoulder seams have the seam allowance spreading to each side and are then fastened to the garment with overcast stitches.

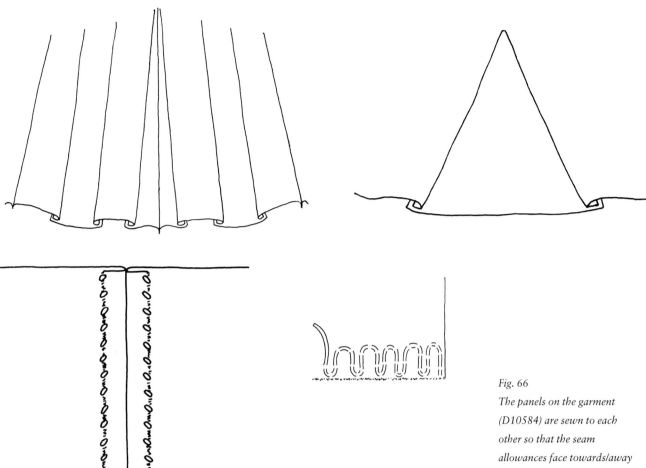

An almost invisible seam is the so-called 'singling'. When the Norse clothes were being investigated, this was quite literally only discovered when the light from the microscope fell diagonally on to a textile fragment. It has later emerged that singling was sewn along edges that were not to be folded, but were terminated with a decorative border, such as tablet-woven piped edging or footweave. The seam appears in particular along hems at the bottom of garments and at right angles to buttonholes to prevent the thread slipping out of the weave.

The decorative seams: stab stitching, tablet-woven piped edging and footweave, besides their ornamental function, also served as reinforcement of garments and hoods where heavy wear could be expected.

Stab stitching can be found along several lengthways seams on garments, on the face-openings of hoods and at the bottom of sleeves. It can also be seen at pocket slits and along necklines. On the whole, stab stitching was much used in Norse clothing, and often appeared together with thick-threaded overcast stitching along a seam allowance.

Tablet-woven piped edging and footweave were also very popular seams for reinforcing a vulnerable edge in a handsome way.

5. Sewing of pleats

On the garment fragments D10590 and D6473, which are unfortunately very poorly preserved, there are narrow pleats folded in parallel with the warp threads in the longitudinal direction of the garments. However, on the 'hip fragment' D6473 the folding follows a warp thread, but not completely. The pleats, which are only 4-5 mm

Fig. 66

The panels on the garment (D10584) are sewn to each other so that the seam allowances face towards/away from each other. On the middle gusset seams, as well as the side seams, the seam allowances face 'inwards'. In order to clarify the principle, the drawing shows unevenness in the width of the seam allowances, but in reality they have the same width.

Fig. 67

Gussets on sleeves and hoods are inserted to lie under the cloth. The seam is the same as the long seams on the garments.

Fig. 68

Shoulder seams are often finished in this way.

Fig. 69

A 'singling' seam is used for reinforcing and is found on many finishing edges. The stitches are pulled 'flat' into the textile and are invisible from the right side.

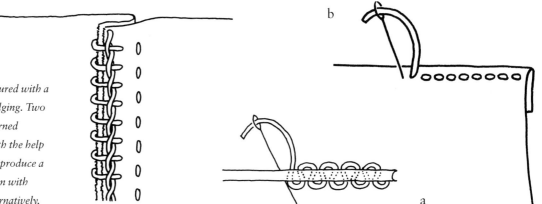

Fig. 70

A seam allowance secured with a tablet-woven piped edging. Two threads – probably turned around each other with the help of a two-hole tablet – produce a cord that is sewn down with overcast stitches. Alternatively, this can be achieved by twisting two threads together with the fingers at the same time as the overcast stitches are sewn. On some of the longitudinal seams the cord is seen innermost, at other times, outermost.

Fig. 71

Stab stitches seen in cross section (a) and from the right side (b). This stitching is found mostly along seams at the top of garments – probably to mark the cut, and as reinforcement for the finishing edges.

Fig. 72

Stitched pleats seen from the reverse side. The pleats, which are only 4-5 millimetres wide, are folded longitudinally, parallel with the warp threads The pleats are sewn as 'false seams' and with almost invisible stitches.

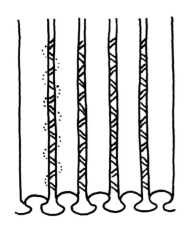

wide – corresponding to seven warp threads – look rounded on the right side, while on the back, where the seam is, they are somewhat flatter. The pleats are carefully folded and then sewn together on the wrong side with stitches that wind from pleat to pleat, only visible as small transverse threads between the individual rows of pleats. In a few places the sewing thread runs across several pleats, but since both pleats and stitches are much decomposed, it is hard to see whether it is an end-stitching or it is sewn over a longer piece, perhaps sewn to keep the pleats close together. Whether the pleats were first folded all over the cloth and then sewn row by row, or whether they were sewn after each pleat was folded, one cannot see. The seam is like the one used for a false seam. One could say that the back of a 'false seam' looks like a narrow 'rounded' pleat.

One single fragment (x2554) from the Farm Beneath the Sand (64V2-III-555) has a few pleats folded in the longitudinal direction, but no seam can be seen.

Pleated fragments like the Greenlandic ones with rounded pleats parallel with the warp have been registered in a woman's grave from the Viking Age at Vangsnes in Vestlandet in Norway. The weaving is in a tabby weave. In Bergen the same type of pleated fragment has been found in both 2/2 and 2/1 twill, dated between the twelfth and fourteenth century. There is also a child's costume with a pleated upper part from a medieval burial in the Norwegian stave church Uvdal.[17]

A skirt found in a bog in the west of Ireland, in Emlagh near Dingle, has tightly folded pleats lengthwise. The pleats were sewn in the same way as the Greenlandic ones, where the back is smooth, while the pleats on the front form 'rounded' pleats on the right side. The skirt is sewn from a thick weave in 2/1 twill and has been dated to the seventeenth century.[18]

Another type of pleat was found on clothing fragments from the Early Middle Ages in both Norway and Sweden.[19] The pleats in these finds have very sharp folds and can be compared with modern 'sunray pleats' that are narrow at the top and increase in width downwards. The cloth used is often worsted in 2/1 twill. But linen too has been used for pleated garments from the Viking Age, as can be seen in the Birka find.[20] At the Bishop's seat Gardar (Ø47) a couple of compacted lumps (100x80 mm and 100x60 mm) of carbonized linen were found. On the smallest piece one can see five-millimetre wide pleats which appear to overlap one another. Perhaps these fragments from Gardar are the remains of the Bishop's alb?

Cloth folded in narrow pleats was already known in ancient Greece, where the finely folded cloth was moistened and left to dry in the sun. From there the pleated garments reached southeastern Europe, and probably continued from there to Birka in Sweden.[21]

Folded skirts, cloaks, aprons and collars are known however from many countries and are depicted in books from the sixteenth century.[22] From an excavation in Roskilde Cathedral there is a small fragment of linen, which is folded in sharp pleats, and sewn with a decorative (smock-like) stitching across the pleats. In Italy since ancient times it has been the nuns who have folded the priests' albs.[23] First narrow, fine pleats were folded along the length of the alb, then it was folded in pleats across – and the process was repeated after each wash.

Future textile research may reveal whether there is a connection between ancient Greece, the alb of the priests, and the secular costume tradition of Viking Age Norway and Greenland.

6. Embroidery

On a small fragment in 2/2 twill from the *Landnáma* Farm (Ø17a) there are some threads sewn down on the right side, which with a little good will can be called an embroidery (D5/1992.8). The fragment is now brownish, but was originally in a blue colour, and across this two or more threads have been laid and sewn fast with small, short stitches. There is only a little left of the embroidery threads, and samples were only taken out for a colour analysis with great caution. This showed that the threads had been dyed in two red shades.[24] The 'embroidery' was done in so-called couching, which was a well known embroidery technique in the early part of the Scandinavian Middle Ages and was mainly used for making picture embroideries. In Iceland, where couching is called *refilsaumur,* 14 *refil*-sewn embroideries are preserved. Most are altar antependia, and the oldest, from the middle of the fourteenth century, is from Stafafell Church in southeastern Iceland.[25] On another Icelandic antependium

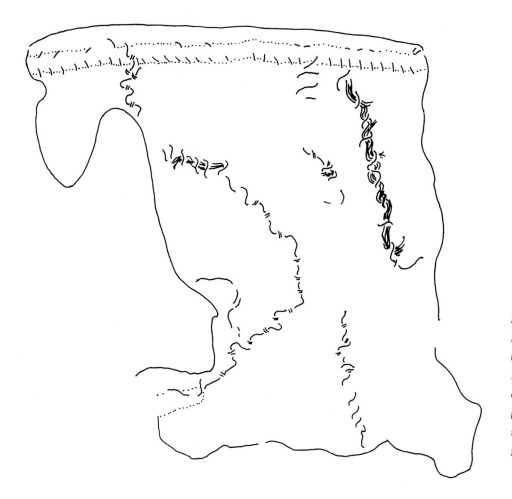

Fig. 73

Preserved threads on the fragment (D5/1992.8) from the Landnáma Farm – the remains of couched needlework? The preserved threads are in two shades of red, sewn on an indigo dyed vaðmál.

101

from the end of the Middle Ages a narrow leather strip forms the contour around appliqué figures. The leather strip is sewn using the couching technique.[26] Some of the couched Icelandic antependia can be seen in the National Museums in Copenhagen and Reykjavík.

In one of the embroideries from the Oseberg find one can see some connected circles consisting of couched threads.[27] The Norwegian name for couching is *leggsøm*. This technique is also found in an embroidery on a fragment from Røn Church in Valdres in Norway. It has been dated to the end of the thirteenth century.[28] Outside the Nordic countries *refil* sewing is known from the famous Bayeux Tapestry in Normandy, which was embroidered at the end of the eleventh century.[29] In the 'embroidery' on the fragment from the *Landnáma* Farm one can see no pattern. It was perhaps just a practice piece.

7. Buttons

A total of about 20 buttons have been found. Seven buttons are sewn from *vaðmál* as in the garment D10583 with which they were found. The tough *vaðmál* was folded around an extra layer of *vaðmál* or a plant(?) material which has now disappeared. To make the buttons stable and firm, small tight stitches were sewn through the layers in concentric rows. The sewing thread is two-ply, very thin and spun from the hair of sheep or goat. On the back of the buttons the cloth is gathered in a bunch through which they were fastened to the garment. Among the other buttons, at Gardar (Ø47) a flat bone button was found, 11 mm in diameter, with head and eye cut out in one piece. The button was found in the small bell tower.[30] Three buttons are from Sandnæs (V51) and are of the same form as the button from Gardar. The Sandnæs buttons are 7-11 mm in diameter; two are of walrus ivory and one of bone. From Nipaatsoq (V54) there are also buttons of walrus tusk which are cut out in one piece, but a few of the eyes are worn right through.[31] All buttons were found lying loose. On the garments where there are buttonholes, it is not possible to see where the buttons were attached, but from preserved contemporary costumes from, among other places, England and France it is evident that in the fourteenth century buttons were sewn on along the outer edge with a long 'stalk'. The buttons are very small, often less than 10 mm.[32]

8. Buttonholes and eyelets

Buttonholes are preserved at the sleeve slits in garment D10583. On the right sleeve of the garment there are 16 buttonholes, while on the left sleeve only seven are preserved. On garment D10591 there are four buttonholes on the left side of the neck opening. The two garments D10594 and D10595 both have buttonholes along the left front edge. On garment D10594 there are three buttonholes at the bottom and 16 at the top, while on the other garment, D10595, there are only two buttonholes at the bottom. How many there once were at the top or whether there were buttonholes spaced equally along the edge from top to bottom, we do not know, since the costume is very poorly preserved.

The buttonholes in the Herjolfsnæs garments are cut at right angles to the edge, that is, on the straight grain of the weft in the weave, with the exception of the buttonholes along the sleeve slits, where they are cut at a slightly oblique angle to the edge. The buttonholes seem very little worn, and no seam is preserved, not even traces of stitches or stitch holes, but there must have been seams. A likely explanation

Fig. 74
Two buttons of walrus tooth with carved eyes (KNK991x620 and –591x624) found on the farm Nipaatsoq in the Western Settlement.

for the absence of thread is that it was a flax thread, i.e. a material that is only in exceptional cases preserved in archaeological textiles.[33] On the other hand at the sleeve slits a singling is preserved – a reinforcing seam that is often found along the lower edges of garments and hoods. The stitches can only be seen on the wrong side, where they follow each or every second weft thread from the outside edge 8-10 mm in. In addition the edge outside the buttonholes is reinforced with a stitched-on twisted cord, which is 3-5 mm wide. On garment D10591 no seam is preserved along the buttonhole edge, while on garment D10594 a four millimetre wide 'ornamental border' has been sewn on at right angles to the buttonholes as reinforcement. On the same garment, along the button edge, stab stitches have been sewn through the folded-over edge, but there is no trace of the sewing-on of buttons. Garment D10595 has stab stitches along both edges, and only a few possible traces of the attachment of buttons.

Buttons have been found in several Norwegian graves from the 8th-10th century – both men's and women's graves. Some are domed, while others are flat iron buttons with bronze-covered heads. Such buttons, used in connection with garments, are known from the thirteenth century. Worked in costly materials, they were used as decoration and only later as closing devices on the clothes.

The very small buttons must have been rather difficult to close, but the alternative to buttons and buttonholes was to close one's garment with pins, so-called costume pins, or to lace up the openings with cords drawn through eyelets. Finally, one could sew one's sleeve slits together every morning, as one can read in the sagas.[34]

On the short-sleeved garment D10581, there is a small slit in front at the neck opening where, according to Nørlund's description, there were two eyelets on each side. In this investigation only faint traces of a single one could be seen.

On a garment fragment (D11920) from Sandnæs (V51) three sewn eyelets are preserved, 3-4 mm long. It is conceivable that on a corresponding piece there were metal hooks for closing the garment, but this fragment has not been found.

A 'buttonhole' in a rather different form has been registered on a woven fragment of wool that is probably from a sail, found with 40 other woven pieces in the loft of Trondenes Church in northern Norway. The fragments had been used as rags to caulk the roof. The textiles have been radiocarbon dated to 1280-1420. As reinforcement around the 15 mm long eyelet, long tight stitches have been sewn with wool thread. On the back there is a hempen cord which runs in under the seam along half of the eyelet. Where the hempen cord comes out again it is worn off, but a few ends show that it is there.[35]

Decoration of Garments

1. Borders

The women of Norse Greenland had several different ways of edging garments and other items of clothing. As can be seen on the short stockings D10616, a natural edge was used as a border. The knee-length stocking has a starting border along the top. This particular border would have been hard-wearing, because the warp threads at the top are double and lie tightly in the weft. Among other 'natural' borders there are selvedges, but they were not used visibly to edge a garment. Theoretically the 'buttoned garments' D10594 and D10595 could have had a selvedge along the straight-threaded front edge, since the warp threads – and thus also the selvedges – run in the longitudinal direction of the garments. All other borders are added, unlike the starting border used on D10616.

'Decorative borders' sewn on the clothes as an addition can be seen on costume D10594, where the cut-off front edge is terminated with a narrow madder-red border, which is sewn around the garment edge as reinforcement. On stocking D10617 a reinforcing decorative border was also sewn along the top edge in another weave than that of the stocking, but this edge no longer exists.

The remaining finishing edges were made, as far as the Norse material shows so far, with a technique that combines sewing and weaving. There are two types: the tablet-woven/stitched and the footwoven. In both, a stretched warp is held along a cloth edge. During the work the warp is manipulated either with tablets or with heddles tied around the warp threads. The weft thread is drawn through the eye of a needle which takes the weft through the shed and on through the *cloth*, around the

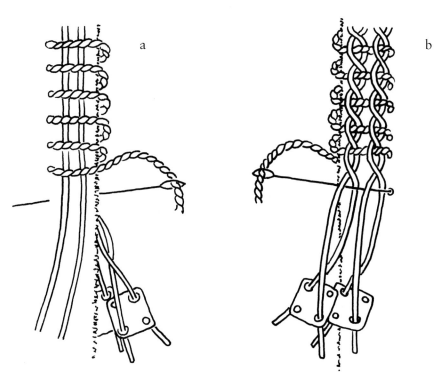

Fig. 75

Tablet-woven piped edging is a combination of tablet weaving and stitching, where the weft thread in the tablet weaving is also the sewing thread that secures the edging to the cloth. On the reverse side (a) only the cross-threads – possibly with filler threads underneath, can be seen. On the right side (b) the edging can be seen as parallel-lying cords, while the weft thread is invisible.

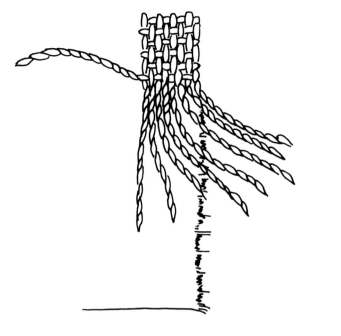

Fig. 76 a
Footweave or 'slynging' is a
combination of weaving and
sewing, where the weft thread
in the weave is also the sewing
thread that secures the woven
edge down to the cloth. On
the right side, the footweaving
can be seen as a tabby weave.
On the reverse side, only the
cross-threads can be seen.

Fig. 76 b
Drawing showing the
footweaving procedure.

cut edge. The weft thread is limited to a 'needle's length', that is the length of thread it is practical to have in the needle to carry out the weaving/sewing work. In many cases the cloth edge had first been secured with a singling and this will, on the one hand, have prevented the threads unravelling and, on the other, supported the edge while the work was done.

In tablet-woven piped edging a few tablets would be used, each with one warp thread drawn through each of two diagonally opposite holes. (See fig. 75). When the tablets are put on the point the warp threads are divided into two layers and a shed appears through which the weft is conducted. Each weaving tablet twists the two warp threads that it holds, and the result is two-ply 'cords' in which the weft is hidden. In some cases these 'cords' have loosened from the edge of the cloth because the weft thread has been worn through. In other cases the 'cords' are quite loose, and it is very hard to tell whether they were originally part of a tablet-woven piped edging.

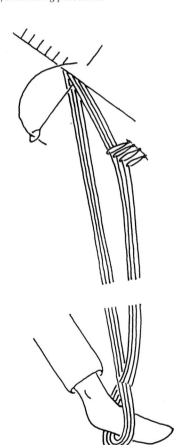

In footweaving, heddles are tied around every other warp thread. As the name suggests, a foot is used to keep the warp tensioned.

Unlike tablet-woven piped edging, which is woven/stitched with the right side of the cloth up, the wrong side of the cloth is turned upwards while the footweaving is carried out. The explanation, according to an Icelandic practitioner of footweaving, is that it is easiest to change shed by means of the heddles when one pulls down, and the weft thread is most easily placed when the 'sewing side' faces upward.[1]

In Iceland footweave is called *slynging*. This kind of weaving/stitching has survived there for centuries. What is perhaps the oldest Icelandic *slynging* in white linen thread is on a liturgical burse from Kálfafell. It is dated to the 1400s or around 1500, now in the National Museum in Reykjavik.[2] An antependium from Hólar church in northern Iceland also has a *slynging* border in wool. The antependium has been dated to the middle of the sixteenth century. A similar border in white flax thread can be seen on an altar-cloth from Hálsi Church. The altar-cloth is dated 1617.[3] Today *slynging* is used as an attractive finishing or closing edge on knitted insoles and is still a living tradition in Iceland. But on other islands in the North Atlantic area footweaving is also known. On Aran and the neighbouring island Inishere, as late as the end of the 1950s, people used footwoven belts, so-called Aran Crois.[4] The belts are independently woven bands, not combined with sewing, which is the special feature of the Icelandic and Norse footweaves.

Footweaving was also used by the Romans in the northern provinces in the third century AD. In Verulamium, the present-day St. Albans in England, a child was buried with its head resting on a pillow in a pewter coffin. The pillow is bordered with a footweave.[5] The weave has been erroneously called a 'darned edge' because of the structure, which looks like a tabby weave.[6]

On the thick *vaðmál* garments and hoods, tablet-woven piped edging and footweave were both practical, and although the edges in this study have almost all disappeared, from the beginning they must have been very hard wearing. Both borders would at the same time have been an ideal solution to the difficult technical sewing problem, which the seam allowance on a rounded cut-off in an unmilled *vaðmál* must have posed. In combination with a subsequent sewing, the result would be clumsy. The Norse woman tablet-wove/stitched or footwove around the edge, and the 'problem' was solved in an elegant way. She also used tablet-woven piped edging when sewing the long garment seams together.

Similar tablet-woven piped edging borders have been registered in finds from London, dated to the fourteenth century.[7]

2. Braiding and cording

Very few braids and cords have been found in the Norse material. The 15 mm wide braid D10624 is a fine representative of what was probably a very common, widespread utility object. The present-day length of the braid is 445 mm, but since it consists of four separate fragments, it may have been longer. One of the fragments was found with costume D10588, the other three close by. On two of the fragments the braid is tied around itself in a knot. The braid is three-stranded, braided from two-ply sheep hair. One can see that the different strands had different shades of colour. Cord D10622, which is wound with twelve individual wool strands in a light brown colour and with a thickness of 7 mm, was like the braid found in Herjolfsnæs Churchyard. Both were undoubtedly used as belts around the waist to hold together loose-hanging garments such as D5674, D10594 and D10595.

A very narrow braid of 4 mm, braided from six strands (hair) is sewn to a neck opening(?) on a child's costume of which only a fragment from the shoulder section is preserved. At the presumed neck opening one can see a sloppy fold with frayed threads on the back – a rare sight in the Norse context. The fragment KNK991x448 is from Nipaatsoq (V54).[8]

Sewn-on cords can be seen on a number of costumes from Herjolfsnæs, partly as reinforcement, partly as decoration – probably a combination of both. On the fragment from the V-shaped neckline on garment D10590, one can see a three mm wide twisted cord, and on the child's garment D10592 there was originally a cord along the bottom edge. It is not possible to tell whether it was an independent cord or part of a woven border, since the cord has now disappeared. In the material from the Farm Beneath the Sand (64V2-III-555) there are a number of loose-lying thick twisted threads which were not necessarily in use as laces, but which are unravelled threads from thick weaves. Many of these twisted threads are of goat hair.

The most common cords, however, are braided – and are called *kríla∂* bands in Icelandic. In Denmark a braided cord is also called a 'Faroe cord', because it is thought to be of Faroese origin. The cord is made such that the long thread loops that are fastened to a fixed point at one end are drawn through one another according to

Fig. 77

Braided cord sewn along a selvedge on the fragment (1950x1426) from the Farm Beneath the Sand. The weave is a 2/2 twill with Z/S spun threads and 11/11 threads/cm.

a particular system, in the diagonal direction. The 'tool' used is the fingers, which hold the loops like hooks.[9] In Iceland such cords are preserved as patterned bands on four sewn laces of wool thread from the 1700s.[10] The braided cords are known from many countries. In Åbo Cathedral there is a braided cord as part of a reliquary, and there is also one in the shrine of St. Erik in Uppsala Cathedral.[11] On other medieval textiles such as reliquary purses and secular purses sewn from gold-interwoven silk weaves one can see cords braided in silk thread or in gold and silver thread. The cords are used as borders around the purses and as draw-strings through the casings above.[12]

Along a neckline(?) on a fragment from GUS (x1341) and on another fragment (x1426) one can see braided cords. From Hvalsey Church the *vaðmál* fragment D12685 is bordered with a cord braided in flax.

Cords, braids and bands worked in various materials were used in innumerable contexts. Textiles bordered with cords can be seen on a blanket from the grave of the Oseberg Queen and in finds from Viking Age women's graves in Vestlandet in Norway as well as from Birka in Sweden.[13]

For putting up hair, ribbons or laces were attached with wooden pins of the same kind as the many Norse pins and, attractively arranged, they could be decorative on the wearer – in Greenland as elsewhere.[14] Narrow ribbons or cords were drawn like laces through eyelets to close an opening in a garment.

To tie up or sew packed *vaðmál*, strong cords were used. In the warp-weighted loom there was also a great need for a strong cord at the top of the loom to carry the many warp threads, and at the bottom of the loom to tie on the weights – one cord for each weight.

In addition, cords and braids were used to tie around the garment, as we can see on many medieval pictures. On the body found in the Skjoldehamn Bog in northern Norway, there was an 11 mm wide braided cord around the waist of the gown, tied in a couple of loops.[15] The monk's habit still has a thick cord tied around the waist with hanging ends.

Accessories

Fig. 78

On excavation of the Farm Beneath the Sand a circlet of hair from a fair-haired Norse Greenlander was found in a recess in a northern wall. The circlet is 575 mm long and 7-9 mm wide.

Fig. 79

Drawing of the circlet of hair. Two by two twisted strands of hair follow parallel, crossing each other in an 'over-under' pattern. An exception to this can be seen in some few places, where two parallel strands cross through the two opposite strands, or cross in through a single twisted strand, as with a 'ply-splitting'.

1. Hairwork

In 1993, in a niche in the weaving room, Room I – from the last phase of the history of the Farm Beneath the Sand (GUS 64V2-III-555) – a 575 mm long circlet was found (x1545), twisted from human hair. It is a very unusual find, perhaps the only one of its kind at all. The circlet of hair is beautifully formed, with almost circular holes like beads on a string. The hairs lie in two strands with some 6-8 hairs in each strand, wound around one another like a Z-twisted cord. The strands were laid parallel in twos around an implement with wooden teeth(?) on which the hair strands were fixed, perhaps with boiling water, and then cooled. The circlet has kept its original form from the time when it was entwined until the time when it was found. This is due to the permafrost in the Greenlandic soil, which has kept it in its frozen grip for 6-700 years. It was probably possible to close it with a small button or bead. The hair strands at one end have opened up and the bead(?) has disappeared. The opposite

end has a corresponding eye for closing. An analysis has shown that the hair is from a fair-haired Norse individual, and it is very conceivable that the circlet was a love-gift.

Since ancient times special qualities and emotions have been associated with human hair – sentimental, magical, symbolic or superstitious. In *Vadstenas Tænke-bok* (1592) one can read that 'Bracelets and rings of hair increase love'.[1] The same thought lies behind the famous English poet John Donne's poem 'The Relique', which he wrote in the seventeenth century. In this poem the 'relic' is a 'bracelet of bright hair about the bone' which can be seen when a grave is reopened gracing the bones of a loving couple.[2]

2. Costume pins

In Herjolfsnæs Churchyard, besides costumes, accessories were also found for two garments, including two pins of copper (D10627), only one of which is complete. It is 55 mm long, thin and pointed with a 6 mm lenticular head. The two pins were found in a grave inside the Herjolfsnæs church ruin (Ø111) along with a thin wooden pin which was probably fastened to a garment. In the grave neither coffin nor costume was preserved, only faint traces of a skeleton.[3]

From most excavations of Norse farms in Greenland costume pins are preserved, some of which may also have been for putting up hair. They are made of bone, wood, caribou antler/bone or walrus ivory in lengths varying from 8 to 20 mm, wide and flat at one end and tapering towards the other end, as can be seen on the bone pins from the *Landnáma* Farm (Ø17a) at Narsaq, while eight wooden pins from Herjolfs-næs (Ø111) are relatively thin and pointed.[4] From Brattahlid (Ø29a), Eric the Red's farm, there are a couple of pins with fine patterns carved in them and holes bored through them – perhaps used to pin down a ribbon or band in the hair. The pins are flat, and are cut off straight with a slight tapering towards the opposite end.[5]

A pin of walrus ivory from Sandnæs (V51) measures 44 mm, but only the pointed part has been preserved. In addition a total of 14 costume pins of bone as well as a number of pins with eyes have been found at this farm and the neighbouring farm Umiiviarsuk (V52a).[6]

Pinning a costume – that is, fastening the clothes with a thin pin cut in wood or other material – was not a novelty in the Middle Ages. A leather cloak from Huldre-mose in Jutland, dated to the year 30 AD, is held together by an 80 mm long pin formed from a bird bone, and the almost contemporary skirt from Lønne Hede is also closed with a long pin of bronze.[7]

The so-called costume pins with heads probably had more functions than those mentioned. The pins may have been used in connection with looms as a tool that helps to maintain a standard weaving width throughout the weaving.

In the Faroes such edge pins were called *tiglar* and can be seen in drawings of the oldest Faroese warp-weighted loom.[8]

3. Buckles

At Sandnæs (V51) and at Umiiviarsuk (V52a), among the incredible number of objects found, there are two belt buckles carved in walrus tusk, the 'ivory of the North'.[9] One is like a flat 'hook' 51 mm long and 17 mm at the widest point, where there are five holes for sewing it on to the belt (D11757.269). The second is 43 mm long, 26 mm wide and 15 mm thick (D12363.270).[10]

Fig. 80

Buckle of walrus tooth found at the excavation of Ø34 at the end of the 1990s. Note the attractive carvings on the 27 mm wide buckle. (Ø34x1321).

Fig. 81

The undecorated buckle was probably discarded after it broke during the boring of the hole for the spindle, which must be proof that the buckle was made in Greenland. (Ø34x1322).

At a third farm, Nipaatsoq (V54), a buckle of brass(?) was found on a piece of leather (KNK991x191). Perhaps this is the remains of a belt. In addition a finger ring of silver was found, and a quite extraordinary silver escutcheon associated with the Scots clan Campbell. How this ended up at Nipaatsoq is an enigma. It may be an imitation, and since there are no holes for sewing it on, it was perhaps never finished.[11]

In the churchyard at Herjolfsnæs two buckles or brooches were found with a diameter of 48 mm, formed of thin circular brass rings (No. 100). On each ring there is a pin for fastening on a garment. The buckles/brooches lay beside each other at the presumed belt position 10 cm apart and at a depth of 116 cm, but both costume and skeleton had almost disappeared. The items may belong with D10621, a textile fragment in a very fine grade of Greenlandic *vaðmál*. Nørlund did not think that they belonged to a belt.[12]

Fig. 82

Silver shield (KNK991x109), measuring 18x24 mm, found during excavations at Nipaatsoq. The intended use of the shield is unknown, as the means by which it could be sewn or attached to an object is not visible.

Implements

1. Needles

In all excavations in Norse ruins needles and pins have been found, most of them relatively crude. They are made of bone, wood or caribou antler. We do not know what all these crude needles were used for, but since in the Middle Ages people used to pack their 'goods' in coarse weaves *(pakkaváð)*, which had to be sewn together, many of the needles must have served this purpose.[1] Others are the so-called costume pins which in various ways held parts of costumes together, and would have been an alternative to buttons and buttonholes. The crude, strong pins may also have been in use as awls, when thick seams had to be sewn where the holes were already pricked.[2] At Bryggen in Bergen many pins and needles of different sizes have been found corresponding to the Norse Greenlandic ones.[3]

Coarse needles were also used for *nålebinding* (knotless netting) or looped needle-netting, a much used technique in the Middle Ages in northern Europe for stockings and gloves. However, straining-cloths for milk, and so on, were also made this way, and many milk strainers are preserved in Norway in particular.[4] So far not a single Norse Greenlandic fragment in *nålebinding* has been preserved, although the Norse Greenlanders had cows, sheep and goats, all of which were milked. One might therefore expect to find milk strainers or straining cloths in Greenland. In an excavation of Inuit settlements in the Thule district various Norse-related objects were found, including a bowl-shaped funnel of wood. At the narrow opening of the funnel there is a projecting edge on the outside, as if something was to be tied to it. There can be no doubt that the object is a milk strainer, where the straining-cloth was tied around the end of the funnel.[5] There are no mittens found in *nålebinding* either. In fact mittens are an object group that is missing on the whole in Norse Greenland, and one for which we must assume there was a great need.

Bodkins and middle-sized needles worked in a hard material like caribou bone and antler were probably used as tools for sewing shoes and furs and for other skin work of various kinds. At the Farm Beneath the Sand (64V2-III-555) as on most Norse farms, several bodkins were found.

For obvious reasons the fine metal sewing needles have disappeared, but the seams are proof of their existence. In excavations fine needles are difficult to see, but a pair of verdigrised sewing needles of bronze from Norwegian Viking Age graves stood out so much that despite their small size they were still found. One is intact and only 20 mm long, while the other, which was broken off at the eye, was a little longer. In other contemporary graves larger needles of iron have been found.[6] The sewing needles of the Middle Ages were hammered, drawn or cast from various metals such as iron, copper, steel and brass.

In an archaeological excavation in Aalborg in 1957 a needlemaker's workshop was found, and from this came much information about the production of among other things needles at the end of the thirteenth century. The workshop was highly versatile. Small fine spindle whorls of lead as well as unfinished costume clasps in

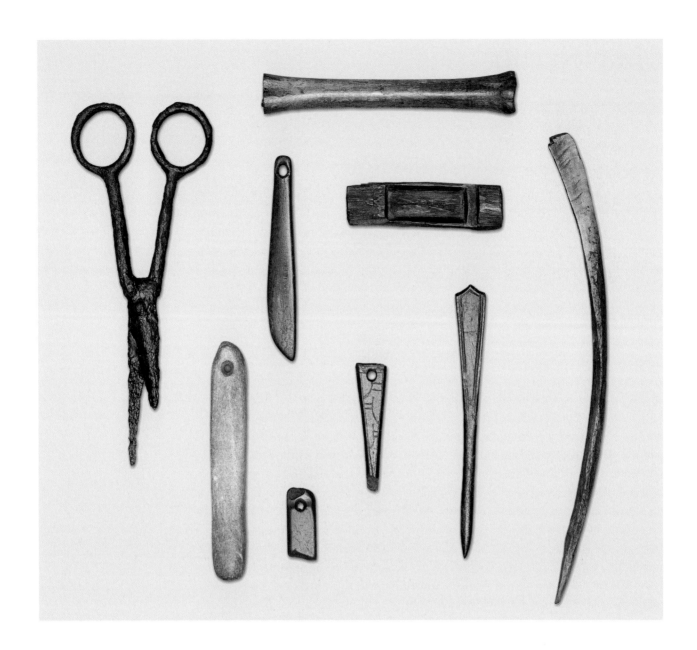

Fig. 83

*Various sewing and weaving
implements. Top: a bone used as
a needle case, and under, a
wooden needle case without lid.
To the right of the scissors: a
small seam smoother made of
bone. Bottom row, from the left:
two grinding stones, the reddish
is Igaliko sandstone, together
with a finely decorated needle of
bone. The stiletto and the curved
weaving pin are both made of
bone.*

copper and other metals were among the many interesting small articles the needle
maker also made.[7] In excavations of Benedictine convents in Denmark a total of
more than a hundred sewing needles have been found, mostly in bronze. The needles
are of different sizes, and with round or oblong eyes.[8] Of the preserved Norse needles
only very few were fine enough for the seams that are found, and the sewing needles
must have been very narrow at the eye end.

2. Needle whetstones

The finest needles had to be kept sharp. For this a small whetstone was used, a *nåle-
bryne*. At Brattahlid (Ø29a) a 30 mm long rectangular needle whetstone (D12205) of
Igaliko sandstone has been found.[9] At one end it has been furnished with a hole
through a flatter-formed ending. Igaliko sandstone is reddish and beautiful as a gem-
stone. With a cord through it, hung around the neck or at one's belt ready for use, it
would have been decorative on any Norse Greenlandic woman.

In most excavations of Norse ruins whetstones or needle whetstones have been
found, often of Igaliko sandstone.

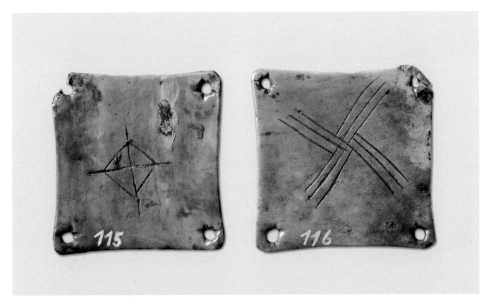

Fig. 84

Decorated four-hole weave-
tablets of bone (50x50 mm)
for tablet weaving. In Greenland tablet-woven piped edging on garments has been
found, but an independent
tablet weaving has not yet
been registered. The weave-
tablets (D23/1991.115 and
–116) are from Russip Kuua.

3. Needle cases

The fine, costly needles were kept in needle cases, which were small boxes or cases of
bone, metal or wood. Needle cases have been found on most Norse farms in Greenland. They are usually exquisitely worked. From Sandnæs (V51) a 112 mm long hol-
low bone (D11715.348) has been preserved, and although the opening at one end
was closed with a small peg, the needles had still disappeared.[10] In the excavation of
GUS three small boxes were found which were probably for storing needles (x620b),
120x24x20 mm; (x1013), 92x33x25 mm; and (x1753) 49x20x14 mm. They were
all made of wood.

4. Weaving tablets

Only a few weaving tablets have been found in Greenland. Two flat bone tablets
(D23/1991.115-116) with fine decorative patterns carved on both sides have been
registered among the finds from Russip Kua (Ø71). The tablets measure 50x50 mm
and have four holes, one in each corner.[11] At GUS two four-hole tablets have also

113

been found, made of baleen, and unfortunately in a poor state of preservation. In addition, in the farm Ø34 at Qaqortoq, a single weaving tablet was found. Thus there are tablets, but so far no complete tablet-weaving has been registered among the Greenlandic weaving items.

Spjaldvefnaður is the Icelandic name for weaving with tablets *(spjald = 'tablet, square')*. It is likely that this textile technique too was brought from Iceland to among other places the Farm Beneath the Sand (64V2-III-555), where traces of tablet weaving were found, but only in the form of a 'thin cord' consisting of four warp threads. The cord would have been outermost on a larger tablet-weaving, since there are remains of weft threads turning along the cord (x3103). The material is flax, and it is something of a miracle that this two-millimetre wide tablet-woven edge cord was preserved in Greenland. Threads of flax were frequently used for tablet weaves, but since vegetable materials such as flax often disappear and leave only small holes or at best a few fibres, they are very difficult to see.[12] In the garment finds from Lønne Hede it was holes like these that revealed that in the cylindrical tablet-woven edge there had originally been a plant-fibre thread.[13] It was probably the white colour of the flax that was attractive as a contrast to the coloured wool threads. Wool could not have the same whiteness. In Viking Age finds from Mammen it was small fibres left in some holes in a 15 mm wide wool band that showed that there had once been flax thread there.[14] But in tablet weaves of costly material like silk, too, flax threads could be used as a supplement to the rare, imported silk. From a find in York there are some 1470 mm long unravelled silk threads that are only held together by two knots at one end. However, closer scrutiny revealed that there were remains of a weft thread in a plant-fibre material, and that the silk threads had once formed a narrow, flat band.[15] There are many medieval tablet weaves in gold and silver thread where flax threads have been woven in as a kind of filler thread. These costly bands graced the church textiles and the vestments of the clerics.[16]

In archaeological textile finds with tablet weaves in metal threads, the flax threads are almost always preserved because of the metal salts. Tablet-woven bands of gold and silver thread have not so far been found in Norse Greenland.

In principle a four-ply tablet weave in its simplest form consists of a number of cords, which are tied together with one or more weft threads. Tablet weaves are found as independent bands or as woven-in borders on weaves, and as such tablet weaving has existed for millennia.[17]

In the Norse textiles there are borders and long garment seams that have been made with one or two tablets combined with sewing. This technique is called tablet-woven piped edging.

5. Seam smoothers

To smooth and press the many narrow seams found on the garments from Herjolfs-næs, the Norse Greenlandic women probably used a tool which is called a *slikisteinn* in Iceland. Such an implement is mentioned among the church inventory in Icelandic priests' contracts, and in that connection it has been interpreted as a tool for smoothing the church's altar-cloths and other linen items.[18] In modern Icelandic the verb *slikja* means to polish, smoothe, make shiny. From Norway there are finds of seam smoothers in Viking Age women's graves. Most are made of black or green glass and are hemispherical. The curved face is smooth and worn. A pebble of almost the same shape as those of glass has been interpreted as a seam smoother.[19] In Norway in recent times other types of seam smoother are also known, for example a so-called *slikjekjake,* called after the jawbone of a cow. The tool could also be a pig's tooth, a horn spoon or a piece of bone.[20] In Greenland there are a few finds of fine, smooth wooden objects which may be interpreted as seam smoothers. Whether any of the animal bones found could be suitable as a *slikisteinn* will perhaps be revealed by further investigations.

6. Smoothing boards

As an underlay for the textile that was to be smoothed, a board or hard sheet of some kind had to be used, otherwise one could not obtain a satisfactory result. Head-dress and shirts of linen had to be rubbed smooth, a living tradition known for example from Scania.[21] But the thick *vaðmál* seams also had to be smoothed. When one was working with hides or skins a smooth underlay would also have been necessary.

In northern Norway no fewer than 35 'boards' of whalebone have been found, which are thought to have been a kind of ironing-board. The boards are rectangular, measuring around 270x200 mm, and since most of them were found in women's graves, they have been interpreted as having been associated with women's work. Some of the boards are splendidly carved with animal heads at one end. That such a large number of whalebone boards in particular have been preserved in northern Norway is partly because the material was easily available, and partly because of the good preservation conditions. Similar 'rubbing boards' of oak or beech wood were used in Scania in the 19th century.[22]

In Greenland there has been a single find of a rectangular wooden board with a ship motif on one-third of the board. The carved part forms a kind of handle. The board (D12809.415) measures 212x73x14 mm. It was found at the farm V53d in Austmannadalen, and since there are many cutting-marks on it, it has been registered as a cutting-board.[23]

Similar boards, but without decoration, have been found in most Norse-Greenlandic farms and have also been described as cutting-boards.

However, one might ask whether these boards always had this function. In favour of this we have the many cutting-marks, but in the case of some of the boards the marks could be from secondary use. The finest of the 'cutting-boards' are probably smoothing-boards.

Other uses of Textiles

1. Sails

It was on ships that Eric the Red and the other Icelanders came to Greenland at the end of the tenth century. Over the next few centuries the Norse Greenlanders continued their dangerous voyages, on the one hand along the west coast of Greenland to Nordrsetur, on the other to Vinland – today better known as North America. Columbus was not the first European to reach the American continent.[1]

In *The King's Mirror* from the thirteenth century, the father instructs his son how important it is to have 2-300 *alen* (ells) of extra *vaðmál*, needles and rope with him on a voyage.[2] Sails were an absolute necessity – otherwise the Norsemen's voyages would only have been Utopian, and indeed several wooden parts from ships have been found at Sandnæs (V51) up the Ameralla fjord.[3] The connection between the more northerly Western Settlement and the Eastern Settlement towards the south was made by ships along the coast and it took six days of rowing in a six-oared boat between the two settlements.[4] Traffic among the remote farms in the individual settlements was probably also by boat where this was possible.

The Norse Greenlanders must necessarily have had woven sailcloth, and it is reasonable to regard the textile 'dressing' of a ship to have been just as demanding a job as providing clothes for the family. However, we do not know of a single textile fragment from Greenland that can safely be identified as sailcloth. If this has not been possible so far, it is first and foremost because we do not know how a Viking Age sail or a sail from the earliest post-Viking Middle Ages looked. From the archaeological ship finds at Oseberg and Gokstad it has been possible to estimate that the larger ships had sails of 100-125 m². For a medium-sized vessel one needed around 50 m². Textile fragments from the Oseberg Ship, woven in wool in a 2/2 twill, have been interpreted as remains of sails or a tent, because they lay together with some rope.[5]

For many years now the Viking Ship Museum in Roskilde has been the base for a series of inter-Nordic experiments where, on the basis of preserved remains, ships and sails have been reconstructed and then tested on long voyages similar to voyages that the Vikings and Norsemen made. One of the most recent experiments has resulted in a wool sail of 90 m² with a weight of 90 kg. The consumption of spun yarn was 897 metres per woven metre with a width of 69 cm. It took a practiced spinner (with a hand spindle) and weaver 4½ years to produce the sailcloth on a warp-weighted loom. Wool from at least 200 sheep was used.[6]

Could the typical Greenlandic *vaðmál* in 2/2 twill perhaps have been used as sailcloth? This unmilled *vaðmál* has a hard-spun hair warp and a relatively dense weft which almost covers the warp, and which gives both sides of the cloth the same 'woollen' character. The other twill-woven Greenlandic *vaðmál*, the dense 2/1 twill, has a 'smooth' right side with a dominant warp thread, while the weft is dominant on the back. A test of the Greenlandic *vaðmál* types as sailcloth would probably prove their usefulness.

2. Textile fragments from Inuit settlements on Ellesmere Island and in Greenland

At the end of the 1970s on Ellesmere Island in Arctic Canada, a couple of rusty iron rings from chain-mail were found, as well as ship's nails, wooden objects and other Norse-related objects. Among these remains is a textile fragment of 150x700 mm radiocarbon dated to 1220-1330 AD (Site SfFk-4-1234).[7] The weaving is a *vaðmál* in 2/2 twill. Some threads were taken for an analysis, which showed that the threads had originally been white and were spun from sheep's wool with an admixture of fur from the Arctic hare. Could this have been a coincidence?

A very unusual textile fragment (L3.2591), which measures 520x360 mm, was found at an Inuit settlement on Ruin Island in the Thule district at 79°N and radiocarbon dated to 1150-1450 AD. It is a greyish weaving in 2/1 twill, and the material in both warp and weft is probably dog-hair, spun together with a little sheep's wool. At this settlement in Inglefield Land, too, Norse objects were found, among other things a fragment of a coat of mail, a chess piece and a comb.[8]

Further south in the Upernavik district at 73°N at Inussuk, an Inuit settlement, a small textile fragment (L4.4892) measuring 40x150 mm was found along with other Norse objects. In addition some small carved wooden figures showing Norse Greenlanders were found. The figures were probably carved by an Eskimo. The textile fragment has now unfortunately disappeared, but judging from a photograph, it is a weave in 2/2 twill.[9]

Finally, all the way south at Narsaq, at the Inuit settlement Tuttutuup Isua, a *vaðmál* fragment in 2/2 twill (L15.187) measuring 70x60 mm was found among spindle whorls, needle whetstones and other Norse objects.[10]

Three of these textiles from Inuit settlements are typical Norse weaves, but without having the dense weft. By contrast the fibre analyses show that the usual fibre combination Hairy/Hairy Medium in warp/weft, which is characteristic of combed wool, is present. A similar fibre distribution has been registered in textile finds on Papa Stour in the Shetlands. This characteristic identifies North Atlantic textiles in English Viking Age finds.[11]

The fourth fragment, the dog-hair weaving from Inglefield Land, is so far the only one of its kind known in Greenland. A three metre long spun thread from a Late Dorset dwelling in Nunguvik, Baffin Island, in Eastern Arctic Canada is an interesting find in this context.[12] The Dorset people had no tradition of spinning and did not use textiles. The thread was spun from fur from the Arctic hare and can thus be compared to thread from GUS. Whether the thread was intended for use in a weave we do not know. Incidentally, there are now well over 100 examples of this form of cordage from Dorset Culture sites in the Canadian Arctic.[13] Further investigations of hair from relevant dog races or finds of similar textiles in other countries might perhaps explain whether this fragment is Norse or not.

The archaeologists interpret the textiles from the Inuit settlements as sailcloth because of the find circumstances. All of them except the fragment from Narsaq come from settlements that lie far from the settlements of the Norse Greenlanders. One can therefore conjecture that a Norse ship was wrecked, and that the sail was a curious find for the Inuit, who knew nothing of woven textiles, since they dressed in furs or skin clothes. But it is equally likely that the Norse objects, and especially the textiles, had great attraction in bartering with the Inuit, as we hear from *Thorfinn Karlsefnis saga* (also known as 'The Saga of Eric the Red') which says that when the

Icelander Thorfinn and his men, on their journey from Greenland to Vinland, met *skrællinger* (Eskimos/Native Americans) the latter preferred to barter for *rautt skrúð* (red cloth). In return Karlsefni got furs and 'grey pelts'(genuine miniver).

3. Tents

A worn sailcloth could be used as a tent and as a tarpaulin, like the Sámi's use of *grener* (blankets), which when worn thin ended up as an extra layer over their huts. The Skolt Sámi from Suenjel in Russian Lapland sometimes also used their *grener* as sails when sailing on the large lakes.[14]

Norse remains have been found at landing places along the west coast of Greenland towards the north up to Ellesmere Island – a long voyage of a couple of thousand nautical miles, where it was sometimes necessary to seek shelter in rough weather, or some of the seamen would sleep while others manned the ship. On land they camped for short or long periods depending on wind and weather and provisioning considerations. Perhaps it was necessary to winter. The sailcloth, new or worn, may have been indispensable as a roof over their heads or as extra covering for the body. From Queen Aase's Ship in Oseberg, which was found in the Oslo Fjord, there is a framework of wood for a tent.[15]

An old Nordic name for a tent is *tjeld* or *tjald,* and this was part of the equipment of the Vikings. The sagas have the expression 'to tent one's ship'. In *Grágás* one reads that each of the booths of those assembled at the Thing (Assembly) was to have a *tjeld* all the way over it.[16] These tents could also be used in church services. According to the saga of Håkon Håkonssøn, on Easter Sunday 1240 in Grønningesund a mass was celebrated in two *landtjeld* which the King had with him. And similarly, a few years later when the King was in Ellidarvik on the Orkneys, a mass was said in a *landtjeld.* During the Coronation in Bergen in 1247 many people had to live in tents around the houses, since there was no room for them indoors. Tents were in general use in the Middle Ages and can often be seen depicted in illuminated manuscripts.[17]

Landtjeld ('country tents') were probably also in use at the Norse settlements which were near the busiest harbours. There, tent-booths could be set up with goods that the Norse Greenlanders wanted to sell to foreign seamen and travellers who, after many weeks or months at sea, had finally reached land.

Furs and Skins

The preserved costumes from Herjolfsnæs are all sewn from Greenlandic *vaðmál*, but there can be no doubt that the Norse Greenlanders also used furs and skins for clothing and in their dwellings. They also had leather footwear.

At the Farm Beneath the Sand, besides textile fragments, fur hairs have also been found which do not come from sheep or goats. These are hairs from the Arctic hare, from the fox, the seal and the wolf, animals which must have lived in the close surroundings of the farm.

Thorfinn Karlsefnis saga says that when the *völva* (sibyl) Thorbjörg, who lived at Herjolfsnæs, visited Thorkel Leifson, she had to be given a warm welcome. A 'high-seat' was prepared for her and on it was laid a cushion which was stuffed with hen's feathers. She herself arrived wearing a black lambskin hood lined inside with white cat fur, and at her belt hung a large skin pouch in which she kept the charms she needed for her magic. On her feet she wore hairy calf-skin shoes and on her hands cat-skin gloves which were white and furry inside.[1]

Another account says that Thormod Kolbrunarskjald had a double-sided fur, white on one side and black on the other. Whether these accounts are true we cannot know, but since the first clothes of fur and skin are mentioned in this way they must have been something known to the listeners when the sagas were told.[1a]

Cowhides, buckskin and sealskin were used by the Norse Greenlanders among other ways as payment of tithes to the Norwegian king.[2] This must mean that there was organized production of a certain volume. A Norse family's own use of hides, skins and furs must also have been extensive, and the time-consuming work of preparing and sewing it would certainly have been done by people with special skills in the same way as textile production. Skins were very likely more costly than *vaðmál*, as one can perhaps infer from a collection of laws from the end of the thirteenth century for Gotland, the so-called *Guterlov,* which forbids the covering of walls with skins.

Regulations covering prices and work areas for skinners/tanners in Bergen in 1282 show how many different skins they worked with: there were stoat/ermine skins, 'greyskins' (the squirrel's winter coat), caribou calf hides and kidskins. It also mentions prices for good 'neck-skins' for lining a mantle on a gown of the best English lambskin and on a 'greyskin' hood. On the other hand the skinners were not allowed to sell *bryddinger* (skin edges).[3]

From Iceland we only have scattered information about the preparation of skins in the Middle Ages. The Arctic fox was the only wild fur-bearing animal apart from the few polar bears that came to the north coast. *Grágás* has a list of different kinds of skins used as legal tender and their value is given. These were fox-skin, lambskin, sheared sheepskin *(klippingar),* cat-skin and cow and ox hides, as well as the skins of old tomcats, which were three times as expensive as fox and lamb skins.[4]

In Greenland the soil conditions – and the freezing – could not preserve furs and skins in the same way as wool, so not a single garment part of skin or fur was found in the excavations. But there are some fragments, most of which are remains of leather from footwear.

A fur fragment from a caribou found at GUS illustrates how the soil 'sorts' things through the preservation conditions. Of this fragment (x846) the hairs can be seen as a dense mass, while the skin layer has completely disappeared.

One can also see innumerable caribou hairs in many textiles, testifying to close contacts if not with the caribou, then at least with its hide. Caribou skin probably served many purposes: as clothing or as bed or bench covering in dwellings. At GUS hairs from a polar bear *(Thalarctos maritimus)* have also been registered (x469), and this is not so surprising considering the location. On the other hand, brown, black and greyish hairs from bears (Ursus sp.) (x1925, -x2519, -x1439) are surprising finds. And there were finds of bison hair too: a thick cord twisted from long black hairs turned out to be from bison. The cord was tied in a hook (x633), a kind of buckle or tightener called a *högld* in Icelandic.[5]

In the excavation of Herjolfsnæs Churchyard (Ø111) it was found that an almost completely decomposed sealskin had been spread over the short-sleeved garment D10581. Along with the costume a fragment of ox-hide or goat-skin was also found, and in the western part of Herjolfsnæs Churchyard remains of red-coloured (later called 'brown') polar bear skin were identified together with a wooden cross (No. 127) from a destroyed grave. Another garment fragment (D10621) is described as edged with skin, and down too was found with the fragment.[6]

In Iceland, bearskin *(berfjall)* is mentioned in parish registers from the fourteenth century along with carpets *(fótaklæði)*.[7] The bearskins were placed individually on

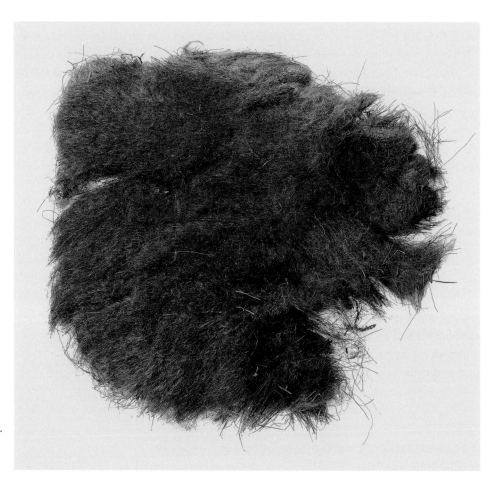

Fig. 85
A clump of fur/hair (1950x846)
from the Farm Beneath the Sand.
The underlying skin has disap-
peared.

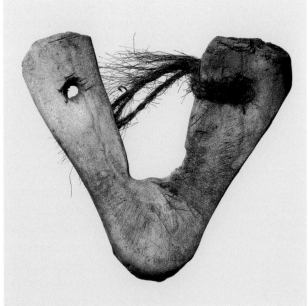

the floor, for example in front of the altar as protection against the cold. Bearskin is also mentioned in the Vadstena Convent rules, written down in 1451, which say that the nuns must not sleep on ticking, but should have straw in their beds and over this a blanket or a bearskin.

A bearskin is very large, and because of its weight it was rarely used for long cloaks, as one perhaps can read into the Icelandic male name *Bjarnheðinn*, which means 'bearskin-tunic'. The name suggests that such a tunic was so rare that it could characterize the person who wore it.[8]

In the Middle Ages cloaks – with and without sleeves – were lined with skin/fur. The priest's garment for winter use was also fur-lined.[9] The everyday costume of the priest did not differ substantially from the layman's and thus reflects ordinary people's clothing, while the bishop stood out with his finer vestments. This is evident from a letter of 1308 in which Bishop Arni from Bergen says that he has sent the following to the Bishop at Gardar in Greenland: *'er skingrit, syrkot, kaprún fódrat med blám skinnum'*, which can be translated as a cloak of rich fabric lined with fur, a tunic and a black hood lined with fur.[10]

Fig. 86

A tuft of hair from a reindeer. Loose reindeer hair is often found between the threads in the Norse textiles. The tuft of hair (1950x497) was found at the Farm Beneath the Sand.

Fig. 87

A cord-tightener of reindeer tooth (135x155 mm) with a twisted cord of bison hair. The Icelandic word is högld. Used in pairs. The Farm Beneath the Sand (1950x633).

1. Caulking

Animal hair and textile remains mixed with tar were used in the Middle Ages to caulk the seams of ships and houses. The Icelandic word for this sealing material is *síþráðr*.[11] At GUS a single find of caulking material was registered, attached to a smallish piece of wood (x2349), where there are still a few wool fibres left.

In Greenland hair from animals may also have been used as a kind of 'toilet paper', as it was in Copenhagen in the Middle Ages. In an excavation in the Copenhagen street Vestergade a latrine barrel was registered where, besides caulking for sealing the barrel, large quantities of animal hair were also found.[12]

2. Footwear

A 275x145 mm leather fragment (D10619) was found in Herjolfsnæs Churchyard (Ø111) in the northeastern corner close to the churchyard wall, partly folded around some metatarsal bones from a young person. The leather was cut as a sole, slightly too large and worn through at the heel, but the upper surface of the leather bears no traces of wear. There are no holes from sewing, but it could still have been a primitive kind of shoe that was tied around the foot. The leather fragment also has an odd 'decoration' in the form of many small crosses carved in it.[13] At the *Landnáma* Farm (Ø17a) at Narsaq an almost intact sole was found, measuring 160x80 mm, with holes and remains of sewing along the edge, and three pieces of an upper; in slits cut in the flap in front and on a side piece there is a small leather strap remaining from what was a closing mechanism.[14]

At Brattahlid (Ø29a) too, a few small pieces of leather have been found as well as a 150x25 mm long strap with traces of fastenings at both ends.[15] In the Western Settlement, at the two farms Sandnæs (V51) and Umiiviarsuk (V52a), besides leather fragments from soles, a total of seven lasts were found, quite clearly showing the size and shape of the shoes. One last is for a wide shoe with a pointed toe, the others are a little more rounded.[16] Several lasts were registered at the Farm Beneath the Sand (64V2-III-555), among others a 20 cm long finely foot-shaped last (x1342).

Among the Norse products the few finds of fur and skin remains represent invisible craftsmanship, which seems insignificant compared with the richly represented textile products. When the visible proofs are not found, the object material is easily forgotten in the larger context, and it is hard to establish how much importance – including economic importance – such a craft had.[17]

For example, in the Norse farms scrapers for scraping and cleaning skins have never been found, despite the fact that awls and stilettos make it likely that there was some sewing of skins and furs. A few vices or clamps of whalebone and other bone material may have been implements for tanners or shoemakers. From Sandnæs (V51) a 100 mm long clamp has been registered, consisting of two identical long pieces of bone held together in the middle by an iron rivet. The clamp functioned with a wooden wedge which when stuck into the 'jaws' tightened the opposite end. From the same farm we have several seam smoothers which as a rule are interpreted as textile-working implements, but which could quite conceivably have been used to 'press' a thick seam in a boot. The seam smoothers are of worked antler or bone and measure from 150 to 180 mm. In addition an attractive bodkin-like bone implement has been found, 72 mm long, 21 mm wide at the top. The pointed bottom end is worn but sharp, and would have been suitable for embossing lines and ornaments in leather. A hole has been bored down through the tool.[18]

The spey-wife Thorbjörg had skin gloves. Perhaps this reflects reality, but since skin is not preserved in the Greenlandic soil, there are no gloves. Nor have mittens of *vaðmál* been found, not even a thumb. It is beyond all doubt that the Norse Greenlanders must have had to protect their hands through the cold winter. Fur-lined skin gloves are the most logical explanation.

Textile Fragments from Greenland

1. Viking Age

How are we to imagine they were dressed – the Norwegian-Icelandic *landnáma* people who in the Viking Age, more than a thousand years ago, settled in the southwestern part of Greenland? And how was the last Norse Greenlander dressed?

Textile fragments from the *Landnáma* Farm at Narsaq (Ø17a), from the oldest building at 'the Farm Beneath the Sand' (64V2-III-555) and from other Norse localities show that the settlers' clothes had elements known from the 'Viking costume'. For example there are pleated fragments of both linen and *vaðmál*, linen drawstrings with overhand knots, dyed wool textiles and korkje-coloured piled weaves as well as madder-red diamond twill. There are also many 'piped' garments.[1]

But although the Greenlandic *landnáma* textiles have a Viking Age element, they are difficult to place as belonging to the costume of that age, since they are stray finds without established relationships. No whole Greenlandic Viking Age costume can be assembled, so it is necessary to look at garments or parts of garments found outside Greenland if we are to form an impression of the clothing of the settlers.

Comparison with preserved fragments and whole garments

A large textile find from Birka in Sweden, supplemented by finds from Haithabu in Schleswig and from west Norwegian graves, especially women's graves, is the basis for the reconstructions we today call 'Viking Age costumes'.[2] The finds have been dated to the 9th-10th century. Contemporary metal brooches/buckles found in graves can have one or more textile layers attached to the back, which tell us about the clothes in which the deceased was buried and about the relative positions of the clothing fragments on the deceased. These brooches or buckles have therefore been important details in the reconstruction of women's clothing from the Viking Age, and new finds are constantly adding important information.[3]

Textile fragments from the large find in Birka – and from the man's grave in Mammen – mainly consist of ornamental weaves in wool and silk, richly decorated with gold and silver work.[4] Not unexpectedly, these are interpreted as belonging to the ruling class of society, but most textile fragments from Haithabu are of a more humble kind: everyday clothing thought to have belonged to people from the middle and lowest social groups. However, among the Haithabu finds there are also exquisite textiles. In one grave, for example, the deceased, a young girl, was dressed in a red garment woven of wool in diamond twill. Under this she had a skirt with shoulder straps and a light blue shift, both made of linen. The shift was lozenge-patterned in red or white. In another grave lay a woman, equally well dressed, with a blue garment outermost, woven of wool in diamond twill.[5] The finds from the western Norwegian women's graves show that the Viking Age women could have two skirts with shoulder straps over a wool shift, folded in narrow pleats. In a few cases cords were

Fig. 88

A reconstruction of the linen
shirt from Viborg Søndersø.
The length is c. 950 mm. The
shirt is dated to around 1050.

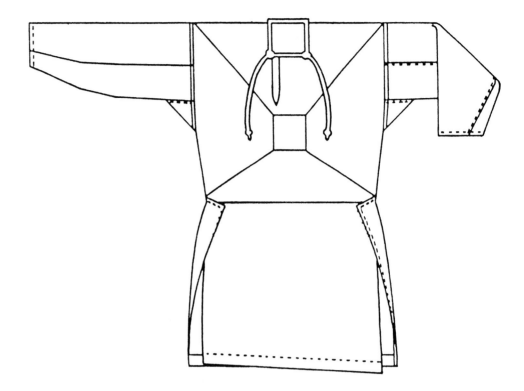

used instead of straps. On other fragments, probably from cloaks, cords are sewn on along the edges. All the garment fragments are woven from wool in different twill weaves.

The unique Viborg find from Søndersø is an example of what a linen shirt, used around the year 1000, looked like.[6] It is not completely preserved, but there are such large pieces that it has been possible to reconstruct the cut. The garment: a shirt or kirtle, is designed to be pulled over the head. The square neck opening with an asymmetric slit has an edging consisting of a narrow piece of linen that continues as two free ties, each with its own preserved overhand knot fixed to the front corners of the neck opening. The shirt has no shoulder seam, and its cut, with straight lines and long added sleeves without doming, is in principle a repetition of the 800-year-older shirt or gown from the famous find in Thorsbjerg Bog in Schleswig just south of the present Danish border. Shirt and gown are both knee-length. Along with the Thorsbjerg gown two pairs of broge trousers were found which can best be described as a kind of sewn tights. Gown and trousers are sewn from weaves in diamond twill and in 2/2 twill in wool.[7]

The Kragelund gown, found in 1898 south of Viborg in the bog Kragelund Fattigmose, and radiocarbon dated to 1045-1155 AD, can be seen as a variant or a further development of the shirt. The gown is sewn from twill-woven wool. Like the Viborg shirt it has no shoulder seam, but has waist-high gussets in the sides, in the middle at the front, and in the middle back. The gusset in front is divided. At the time of the find it was registered that the 1140 mm long Kragelund shirt reached down to the middle thigh of the male corpse. On the basis of this measurement the man's height was estimated as c. 190 cm.[8]

Comparison with Nordic pictorial material from the Viking Age

By combining textile finds with images of clothed people from the same period, costume researchers have tried to fill in the 'costume gaps' left by the lack of complete

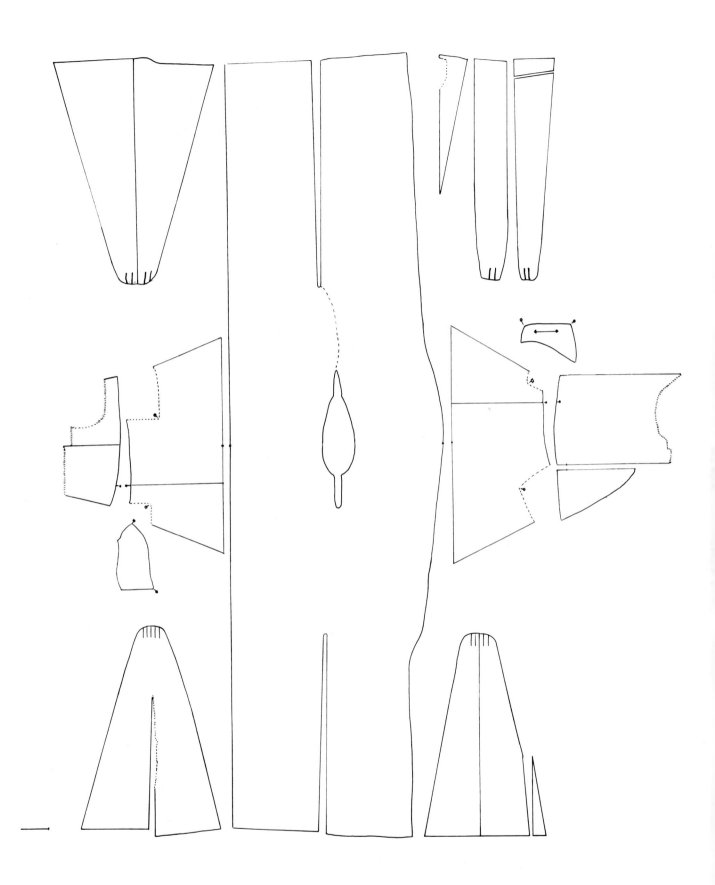

Fig. 89
*Measurements of the Kragelund gown. The length is 1140 mm, and shoulder width is 630 mm. There is a
selvedge along one side of the gown. The front middle gusset, which is split up, is illustrated bottom left. The
seamed middle gusset of the back is shown at the top left. The gown's seamed side gussets are placed to the right
in this illustration: the left is shown above, and the right at the bottom. The measurement specified is 100 mm.*

costume finds from the Viking Age and the Early Scandinavian Middle Ages.

The small *guldgubber* (votive figures of gold leaf) found in recent years in large quantities are like a miniature catalogue of the Viking Age costumes.[9] Similarly, there are many representations of costumes on picture-stones in churches.[10] Textile images of human figures can be seen on woven *bonader* (long narrow wall hangings) from Skog and Överhogdal in Sweden and on the Norwegian *refil,* the frieze from Queen Åse's ship grave at Oseberg.[11] In figures that are 5-10 cm tall, the frieze shows a woman in a long dress with a train as well as a long cloak, while the men can be seen in knee-length gowns as well as tight, or long loose, trousers. Outermost there is a cloak, probably a rectangular piece of cloth wrapped around the body. On their heads they have a cap. All these are in different colours. A common feature of these early representations is that they are more or less convincing.

The landnáma *people in Greenland*

The male settlers may thus have worn a linen shirt, as well as one or two long-sleeved knee-length *vaðmál* gowns and trousers, or possibly leg-wrappings. The women may have been dressed in a pleated linen or wool shift as well as a long strapped skirt consisting of one or two rectangular pieces of cloth that were wrapped around the body and held up by straps or cords over the shoulders. On their heads the men would have had round or pointed caps (small caps resembling pill-box hats). Both men and women had shaggy-pile woven cloaks. On their feet they wore leather shoes or boots.

2. The Middle Ages

Thus, although we only have fragments of the clothes of the Viking settlers, we do have a rich selection of the costumes of their descendants as used by children, women and men in the Middle Ages. These clothes are represented in the large find from Herjolfsnæs Churchyard (Ø111). Several of the textiles have been radiocarbon dated to the period 1180-1530 AD. The textile find in Herjolfsnæs Churchyard comprises at least 69 registered garments, parts of garments and other parts of clothing, which Poul Nørlund grouped in 1924 according to types. What is common to all the garment types are the domed sleeves that are set in, and the shoulder seams that flare slightly outwards.

The Herjolfsnæs garments grouped according to types

In the costume catalogue there are detailed descriptions of the individual finds.

Nørlund Type Ia. To this group belong garments D5674, D10577, D10578 and D10579, which are designed to be pulled over the head, and have side panels but have no middle gusset. Oval neck opening. The first and the last of these garments are almost complete, but the other two are only preserved with a single panel or as a larger fragment.

• *Comments:* We have no radiocarbon datings of the textiles from this group. The lengths of the two complete garments are 1090 mm and 1220 mm respectively; with a belt or a cord around the waist the garments would have reached the knees or the middle of the calves. In pictures throughout the Middle Ages we can recognize the garment as clothing for men in various working situations.

Fig. 90 (on the opposite side) Kragelund gown (D3956) of wool, sewn from a textile in 2/1 twill with a light grey-brown warp and a white weft. (Z/S, 12/8 threads/cm). The gown is radiocarbon dated 1045-1155. The split-up middle gusset is torn apart and tacked together almost up to the top rounding. Each of the four 600 mm long gussets have been gathered in five parallel upright pleats before being sewn into the gown

Fig. 91 Kragelund gown (D3956) seen from the back.

Nørlund Type Ib comprises the garments D10580, D10581, D10582, D10583 and D10584, which are tight-fitting with gussets inserted in the front and back and with between four and eight side pieces which give them outward-flaring fullness from around waist height. The garments are for pulling over the head, with round or oval neck openings.

• *Comments:* One garment (D10581) in this group has been radiocarbon dated to 1380-1530 and identified by Nørlund as a woman's garment. Nørlund registered the garments D10580 and D10583, on the basis of the relatively well-preserved skeletons, as a woman's and a man's garment respectively. Garment D10582 was found together with a cap (D10610); Nørlund interpreted this as a man's cap, and thus described the garment as a man's. He concluded, however, that the garment might still be for a woman, since the skeleton is gracile. The latter garment (D10584) was identified by him as a male garment, because the sleeves are relatively long and the pocket slits are low – at the middle of the thigh.

The late dating of the short-sleeved woman's garment D10581 does not necessarily date the other garment in the group to the same period. The garments have a length of 1190-1280 mm and a waist width of 940-1000 mm. Of all the Herjolfsnæs garments the male costume D10583 has the greatest width, 4250 mm measured along the bottom edge.

These close-fitting garments with great fullness were popular with both sexes from the end of the thirteenth century until at least a century later, after which they became restricted to women. The description of the garments as close-fitting must however be viewed in terms of the high or low position of the middle gusset, since this influences how close-fitting the garment is. The women of the Middle Ages were probably pregnant most years throughout their child-bearing life. It is therefore realistic to assess the garments on the basis of how suitable they were as 'maternity wear'. Incidentally, how was it possible to breast-feed in these garments? In garments D10580, D10581 and D10584 the middle gussets are inserted in such a high position that there is room for a pregnant stomach. Thus in Nørlund's 'gender determination' it is only garment D10584 that does not quite meet the criteria. His argument for the garment as a man's includes the length of the sleeves, but since both the sleeve armhole and the wrist width are small, the garment seems more like a woman's.

Nørlund Type Ic comprises garments D10585,1, D10586, D10587, D10588 and D10589, which are less close-fitting with gussets inserted at the front and back. In the sides there are from four to eight panels which give it a moderately outward-flaring fullness from chest height. The garments are for pulling over the head with round or oval neck openings. Garment (D10586) is for a child 8-10 years old, and numbers D10588 and D10589 represent garment panels and larger fragments. To this type too belongs the 'newly found' Herjolfsnæs garment Rønbjerg D2625a-e.[12]

• *Comments:* The garment D2625a-e has been radiocarbon dated to 1180-1310. It is thus the oldest dated garment from the churchyard. The lengths of the two best preserved garments (D10585,1 and D10587) are 1160 mm and 1200 mm. Nørlund identified the former garment as a man's, partly because it was found together with a hood that he considered a man's, and partly because the sleeves seem long compared with the garment. Also, he thought that it was an undergown, referring to marks of wear from a sword that had hung from a belt, and thought that the deep neck opening also characterized the garment as an undergown.

The short-sleeved garment D10587 looks like a robust working garment, quickly sewn with a number of mock seams. Nevertheless the garment has many fine, time-consuming details. The short sleeves and the length suggest that it is a woman's garment.

Under Nørlund Type Ib or Ic belong garment fragments D8080-D8081, which were found in the churchyard in 1900. The former (D8080) almost makes up a whole garment, while the latter only consists of some large fragments.

The garments (Nørlund Type Ib and Ic) which consist of many panels and gussets sewn together were called *fjolgeirungr* on Iceland in the fourteenth century.[13]

Nørlund Type Id consists of the pleated garment pieces D10590 and D6473. The former comprises most of an upper part and the latter is probably a 'hip piece'.

• *Comments:* The garment fragments have been radiocarbon dated to 1300-1410 and 1300-1370 respectively with 'reduced likelihood for the decade around the 1370s'. In photographs taken at Herjolfsnæs in 1921 one can see garment D10590 lying in some sackcloth, which was used to lift the textiles out of the excavation. The V-shaped neck opening, the left sleeve and the pleated upper part are recognizable from drawings in *Buried Norsemen at Herjolfsnes*.[14] In the pictures from 1921, which have not been published before, one can see both sleeves – unfortunately they are placed so that they hide important parts of the garment. The most interesting thing, though, is that one can see that the narrow pleats continue down into a skirt, but how long? The pictures only show the garment to around knee height.

Nørlund describes the shape of the garment as the usual one for pulling over the head, and says that a number of seams in the bottom part also correspond to those on the other garments. He further writes that the details are difficult to explain, since only the upper part is preserved.

The details are still difficult to explain. On the preserved upper part the parallel pleats are sewn. If the garment was pleated along its whole length, the pleats would probably have been open on the bottom piece to give the skirt fullness. A similar opening of sewn pleats can be seen on fragment D6473, the 'hip piece', which is sewn together from two pieces with a slightly outward-sloping seam. To clarify whether the two pleated garment pieces originally belonged together, thread samples were taken from both for dye and wool analysis in York. The results showed that the fragment D6473 was woven with a brown wool that was strongly affected by a red (iron salt) colour, while the upper part (D10590) was woven with a black wool with no subsequent red-colouring. The two pieces were in all likelihood not from the same garment. The fragment D6473 was found in Herjolfsnæs Churchyard fifteen years earlier than the upper part.

An Irish costume with a pleated shirt has been found in Emlagh Bog near Dingle, County Kerry, and has been dated to the seventeenth century.[15] In addition, in a burial under the floor of the east Norwegian stave church Uvdal in Buskerud, a child's garment has been found with a pleated upper part. The Norwegian find has not yet been fully described and dated, but may be from the 13th-15th century.[16]

Nørlund Type Ie, the fragment D10591, is the top part of a garment with remains of side panels. The neck opening is small, and there is a short slit in the middle front with buttonholes. With the exception of the buttonholes the neck opening corresponds to the one that can be seen on the garment D10581.

Nørlund Type If comprises the small children's garments D10592 and D10593. The former has middle gussets inserted and side panels. The garment D10593 has inserted middle gussets and a yoke in front.

• *Comments:* The two garments are miniatures of adult garments, the first being the most pronounced. The absence of sleeves and the fragmentary neck opening make it difficult to determine what age the garment was intended for. Among the Herjolfsnæs garments this is the only one that was found in a coffin. The length is 450 mm and compared with the inside of the coffin which measures 880 mm, the child may have been bigger than the immediate impression given by the garment. But perhaps the coffin was far too long?

The second garment (D10593) is for a smaller child, since its width across the chest is only 440 mm. The length is 495 mm.

Nørlund Type II comprises the buttoned garments D10594 and D10595, each of which has eight panels and outward-flaring fullness from the shoulder. There are buttonholes along one front edge. The first garment has a small upright collar.

• *Comments:* The garment D10594 has been radiocarbon dated to 1280-1400. The lengths of the garments are 1050 mm and 1250 mm respectively. Nørlund described the former as a man's garment, because it is large and short. The latter garment (D10595) he described as a woman's because it is smaller and longer. The skeletons were not preserved. Nørlund's 'gender determination' of the garment D10594 on the basis of the length is not possible, since the length is doubtful. The original hem can only be seen on a fragment that is no longer joined to the garment. Both buttoned garments may therefore have been of more similar length from the outset. The garment D10594 has been described as a buttoning coat. This is due to a reading of the words 'kiutell knappadhan'. But the term is a little misleading, since it is associated with outer clothing, and since none of these buttoned garments is sewn from thick *vaðmál*, we must assume that like all the other garments they are not for outdoor use in a wet or cold climate.

The garment D10594, which was originally dyed brownish-black and had madder-red borders as well as many stab-stitched seams, must have been a stately garment. There are no comparable garments in the Nordic countries, but some wool shirts from Skjoldehamn and Guddal in Norway have similar high collars.[17] In an Italian painting by Altichiero from 1385 one can see an older child in a buttoned garment with a belt. The buttons can be seen both in the bodice of the garment and below the waist, where there are two sets of three buttons corresponding to those on the Greenlandic garment. The painting is in the Chapel of San Giorgio in Padua.[18]

Hoods

Nørlund Type I This includes the liripipe hoods D10596, D10597, D10598, D10599 and D10600 with shoulder capes. The first of these hoods has a small gusset at both front and back, while the others have just one gusset in the middle front.

• *Comments:* None of the large liripipe hoods with shoulder capes have been radiocarbon dated. Nørlund describes the hood D10596 as the oldest, since it has a clumsy cut with a baggy transition between liripipe and hood. A similar hood with a shoulder cape – farthest back – can be seen on a 50 mm carved wooden figure found at the Eskimo settlement farthest north in Upernavik District.[19] The doll is thought to show a Norse Greenlandic woman and is probably from the fourteenth century. Nørlund dated the more elegantly designed large hoods with a narrow liripipe to the fourteenth century. In Greenland they were worn throughout the Norse period. The last hood mentioned (D10600) is quite special, since it is cut diagonally to the weave. The liripipe hoods with shoulder capes, which were also called cape hoods, have the

Fig. 92
Detail of the Altichieros painting from St. George's Chapel in Padua, Italy. The small boy to the left of
the picture is wearing a costume that bears a great resemblance to the button garment (D10594).

longest liripipe 'tails'. On the hood D10600 a length of 870 mm has been measured. In the Middle Ages the liripipes could be very long, as can be seen from the prohibitions that were issued in several places. In 1357 in Iceland, the Bishop at Skalholt had to issue the prohibition that priests and sacristans were not to wear hoods on which the liripipe was more than two fingers wide, and the length was to be no more than one alen.[20]

Similar hoods have been found in the Bocksten and Skjoldehamn bogs. Only the hood from Bocksten has been radiocarbon dated, to 1290-1420.[21]

Hoods, Nørlund Type II

This group comprises eleven hoods (D10601, D10602, D10603, D10604, D10605, D10606, D10607, D10608, D10609 and D10585,2 and Nørlund No. 75). They are small, short hoods that end at the shoulders, and which have two gussets, one on each side. All the hoods are for pulling over the head. They have, or have had, liripipes.
• *Comments:* The hoods D10605 and D10606 have been radiocarbon dated to 1390-1490 and 1380-1440 respectively. In view of the large number of preserved short hoods, they must have been very popular among the Norse Greenlanders. One of the hoods (D10608) was found with a cap inside, and both are for a grown child. On some of the hoods one can see wear-marks along the front edge after folding. Nørlund incidentally thought that all the hoods were male garments, but from medieval texts like 'I gave Gudrid a hood' and 'the women's hoods were double, blue and red inside' it is evident that women too used hoods.[22] In illustrations and wood-carvings from the fourteenth century one can see that the women's hoods were open at the front.

In Norway there are a large number of women's hoods from the nineteenth century. As a living tradition, they have a form which represents a link back in time to the Greenlandic hoods. The Norwegian hoods, which have no liripipe, were used with a rolled-up front edge and were hooked under the chin. They are sewn from home-woven and stamped *vaðmál* in black or dark-blue colours, often with a lining in a different colour. The hoods were mainly used in bad weather during work in the fields and for example on the way to church, above a cap (a girl/woman cap). In the church the hood was taken off.[23] The Norse closed hood, which is for a relatively small head size, would have been close-fitting around the head with the liripipe wound round the neck – practical in cold, windy Greenland.

The caps ('Pill-box' caps)

D10608, D10610 and D10611 consist of rectangular pieces sewn together with a round crown. One cap (D10608), which was inside a hood, is for a grown child, and D10611 is for a smaller child. All of them have a transverse seam across the middle of the crown.
• *Comments:* None of the caps has been radiocarbon dated. A small self-portrait of a Norse Greenlander wearing a cap was found at Sandnæs (V51).[24] It is carved in walrus ivory, only 45 mm tall and perhaps shows the popularity of the cap among the Norse Greenlanders. It was headgear for boys and men, used by laymen as well as clerics and with ancient roots.

Tall (brimless) hat

The tall hat D10612 is in principle a cap with a slightly outward-flaring extension sewn on. The extension combined with a gusset gives the cap fullness below.

• *Comments:* The hat has been radiocarbon dated to 1250-1410. Nørlund describes the tall hat as on top of 'another piece', which he assumes is some kind of head-dress since there were teeth inside the piece. There was no longer any skeleton. The hat is sewn together from two different pieces of *vaðmál*, woven in some places from many joined ends of dark and light wool and goat hair. In front one can see a seam and at the back a gusset. All this gives the hat a slightly shabby appearance.

In 1921 Nørlund tried to date the hat on the basis of pictures of women and men with tall hats. Among other things he compared it to the Icelandic woman's headgear *faldur, skaut* or *skautfaldur,* an odd item of head-dress that was used from the sixteenth century until the present day. Over this head-dress one wore a cap. The head-dress was formed from white linen kerchiefs, 1½ *alen* (855 mm) wide and folded diagonally, which were wound around the head. Outside the first, another was added until the desired height had been obtained. These white wound headcloths were also called *vaf* (= winding). The oldest drawings from the sixteenth century show a tall hat, but it is not evident that the hat is wound.[25] The Greenlandic tall hat probably had nothing to do with this wound head-dress.

To enable a better dating, Nørlund also compared the tall hat with painted portraits from the sixteenth century. He found many similarities and concluded that the

Fig. 93
The 61 mm high wooden figure from Sermermit is shown here in full face and in profile. The figure, embellished with a turned-up cap, has been given the name 'The distinguished gentleman'.

Fig. 94

A portrait carved in wood from
Inussuk. The 63 mm high Norse
head is portrayed wearing a hat
or headscarf, possibly both.

Greenlandic hat must have been from this period, and that it must thus represent the latest date for the burials in the churchyard.

Posterity has named it the 'Burgundian cap'. Nørlund's reference to the Burgundians did not apply in particular to the tall hat (D10612), but to the use of a hood above a cap, as was the case with the hood and cap D10608 for a grown child in another burial. He illustrated this by referring to two figures, so-called 'weeping brothers', from c. 1425, set up at the sarcophagus of the Duke of Burgundy.[26] On one figure one can see the weeping brother with a cap on his head and a hood that is pushed down from the head, covering neck and shoulders. The other mourning brother is shown in mourning for the dead duke, with a hood that is pulled down over his head. In 1934 when Poul Nørlund published the book 'The Old Norse Settlements at the End of the World' he had apparently forgotten(?) his original reference to Burgundy, where this particular use of the cap with a hood was typical. In the book he himself now called the tall hat a 'Burgundian cap'.[27]

Experiments with a reconstructed tall hat have shown that it can be positioned in several ways. If one puts the hat on an adult head with an extra hat or something else below it, the width fits fairly well, and the hat seems tall. If, however, the bottom edge of the hat is turned up, its width is reduced to such an extent that when there has to be room for an under-cap, or the like, the hat can fit a grown child. The gusset is woven in twill, unlike the hat itself; this means that the gusset is slightly elastic, which may have been deliberate. Or was the *vaðmál* used for the hat chosen from other worn items of clothing as recycling?

It is tempting to compare the hat to some small portraits of Norse Greenlanders with head-dress. These are 61 mm and 63 mm tall wooden figures found at Eskimo settlements in two places: Sermermiut in Disko Bay and Inussuk in Upernavik. On one of the figures one can see a hat with a small folded edge, and on the other one can see a hat or headscarf(?) placed over another hat.[28]

The Norse people are always portrayed with something on their heads. In this burial the deceased had head-dress in the grave as burial clothing – a widespread tradition in other places outside Greenland too.

Stockings

There is one pair of long stockings (D10613 and D10614), the latter of which is very fragmentary. Of short stockings, so-called *stunthoser* or 'hoggers' four without feet have been preserved (D10615, D10616, D10617 and D10618).

• *Comments:* None of the stockings have been radiocarbon dated. Long stockings with similar diagonally cut legs and feet formed from one or more pieces are known from other archaeological excavations, such as Bocksten Bog. The long stockings are imitations of the so-called pontifical stockings, which were sewn from ornamental weaves in silk. In many medieval murals one can see how the long stockings were attached to a belt or the edge of a garment. The short stockings were fixed below or above the knee, and the stockings often sagged down around the legs.

During the period one rarely sees women depicted so that the stockings are visible, but they must have had them, at least in Greenland. Among the short stockings, D10615 is doubtful with its present-day assembly, and the 'stocking' D10617 was never a stocking.

The Herjolfsnæs garments compared with other preserved Nordic medieval garments and parts of garments

The garments from Herjolfsnæs Churchyard were preserved because they ended up in a soil which in time froze solid. Each garment or part of a garment was used as grave clothing or shroud and therefore does not represent a complete costume as used by Norse Greenlanders. The textiles make up a large body of individual items showing variants of garments for children and adults.

In the other Nordic countries there have been similar finds. In these cases it was not the ice, but other favourable soil conditions that had a preservative effect.

The Moselund Gown (C5238-39) was found in 1884 when a male corpse (180 cm tall) was registered in Moselund Bog south of Viborg. It was dressed in a brownish *vaðmál* gown.[29] It has been radiocarbon dated to 1050-1155 AD and has great resemblances to the Herjolfsnæs garments, Nørlund Type Ic.

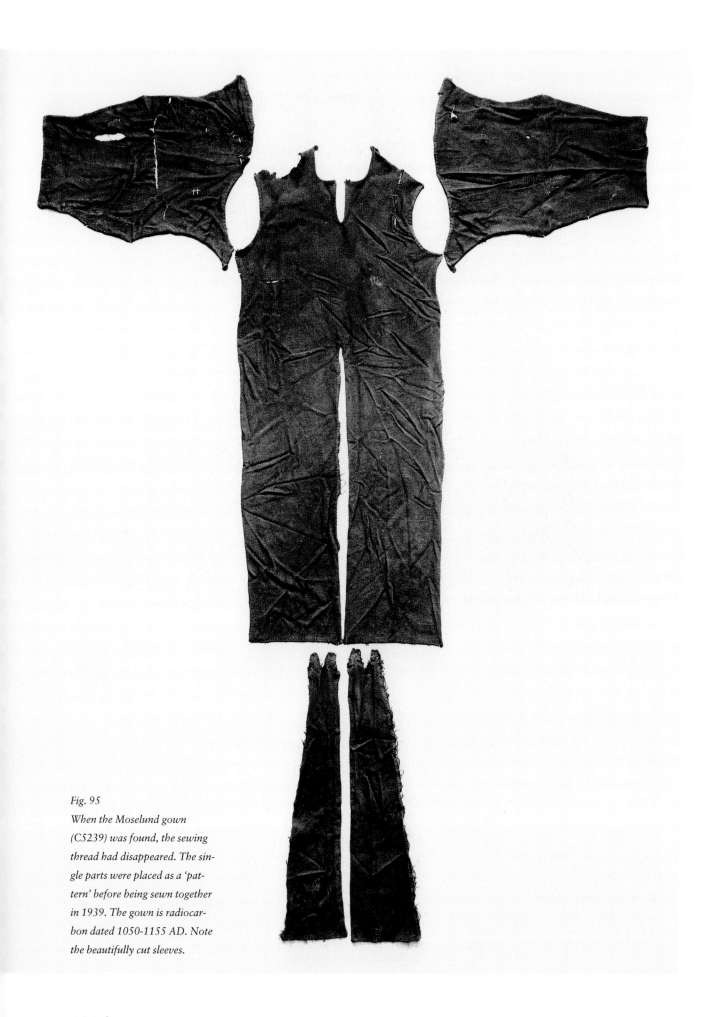

Fig. 95
When the Moselund gown (C5239) was found, the sewing thread had disappeared. The single parts were placed as a 'pattern' before being sewn together in 1939. The gown is radiocarbon dated 1050-1155 AD. Note the beautifully cut sleeves.

Fig. 96
Moselund gown (C5239). Back,
side panels and middle gusset.

Fig. 97
Moselund gown (C5239) photographed in 1999. The material
is wool and the textile is a 2/1
twill, (Z/S, 14/10 threads/cm),
that is felted.

Fig. 98
Moselund gown (C5239) seen
from the back.

Fig. 99

*'Rønbjerg Garment' (D2625a-e),
the oldest dated garment from
Herjolfsnæs, radiocarbon dated
to the end of 1200s. There is a
half front piece (the garment's
left), on the one side of which is
sewn a two-part middle-gusset
and on the opposite side a piece
of the garment's left side-panel.
Also preserved is the top of half a
back, together with two smaller
pieces.*

The Moselund find was in many pieces, since all the seams had come apart. In 1939 all the pieces were sewn together according to the best knowledge available to create the present-day appearance of the gown. It has later been declared to be the only preserved *blaðakyrtill*. This term occurs in medieval Icelandic texts and is applied to garments with a division in the middle front and middle back – a convenient garment for riding.

It is likely, but not proven, that the Moselund Gown is such a *blaðakyrtill*. It has also often been compared to the fragmentary 'Rønbjerg Garment' (D2625a-e), which has however turned out to be a garment from Herjolfsnæs.

A misinterpretation of the sleeve hole of the 'Rønbjerg Garment' (D2625a-e) as a neck slit and a side seam as a division of the front piece made comparisons possible. The 'newly found' Herjolfsnæs garment D2625a-e has a rounded neck opening and the front is not sewn together from two (different coloured) parts. It cannot therefore be described as a *hálfskiptr* gown. (See below). Neither a *blaðakyrtill* nor *hálfskiptr kyrtill* have been registered in Greenland.

The fragmentary Söderköping Gown from Öster-Götland in Sweden is a contemporary garment for pulling over the head.[30] It has slits in the middle-front and middle-back gussets, and high side gussets, the longest of which measures 780 mm. It has high side panels, of which the longest measures 780 mm. On this basis the length of the gown has been estimated as 1200 mm. There is a partly preserved sleeve. The colour of the gown is brownish-black, but originally it was two-coloured, probably red and blue. The colours changed along a vertical middle seam. Each half thus had its own colour. The gown was found under some wood and pottery that have been dated to the period 1200-1243. On this basis the gown has been dated to the beginning of the thirteenth century. The Söderköping Gown is a so-called *hálfskiptr* gown.

Costume fragments with no connection to other garment fragments are also known from Leksand in Dalecarlia in Sweden.[31] A fragmentary ornamental cloak was found in a woman's grave there, semicircular and open at the front, where it is decorated with wide tablet weavings. It could be held close around the body by a band or cord tied through a pair of eyelets at the top of the front edge. The cloak is woven from wool in a diamond twill, and its length has been estimated as around 1450 mm. A radiocarbon dating puts its age at the beginning of the thirteenth century. A cloak of this type was called a *tuglamǫttul* or *seilamǫttul* in Icelandic.

In Norway at Guddal Church in the county of Sogn and Fjordane two garments were found, a shirt and a tunic.[32] Both are sewn of twill-woven wool without shoulder seams, and are for pulling over the head. The shirt narrows at the waist and has short slits at the bottom of the side seams. It has a high collar with two small slits in front. Over this was a tunic with stripes on the bottom part, in which slits had been cut. The gown must have reached the middle of the thigh, while the shirt was rather shorter. We still lack a complete analysis and description of the find, but they are thought to be male garments from the end of the Middle Ages.

Fully dressed male bodies

A better picture of how the living Norse Greenlanders may have dressed is shown by two fully dressed bog bodies – important finds from the Middle Ages – which literally illustrate how a couple of men were dressed on the day they were killed or in some other way ended their days in a bog.

Both bog bodies were found on a June day in 1936 in Norway and Sweden respectively. One was found in Skjoldehamn on Andøya in northern Norway and the other in Bocksten in Halland, southern Sweden. They were both fully dressed, and the clothes have today been radiocarbon dated.

The bog body from Skjoldehamn lay on a bed of birch branches and bark, covered by a reindeer skin.[33] The skeleton was almost wholly decomposed with the exception of a radius bone, from which it has been calculated that the body height was around 155 cm. A likely age is 40-45 years. The body was wrapped in a large-checked blanket which was lashed around the legs with leather straps. Under the blanket the body was dressed in a brownish gown with a narrow belt braided of red yarn tied around the waist. The long-sleeved gown is for pulling over the head. It has a small three-sided neck opening, has no shoulder seam, and has gussets in the middle front and middle back as well as at the sides. The gussets are waist-high. Inmost there was a patched shirt with a 50 mm high collar. The shirt is for pulling over the head, has long sleeves and side gussets. It has no shoulder seam and is for closing over the chest with a square flap. A pair of long-legged trousers, which were held up by a band drawn through a fold, completed the costume. On the head was a hood with a shoulder cape. Around the legs were wound narrow bands and on the feet there were ankle cloths and so-called *lester,* a kind of short stocking. Of the footwear only the leather soles were left. All the cloth was woven from wool. None of the garments is completely preserved; poorest preserved are the trousers. The length of the gown is 1060-1080 mm, and the shirt is rather shorter, around 900 mm. The trousers are 1000 mm long and have a waist width of 13-1400 mm.

A radiocarbon dating of the gown gave the result 995-1029 AD. The blanket is probably older.[34]

The relatively well preserved radius bone shows that this was a slender person, probably a male Sámi (Lapp).[35]

The man from Bocksten was c. 25 years old when he ended up in the bog.[36] He was dressed in a reddish-brown cloak, semicircular with a round neck opening. A seam on the right shoulder holds the cloak in place. Under this he had a yellowish-brown gown with a leather belt around the waist. The long-sleeved gown has a round opening at the neck, gussets in the middle front and middle back, and in the sides. The gussets are waist-high. It has no shoulder seam. On his head he has a lirip-ipe hood with a shoulder cape and on his legs long stockings with foot-patches as stocking feet. The long stockings were held up by leather straps. A small bag was also found. On his feet he had a pair of front-lacing shoes of leather. All the cloth was woven from wool. The length of the cloak is 1100 mm and that of the gown is 1150 mm. The height of the man was estimated as 172.4 cm.

A radiocarbon dating of garments, leather and skeleton gives us a dating within the period 1270-1390. The conclusion was that the garment should be dated to the fourteenth century.

These two bog bodies are the only ones representing fully-clad male individuals from the Middle Ages. There are no corresponding women's bodies in the Nordic area.

Garment lengths relative to the heights of people from the Middle Ages

The investigations in the 1920s of the skeletons from Herjolfsnæs Churchyard concluded that the Norse Greenlanders had been malnourished with a miserable state of health as the result. In the end they were a degenerate population. However, recent research has shown that in the 1920s not enough attention had been given to the

external circumstances that had affected the bone material. The changing seasonal temperatures with alternating frost and thaw and an unfavourable soil, which resulted in a decalcification of the skeletons, led to misinterpretation as deformities. The body heights given by Nørlund are therefore incorrect, but the gender determinations may be correct. In excavations at Brattahlid Churchyard in the 1960s and 1970s a total of 155 skeletons were found.[37] From this find and from skeletal finds in other Norse churchyards it has been possible to estimate that the average height for women was 166 cm and for men 177 cm. There were even men who measured 18485 cm. This means that the Norse men's average height matches more or less the height of the men from Kragelund, Moselund and Bocksten, who were 190 cm, 176 cm and 172.4 cm in height, respectively.

The length of the male garments D5674 and D10583 from Herjolfsnæs is between 1090 mm and 1280 mm, measured on the shortest and longest. By 'dressing' the Norsemen in these garments, it would be possible to see that the garments reached the knee or just below. Probably none of the garments reached farther than to the middle of the calves. These were the working clothes of the Middle Ages, which had to be practical.

The length of the garments, which seem most likely to be women's, lies between 1185 mm and 1265 mm, measured on the shortest garment (D10587) and on the longest (D10584). 'Dressing' the Norsewomen would show that most garments reached the middle of the calves or just below.

Anthropological investigations from the 1990s of Norse skeletal material suggest

143

that the Norse average height declined over the centuries. With the most recent skeletal measurements the length of the garments will thus change; they will seem longer on a 'dressed' body.

The last Norse Greenlander

The Norse Greenlanders are thought to have disappeared from the Norse settlements in the last half of the fifteenth century. A radiocarbon dating of the garment D10581 and of the hood D10606 puts the date around 1434, the latest date documented so far. The textiles had been used when they ended up as burial clothing, so this date cannot be taken as dating to the last decade of the Norsemen in Greenland.

An often-quoted account speaks of the Icelander 'Jón Greenlander', who within 'living memory' had been driven off course on one of his voyages to Greenland. On a small island deep within a Greenlandic fjord, where he and his crew landed, they saw stone circles of the type they knew from Iceland, and 'there they found a dead man lying face down; on his head he had a well sewn hood; his other clothes were partly of *vaðmál*, partly of sealskin'.[38]

'Living memory' is a rather uncertain dating, so it is uncertain when the dead Norseman was found.

In the context of this book, however, it is interesting to get a description of how he was dressed. Whether the man was in fact the last Norse Greenlander, abandoned by the others, cannot be documented. In Jón Greenlander's time, as in our own, there are no bounds to the imaginative explanations of how this people disappeared. There are few facts. But the last Norseman or the last Norsemen were undoubtedly dressed on their departure in well sewn gowns, hoods and stockings of Greenlandic *vaðmál*. The outer clothing would be sewn from fur or skins.

Summary

It was Icelandic Vikings who settled in the tenth century in the southwestern part of Greenland. The *landnáma* men were magnate farmers who owned people and animals and were so well off that they could equip ships for a dangerous voyage and settlement in an uninhabited part of the country. They built their farms and churches on carefully selected points and at places with a magnificent view and with a good grassy hinterland. From the saga literature we know the names of some of the settlers. The first was Eric the Red, who built Brattahlid. With him came Herjolf Bårdson, who gave his name to Herjolfsnæs, and then there were the sons: Leif the Lucky (Leifr inn heppni Eiriكksón) and Bjarni Herjólfsson, who accidentally – but later very deliberately – sailed to the south west and came to Vinland, the present-day L'Anse aux Meadows on Newfoundland.

Specific Norse Greenlandic names are carved in runes on grave crosses and on implements – unknown Norsemen who, once named, become present to us just as the clothing they left behind makes them visible to us.

Iceland and Norway became Christian at the end of the Viking Age, but before this there had been Christian Celts in Iceland, and it is thought that the first church there was built late in the ninth century of timber brought from the Hebrides. In the North Atlantic countries the initiative for and funding of the church construction came from chieftains or magnate farmers. And so it was too in Greenland. The Norwegian Arnald became Greenland's first bishop. He was consecrated in Lund in 1124 and two years later had his seat at Gardar, the present-day Igaliku. Greenland, like Iceland, Norway, the Faroe Islands and the Orkneys, was subject to the archbishopric of Nidaros in Norway founded in 1152-53.

The Catholic Church was international. In many medieval churches in Iceland and Norway, a rich and carefully wrought inventory is preserved; some of it was imported from northern European countries and especially from England. Fittings had a special function in the liturgy of the church. They not only helped to illustrate the sacred texts, but were also pleasing to the eye. Ordinary people could come into contact with pictures and colours, as well as song. Magnificent textiles for the altar, the church interior and the clerics were part of all this.

Many crafts in the Middle Ages were closely associated with monasteries and bishops' seats, and excellent objects were made at these workshops. Icelandic and Norwegian craftsmen travelled abroad to enhance their skills, and foreign artists-craftsmen came to the Nordic workshops. In Iceland the art of making and illuminating the liturgical books necessary for the Christian ritual flourished. Greenland was part of this cultural sphere, and the *landnáma* people there had some knowledge of such books. This is indirectly evident from a small crucifix which was found at Sandnæs in the Western Settlement. On the crucifix one can see the Virgin Mary depicted with a book in her hand – an unusual picture which is only known from a few other crucifixes.

Icelandic sagas tell us how dexterous the women were at embroidery and artistic weaving. One of them was Margrét hin haga (the ingenious). She was married to the priest at Skálholt and was given her byname because she was Iceland's ablest wood-carver. Of the learned maiden Ingunn, who studied in the twelfth century at a school at the Hólar bishop's seat, it is said that as well as her own studies she was able to teach grammar and correct Latin books while she was embroidering or doing other handwork. It was such Icelandic women – we must imagine – who trained the Greenlandic *landnáma* women.

The church was part of life in the Norse settlements in Greenland. This was where people met, and this was where one drew inspiration for everyday life. People gathered for the festivities of the liturgical year, and foreigners came on visits, presumably mainly to the bishop's seat at Gardar. This afforded opportunities for exchanging or trading goods, and people heard news from the world outside. The foreigners were received by Norse Greenlanders, dressed in *vaðmál* in the natural colours of the wool, but there were also those who could appear in more prestigious costumes where blue, red and red-brown as well as black were possible colours. The domestic red-mauve lichen colour, *korkje,* could for a short while vie in radiance with the imported colours, but its durability was limited.

As soon as the *landnáma* farms had been built, the warp-weighted loom that had been brought with the settlers was set up leaning at an angle against the back wall of the *dyngja* in the farm with light coming from the fireplace in the middle of the room. From archaeological investigations it can be seen that the floor in this particular room had been dug deeper than in the adjacent rooms to allow for the height of the loom. Finds of loom parts from the farms show the width, but not the height of warp-weighted looms.

The sheep and goats that they had brought with them supplied the necessary raw material for the *landnáma* people's clothing, but over the years – for both decoration and in weaves for special purposes – the women also made use of fur from the Arctic hare.

The 'Little Ice Age' in the thirteenth century made the Norse Greenlanders change their Icelandic traditions for weaving *vaðmál*. A new, characterful Greenlandic product arose with a dense, often warp-covering weft.

The Greenlandic *vaðmál* was of a quality that made it suitable for exporting. It was woven with the most suitable weave for the warp-weighted loom: 2/2 twill. But weaves in tabby and 2/1 twill were also used. With a light-coloured weft beaten closely around a dark warp 2/1 twill could result in a *vaðmál* with two different-coloured sides, and in Greenland – as in other places – striped and checked weaves were possible pattern compositions. In addition the warp-weighted loom was used experimentally.

From the warm *vaðmál*, garments were sewn according to the latest European cuts. Garments and hoods were edged with hard-wearing borders in a combination of stitching and weaving. Textile production in Greenland was so professional that specialization seems likely. Able women must have trained children and servant-girls who had a talent for the textile crafts, and it is conceivable that on the large farms there was organized instruction.

The strong relations in the earlier part of the Middle Ages between England and western Norway also affected the textiles in Greenland. The reddish diamond twill is a weave of English origin, the pile-weaving – also red-coloured – makes the connection with Ireland, and the stitching/weaving technique *slynging,* which the settlers took with them, has survived until today as an old tradition in Iceland and on the

Aran Islands off the west coast of Ireland. The association with western Norway is most apparent, however, from the textile implements in Greenland.

The clothing of the Norse Greenlanders included other items than those we know from the churchyard at Herjolfsnæs, where the garments were re-used as burial clothing instead of coffins. Solid and warm outer clothing has not yet been found, although it must have been an absolute necessity in the cold windy Greenlandic weather. Innermost in Godthåb Fjord, where the Farm Beneath the Sand lay, the temperature in one winter in the 1990s was measured as minus 45°C, and although it was not quite so cold at the beginning of the Middle Ages, garments like those from Herjolfsnæs would not have been suitable as outer clothing in the winter. The Greenlandic soil preserved textiles, but not furs and skins. However, hair from wild animals not native to Greenland has been registered; it must have come from barter with Eskimos or Indians from North America. This is probably where the material came from for the missing outer clothing.

Poul Nørlund, who excavated the churchyard, described all liripipe hoods as headgear for men. This is doubtful. In the Middle Ages women had many differently designed types of head-dress, including hoods. Among the many textile fragments from the excavations there is certainly also a corner of a headscarf, an ancient item of head-dress for women.

The fragments from the *Landnáma* Farm in Narsaq and from the farms in the Western Settlement supplement the garments from Herjolfsnæs with other *vaðmál* types and with many fine sewing details, which in future will become just as well known as the garments are now.

The Herjolfsnæs garments show that although the economic basis for the sustenance of life at the Norse farms in Greenland diminished, the Norse Greenlanders maintained their textile tradition and formed their clothes according to European models, as they had always done.

Radiocarbon datings of the textiles indicate the period within which the wool was taken from the sheep, but this does not necessarily mean that the clothes were sewn in the same decade. Some of the garments were worn and patched, others were relatively new when they were used as grave clothing, but the weaves and seams testify that it was people with a certain surplus who made them. People in dissolution or in flight do not make products of such a high standard. The textiles are therefore tangible proof that 'all was well', as Icelandic guests related in 1408 about the Norse Greenlanders, after they had attended a wedding in Hvalsey Church in Greenland.

Explanation of the Catalogue text

The sequence of preserved and D-numbered textiles in this catalogue follows the presentation in Poul Nørlund's *Buried Norsemen at Herjolfsnes*, where the numbering is prefixed with "No. –"

There is also one D-numbered and two unnumbered fragments placed in the D-number sequence, which Nørlund does not mention, including the newly discovered garment from Herjolfsnæs that is described under 'Rønbjerg' in Margrethe Hald's *Olddanske Tekstiler* from 1950, p. 58-59 and p. 352-354. *Ancient Danish Textiles from Bogs and Burials* from 1980, pp. 62-63 and pp. 342-343.

Furthermore, included is the find of 12 garments from the Herjolfsnæs churchyard that Poul Nørlund described, but which could not be preserved, p. 231.

NØRLUND:	MUSEUM NUMBER
GARMENT TYPE Ia	
pp. 96-100	pp. 155-159 (in this book)
No. 33	D5674
	D5677
No. 34	D10577
No. 35	D10578
No. 36	registered, but not preserved
No. 37	D10579
GARMENT TYPE Ib	
pp. 100-113	pp. 160-173
No. 38	D10580
No. 39	D10581
No. 40	D10582
No. 41	D10583
No. 42	D10584
GARMENT TYPE Ic	
pp. 113-123	pp. 174-185
No. 43	D10585,1
No. 44	D10586
No. 45	D10587
No. 46	registered, but not preserved
No. 47	registered, but not preserved
No. 48	registered, but not preserved
No. 49	registered, but not preserved
No. 50	registered, but not preserved
No. 51	registered, but not preserved
No. 52	D10588
No. 53	registered, but not preserved

Where the Garments were placed

In relation to one another upon excavation from Herjolfsnæs Churchyard

(Se pages 23-25)

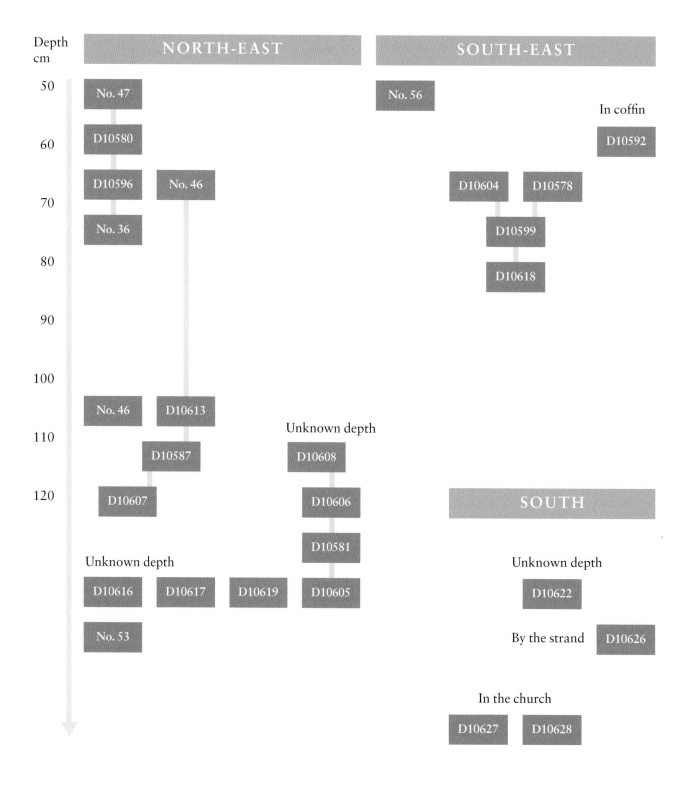

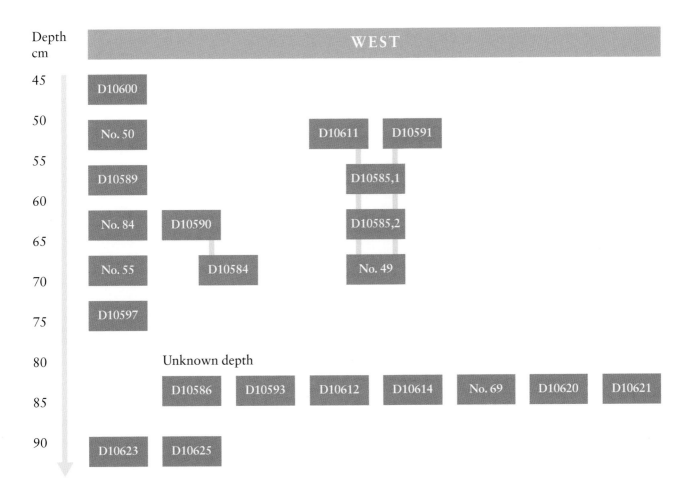

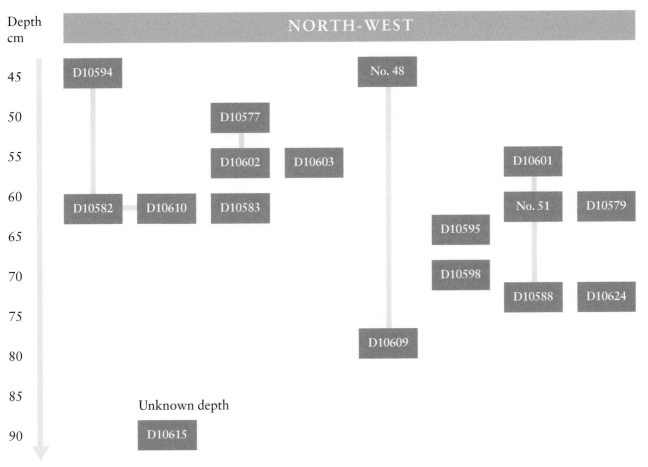

Garment Type | Ia

Nørlund No. 33. *(Figs. 1-6)*
Museum No. D5674

Garment sewn in Greenlandic vaðmál in 2/2 twill. The present-day colour is brown, but originally the textile had a light grey warp and a white weft. The length in front is 1090 mm, at the back 1110 mm. The original width along the bottom hem was c. 2700 mm. The garment consists of a front and back. The right side consists of two panels, divided at the side seam by a 'false seam'. Of the front side panel only 115 mm are preserved at the

Fig. 1
The so-called 'sailor's jacket' was found in the Herjolfsnæs church ruins already in 1840. The right sleeve and two side panels are missing. The preserved left sleeve consists of two lengths.

armhole at the top, but the back part (the right side panel) is intact. The left front panel is missing, as is most of the left back panel.

Fig. 2
The garment viewed from the back. The length is 1110 mm The sides at the front and the back of the garment are slightly flared. The gusset in the sleeve is placed rather high.

Sleeves: Only the left sleeve has been preserved, but in rather fragmentary form down towards the wrist. It is therefore not possible to see whether there was a sleeve slit. The sleeve is 560 mm long and consists of two lengths with the front seam at a distance of 155 mm from the shoulder seam and the back 80 mm from the shoulder seam. A 175 mm long and 83 mm wide gusset has been inserted in the back sleeve seam. This is the only garment that has a two-part sleeve.

Stab stitching: The 730 mm neck opening is edged with stab stitching, sewn through a 10 mm wide crease sewn down to the garment with close overcast stitches.

Singling: Along the bottom edge of the garment there is a 10-12 mm wide singling which is only visible on the back. The edging that was sewn across this has disappeared, but the singling shows that the garment has kept its original length.

Nørlund: The garment is the so-called 'sailor's jacket' found at the Herjolfsnæs church ruin in 1839 by the clerk Ove Kielsen. The garment consisted of several pieces that were sewn together, and as such they feature in several earlier publications on the Norse culture. Nørlund writes in 'Buried Norsemen at Herjolfsnes' that it was described in the National Museum's catalogue as a shroud of wool (front piece, back and a right sleeve) and 'two long triangular pieces, probably panels for a woman's garment'. Later the two triangular pieces were sewn into the garment, and as a replacement for the missing sleeve, *vaðmál* from other garment parts was used. At a later juncture – perhaps in connection with the publication of *Buried Norsemen at Herjolfsnes* in 1924 – these pieces were removed again and the garment was given its present appearance. Nørlund writes that the right sleeve has been preserved. However, it is in fact the left one.

Repairs: All seams are 'museum seams'. A brown lining of shirting has been sewn in the preserved sleeve.

Weight: The garment weighs 1000 g in its present state of preservation. It was weighed because it is the only garment that is not fully lined, but since the garment lacks more than two side panels and a sleeve, the weight must have been rather more when it was new.

Under the same number as the 'sailor's jacket' (D5674) there are also two lengths from a sleeve, measuring 580x240 mm and 580x310 mm, and a smaller piece perhaps used as a gusset(?), measuring 170x160 mm. All three pieces are in Greenlandic *vaðmál* in 2/2 twill. The present-day colour is reddish-brown. The first sleeve length and the smaller piece have the same thread count per cm, while the thread count of the last-mentioned lengths is different.

These pieces were probably taken from other garment parts and

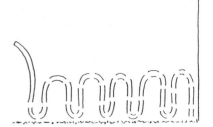

157

Fig. 5

Section showing the edge of the neck of the garment, where the remains of stab stitches can be found in some few places. The difference in weaving structure between the right and reverse sides can be clearly seen. The strong slanting line of the S-twill grain – reverse side, is more prominent than the corresponding Z-twill grain on the front.

Fig. 6

Drawing illustrates the finishing of the neckline with stab stitches sewn through a seam allowance, and overcast stitches that secure the raw edge down to the garment.

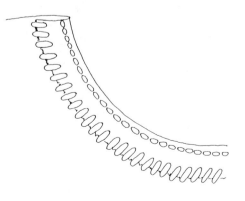

inserted in the 'sailor's jacket'. Thread remains and folds show that it was necessary to turn the reverse side of one sleeve length out to get a whole sleeve pieced together.

Museum No. D5677

A fragment of Greenlandic *vaðmál* in 2/2 twill. The present-day colour is brown.
Dimensions: 75x50 mm.

Nørlund No. 34.
Museum No. D10577

Part of a garment, a side panel, in Greenlandic *vaðmál* in 2/2 twill. The present-day colour is reddish-brown. The length is 870 mm, and the width above is 30 mm, flaring out to 420 mm below. One side of the fragment is on the straight grain, and in several places one can see the original seam allowance along a seam, but with no remains

of sewing thread. The opposite side has been cut off diagonally. The bottom hem is slightly rounded, and on the back there are traces of a singling sewn in a width of 12 mm.

Nørlund writes that the whole garment could unfortunately not be saved, but that it corresponded in type to D5674.

Under the same number (D10577) there are a further two largish fragments of Greenlandic vaðmál in 2/2 twill, measuring 390x335 mm and 280x270 mm, and a few smaller fragments. The present-day colour is reddish-brown with many black fibres in the threads. Finally there is a small fragment measuring 50x50 mm in 2/2 twill, in a reddish colour. These fragments are all in the same weave, but from different textiles.

Nørlund No. 35.
Museum No. D10578

Part of a costume, side panel, of Greenlandic *vaðmál* in 2/2 twill. The present-day colour is reddish-brown. The length is 770 mm, the width above is 70 mm, flaring out to 300 mm. One side of the fragment is cut off diagonally, and one sees remains of a seam allowance from a seam with a few stitches preserved. The opposite side is very fragmentary. The bottom edge is slightly rounded, and there are traces of a singling.

Nørlund describes this side panel as a part of a whole garment which could not be preserved, but says that it corresponded in type to D5674.

Nørlund No. 36.

Registered, but not preserved.

Nørlund No. 37. *(Fig. 7)*
Museum No. D10579

Fragmentary garment sewn in Greenlandic *vaðmál* in 2/2 twill. The present-day colour is dark brown, but originally the garment was white, possibly with a tannin-dyed warp.

The garment consists of a back with one panel sewn in on each side. Of the front only the left side panel of the garment is preserved. Both sleeves are missing. The length of the garment is 1220 mm and its fullness is 1800 mm, of which the back alone makes up 940 mm, measured parallel to a weft thread at the bottom of the garment. It is the greatest existing width registered on a Norse textile. No selvedge can be detected since the back is cut off diagonally at both sides. The neck opening on the preserved back is oval and measures 330 mm.

Tablet-woven piped edging and singling: The back is sewn to the side panels with tablet-woven piped edging. Along the front side panel the remains of a seam allowance, sewn down with overcast stitches, can be seen. At the neck opening there are a few stab stitches. At the bottom of the garment there is a singling with tablet-woven piped edging (over the cut-off edge).

Nørlund writes that the garment was cut into pieces and used as a shroud. He thinks that a seam in the right side of the garment is from a pocket slit. This is however highly doubtful, since the seam in question consists of overcast stitches sewn over a seam allowance. In addition the side panel on which the pocket slit should be is on the left, not the right. The 'false seam' Nørlund mentions is also a misunderstanding. There are no mock seams on this garment.

Repairs: There are 'museum seams' in several seams and darns with brown and black wool yarn. Probably in the 1920s, the garment parts were lined with brown shirting.

Fig. 7 The garment seen from the back. On the left side one panel is preserved from the front and one from the back, separated here by the light-brown lining that forms a line where the side seam has been.

Garment Type | Ib

Fig. 8

In contrast to the other garments, this garment has diagonally cut side panels at the side seams. There are four panels in each side, narrow at the waist and increasing gradually towards the bottom edge, increasing the fullness. Pocket slits, originally trimmed with braided cords, are cut in the two front panels.

Nørlund No. 38. *(Figs. 8-11)*
Museum No. D10580

Long-sleeved garment sewn of Greenlandic *vaðmál* in 2/2 twill. The present-day colour is dark brown, but originally the textile had a dark grey warp and a light grey weft. The garment consists of a front piece and a back, each with an 880 mm high two-part gusset. On the front gusset one sees piecings, which are 150 mm and 140 mm respectively from the bottom edge.

Fig. 9

Magnified section of tablet-woven piped edging at the bottom of the garment, originally with three cords. The warp threads in the tablet weaving, which lie on the right side, have almost completely disappeared, meaning that the weft (S-spun) threads have become visible. In the middle of the picture a couple of bows from the underlying singling can be seen.

Fig. 10

Schematic presentation of tablet-woven piped edging with three 'cords' on the right side. On the reverse side the S-spun thread lies as the transverse stitch.

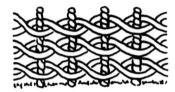

The round neck opening, which is deepest at the front, measures 710 mm. The length of the garment is 1230 mm.

The four panels in each side are cut very narrow above with an increasing fullness from hip to bottom edge, where they increase the fullness of the garment to 3400 mm. A 'false seam' divides the two hindmost side-panels from the waist down.

Unlike all the other garments, this garment has diagonally cut-panels at the side seams.

Pocket slits: On the two front side panels parallel with the warp threads, 170 mm long pocket slits have been cut at a distance of 20-30 mm from the seam to the front piece and beginning at waist height. Both were trimmed with braided cords, of which 25 mm has been preserved on the right panel, while at the left pocket slit of the garment only stitches from the attachment of the cord have been preserved. In addition large parts around the left

pocket slit have disappeared altogether.

The sleeves: The right sleeve is 540 mm long and has a 10-15 mm wide piecing at the bottom, from which the outermost edge has disappeared. The seam of the sleeve ends in a long uneven slit, which measures 105 mm at the front and 130 mm at the back. The slit is attractively bordered and seems to have been left open, perhaps because the fullness at the wrist is very narrow.

The left sleeve is 40 mm shorter than the right one, and the slit is only partly preserved. A 20 mm wide piecing is sewn into the sleeve at the bottom. The piecing is trimmed with a braided cord, of which 50 mm is placed up along the slit and 20 mm at the rounding down towards the hand. Both sleeves have 210 mm long, 140 mm wide gussets inserted at the top back at a distance of 160-170 mm from the shoulder seam. The gusset on the right sleeve of the garment consists of two pieces sewn together.

Stab stitching: To underscore the shape of the garment there is a row of stab stitching parallel to the sewing of the side panels. On the right sleeve slit of the garment one sees two rows of stab stitching, sewn to the sleeve through a 7 mm wide seam allowance held down with overcast stitches. Outermost along the edge of the sleeve slit one can also see a seam that probably held a braided cord.

The neck opening is edged with stab stitching in two rows, sewn through an 8 mm wide seam allowance which is sewn down with close overcast stitches. There was probably also a braided cord along the outside edge, corresponding to the trimming of the sleeve and pocket slits, but since the edge of the neck is worn, there are no traces of cord or stitching.

Tablet-woven piped edging: Below, the garment is bordered with a 12 mm wide singling. There is also a 7 mm narrow strip of tablet-woven piped edging, three rows on the right side with a couple of twisted (filler) threads laid under the stitches on the back, parallel to the cut-off edge. Some of the lengthwise seams have two rows of tablet-woven piped edging, while others have an ordinary seam and overcast

stitching, so that the seams are 'upright'.

Finally there are seams where the overcast stitches sew the seam allowance down to the cloth.

Nørlund writes that the garment was pierced through by plant roots, and that it was one of the most tightly fitting garments at the waist.

Repairs: There are 'museum seams' sewn over almost all original seams, and many darns with brown and

black wool yarn. A net has been glued to the back of the garment, and brown shirting has been sewn in as lining, probably in the 1920s.

A fine garment: Despite large missing sections and damage, one can still see that this was an impressive garment. No other garment has such a distinctive cut as this one. The waistline and hipline are clearly visible and there are many decorative details in the sewing.

Fig. 11
The garment seen from the back.
The darns and lining are from the 1920s.

Nørlund No. 39. *(Figs. 12-15)*
Museum No. D10581

Short-sleeved garment sewn in Greenlandic *vaðmál* in 2/2 twill. The present colour is reddish-brown, but originally the textile had a brownish, tannin-dyed warp and an undyed weft. The garment consists of a front piece and a back, each with an 820 mm high two-part gusset inserted. The gussets are terminated above with rounded points which are fitted in a sophisticated way to the front and back. In front the garment measures 1230 mm in length, and at the back 1210 mm. There are also differences on the front itself, where the right side is 40 mm longer than the left side. The fullness measured along the bottom edge is 3600 mm. At chest height in front, a patch of 150x240 mm has been inserted. The original colour of the patch is white. The garment has two panels in each side; all four

Fig. 12

From the first time this short-sleeved garment was exhibited in the National Museum, it has been one of the most frequently shown and copied garments. On the left sleeve some few millimetres of the finishing edge has been preserved. The Greenland vaðmál from which the garment has been sewn, had originally a brownish warp and a weft with the colour of natural fleece. The patch on the breast was white. After nearly five hundred years in the churchyard soil at Herjolfsnæs, the garment now has a beautiful reddish-brown colour.

163

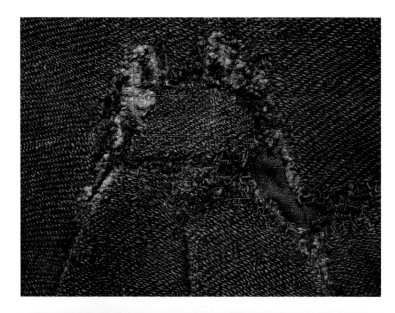

Fig. 13

Section showing the finish at the top of the middle gusset, front of the garment. The inserted two-part gusset has been extended with a transverse piece, which upwards has two rounded points. The light coloured edges along the gusset are discoloured threads, caused by chemical attack.

Fig. 14

Section showing the inserted middle gusset at the back of the garment, of which most of the upper finishing has disappeared. The thin transverse threads are stitches that secure the weakened textile to the supporting material. From the restoration in the 1980s.

of these are widened towards the armhole with 80-230 mm long pieces. The longest piece in the left side is cut with the warp in the transverse direction.

In the left side seam of the garment there is a 'false seam' from the bottom edge up to the piecing. The neck opening measures 590 mm, and there is a 45 mm long slit in the middle front.

The sleeves: The sewn-on sleeves are 270 and 300 mm long respectively; the left sleeve is longest and on this a couple of centimetres of the original edging are preserved. The sleeves have 115 mm long and 110 mm wide gussets inserted at the top of the back at a distance of 140 mm from the shoulder seam. The gusset of the left sleeve is however 130 mm wide. The right sleeve is sewn together from two pieces with a longitudinal seam, and an oval patch has been inserted along almost the whole sleeve length.

Stab stitching: On the bottom edge of the garment and at the neck opening there are stab stitches, sewn through a 7 mm wide seam

allowance. Close overcast stitches sew the seam allowance in to the garment. One sees the same edging on the left sleeve, although the stab stitching has disappeared here. In addition there is stab stitching at the top along the seams at the middle gusset and through the back and the right side panel.

Nørlund writes that this garment was the best preserved of all when the Herjolfsnæs clothing was found. Unfortunately many years on display have worsened its state of preservation.

Of the two pairs of finely bordered eyelets at the neck vent, which he mentioned, it is only pos-

sible to faintly see one now, and the seam allowance at the sleeves is no longer there. Nørlund believed that the asymmetries of the garment were due to the fact that the person who wore it was hunchbacked or had some other deformity, and that the patch on the front piece and the four piecings in the side panels were sewn in to fit the garment to the person. He further suggests that the patch on the front piece and the piecings may be repairs after wear. He does not mention the patch under the sleeve. On the other hand he suggests that a so-called vimpel (streamer) may have left a tear in one sleeve.

Repairs: In the 1920s various repairs were done with a grey sewing thread as well as 'museum darns' with wool yarn. Among other things the patches were sewn on firmly.

Restoration: In connection with a restoration in 1986, when the garment was lined with a dyed wool material, many of the old darns and repairs were removed.

On the garment there are many light-coloured edges at the seams where the wool threads seem 'withered', a phenomenon one sees on a few other garments and fragments along seams or in seam allowances.

Fragment without museum number: A fragment of Greenlandic *vaðmál* in 2/2 twill in a reddish colour, 10/14 threads per cm, has a yellowed note attached which says in Gothic script 'Found in the church ruin of ... in Herjolfsnæs, 27 April 18 ...'. The fragment (measuring 55x165 mm) is made of the same *vaðmál* as the garment D10581. But that this fragment is part of a vimpel (streamer) is just as inconceivable as that this outlandish fashion was ever in use in Greenland. Another garment or hood could have been sewn from the same *vaðmál*.

Fig. 15

Short sleeved garment seen from the back.

165

Under the same number (D10581) there is a fragment of 100x37 mm with an 8 mm wide seam allowance sewn down with close overcast stitches. Above the seam allowance, but below the stitches, one sees a light Z-twisted thread. The fragment is not part of the garment D10581, since the colour and thread density are different.

Nørlund No. 40. *(Fig. 16)*
Museum No. D10582

Fragmentary garment sewn of Greenlandic *vaðmál* in 2/2 twill. The present-day colour is reddish-brown, but originally the weave had a grey warp and a light grey weft. The garment consists of a front piece and a back, each with a 740 mm high two-part gusset inserted. Two panels, one from the front and one from the back, have been preserved in the right side of the garment. Both panels have selvedges out towards the side seam, while the opposite sides are cut with a relatively large rounding at the hip. From here the panels flare downward to a fullness of 940 mm. The original fullness of the garment below may thus have been c. 3480 mm. The length of the garment is 1195 mm.

The sleeves and the left front part are no longer there, and of the left side of the garment only a smallish fragment remains. The oval neck opening is only intact at the back, where it measures 350 mm.

Tablet-woven piped edging and singling: In the sewing of the middle gusset in front one sees tablet-woven piped edging. In addition there are a few original lengthwise seams.

At the bottom of the garment there are remains of singling, which show that the garment has preserved its original length. The border at the neck opening has disappeared.

Nørlund writes that when the garment was excavated most of the seams had come apart, and it had to be sewn together again.

Repairs: Almost all the seams are 'museum seams', and many holes

Fig. 16
Garment seen from the back. Originally the garment was greyish with a light weft on a dark warp. From the right side of the garment only one panel from the front and one from the back have been preserved, both with selvedged side seams.

are darned with black wool yarn through a glued-on net, probably during repairs in the 1920s.

A loose-lying fragment of 510x310 mm is probably part of the garment, but it has not been possible to place when the garment was repaired.

Nørlund No. 41. *(Figs. 17-23)*
Museum No. D10583

Long-sleeved garment sewn of Greenlandic *vaðmál* in 2/2 twill. The present-day colour is dark brown, but originally the textile was almost black in both warp and weft. The garment consists of a front piece and a back, each with a 710 mm high two-part gusset inserted. The gussets are terminated above with rounded points which

Fig. 17
Originally, this garment was almost black. Four panels on each side have given a fullness of slightly more than four metres. With so many fine sewing details, this garment was once very beautiful. The garment is shown here from the front, where the light coloured lining from the 1920s particularly disturbs the overall impression.

are sophisticatedly fitted to the front piece and the back. The length of the garment is 1280 mm. Four panels in each side increase the fullness of the garment to 4060 mm, measured along the bottom edge. The neck opening is oval and measures 880 mm. Large sections of the

garment have disappeared, including the top of the right sleeve and the side panel, and the left middle gusset.

Sleeves with buttonholes: The sleeves have 220 mm long, 135 mm wide gussets inserted in the top back at a distance of 115 mm from the shoulder seam. The right sleeve measures 640 mm. The sleeve seam ends in a 270 mm long vent. In the front of the slit there are 16 hori-

zontal buttonholes, 7-10 mm long, placed at intervals of c. 15 mm. Most are worn away at the outermost end. There is no seam around the buttonholes.

The left sleeve measures 638 mm. The slit in the sleeve seam is 260 mm long, and the buttonholes are positioned in the same way as on the right sleeve, but since the bottom part of the sleeve is much worn, there are only seven buttonholes left – most of them poorly

Fig. 18
Garment seen from the back. Length is 1280 mm and the sleeves are 640 mm.

preserved. Singling and remains of cord can be seen in a few places. At the opposite end of the vent, the button side, the border has disappeared. The edging of the sleeve at the wrists has also disappeared.

Singling: On the buttonhole side the slit on both sleeves is reinforced with an 8 mm wide singling, where the stitches are sewn into each weft or every other weft. Outermost along the edge of the right sleeve one sees remains of a 3–5 mm thick cord, possibly attached with the stitches that form the singling.

A similar edging with singling and cord has been preserved in a few places at the bottom of the sleeve.

On the button side the slit is also edged with stab stitching sewn through a 6 mm wide seam allowance, which is sewn down with close overcast stitches to the sleeve.

Stab stitching: Along the seams of the side panels from the armhole down to the waist there are stab stitches which have been preserved in a few places to lengths of up to 290 mm. In addition, as mentioned above, there is stab stitching at the bottom edge on the right sleeve slit.

The neck opening is bordered with stab stitching sewn through a 6 mm wide seam allowance which is itself sewn down with close overcast stitches.

In 1921 Nørlund had a drawing made of the garment as it was found, with the sleeves laid crosswise over the chest.

Repairs: The garment is lined with brown shirting, and there are many 'museum seams', probably from the 1920s.

Fig. 19
Section showing the top finish of the middle gusset on the front of the garment. The 17 mm wide 'tongue' has a transverse piecing.

Fig. 20
Section showing the very worn out top finish of the middle gusset on the back.

Fig. 21
In the right sleeve slit 16 buttonholes have been preserved, 7-10 mm long, placed at intervals of c.15 mm. No trace of sewing around the edges of the holes has been found

Fig. 22
The seam at the shoulder has been flattened out to either side and sewn to the garment with overcast stitches.

Fig. 23
Schematic presentation of the edging along the sleeve slits. The reinforced singling must have been sewn after the buttonholes were cut, but it is not possible to see whether the stitches in the singling have also secured the cord to the edge.

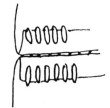

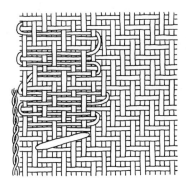

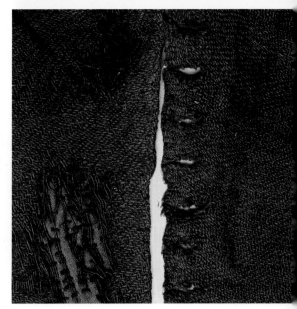

An impressive garment: Despite the garment's poor state of preservation and the many repairs, one can still see that it was a very impressive garment, beautifully woven with many fine seams.

Nørlund No. 41. *(Figs. 24-25)*
Museum No. D10583 (Buttons)

Seven buttons have been preserved. According to a note attached, five are from a right and two from a left sleeve. The buttons, which measure 10-12 mm in diameter, are made of the same *vaðmál* as the garment D10583. They are formed such that the upper surface is smooth, while the cloth of the underside is gath-ered in a bunch. On the buttons one can see that they were sewn through with small stitches in concentric cir-cles. The thread has gone, but the holes from sewing are there. The buttons, which are stored in two round glass cases, have at some point been treated with a substance which is now greasy.

Nørlund writes that there were six buttons, and that the cloth in the buttons was glued together.

Fig 24

Seven buttons, sewn from the same vaðmál as the garment (D10583) with which they were found.

Fig. 25

The three best-preserved buttons from the garment. The front of two of the buttons is displayed, and the back of the third. Very small holes from the stitches that were sewn through the buttons in concentric circles are still visible. Diameter: 10-12 mm.

Nørlund No. 42. *(Figs. 26-30)*
Museum No. D10584

Long-sleeved garment sewn in Greenlandic *vaðmál* in 2/2 twill. The present-day colour is dark brown, the original colour of the textile. The garment consists of a front piece and a back, each with a two-part gusset inserted at a height of 840 mm and 880 mm respectively. The front piece had been pieced out by 50 mm on each shoulder.

The length of the garment in front is 1195 mm and at the back 1280 mm. Two panels in each side increase the fullness of the garment to 3335 mm, measured along the bottom edge. In the right side of the garment the two outermost panels are cut in one piece, which in itself gives this piece a fullness of 815 mm. A 'false seam' divides the piece lengthwise and forms a side seam.

The round neck opening measures 640 mm, but since the edge of

the neck is very fragmentary at the front, these measurements are rather uncertain.

Pocket slits: In the front side panels, 170 mm long pocket slits are cut parallel to the warp threads at a distance of 20-25 mm from the seam to the middle piece. The right pocket slit ends 540 mm from the bottom edge of the garment, and the left one 570 mm. Since the garment is poorly preserved under the armholes, the distance from pocket slit to armhole cannot be given.

Sleeves: The sleeves have 170 mm long, 75 mm wide gussets inserted in the back at a distance of 125 mm from the shoulder seam. The right sleeve is 430 mm long and measures 250 mm at the wrist; a 7 mm wide seam allowance is sewn down to the sleeve with overcast stitches. The sleeve seam ends in a 12 mm long 'slit' or opening.

The left sleeve is 530 mm long, and the fullness below is 155 mm. The sleeve seam ends in a 140 mm long slit. Along the bottom edge

and at the slit two rows of stab stitching are sewn. One side of the slit is however fragmentary. At the top, by the slit, a patch or reinforcement has been inserted.

Tablet-woven piped edging and singling: At the bottom of the garment there is a partly preserved singling, 8-10 mm wide and with 5 mm between the arches. Above the singling and along the raw edge, tablet-woven piped edging can be seen.

Braided cord: The neck opening is bordered with a 5 mm wide seam allowance, to the outermost edge of which a braided cord is sewn.

Remains of a similar cord can be seen at the pocket slits. Nørlund writes that when the garment was found, the sleeves were laid crosswise over the chest, and the fullness of the skirt was attractively folded in deep pleats. He also writes that the gusset in the middle back is divided by a 'false seam'. This is wrong, however. It is an ordinary seam. His information that the right sleeve was longer than the left is doubtful, since the original edging at the bottom of the left sleeve is still there.

Repairs: The garment is poorly preserved, especially the upper part and the top part of the sleeves, and, probably in the 1920s, a net was glued to the back of the garment. In addition the garment is lined with brown shirting, through which there are many 'museum darns' in both wool yarn and grey sewing thread.

Restoration: In 1996 the most disfiguring 'museum darns' were removed from the front of the garment, and the threads in the weave were laid parallel as far as possible and then sewn down to a dyed wool material. For reasons of preservation, however, the old lining was not removed from the back of the garment, since there was a risk that many threads in the textile would disappear.

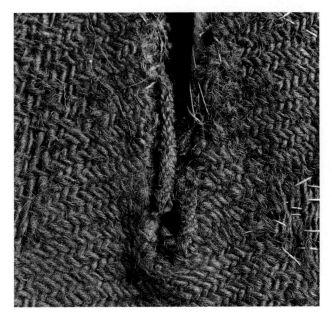

Fig. 28
Section from the left sleeve, bottom. At the rounding towards the slit there are some few stitches from two rows of stab stitches. The Z-twill grain is beautifully outlined in the worn vaðmál.

Fig. 29
Section of the left sleeve, bottom. A corner of the sleeve is folded in to display the seven mm narrow seam allowance on the reverse side. The seam allowance is sewn down to the woven cloth with very close overcast stitches. A newer lining is visible along the folded part.

Fig. 30
Section of the right pocket slit of the garment, which is bordered with a braided cord, a 'Færøsnor'. The textile has nine threads per cm. in the warp. The white stitches are from repairs carried out in the 1920s.

173

Garment Type | Ic

Nørlund No. 43. *(Figs. 31-36)*
Museum No. D10585.1

Long-sleeved garment of Greenlandic *vaðmál* in 2/2 twill. The present-day colour is dark brown, but originally the textile had a grey warp and a light grey weft. The garment consists of a front piece and a back, each with a 700 mm high two-part gusset inserted. The gussets are attractively terminated above with rounded points, sophisticatedly fitted to the front and the

back. The length of the garment is 1160 mm. Two relatively narrow panels in each side increase the fullness of the garment at the bottom to 2020 mm. The oval neck opening, which measures 645 mm, is terminated at the front with a 185 mm long slit.

In the side seams there are 120-130 mm long openings (pocket slits) at a distance of c. 70 mm from the armholes. The garment is much worn and large patches of various

pieces of *vaðmál* are sewn under it.

Sleeves: The right sleeve has been preserved, but much pieced together and patched. Stitch holes and remains of thread through an 8 mm wide seam allowance at the bottom of the sleeve show that the original length of the sleeves was 580 mm. On the other hand, the existing 70 mm long slit at the bottom of the sleeve seam is probably not original. Of the left sleeve only a small

Fig. 32
The garment seen from the back. Length is 1160 mm. When the garment was found there were loose patches inside, which in the 1920s were again placed under the holes. A large section of the lower part of the skirt has disappeared. The lining of shirting is visible.

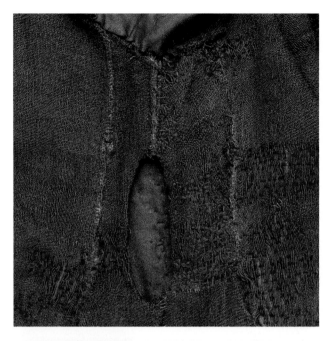

Fig. 33
Section of the garment's right side with an opening that begins 70 mm from the armholes. Nørlund considered the opening to be a pocket slit. The many darns are from the 1920s.

Fig. 34
Section of the sewing on the middle gusset seen from the reverse side, back. The sewing is either tablet-woven piped edging with two threads in a tablet, or sewing where two threads are twisted together using the fingers, simultaneously with the overcasting of the raw edge. The twisted thread is seen outermost on the seam.

strip of 20-90 mm is preserved in the armhole. In both sleeves on the back, gussets have been inserted. These are also pieced together and only partially preserved.

Stab stitching: On the back there is stab stitching at the top of the middle gusset and along the seams of the side panels for the back. At the neck opening and at the bottom of the right sleeve there are stitch holes and remains of thread, probably from stab stitching. A few threads

at the bottom edge can be interpreted as remains of an edging seam. On the other hand there are no traces of sewing along the pocket slits or along the neck slit.

Nørlund writes that when the garment was found, several patches were lying inside it. Around the right leg some rags were wound, which could later be sewn together to form the right sleeve. During the subsequent lining the patches could no longer be placed. Nørlund also thought that the garment was a

kind of under-tunic, partly because the textile is thinner than that of the other garments, and not so carefully done, partly because of the long neck slit. He further believed that wear from a belt with a sword attached indicated that the garment was an under-tunic.

From the examination of 1997 it could be established that the most visible wear in the garment is in an area that goes from the bottom of the 185 mm long neck slit 170 mm down – an area which must have

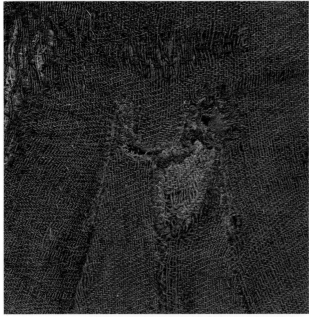

been above the belt area, and which cannot have been worn away by a belt or by an attached sword.

The few preserved stab stitches and the fine edging of the middle gussets suggest that the garment was originally more carefully made than one can now see. However, there can be no doubt that the garment is worn out.

Repairs: Almost all seams are 'museum seams', probably from the 1920s, when a net was also glued to the back of the garment. Moreover, innumerable 'museum darns' with brown wool yarn attach the garment to a lining of brown shirting.

177

Nørlund No. 44. *(Figs. 37-38)*
Museum No. D10586

Long-sleeved child's garment, sewn in Greenlandic *vaðmál* in 2/2 twill. The present-day colour is brown, but originally the garment was white. The garment has a front piece and a back, each with a 560 mm high two-part gusset. The length is 880 mm. Two panels in each side increase the fullness of the garment to 2300 mm measured along the bottom edge.

Sleeves: The sleeves were c. 390 mm long, but the length is uncertain, since the garment is very poorly preserved. For the same reason the two gussets from the back of the sleeves are also missing, but on the basis of the preserved armholes one can see that they were once there.

No original borders have been preserved.

Nørlund writes that many roots had grown through the garment, its state of preservation was poor, and it had come apart at all seams.

Repairs: In the 1920s the garment had a net glued to the back and was given a lining of brown shirting. In addition one can see many 'museum darns' made with brown and black wool yarn.

< Fig. 37

A six- to eight-year-old child's garment, seen from the front. The garment, which originally was white, is in a very poor state of preservation and in many places the textile is decomposing.

Fig. 38

The child's garment seen from the back. The gussets from the sleeves are missing, but the width of the armholes suggests that they once existed.

Nørlund No. 45. *(Figs. 39-41)*
Museum No. D10587

Short-sleeved garment sewn in Greenlandic *vaðmál* in 2/2 twill. The present-day colour is dark brown, which was also the original colour. The garment consists of a front piece and a back, each with an inserted two-part gusset at a height of 840 mm and 860 mm respectively. The length in front is 1185 mm, at the back 1200 mm. Two panels

in each side increase the fullness to 3050 mm measured along the bottom edge. A pocket slit is positioned in the seam between front and side panels. The right pocket slit is 190 mm long and 220 mm from the armhole, while the left pocket slit is only 160 mm long and is 215 mm from the armhole. The round neck opening measures 650 mm.

The garment has unusually many so-called 'false seams'. On the left side of the garment one can see

three (side seam and one on each side of this) and on the right side two (one on each side of the side seam). In addition there is a false seam in the back middle gusset.

Sleeves: Only the right sleeve with 15 mm of the original border along the bottom edge has been preserved. The sleeve length varies from 205 mm to 370 mm with the shortest length at the front of the arm and the longest at the back seam, where a 155 mm long, 120 mm wide two-part gusset has also been inserted. The sleeve is placed such that the bottom gusset seam is opposite the side seam of the garment.

Braided cord: The border seam at the bottom of the sleeve consists of a 5 mm wide seam allowance towards the reverse side, sewn to the cloth with overcast stitches. Outermost on the edge a braided cord is sewn.

Fig. 39
Short sleeved garment. Pocket slits are in the seam on the front between the middle and side panels. The neck opening, pocket slits and the bottom edge of the garment are all beautifully finished with stab stitches, two rows at the slits, and one row on the rest.

Stab stitching: The neck opening is bordered with stab stitching, sewn through a 6 mm wide seam allowance that is attached with close overcast stitches to the garment. One can see a similar border at the bottom edge of the garment, where the seam allowance is 8 mm. There, too, a thick (filler) thread had been laid under the stitches, above the raw edge. Both seams can be seen at a distance of 2.5 mm from the outermost edge. The stitches are 2-3 mm long and sewn very closely.

At the pocket slits there are two rows of stab stitching sewn through an 8 mm wide seam allowance, sewn with close overcast stitches to the garment.

Tablet-woven piped edging: The lengthwise seams are sewn either with tablet-woven piped edging or with running stitches and overcasting of the seam allowance with

Fig. 40
The garment, seen from the back, is of a rough vaðmál quality. 15 mm of the original seam allowance with sewn-on braided cord is preserved on the right sleeve. Note the two-part sleeve gusset. The lining of shirting was sewn in during the 1920s.

181

Fig. 41
The right sleeve folded upwards. The gusset of the sleeve is placed so that the seam at the bottom of the gusset meets the garment's side seam. The other seams on the gusset meet at the back where the middle and side panel seams are found. The length of the sleeves varies, shortest in the front and longest at the back. Thoroughly functional.

a thick (filler) thread laid under the stitches. Some of the 9 mm wide seam allowance is 'upright'.

Nørlund writes that when the garment was found, it was in several pieces which were found scattered at distances of a few metres. With the garment were the stockings D10613 and D10614. Nørlund thought that garment and stockings belonged together.

Repairs: Some seams are from the 1920s, when a lining of brown shirting was also sewn in. In addition there are many 'museum darns' with brown and black wool yarn.

From the examination of 1997 it could be established that the garment is still of very solid quality and in a good state of preservation. The cloth and seams are worn smooth and are very beautiful.

Nørlund No. 46.
Registered but not preserved

Nørlund No. 47.
Registered but not preserved

Nørlund No. 48.
Registered but not preserved

Nørlund No. 49.
Registered but not preserved

Nørlund No. 50.
Registered but not preserved

Nørlund No. 51.
Registered but not preserved

Nørlund No. 52.
Museum No. D10588

Parts of a garment sewn in Greenlandic *vaðmál*. The present-day colour is light brown. There are four panels sewn together into one piece which measures 560 mm in height and 1230 mm in width, measured along the bottom edge. A loose-lying fragment measures 320x320 mm.

Tablet-woven piped edging and singling: The lengthwise seams are sewn with tablet-woven piped edging. As a border on the bottom edge one sees a 12 mm wide singling, and stitches from tablet-woven piped edging, which are almost completely worn off. On the back one can also see some thick (filler) threads under the stitches.

Nørlund writes that a smallish piece of the braided cord D10624 lay with the garment. He also writes that these garment parts with many seams and narrow panels were in a very poor state of preservation, and that only four panels were preserved from the lower part of a garment.

From the examination in 1997 it could be established that these preserved parts are from a good, solid garment and are in a very fine state of preservation.

Nørlund No. 53.
Registered but not preserved

Nørlund No. 54.
Museum No. D10589

Fragment of a child's garment – a yoke or top piece of a garment – sewn in Greenlandic *vaðmál* in 2/2 twill.

The present-day colour is dark brown. Dimensions: 190x265 mm. On the fragment one can see a 250 mm deep neck rounding with stab stitching sewn through a 6 mm wide seam allowance which is sewn with close overcast stitches to the fragment. Under the stitches a thick (filler) thread has been laid. Similar narrow borders can be seen at the armholes, but with no stab stitching. There are seam allowances along the very diagonally cut-off shoulders, but no stitches are preserved from a seam.

The direction of the warp is transverse to the garment fragment. This is unusual, since all the other garments are cut with the warp thread lengthwise.

Nørlund writes that other garments and the 'pill-box' cap No. 84, which had a two-part circular crown, were found with this garment. The cap was 100 mm tall and had a diameter of 145 mm. Neither the cap nor the other garments could be taken up and preserved.

Nørlund No. 55.
Registered but not preserved

Nørlund No. 56.
Registered but not preserved

Nørlund No. 57.
Museum No. D8080

Small and large fragments of Greenlandic *vaðmál* found in 1900 at Herjolfsnæs Churchyard by the district medical officer Gustav Meldorf. There are a total of 20 reddish-brown fragments in 2/2 twill, positioned such, that in an assemblage they make up the top part of a garment. However, this

positioning is very doubtful, since some of the fragments have the reverse side turned up and others are placed with the thread directions at odds with one another.

It is likely that after making the assemblage Gustav Meldorf himself sewed the fragments to a grey linen material with white sewing thread. No original seams or stitches are preserved. Together the fragments measure 1300 mm in width. The longest piece measures 500 mm.

Nørlund No. 57.
Museum No. D8081

Fragmentary garment sewn in Greenlandic *vaðmál* in 2/2 twill. The district medical officer Gustav Meldorf found the fragmentary garment along with the above-mentioned 20 fragments (D8080) in Herjolfsnæs Churchyard in 1900. The present-day colour is dark brown, but originally the garment was white and sewn with an almost black thread. At least 14 'panels' have been preserved, and two of these are front and back with two-part middle gussets; the other eight are side panels (four from each side). The 14 panels are sewn together in two large pieces with five and nine panels respectively. In addition there are some long narrow strips, which may be remains of panels. Two largish fragments of 540x340 mm and 500x315 mm are probably remains of the sleeves.

The fullness measured along the bottom edge of the five plus nine panels sewn together is c. 2650 mm, and the greatest height is 740 mm. The many panels and fragments almost make up a whole garment, but the top part is missing except for one preserved fragment. Probably a shoulder part.

Great fullness: Looking at the garments D10580 or D10583, each of which has eight side panels, with a split front piece as well as back and middle gussets, one can count a total of 16 'panels' on each garment. This gives them a fullness of 3400 mm and 4060 mm respectively. Looking at a whole garment, there is no doubt about differences or uniformities in the individual panels in terms of belonging together with adjacent panels. But if one looks at a fragmentary garment like D8081, where the top borders of the panels or complete sewing to the adjacent panels are missing, it is not possible to tell precisely which 'panels' are represented here.

Tablet-woven piped edging: The bottom hem of the garment is attractively finished with a 10 mm wide seam allowance towards the reverse side, but without being sewn on.

Along the cut-off and turned edge one can see tablet-woven piped edging, sewn with an almost black thread. Similar tablet-woven piped edging with the same dark thread was used to sew together the many panels where the 7 mm wide seam allowance is 'upright'. All these decorative seams are only visible on the reverse side of the garment.

It was probably Gustav Meldorf who sewed the garment parts – many of which are much frayed at the top end – to grey linen lining with long white stitches. One of the sleeve fragments is tacked on with white sewing thread and is not sewn to lining.

Along with the garment D8081 there are two smaller unnumbered pieces measuring 260x150 mm and 400x60 mm packed in blue paper. Outside the packing one reads 'Mr.

District Medical Officer Meldorf. Julianehaab'. On the paper there is red sealing wax in which one can read 'K. Bugge'.

The former piece is in a coarser weave (2/2 twill, 10/9 thr./cm) and is not part of this garment, whereas the latter (400x60 mm) has the same weave and thread count as the garment D8081. Both pieces have stab stitching along an edge, and both are tacked with white sewing thread.

'Rønbjerg' D2625a-e *(Fig. 42)*

Fragmentary garment sewn in Greenlandic *vaðmál* in 2/2 twill. The present-day colour is dark brown, which is also the garment's original colour. The garment consists of a half front piece, 1135 mm high and 180 mm wide, with a two-part gusset, 800 mm high and 475 mm wide, sewn on. Of the other half front, 570x190 mm has been preserved. In addition there is a largish fragment with remains of an armhole, probably from the left back. The other fragments from the garment have no seams or borders that can place them.

This garment is not included in Poul Nørlund's catalogue of preserved garments, nor has it been possible to recognize it in list of non-preserved garment finds. However, in her publication Olddanske tekstiler from 1950 (English edition Ancient Danish Textiles from Bogs and Burials, 1980), Margrethe Hald has described the garment under 'Rønbjerg' (D2625a-e). From her description it is evident that she has actually stood in one of the National Museum's storage rooms with a cardboard box marked Rønbjerg, in which there were several large and small garment fragments with no museum number or other information. She could identify a sheepskin and a strap as belonging to the real Rønbjerg find. She numbered the other pieces D2625a-g, although she did not think they belonged together or were from the same time. She compares the gar-

ment D2625a-e plus some small fragments to the gown from Moselund and says: 'To the front, which is hardly complete, a gusset-shaped sewn-on piece fits, which reveals the medieval cut of the garment ... The shoulder seam and the slit at the neck opening are placed in the same way as on the gown from Moselund (see pp. 135-139) and in terms of the cut the fragment also shows similarities to some of the famous garments from Herjolfsnæs.'

In connection with the publication of the book in 1950 the Rønbjerg garment was photographed (Hald 1950 Figs. 43. and 44.) and here one can see that the garment has been placed with the armhole as a slit in the middle front, and the two-part middle gusset as a side panel. The assemblage is correct if one focuses on the two-part gusset as the central axis of the garment. The garment is thus given an appearance that wholly matches that of the Herjolfsnæs garments (Nørlund Garment Types Ib and Ic), which also have the oval neck openings.

A technical analysis of the garment in 1999 showed that fibres and weave (more threads in the weft than in the warp) have the same characteristics as the Greenlandic *vaðmál*. In addition the few preserved seams (stab stitching and singling) are identical to the seams on the Herjolfsnæs garments. Finally, a radiocarbon analysis has confirmed that the garment is from the end of the 1200s. It is thus the oldest dated of the garments from Herjolfsnæs.

Nørlund No. 58. *(Figs. 43-49)*
Museum No. D10590

Parts of a long-sleeved, pleated garment of Greenlandic *vaðmál* in 2/2 twill. The present-day colour is brownish-black, but originally the garment was completely black, and the threads were probably spun from goat hair. After the excavation in 1921, Poul Nørlund described the garment as 'grown through by plant roots – the garment appears to have been cut according to the usual pattern for a garment to pull over the head, but the details are difficult to explain, since only the top part has been preserved'. And further: 'a number of seams in the bottom part fit well compared with the other garments'. What was noted in the examination in 1997 was an upper part consisting of a front and back, both with large sections missing. The front and a narrow panel on each side measure together 290 mm in width. The height of the front, measured from shoulder seam to bottom edge, is 435 mm on the left side of the garment and 465 mm on the right side. The back measures 450 mm in height and the incomplete neck opening on the back measures 350 mm.

Sleeves: Only the left sleeve has been preserved to a length of 485 mm. There are no original seams or borders at the bottom of the sleeve. At the top there are remains of a 165 mm long gusset, positioned at a distance of 60 mm from the shoulder seam. The gusset width is uncertain. The fragmentary armhole is very large, and the present placing of the sleeve in the armhole is uncertain.

Sewn pleats: There are narrow pleats on both front pieces and on the fragmentary side panels to a height of 220 mm measured from the bottom edge. There are thus no pleats at the top towards the shoulder seams. The pleats are c. 4 mm wide and folded on the straight thread with the warp threads. They are attached by sewing on the reverse side. On the right side of the garment – up towards the armhole – one can see, crosswise to the pleats, a 16 mm wide seam allowance towards the back, but there is no seam.

Along the neck opening on the back a 150 mm long seam allowance is preserved with a few stitches.

Repairs: The present-day sewing-in of the sleeve was probably done in the 1920s, when a net was also glued on. In addition the upper part has been lined with brown shirting, and there are many 'museum darns'.

Comparing the existing garment with the drawing of the upper part (Fig. 74, bottom) in *Buried Norsemen at Herjolfsnes*, one sees that a large section in the middle of the front has disappeared after the drawing was made in the 1920s. The state of preservation was registered in 1997 as very poor.

Under the same museum number (D10590) there is a fragment of

Greenlandic *vaðmál* in 2/2 twill which belongs with the pleated upper part. The fragment is triangular in form, 135 mm long, 50 mm at the widest point. It has narrow sewn pleats parallel to the longest side of the triangle. Along the diagonal – crosswise to the pleats – one can see remains of a border, probably done as tablet-woven piped edging. This border was part of the neck opening, as Nørlund describes it, 'cut in a low V'.

The fragment with the triangular form and the sewn border diagonal to the pleats could be positioned on the front piece in relation to the pleats that are still left on the right front piece. Here it could form one side of the low 'V', which can no longer be seen in this examination.

The fragment is kept between two sheets of glass held together by a black wooden frame (measuring 170x80 mm). For preservation

< Fig. 43.
Bodice of garment with the left sleeve preserved, dated to c. 1370. The threads in this vaðmál are probably spun from goat hair. On the front, and on a narrow panel at each side, a sewn pleat can be seen.

< Fig. 44.
Bodice, seen from the back. The remainder of a gusset is found on the relatively large sleeve, which probably has been sewn in again when the garment was lined in the 1920s. There is no pleat on the back.

Fig. 45.
Section of pleat on the right front piece. Each pleat is sewn as an inverted 'false seam' with the seam placed in the middle under the pleat and straight along the grain. The pleats are c. four mm deep.

Fig. 46. og Fig. 47.
A 135 mm long fragment from the V-formed neck opening. On the fragment the original border, folded diagonally to the sewn pleats, can be seen. Along the seam allowance on the reverse side there are remains of a three mm thick cord, which is the same as the finishing that can be seen on the sleeve-buttonhole side of the garment. (D10583) (See Fig. 23). Right side and reverse side.

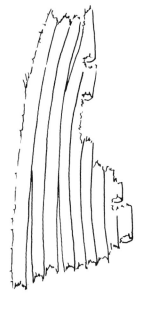

reasons, the fragment was not taken out of the glass framing during this examination.

Under the same number (D10590) there is a fragment, 520 mm long, 20 mm in width, flaring out to 345 mm, sewn in Greenlandic *vaðmál* in 2/2 twill. The state of preservation is so poor that the weft is only preserved in small segments. The present-day colour is blackish-brown. A small fragment of the same *vaðmál* is sewn on at the bottom of one side. As an extension of this, yet another fragment is glued on in the same weave and colour, but there are no threads connecting the latter fragment with the other pieces.

Border: At the wide end the largest fragment has a 10 mm wide seam allowance where a couple of (filler) threads held by overcast stitches hide the raw edge. This border sewing can be seen on other whole garments, among other places along the bottom edge. It is therefore possible that this fragment is from the 'skirt' for the pleated upper part D10590. The two textiles have the same thread count per cm.

Repairs: The reinforcing net was probably glued on in the 1920s.

Another 30 fragments of Greenlandic *vaðmál* in 2/2 twill are also numbered with D10590. The present-day colour is brown. The lar-gest fragment measures 270x265 mm. On one of the fragments one can see remains of an 11 mm wide singling sewn with 5-7 mm between the curves. The state of preservation is very poor. It must be accidental that these fragments have been given the same museum number as the above-mentioned garment parts; they have nothing to do with one another.

Nørlund No. 59. *(Fig. 50)*
Museum No. D6473

Part of a garment ('hip yoke') of Greenlandic *vaðmál* in 2/2 twill. The present-day colour is dark brown. The length is 460 mm and the width is 280 mm. The garment parts consists of two pieces which are sewn together with a 380 mm long seam lengthwise. On one piece the warp threads are parallel to the seam. On the other, a cut-off diagonal edge can be seen in the seam. These 'diagonal-against-straight' cut-offs at the lengthwise seams are something one sees on the whole garments.

Tablet-woven piped edging: A fragmentary tablet-woven piped edging can be seen on the longitudinal seam.

Pleats: Lengthwise, narrow sewn pleats cover almost a third (120 mm) of the garment parts in a transverse section at the top of the piece, and at the top edge the pleats are turned towards the reverse side with a 12-18 mm wide seam allowance, almost parallel with the weft. The seam allowance was originally sewn to the cloth, but only a few stitches of this seam have been preserved.

Nørlund writes that the pleats are like those one sees on D10590, but he does not consider the free edges of this garment part suitable as a neck or sleeve slit. He also writes that it is conceivable that the piece forms the skirt matching an upper garment.

The cutting of the two panels on this garment part, 'diagonal-against-straight', and the border sewn crosswise to the pleats, show that this is a piece from an independent skirt. It must thus be the 'first' known lower part of a medieval cut-off garment!

The garment part was sent in to the National Museum in Copenhagen in 1906 by the district medical officer H. Deichmann with the information that the piece was found in a grave at Herjolfsnæs.

Repairs: A net is glued under the whole piece as reinforcement. In addition there are many 'museum seams and darns' with yellowish-brown sewing thread, probably from the 1920s.

Fig. 50
Pleat fragment, probably a part of a skirt. Crosswise to, and above the pleats there is a 12-18 mm wide seam allowance with some few preserved stitches where it is sewn down.
This 'hip piece' is not woven in the same thread materials as the upper section of the garment (D10590). From the 1920s there are many darns with a yellow-brown thread, and a net has also been glued underneath.

Garment Type | Ie

Nørlund No. 60. *(Figs. 51-52)*
Museum No. D10591

Garment parts sewn in Greenlandic *vaðmál* in 2/2 twill, consisting of a fragmentary upper part and some side panels, four of which are sewn together while three are loose-lying. The present-day colour is brown, but originally the garment was dark grey. The upper part is 420 mm in

height measured on the best-preserved part. The sewn-together panels measure 410 mm in height and the fullness is 690 mm. Three loose panels measure 420x230 mm, 410x340 mm and 180x130 mm.

On the upper part there are 30-60 mm large fragments left of the sleeves, among other things the top of a sleeve gusset. The round neck opening, which measures 500 mm,

Fig. 51
Upper part of an original grey garment, 420 mm long. In the armholes there are remains of sleeves with gussets. In the middle of the front of the garment the neck opening is provided with a 100 mm long slit with four buttonholes on the left side. There are stab stitches on the neck and slit, and around the armhole.

has a 100 mm long slit in front which is torn apart below. In the left side of the slit there are four 12 mm long buttonholes. The top buttonhole is placed 15 mm from the neck opening, the others at intervals of 20-25 mm.

Stab stitching: Along the neck opening and slit there is a 7 mm wide seam allowance with stab stitching. A few millimetres from the armholes there is also stab stitching, sewn such that the stitches go through both the upper part and the sleeves (the fragments). The stab stitching continues from the armholes down along a side panel.

On the four sewn-together panels one can see a 10 mm wide seam allowance at the longitudinal seams, but the bottom hem only measures 7 mm.

Fig. 52
Upper part of garment seen from the back. Under the armhole in the right side it can be seen how beautifully the side panel has been placed in under the front piece and back. The side panel becomes narrower at the bottom, and this is emphasized by the stab stitches along the seam. The seam allowance at the bottom of the back is probably from the 1920s when the lining was set in.

191

Garment Type | If

Fig. 53

Child's garment sewn in a very densely woven Greenland vaðmál and in the same cut as an adult garment. The original colour was white. The garment is in a very poor state of preservation and decomposition is probably the reason for the missing sleeves. The V-formed neck opening must have come about in connection with the lining of the garment in the 1920s, where a net was also glued underneath.

Nørlund No. 61. *(Figs. 53-54)*
Museum No. D10592

Garment for a small child sewn in Greenlandic *vaðmál* in 2/2 twill. The present-day colour is light reddish-brown, but originally the garment was white. The garment consists of a front and back, each with a 350 mm high two-part gusset inserted. The length is 540 mm.

Two panels in each side increase the fullness of the garment to c. 1480 mm, but since the garment is very poorly preserved this measurement is uncertain. It is equally uncertain whether the garment had sleeves, and how the neck opening was shaped. Nørlund writes '… edged below with a thin cord which is sewn on with long darning stitches, forward and back'. In the examina-

tion in 1998 the cord mentioned was no longer there. It was probably the remains of a tablet-woven piped edging which – when the garment was found – was in the process of decomposition, leaving the characteristic 'cords'. The small garment is sewn in a fine, thin *vaðmál* (10/15 thr./cm) and would certainly have had beautiful borders. *In a coffin:* This was the only garment from the churchyard at

Herjolfsnæs to be found in a wooden coffin (Nørlund No. 15). On the chest lay a 210x160 mm wooden cross (Nørlund No. 154).

Repairs: There are new 'museum seams' everywhere, probably from the 1920s. A net has been glued on to the back of the garment. Later it was lined with brown shirting, and there are innumerable stitches with brown and black wool yarn. In addition repairs with grey and black sewing thread can be seen. A complete measurement of the garment is not possible, since it is too fragmentary.

Nørlund No. 62. *(Figs. 55-56)*
Museum No. D10593

Garment for a small child sewn in Greenlandic *vaðmál* in 2/2 twill. The present-day colour is reddish-brown, but originally the textile had a light grey warp and a white weft. The length is 495 mm and the fullness below is c. 980 mm, but since the garment is fragmentary this measurement is uncertain. The garment consists of a front piece and a back, each with a gusset inserted. The front has a piecing at 'yoke height'. In addition the 350 mm high gusset in the front piece is

composed of three pieces. The gusset on the back is 360 mm high and consists of one whole piece which is divided lengthwise by a 'false seam'. There are no side panels in this garment. Large parts of the back have disappeared, and no original borders are preserved.

Sleeves: There are added sleeves. The left one is 185 mm long, while the right one has only been pre-served to a length of 20-60 mm.

Restoration: In a restoration in the 1980s repairs from the 1920s were removed. These were 'museum seams', a glued-on net and a lining of shirting. Through this lining there were many darns with brown and black wool yarn, and with grey and black sewing thread. Instead the garment was underlaid with a thin dyed woollen material.

< Fig. 55.
The smallest of the three preserved children's garments has a length of 495 mm. The garment was originally light grey. The front has a piecing at 'yoke height'.

Fig. 56.
The child's garment seen from the back with the left sleeve being the best preserved. The sleeve length is 185 mm, but the original finishing at the bottom of the sleeve is missing. Restored in the 1980s.

Garment Type | II

Nørlund No. 63. *(Figs 57-61)*
Museum No. D10594

Garment sewn in Greenlandic *vaðmál* in 2/2 twill with buttoning down the middle front and with a small high collar. The present-day colour is dark brown, but originally both warp and weft were dyed almost black with an unidentified tannin dye. Along the front edge there are remains of a lighter, narrow edging in 2/1 twill, originally madder-coloured.

The garment consists of eight panels, narrow above and flaring to a total fullness of 3000 mm. The length is 1050 mm.

Each panel has an edge on the straight grain and a side edge cut off diagonally, placed by the seams such that a diagonal edge touches a

Fig. 57.
The so-called button garment with a small upright collar was almost completely black originally. It is dated to c. 1350. A narrow madder dyed border is sewn along the left side of the garment where 19 buttonholes – 16 in the upper and three in the bottom part – can also be seen. On the opposite side there are no visible holes or stitches from buttons, which must have been there. The edge of the button side is finished with stab stitches.

Fig. 58.

The button garment seen from the back. At the middle seam both panels are cut diagonally. The sleeves have been sewn in wrongly during restoring in the 1980s, and the finishing at the bottom of the best-preserved sleeve is likewise incorrect. The gusset should sit c. 80 mm from the shoulder seam. A large fragment with tablet-woven piped edging is placed at the bottom of the right side. The border shows that the fragment is a piece of the lower part of the garment.

straight one. In the middle front and middle back the panels are joined in the opposite way, i.e. the front edges are on the straight grain and the edges at the seam in the middle back are diagonal. Most of the right-half of the garment and a large piece of the left-half have disappeared. A loose-lying fragment with the same museum number, weave and colour as the garment has a hem which shows that the fragment is from the bottom part of the garment.

The collar, cut from one layer of *vaðmál*, is 27 mm high, but was probably once higher since it is now worn away at the top.

Buttonholes: In the left front edge of the garment there are 19 button-holes, 3 below and 16 above, including one in the collar. The bottom one is 140 mm from the present edge of the garments, the next two are placed at intervals of 16-17 mm. The other 16 buttonholes are spread over 265 mm, measured from the top on the collar with intervals of 15-18 mm. The length of the buttonholes is c. 15 mm, and no seams are preserved around them.

The sleeves: Of the right sleeve the top half is preserved. The left sleeve

Fig. 59
Section of button garment. The buttonholes are 15 mm long and placed at intervals of 16-17 mm. There is no visible trace of sewing around the buttonholes.

is intact. It is 570 mm long, sewn together from a dark brown and a light brown *vaðmál* with a transverse seam at elbow height. Two gussets have been inserted, one in the top back and one just above the slit at the bottom of the sleeve. In the sleeve seam down towards the wrist there is a 100 mm long slit, but without any original seam preserved. It is therefore uncertain whether the slit was there from the beginning.

Stab stitching: The garment was undoubtedly decorated with stab stitching along all seams. One can still see this seam along the bottom edge of the collar and along most longitudinal seams from the shoulder and 110-180 mm down. In addition there is stab stitching at the shoulder seams, at the sleeve seams and at the top gusset. In a few places, however, there are only holes and remains of thread from the stab stitching. Along the right front edge, where the buttons must have been (no buttons have been preserved), the garment has a 6 mm seam allowance through which there is stab stitching, with overcast stitches over the raw edge on the reverse side.

Tablet-woven piped edging: The loose-lying fragment, which during a restoration was placed at the bottom of the back on the right side panel, has tablet-woven piped edging preserved which shows that it is the original bottom hem of the garment.

Decorative border: Around the left front edge (the buttonhole edge) there are remains of a lighter edge in a finer weave (2/1 twill, originally madder-coloured). The decorative border measures 4 mm in width on the right side and is two millimetres wider on the reverse side. The border is so poorly preserved that it is not possible to see whether there were seam allowances along the edges.

Nørlund writes that the garment had a lighter brown edging along both front edges and the collar edge.

In the 1980s the collar was much worn, and the edging mentioned was not there any longer with the exception of a few small sections at the left front.

It is doubtful whether there was any bordering at all on the right edge, since this is beautifully hemmed with stab stitching. Nørlund also writes that when the garment was found, it had been cut to pieces and used as a shroud – for example, the sleeves were wrapped around the feet of the corpse. However, a few original seams are preserved under the new ones, and the garment must therefore have been more or less intact.

Restoration: Several 'museum darns', a glued-on net and lining of brown shirting were removed when the garment was restored in the 1980. Instead the garment was lined with a dyed thin woollen material. During the restoration the sleeves were loosened and sewn on again such that the back gusset is now – incorrectly – adjacent to the

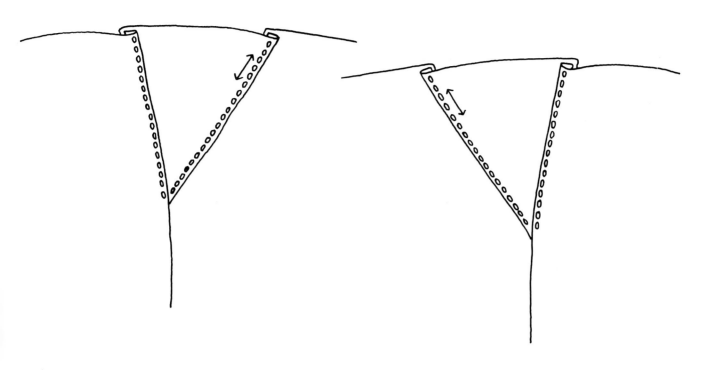

Fig. 61a+b.

The gussets of the sleeves, when sewn in, were laid under the front part of the sleeve where stab stitches can be seen. The hindmost gusset seam (on the grain, marked with an arrow) lies on top of the sleeve. On the opposite sleeve the insertion of the gusset and the sewing are laterally reversed.

Fig. 60

Drawing from Nørlund's book, Buried Norsemen at Herjolfsnes, *which perhaps shows the original shape of the sleeve.*

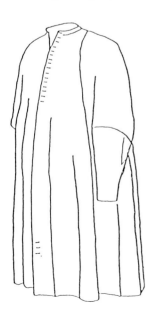

shoulder seam. Whether the placing of the sleeves in the 1920s with the gusset some centimetres from the shoulder seam, as we can see on a picture, was more correct we cannot know, since the sleeves were found, as mentioned above, wrapped round the feet of the corpse. The great fullness of the sleeve is due to the restoration in the 1980s. The drawing of the garment in *Buried Norsemen at Herjolfsnes* (p. 129) probably shows the original design. A reconstruction of the garment has shown that it gives a better fit when the sleeves are placed as they were on the sewn-together version from the 1920s.

During the restoration the above-mentioned loose-lying fragment was also sewn on lining with no direct connection with the garment, since it is not possible to see its original placing.

Nørlund No. 64. *(Figs. 62-63)*
Museum No. D10595

Garment sewn in Greenlandic *vaðmál* in 2/2 twill with buttoning in the middle front. The present-day colour is light brown, the original colour of the garment. The garment is of the same type as D10594 above, with a total of eight panels. Sleeves and collar have disappeared, and the garment is in a very poor state of preservation. The length in front is 1135 mm and at the back 1240 mm. The difference in the two lengths is partly due to the fact that the panels at the back seam are cut off diagonally, while the front is on the straight grain at the middle. The fullness at the bottom was c. 3200 mm, but since large parts of the side panels are missing, this is uncertain.

Buttonholes: There are 12 buttonholes – possibly 13 – in the left side of the garment, distributed over 270 mm. The thirteenth, top buttonhole, which is 10 mm from the

Fig. 62

The button garment in a light brown colour with the same cut as garment (D10594). The finishing edge on the sleeves and neck is missing. Like the above-named garment, the buttonholes are placed with the majority at the top and some few at the bottom. The front edges are cut on the straight grain and finished with very narrow seam allowances, through which fine stab stitches are sewn.

present neck edge, is doubtful, since the front edge is very fragmentary up towards the neck. In addition there are two buttonholes below, placed 240 mm and 262 mm respectively from the bottom edge. There are no buttonholes in the piece in between, as on the garment D10594.

The 12 mm long buttonholes are cut parallel to the weft threads and are at intervals of 20-22 mm. Only the bottom two and one of the top ones are relatively intact out towards the edge. The others are

worn away. There is no trace of any seam around the buttonholes.

Stab stitching: Along the buttonhole edge in the left side of the garment stab stitching has been sewn outermost in two rows through a 6 mm wide seam allowance. But the seam with overcast stitches which otherwise always accompanies the stab stitching is not there. It may however have been worn off, since the seam allowance is much frayed.

On the opposite side – the button side – there is stab stitching sewn

through a 7 mm wide seam allowance with close overcast stitches over the raw edge on the back. At the front edge in the top half one can see holes as if from needle or thread, but the holes are not at regular intervals, and it cannot be demonstrated that these holes are traces of the sewing-on of buttons.

Stab stitching: Along the left armhole on the back, 85 mm of stab stitching has been preserved.

Nørlund writes about the garment that it was cut up and incomplete. The sleeves had disappeared except for a small piece (25-30 mm) at the top of the right sleeve, and the collar was missing. In addition he writes that the garment was mended with large ugly patches, especially at the front.

Repairs: There are 'museum seams' in all seams, where the patches are sewn on, at the neck edge and at the bottom edge, probably from the 1920s. In addition the garment is lined with brownish shirting, to which it has been darned with a brownish wool yarn.

Beautiful garment: Despite the poor state of preservation it is still possible to see that it was once a very handsome garment. The weave is close and the threads are of fine quality.

Fig. 63
The back of the button garment with panels that are diagonally cut against the middle seam. There are large sections missing, but the preserved parts are witness to the excellent workmanship and beautiful weave of the garment.

Hoods Type | I

Nørlund No. 65. *(Fig. 64)*
Museum No. D10596

Liripipe hood with shoulder cape of Greenlandic *vaðmál* in 2/2 twill. The present colour is brownish-black, the original colour of the hood. The length is 455 mm. At the bottom of the shoulder cape at the middle front and middle back a smallish gusset has been inserted, which increases the fullness to 1260 mm. The liripipe is sewn together from two pieces to a length of 400 mm, of which the top piece measures 135 mm and is sewn in with the reverse side (S-twill) outwards. The liripipe hood differs from the other Norse hoods in having large head dimensions and a relatively wide – 200 mm – liripipe, which is sewn on to the top of the diagonally cut-off hood. The hood cape is longest at the back. The liripipe

Fig. 64
Hood with shoulder cape and broad liripipe. Stab stitches along the face opening. Poul Nørlund considered the hood to be the oldest of those preserved in that it has a slightly clumsy appearance. The upper part, an extension of the liripipe, has been sewn in with the reverse side out – a mistake which has only happened a couple of times in all the Herjolfsnæs material.
Before restoring.

203

hood is not intact: in several places large or small pieces are missing.

Stab stitching: Two rows of stab stitching can be seen along the face edge, sewn through a 7 mm wide seam allowance which is sewn with close overcast stitches to the reverse side. At the back gusset there is a very narrow piecing, attractively sewn in. This seam and the stab

Fig. 65
Hood with shoulder cape and a 500 mm long liripipe, of which the outermost 330 mm is additional. The hood has originally been white. Sewing along the edges has disappeared. Restored in the 1980s.

stitching are the only originals. Nørlund writes that this hood is probably the oldest of the preserved hoods from Herjolfsnæs.

Repairs: Most of the seams are 'museum seams'. A net is glued under the hood. The net is attached all the way in under the bottom edge of the hood, after which the cloth is turned. In addition the hood is lined with brownish-mauve shirting. The repairs are presumably from the 1920s.
Restoration: In a restoration in 1994 the old linings and most darns were removed. Instead the hood was lined with a dyed wool material.

Nørlund No. 66. *(Fig. 65)*
Museum No. D10597

Liripipe hood with shoulder cape sewn in Greenlandic *vaðmál* in 2/2 twill. The present-day colour is reddish-brown, but originally the hood was white, with the warp threads possibly tannin-dyed.

The height is 685 mm, and the fullness below 1400 mm. The width of the liripipe is 40-60 mm and the length is 500 mm, of which 170 mm is cut in one with the hood. A 195 mm high gusset has been inserted in the middle-front of the shoulder cape. Parts of the left front edge and large sections on both sides of the

hood have disappeared. The original hem along the bottom edge has also disappeared.

Restoration: In a restoration in the 1980s a lining of shirting and 'museum darns' from the 1920s were removed, and the hood was lined with a fine dyed wool material.

Nørlund No. 67. *(Fig. 66)*
Museum No. D10598

Liripipe hood with shoulder cape sewn in Greenlandic *vaðmál* in 2/2 twill. The present-day colour is reddish-brown, but originally the weave had a light grey warp and a white weft. The height is 600 mm, and the fullness at the bottom is 1540 mm. The width of the liripipe is 45 mm and the length is 500 mm, of which 230 mm is cut in one piece with the hood. A 140 mm high gusset has been inserted in the middle front of the hood cape. Along the face edge there are traces of a selvedge, but one can see no seam. Large sections along the face opening and on the right side of the hood have disappeared. At the bottom edge a few original sewing threads are preserved, probably from the hem. One can see some loose threads at the edges.

Repairs: The hood is lined with brown shirting, with many 'museum darns' in brown and black wool yarn, and thin cotton threads through it. The repairs are probably from the 1920s.

Fig. 66
Hood with shoulder cape and liripipe of which the outermost 270 mm is an addition. Along the face opening there are the remains of a selvedge, which has not been turned. Lined in the 1920s. In connection with a later exhibition, the lining – which had obviously faded – was repaired with aquarelle colour. Nobody gave a thought to the fact that the threads in the hood had also received too much light. The hood was displayed again.

Nørlund No. 68.
Museum No. D10599

Fragmentary hood with shoulder cape sewn in Greenlandic *vaðmál* in linen repp. The present-day colour is reddish-brown, but originally the hood was white. Only one side is relatively intact, and there the height is 470 mm. The width is 260 mm. The liripipe measures 55 mm in width and of the length a 100 mm long fragment is preserved. It is cut in one piece with the hood. A few stitches have been preserved at the face opening and the crown and neck seams.

Nørlund writes that there was probably a gusset in the middle front, and the hood thus belongs to the group with a shoulder cape.

Nørlund No. 69.
Registered but not preserved

Nørlund No. 70. *(Fig. 67)*
Museum No. D10600

Hood with shoulder cape and liripipe sewn in Greenlandic *vaðmál* in 2/2 twill. The present-day colour is dark brown, the original colour of the hood. The height is 515 mm, and the fullness is 1280 mm measured along the bottom edge. The liripipe is 870 mm long, 15 mm wide. In the middle front a 100 mm high gusset has been inserted, with the reverse side (S-twill grain) facing outward.

The hood differs from all the others in being cut diagonally to the weave, making its shape 'rounder'. The narrow whip-like liripipe is also cut diagonally. No original hems are preserved.

Restoration: In a restoration in 1997 old lining and 'museum darns' from the 1920s were removed, and the hood is instead (partly) lined with a fine brown wool material.

Hoods Type | II

Nørlund No. 71. *(Fig. 68)*
Museum No. D10601

Hood sewn in Greenlandic *vaðmál* in 2/2 twill. The present-day colour is dark brown, but originally the hood was almost black. The height is 400 mm, and the fullness along the bottom edge is 1085 mm. Shoulder gussets have been inserted

on each side of the hood. The left one measures 140 mm in height and the right one 130 mm. Both gussets consist of up to four pieces. In addition there are two piecings at the bottom of the left side of the hood – towards the chin seam. The hood is cut above with a slope that rises slightly from the neck towards the face opening. There are marks of

Fig. 68
A poorly preserved hood. The hole at the top, by the neck, indicates that a liripipe was once there. Wear marks from a turned-back front edge can be seen close to the face opening, which is finished with two rows of stab stitches. At the bottom, remains of a footweaving can be found, with ten warp threads and eight weft threads per cm.

wear from a seam allowance of the front edge at a distance of 20-30 mm from it. The liripipe is no longer there, but there is a hole at the top by the neck, which shows that there was a liripipe. On the right side of the hood up towards the crown seam a patch has been inserted. In addition there are many breaks and holes in the textile.

Fig. 69
Hood with strange holes above the gussets. The holes were probably cut to give the hood more fullness, thereby making it easier to pull over the head. The textile is so close that the weft threads completely cover the warp threads.

Stab stitching: At the face opening the hood is edged with two rows of stab stitching, sewn through a 7 mm wide seam allowance, which is sewn down with close overcast stitches to the hood.

Footweaving: The bottom edge of the hoods is bordered with a 10 mm wide footweaving.

Repairs: There are 'museum seams' on the crown, under the chin, along the back of the neck and at the patch – probably done in the 1920s. The other seams are original. In addition a net has been glued to the back of the hood, as well as a lining with brown shirting. Finally,

there are many 'museum darns' with brown and black wool yarn.

Nørlund No. 72. *(Fig. 69)*
Museum No. D10602

Hood sewn in Greenlandic *vaðmál* in 2/2 twill. The present-day colour is dark brown, but originally the textile had a light grey warp and a white weft. The height is 440 mm and the fullness along the bottom edge is 1200 mm. The liripipe, which is 600 mm long, 35 mm wide, is cut with the weft threads in the longitudinal direction of the liripipe. Two 150 mm high shoulder gussets have been inserted. No orig-

inal hems are preserved. At the top by the shoulder gussets there are two large holes, which seem to have been formed deliberately. The hood is much worn.

Repairs: There are 'museum seams' in all seams, and on the hood there are many darns with brown and black wool yarn, probably from the 1920s. A net is glued on the back.

Nørlund No. 73. *(Fig. 70)*
Museum No. D10603

Hood of Greenlandic *vaðmál* in 2/2 twill. The present colour is brownish, but originally the hood had a lighter brown colour. The height is

420 mm, and the fullness measured along the bottom edges is 1120 mm. Two 150 mm high shoulder gussets in a coarser *vaðmál* have been inserted. The left side of the hood is transversely sewn together from two pieces. One can see the seam at a distance of 65 mm from the point of the gusset.

The liripipe is no longer there, but the hood has torn-off edges where the liripipe once was. Above the middle forehead a piece is also missing. In general the hood is poor-

ly preserved on the sides around the top points of the gussets.

Stab stitching: At the face opening one can see two rows of stab stitching sewn through an 8 mm wide seam allowance, held in place by close overcast stitches which sew the raw edge down to the hood. Under the stitches on the back, one or two (filler) threads have been laid.

Footweaving: Along the bottom edge there are a few traces of footweaving to a length of 6-7 mm.

Repairs: The hood is lined with mauve shirting, and all seams are sewn through with 'museum seams', probably from the 1920s.

Nørlund No. 74. *(Fig. 71)*
Museum No. D10604

A hood sewn in Greenlandic *vaðmál* in 2/2 twill. The present-day colour is dark brown, but originally the textile had a grey warp and an almost white weft. The height is 370 mm and the fullness along the bottom edge is c. 1210 mm., but since only the left shoulder gusset has been preserved, this measurement is uncertain. The gusset measures 130 mm in height, but was once higher, since the top point is missing. The gusset seems very large for the relatively short hood, and one can see many errors in the weaving, for example two wefts in the same shed. The liripipe is missing, and the hood is fragmentary

Fig. 71
This hood was originally light grey in colour. The right side gusset, a large piece of the crown and a liripipe are missing. Under the chin the textile has disintegrated and it is not possible to see the original cut. During restoring in the 1980s the hood has been lined, but not sewn together at the front, which incorrectly has given the impression that it was perhaps a so-called open hood.

under the chin and at the top of the crown. No original hems are preserved. Nørlund writes that it is the only hood where he is uncertain as to whether it had a liripipe. In this examination no remains of stitching for any liripipe were observed.

Restoration: In a restoration in the 1980s lining and 'museum darns' from the 1920s were removed, and a dyed lining in fine wool material was sewn in the hood. In that connection the hood was opened up in front but not sewn together again. This is wrong, however, and has given rise to the misunderstanding that the hood is an 'open' hood.

Nørlund No. 75 *(Fig. 72)*

Fragmentary liripipe hood sewn in Greenlandic *vaðmál* in 2/2 twill. The present-day colour is reddish, but originally the hood was white. The height is 445 mm and the fullness below is c. 630 mm. Both liripipe and side gussets have disappeared, but there is no doubt that the hood had both. In addition a large section is missing on the left side of the hood.

Nørlund writes that the hood was dug out of a slope at Herjolfsnæs Churchyard in 1900 by the district medical officer Gustav Meldorf from Julianehåb. The hood was

acquired by the National Museum in Copenhagen along with the garments D8080 and D8081.

Repairs: There are 'museum seams' in all seams and some darns with black wool yarn. The hood has also been lined with brown shirting, probably in the 1920s.

Fig. 72
This poorly preserved hood was excavated from Herjolfsnæs churchyard in 1900. It was originally white. The gussets and the liripipe have disappeared. The lining is from the 1920s.

Nørlund No. 76. *(Fig. 73)*
Museum No. D10585.2

Liripipe hood of Greenlandic *vaðmál* in 2/2 twill. The present-day colour is brownish-black, and the textile has a very shiny appearance. The height is 420 mm. The fullness along the bottom edge is 1080 mm. On each side of the hood a shoulder gusset has been inserted, cut below in wide round curves that 'stand out' from the hood.

The hood is cut above with a gradient that rises slightly from the back of the neck forward to the face opening. The liripipe has disappeared leaving a small fragment at the top.

Stab stitching: At the face opening the hood is bordered with stab stitching in one or possibly two rows, sewn through an 8 mm wide seam allowance, which is sewn down with close overcast stitches to the hood.

Footweaving: In a few places along the bottom edge of the hood, a few centimetres of a 7 mm wide foot-weaving are preserved.

Nørlund writes that the hood was found along with the garment D10585.1.

Repairs: There are 'museum seams' in the neck seam, but the other seams are original. On the back the hood has a net glued on, and above this a lining of brown shirting, probably from the 1920s. A number of 'museum darns' with brown wool yarn can be seen in several places.

Nørlund No. 77. *(Figs. 74-75)*
Museum No. D10605

Hood sewn in Greenlandic *vaðmál* in 2/2 twill. The present-day colour is greyish-brown, but originally the textile had a grey warp and a white weft. The height is 410 mm, and the fullness along the bottom edge is 940 mm. Two 110 mm high shoulder gussets have been inserted. The hood is cut such that from the crown to the face opening it rises slightly upwards into a 'horn'. The liripipe is no longer present.

Stab stitching: The original hems at the face and at the bottom of the hood have been preserved. Both edges have two rows of stab stitching, sewn through a 7 mm wide seam allowance, which is sewn down with close overcast stitches to the hood.

Fig. 73
Shiny, worn hood, woven from the finest combed fleece, which is still glossy after six hundred years in the earth. The wide shoulder gussets, and the crown which rises beautifully from the neck towards the forehead, have given the hood a handsome cut. A piece of the liripipe is still left, as well as the remains of footweaving at the bottom edge.

Fig. 74
The seam at the neck, seen from the reverse side.
The seam is only 7 mm in breadth. Similar narrow seam
allowances can be seen at the bottom edge.

Fig. 75
Beautifully shaped and well-preserved hood in spite of the missing
liripipe. The height is 410 mm. There are stab stitches at the face
opening and along the bottom edge. The weaving is close, with 12 weft
threads per cm.

Nørlund writes that there are various traces that show the liripipe was sewn on according to the same principle as hood D10606.

Restoration: In a restoration in the 1980s, lining and 'museum darns' from the 1920s were removed, and the hood was lined with a fine dyed woollen material.

Nørlund No. 78. *(Fig. 76)*
Museum No. D10606

Hood sewn in Greenlandic *vaðmál* in 2/2 twill. The present-day colour is dark reddish-brown, but originally the hood had a light grey warp and a white weft. The height is 400 mm, and the fullness along the bottom edge is 950 mm. Two 85 mm high shoulder gussets have been inserted. The added liripipe is 695 mm long, 55 mm wide. It is sewn together from two pieces with seams above and below the liripipe. In addition there is a piecing at a distance of 235 mm from the outermost end. The hood is cut such that from the crown forward to the face opening it rises slightly upwards into a 'horn'.

Stab stitching: The original finishing edges at the face and on the shoulder are preserved. Both have two rows of stab stitching, sewn through a 7 mm and a 9 mm narrow hem. The hem is sewn down with close overcast stitches. There are wear-marks 15-40 mm from the face opening, caused by turning back the front edge of the hood.

Fig. 76
The best preserved of all the hoods. Originally it had a delicate light grey colour. Both the face opening and the bottom edge are beautifully finished with two rows of stab stitches.

Almost all the seams are original.

Nørlund writes that the hood belonged with a shroud – probably for a child – which was so poorly preserved that it could not be taken

Fig. 77
Hood with a little piece of the liripipe still visible, and a crown seam that rises upward in a 'horn' to the front over the forehead. Stab stitches are preserved at the shoulder edge and along the face opening where wear-marks from a seam allowance can also be seen.

up intact from the excavation. A number of rags were however taken out: most were of no interest, although three of them could be identified as parts from the left shoulder of the garment No. 45 (D10587).

Restoration: In a restoration in the 1980s the net, lining and 'museum darns' from the 1920s were removed. Instead the hood was lined with a fine dyed wool material.

Nørlund No. 79. *(Figs. 77-78)*
Museum No. D10607

Hood sewn in Greenlandic *vaðmál* in 2/2 twill. The present-day colour is dark brown, but originally the hood was light grey. The height is 340 mm, and the fullness along the bottom edge is 830 mm. Two 65 mm high shoulder gussets have been inserted. The 30 mm wide liripipe has been torn off leaving a 35 mm long piece. The small fragment of liripipe is sewn to the hood with stab

Fig. 78
Section showing a small liripipe piece laid in under the
hood at the neck seam. The visible seam is that of the
crown.

Fig. 79
Child's hood, once white, with the same cut as several
of the adult hoods and with a crown seam that rises
towards a 'horn' above the forehead. Very beautiful
finishing edges at the face opening and at the bottom of
the hood.

stitching, and one can see a seam on the underside. The hood is cut such that from the crown forward to the face opening it rises slightly upwards into a 'horn'. There are wearmarks from rolling back the front edge 20-30 mm from this, and the original hems at the face and shoulder have been preserved.

Stab stitching: Both edges have two rows of stab stitching, sewn through 7 mm wide seam allowances, which are sewn down with close overcast stitches to the hood. The poorest preserved is the stab stitching along the shoulder edge.

Repairs: One can see many 'museum darns' with brown and black wool yarn and some seams with grey and black cotton sewing thread, for example under the chin, probably from the 1920s. The hood is in a relatively good state of preservation and has therefore never had a net glued on or been lined with shirting.

Weight: 120 g.

Nørlund No. 80. *(Figs. 79-82)*
Museum No. D10608

Child's hood sewn in Greenlandic *vaðmál* in 2/2 twill. The present-day colour is dark reddish-brown, but the hood would originally have been almost white. The height is 340 mm, and the fullness along the bottom edge is 670 mm. Two 90 mm high shoulder gussets have been inserted. The added liripipe, which is 470 mm long, 20 mm wide, is cut with the weft threads in the longitudinal direction of the liripipe and with a seam on the underside of the liripipe. The hood is cut such that it rises up at the back in a high neck, and at the front in a small 'horn'.

Stab stitching: The original hems at the face and shoulder have been preserved. At the face edge two rows of stab stitching are sewn through a 7 mm wide seam allowance which is sewn down with close overcast stitches to the hood.

Footweaving: The bottom edge is finished with a 7 mm wide foot-

weaving above a singling, which has however only been preserved in a few places.

Nørlund writes that the cap No. 86 (D10608) lay inside the hood, and that the two items of headgear had been used together. In addition, at the same place some garment parts were found, of which the following could be identified: the bottom of a sleeve with an 80 mm long slit, parts of a stocking leg and remains of a stocking foot and a piece of a liripipe. Nørlund adds that it was not possible to assemble these different fragments so that they could form any kind of garment.

Repairs: One can see 'museum darns' with brown and black wool yarn, and there are some seams with grey sewing thread in cotton, probably from the 1920s. The hood is in a relatively good state of preservation and has therefore never had a net glued under it or been lined with shirting.

Weight: 125 g

Fig. 80
Section of two rows of stab stitches at the face opening. The very narrow seam allowance, with sewing, is seen from the right side (overlying part) and from the reverse side. The close overcast stitching is sewn over a thick (filler) thread in such a way that the edge is also decorative on the reverse side – visible if the hood's front edge is rolled back.

Fig. 81
Section of footweaving along the bottom edge at the left gusset. The footweaving has eight warp threads and seven weft threads per cm. The sewing thread is two-ply, possibly spun and twisted goat's hair.

Fig. 82
Section of the footweaving seen from the reverse side where there are traces of a singling under the footweaving. The singling is sewn flat into the weave in 6-8 mm long bows.

Nørlund No. 81.
Museum No. D10609

Fragmentary hood sewn in Greenlandic *vaðmál* in tabby weave. The present-day colour is dark brown. The height is 410 mm, and the width is 280 mm. The loose-lying liripipe is 480 mm long, 25-30 mm wide. Parallel with the neck seam one can see a 40-50 mm wide stripe formed from light-coloured warp threads.

Stab stitching: At the face opening there are remains of a hem with two rows of stab stitching, sewn through a 6-8 mm wide seam allowance. Tight overcast stitches with a thick (filler) thread laid in below hide the cut-off edge of the seam allowance at the back.

Nørlund writes that the hood is cut such that it has a smallish 'horn' at the front, and that it once had side gussets. Roots had grown all the way through it.

Nørlund No. 82.
Museum No. D12790

Fragment of liripipe sewn in Greenlandic *vaðmál* in 2/2 twill. The present-day colour is reddish-brown. The fragment is the outermost 170 mm of a 30 mm wide liripipe sewn together on the underside and with a beautifully formed rounding at the end. Nørlund writes that this end piece was found in the National Museum's stores, and it is from an excavation at Herjolfsnæs, perhaps from Kielsen's excavation in 1840.

'Pill-Box' Caps

Nørlund No. 83. *(Fig. 83)*
Museum No. D10610

Cap sewn in Greenlandic *vaðmál* in 2/2 twill. The present-day colour is dark brown, but originally the cap was almost white. It consists of a circular crown sewn together of two parts, with a diameter of 170 mm and with a 100-120 mm high edge sewn to the crown. The edge also consists of two pieces sewn together. The fullness along the bottom edge is 580 mm.

Seams: At the bottom of the cap a few overcast stitches are preserved. The other seams are new.

Nørlund writes that one piece of the crown is much worn and patched, first with one patch and then with another patch.

Restoration: In a restoration in the 1980s the cap was lined with fine woollen cloth. At that time only one patch was noted below the crown.

Nørlund No. 84.

Registered but not preserved.

Fig. 83
The adult 'pill-box' cap (D10610) on the left, and a child's 'pill-box' cap (D10611) on the right, were originally white and brown-flecked, respectively. The child's cap is woven with threads that were spun with goat hair. Both crowns are in two parts. Restored in the 1980s.

Nørlund No. 85. *(Fig. 83)*
Museum No. D10611

Child's cap sewn in Greenlandic *vaðmál* in 2/2 twill. The present-day colour is brown, but originally the textile had a dark brown warp and a light brown weft. Both warp and weft threads are spun from goat hair. The cap consists of a two-part oval crown, diameter 120-150 mm, with a relatively high edge of 950 mm sewn to the crown. The fullness below, where one sees a 7 mm wide seam allowance, is 430 mm.

Restoration: In connection with a restoration in the 1980s a glued-on net and various 'museum seams' from the 1920s were removed and the cap was lined with a fine dyed wool material. The state of preservation is very poor; the weft threads in particular have decomposed.

Nørlund No. 86. *(Fig. 84)*
Museum No. D10608

A child's cap sewn in Greenlandic *vaðmál* in 2/2 twill. The present-day colour is dark brown, but originally the textile had a grey warp and a light grey weft, which was later dyed reddish with korkje, a lichen dye.

The cap has a circular crown with a diameter of 180 mm, sewn to an edge that consists of four 850-900 mm high sewn-together pieces of *vaðmál* of various grades. The fullness along the bottom edge is 500 mm. The crown is divided into two unequal large halves by a 'false seam'. Its circumference is rather greater than that of the edge, and the crown is folded over 20-25 mm before the seam for the edge begins.

The edge is finished at the bottom with a 50 mm wide unsewn seam allowance towards the reverse side.

Nørlund writes that the cap was found inside the child's hood D10608.

Restoration: In a restoration in the 1980s lining and 'museum seams' from the 1920s were removed, and the cap was lined with a fine dyed wool material.

Fig. 84
Child's 'pill-box' cap, originally light grey but dyed later with korkje (lichen dye), has a crown that is divided crosswise with a false seam. The cap has the same number as the child's hood as it was found inside the hood.

Nørlund No. 87. *(Figs. 85-87)*
Museum No. D10612

A hat sewn in Greenlandic *vaðmál* in tabby weave (repp) and in 2/2 twill. The present-day colour is light brown, but originally the hat had black and dark brown (tannin-dyed) warp threads with a white or light brown weft. The warp threads, which run crosswise to the cap, are spun from a combed hair material, possibly from a goat. The weft threads are spun from under-wool that contains the remains of root ends, which means that the wool was plucked and not shorn from the sheep.

The hat can be described as a round-crowned 'cap' with a height of c. 270 mm. The high sides are formed from two pieces of 70 mm and 190 mm respectively. At the top, on the crown, the narrowest piece is sewn on, after which the other piece is sewn on. At the side

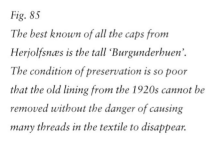

Fig. 85

The best known of all the caps from Herjolfsnæs is the tall 'Burgunderhuen'. The condition of preservation is so poor that the old lining from the 1920s cannot be removed without the danger of causing many threads in the textile to disappear.

Fig. 86

The tall brimless hat is sewn in a tabby weave (repp), with the warp threads running crosswise, and a twill-weave. Likewise, the two-part crown is a combination of two different weaves. A couple of threads from a singling are preserved at the bottom edge. This sewing shows that the hat's highest measurement, 270 mm, is the original height.

Fig. 87
Section of a piece with many thread-ends tied
together. Was a striped effect wished or were
the thread-ends used to be economic? The
dark and shiny warp threads are probably
spun of goat hair.

seam the wide piece flares slightly outward. A 130 mm high, 130 mm wide twill-woven gusset increases the fullness downwards. The gusset is inserted opposite the side seam.

The circular crown, diameter 150 mm, consists of two halves sewn together, one of which is tabby (repp), the other twill-woven. The repp-woven parts of the cap are unevenly woven and in several places the warp threads lie in pairs.

Striped: A striped effect in the warp direction can be seen in three places: in a 140x200 mm section on the bottom part of the cap; on the top narrow piece; and on the crown. The stripes were obtained by alternately using light and dark threads. The warp threads in the same area are in many cases tied one to the next. Whether this striping was deliberate or accidental one cannot tell. Perhaps the explanation is that for reasons of thrift the remains of

thread were used. When the hat was new the close weft probably covered both knots and stripes, but because of wear after use at Herjolfsnæs, or use in displays in Copenhagen, knots and stripes have now become visible.

Nørlund writes that some textile material was found inside the hat. This might be the remains of an item of headgear of another kind which could not be preserved. Nørlund further observes that the bottom edge of the cap has disappeared, and that it is very poorly preserved. He does not think that the hat had any wide (outside) seam allowance because of the gusset, but he does add that there are suggestions of a very narrow (inside) seam allowance, widest in front and narrowest at the back.

In the examination in 1998 it could be established that the hat is in an extremely poor state of preservation, and that possible wear-

marks have disappeared. In a few places there are traces of a 'singling' at the bottom edge of the hat, and since this seam on the other Norse garments and caps is a hem, this must mean that the hat has preserved its original height.

Repairs: There are 'museum seams' everywhere and many darns with black and brown wool yarn. A net is glued on the back of the hat, and it is also lined with mauve shirting lengthened at a missing section at the bottom with brownish shirting.

Stockings

Nørlund No. 88. *(Fig. 88)*
Museum No. D10613

Stocking sewn in Greenlandic *vað-mál* in 2/2 twill. The present-day colour is dark brown, but originally the textile was almost black with a few white warp threads distributed over a 50 mm wide strip at the top of the leg and above the foot. The stocking, which is cut diagonally to the cloth, measures 880 mm in length from the top angle to the tip of the toe. The fullness measured across the top of the leg is 550 mm. The stocking is cut such that the cloth above forms a right angle with a selvedge on one side and a narrow seam allowance on the other side. Along the selvedge a narrow gusset was added, which has not been preserved in its full length. The seam of the stocking is in the middle of the back. When the stocking is put on, the right angle forms the point at which it is fastened to a belt or a garment. The stocking foot consists of six pieces, the two longest of which continue from midway below the foot around the heel up into the leg. Three pieces start from one and the same point under the sole.

Fig. 88
Two stockings, which possibly belonged together. They are twill woven, cut diagonally to the cloth and have piecings at the top of the shank. The feet consist of many pieces, especially the poorly preserved. The best-preserved stocking, which measures 880 mm from the top angle to the tip of the toe, has originally been almost black, while the other has been greyish.

D10613   D10614

223

Fig. 89

The longest stocking in the illustration is woven in tabby weave and has two slits, which were necessary to allow the stocking to be pulled up onto the leg. A tabby weave of this type is not very elastic and therefore was not an especially suitable weave for stockings. The short 'stocking' is a practice piece.

The fourth is a 'heel'. (See p. 297). The stocking foot is open at the toes, but to what extent this is the original opening is difficult to decide.

Stab stitching: There is stab stitching along the 8 mm wide seam al-

lowance at the top of the leg.

Nørlund writes that there are two vents at the bottom of the leg which divide it into three 'flaps'. The two outermost meet behind and under the heel, while the middle incomplete flap lay over the foot. He also writes that the seam in the foot under the heel is a later repair, and that it has nothing to do with the original cut.

When one compares Nørlund's description with the existing stocking and the scale drawing, a number of irregularities become evident. Few of the original seams are preserved, and it is doubtful whether all the pieces were found and assembled correctly in the 1920s. The stocking is glued to a net and was later lined with shirting to which it is sewn with black wool yarn.

Nørlund thinks that this stocking forms a pair with the stocking D10614, since both were found along with the garment D10587 (in the northeastern corner of the churchyard). In the description of the stocking D10614 it is stated that it was found west of the church. Both stockings are however cut and sewn according to the same principle, but the colours were different.

Nørlund No. 89. *(Fig. 88)*
Museum No. D10614

Fragmentary stocking sewn in Greenlandic *vaðmál* in 2/2 twill. The present-day colour is brownish, but originally the textile had a dark grey warp and a light grey weft. The stocking, which is cut diagonally, is sewn together from eleven parts. The largest fragment, which is 480 mm long – measured lengthwise on the leg – is cut diagonally and forms the top part of the stocking. The stocking leg has a border at the top

D10615

D10617

with a selvedge and a sewn-on gusset – like the stocking D10613. The greatest width of the fragment measured crosswise is 255 mm. The foot is composed of six largish pieces, the two longest of which continue from the middle under the foot around the heel up into the leg. The pieces are not sewn together above the foot. The other pieces are more or less sewn together leaving finished seam allowances towards the reverse side as well as torn-off edges.

Nørlund writes of the stocking foot that, apart from the gussets at the heel, it is formed from one single piece with a seam along the sole. However, this does not conform to the appearance of the stocking foot in this examination. All the seams are original, and no new seams have been sewn over them.

Nørlund similarly writes that the overcasting with coarse stitches around the top edge is the same as is found on the stocking D10615. In this examination there were only a few remains of stitches left.

Repairs: There are 'museum darns' with black wool yarn, probably from the 1920s. The stocking leg and half of the foot are glued to a net. Two smallish loose-lying fragments are not glued to a net, since they could apparently not be placed in the right context.

Nørlund No. 90. *(Figs. 89-90)*
Museum No. D10615

Stocking sewn in Greenlandic *vaðmál* in tabby weave. The present-day colour is reddish-brown; the foot piece is lighter in colour, but originally the stocking was white. The weaving is uneven, and the threads vary in thickness. The stocking leg is 455 mm long, and

above the fullness is 420 mm. At the ankle the fullness is uncertain, since this part of the leg is very fragmentary. On the front of the leg one can see two 160 mm long vents that run up from the bottom edge. A foot piece has been sewn on, but the

Fig. 90
The slit on the long stocking is cut on this side parallel with the warp threads. On the opposite side it is cut diagonally. The stocking was restored in the 1990s.

225

Fig. 91

A so-called 'stunthose' – a stocking without a foot. This was originally white with a length of 430 mm. The condition of preservation is very poor, and the stocking was glued to a net in the 1920s. A partly preserved starting border can be found at the top of the shank, and at the bottom two slits can be seen.

placing of the 'foot piece' is very doubtful, since the front part is missing, and the seam to the leg is new (from the 1920s?).

Nørlund thinks that the foot piece was originally a strap behind the heel, and that a real foot was also sewn to the leg, but this has now disappeared.

At the top edge one can see overcasting with 15-20 mm long stitches at intervals of c. 20 mm.

Restoration: In a restoration in the 1980s lining and 'museum seams' from the 1920s were removed, and the stocking was lined with a fine dyed wool material.

Nørlund No. 91. *(Fig. 91)*
Museum No. D10616

'Footless stocking' sewn in Greenlandic *vaðmál* in 2/2 twill. The present-day colour is brown, but originally the stocking was white. The length on the right side is 430 mm and on the left 420 mm. The fullness above is 360 mm and below 250 mm. At the bottom of the leg one can see two vents – vertical but not parallel with the wrap thread – c. 70 mm high. Along the edges of the vents are the remains of a seam allowance towards the reverse side.

At the top, the stocking has a starting border. At right angles to this a few centimetres of a selvedge are preserved. Nørlund describes the stocking as sewn together at the back of the leg, and with a loose strap, for holding the stocking in place on the leg, lying beside it.

Repairs: The toeless stocking was glued to a net, probably in the 1920s.

In the examination in 1997 the state of preservation was very poor.

There are no longer any seams, and the strap has disappeared.

Nørlund No. 92.
(Figs. 89-90 + 92-93)
Museum No. D10617

Stocking(?) sewn in Greenlandic *vaðmál* in tabby weave and diamond twill. The present-day colour is reddish-brown. The length is 350 mm and the fullness 80-100 mm. Spread out, the 'stocking' would measure 700x80-100 mm plus the seam allowance. This long piece is folded at the middle where the weave changes from tabby to diamond twill. After this it was sewn

Fig. 92
This piece of textile is registered as a 'stocking', but the description is doubtful. The textile is a 700 mm long weave that is folded at the middle and sewn together along both sides. Tabby weave.

Fig. 93
The textile seen from the opposite side, with a diamond-twill weave in 2/2 twill. This diamond-twill is the only patterned weave among the textile finds from Herjolfsnæs churchyard.

together along the sides with the exception of 130 mm on one side, leaving an opening towards the folding.

The seams are new, and it is not possible to see whether there are any remains of original seams under the new ones. The seam allowance on both sides is 10-15 mm wide.

Nørlund writes that this stocking(?) lay with the stocking D10616 as if they formed a pair. But he doubts that it is a stocking at all, since the fullness is only 180-190 mm. From Nørlund's description it is further evident that the stocking was finished above with a 40 mm wide sewn-on border in 2/2 twill, which at the time of registration was in a poor state of preservation.

Repairs: In the examination in 1997 there were no traces of the above mentioned sewn-on border. Instead the stocking has a 15-20 mm wide seam allowance towards the reverse side, which is sewn down with running stitches with modern sewing thread.

Weight: 50 g

Nørlund No. 93. *(Fig. 94)*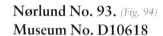
Museum No. D10618

Fragmentary footless stocking sewn in Greenlandic *vaðmál* in 2/2 twill. The present-day colour is reddish-brown, but originally the stocking was white. The height is 440 mm measured on the left side and 420 mm on the right. The length in the middle front at the curve above the foot is 340 mm. The fullness above is 340 mm and below it is 320 mm. The left side of the stocking leg slopes inward towards the foot. Nørlund describes the stocking as sewn together along the back of the leg.

In the examination in 1997 there was no longer any seam in the stocking, but there was a narrow fold which is the remains of a seam allowance. At the top edge one can see remains of thread from a seam.

Repairs: The stocking was probably glued to a net in the 1920s.

Fig. 94

Stunthose D10618. Originally this was white.

Fragmentes of Leather, Cloth and Cords, Ornaments and Accessories

**Nørlund No. 94.
Museum No. D10619**

A leather fragment with a small cross carved in it. Dimensions: 275x145 mm. Nørlund writes that the widest end of the fragment is folded in pleats, and that it is perhaps an item of footwear for a young person, since there were some metatarsal bones inside.

**Nørlund No. 95.
Museum No. D10620**

Two fragments of Greenlandic *vaðmál* in 2/2 twill. The present-day colour is reddish-brown. Dimensions: 332x320 mm, and 330x320 mm. There are remains of a seam allowance with 'withered' edges.

**Nørlund No. 96.
Museum No. D10621**

Fragment of Greenlandic *vaðmál* in tabby weave, consisting of two pieces sewn together, a reddish one of 300x170 mm and a brownish one of 130x45 mm. No sewing thread is preserved in the seam. The fragment is matted, possibly fulled(?). The reddish piece is in a fine, close weave. The brownish piece – unlike all other Norse textiles – has S-spun threads in both warp and weft.

Repairs: The whole fragment is glued to a net.

**Nørlund No. 97.
Museum No. D10622**

Cord of wool. The length is 1150 mm and the thickness is 5-7 mm. The present-day colour is light brown. The cord is formed of 12 threads twined together. The cord is kept in a wooden frame between two sheets of glass with a distance of 8 mm between the sheets.

**Nørlund No. 98.
Museum No. D10623**

Described as a wool cord of felt, shaped like a tube.
No longer exists.

*Fig. 95
Fragments of a triple braiding, 7-10 mm wide. The wool is in different shades, and probably was once a cord to tie around the waist.*

Fig. 96
Magnification of the triple braiding.
The threads in the cord are S-spun
and Z-plied.

Nørlund No. 99. *(Fig. 95-96)*
Museum No. D10624

Triple braiding of Greenlandic wool, consisting of four separate pieces. Lengths: 140, 140, 120 and 45 mm, totalling 445 mm. The width is 7-12 mm. The present-day colour is reddish-brown, but the strands in the braid had different colour shades.

The braid is formed from three elements (cordons), each consisting of four parallel threads. The individual threads are 2-ply (2Z1S) and 1.5 mm thick. On two of the pieces the braid is tied around itself in a knot.

Nørlund No. 100.
Museum No. D10625

Two circular brooches of brass. Diameter 48 mm.

Nørlund No. 101.
Museum No. D10626

A cross of bone with engraved circles. 13x13 mm. The arms of the cross are 4 mm wide.

Nørlund No. 102.
Museum No. D10627

Two costume pins of copper. Length: 55 mm.

Nørlund No. 103.
Museum No. D10628

Eight costume pins of wood. The longest measures 167 mm, the shortest 90 mm.

Nørlund Nos. 104, 105, 106

A tombstone.

Nørlund No. 106 (lb. nr. a-o)

Under this number a collection of 18 textile fragments is registered, with the appearance of having been 'left over'. They almost all have creased edges and given their sizes and shapes should clearly be regarded as patches. The few exceptions, for example lb. nr. f – two large pieces – are probably parts of a garment.

Nørlund writes in *Buried Norsemen at Herjolfsnes* (p. 39) about the packing, sending home and restoration of the many textiles: 'The work was extensive, and it took about 18 months before the restoration was concluded'. He continues: 'Several of the costumes had been cut up to serve as shrouds, some had only survived through the centuries in a very dilapidated state, and often after rinsing and conservation we had merely a heap of loose rags before us which were to be brought into the right relation to each other'. It is certainly from this 'heap of loose rags' that these fragments come. In *Buried Norsemen* the textiles and the few objects related to the garments are registered under Nørlund Nos. 33-103. The next four numbers, No. 104, 105, 106 and 107, apply to tombstones – thus including No. 106.

If this heap of rags (lb. nr. a-o) was given the number 106, there must have been some duplicate numbering. In the book the tombstones have replaced the small textile fragments, which were understandably less interesting to include than all the garments.

The 18 fragments are however good representatives of the cloth from Herjolfsnæs when one considers the weaving and the seams, since almost all of the fragments have one of the seams that occur on the garments. In addition there are a couple of patches with folded edges where there are remains of sewing thread of plant origin. This was not seen in the cloth from Herjolfsnæs.

Garment finds, described by Nørlund, but which could not be preserved

No. 36 Front- and back-piece without middle gussets. Two broad side panels.

No. 46 Back-piece with 'two middle gussets'. Four panels in each side. At the top of the back piece there were two rows of holes, cut with a knife. The holes had probably been used to hold the garment tight around the body.

No. 47 Front- and back-piece, each with a middle gusset, divided by a false seam. There was a single broad panel in the sides, which was divided lengthwise by a false seam. In the seam between the front piece and the side panels there were pocket slits, carefully seamed. The uppermost part of the garment was very badly preserved. Fullness below: 2750 mm, which was finished with a hem.

No. 48 Child's garment. A back-piece with 'two small middle gussets'. Two broad panels in each side, the right in one piece was divided by a false seam. The length, measured from the armhole downwards, was registered to 600-650 mm. The edge was hemmed.

No. 49 Front- and back-piece, 1100 mm long and 330 mm wide, with 860 mm long and narrow (170 mm at the bottom) middle gussets inserted. The neck opening was carefully folded and hemmed. By the upper part of the garment there was a pair of well-preserved pieces, which had possibly formed half-long sleeves. On another piece, probably from a side panel, there was a false seam.

On the chest, under the garment, there was a wooden cross (No. 151), 208x113 mm.

No. 50 Front- and back-piece, each with a two-part middle gusset and two broad side panels. The garment only reached the mid-thigh. The skeleton was almost completely disintegrated, but could however be recognised in the earth.

No. 51 Front- and back-piece with middle gussets, divided by false seams. The length of the gussets was 620 mm. Nørlund notes this as the shortest gusset length of all those registered. The shoulder length was measured to 1120 mm. It was not possible to see if the garment had had side panels.

No. 53 A 350 mm narrow back-piece with an inserted gusset, which was divided by a false seam. The gusset was the longest that was registered (no measurement was given). The left side panel was divided with the help of false seams into two – probably three – panels. The remains of sleeves were found.

No. 55 A small fragment from a back-piece was registered along with the remains of side panels and a sleeve gusset. The hems were carefully folded.

No. 56 The back-piece with 'two middle gussets' of 'normal' length. In each side there were two panels that were divided by false seams in the left side. Remains of a sleeve with an extremely large gusset were also found.

No. 69 Remains of a hood with an inserted gusset at the front. The hindmost part of the hood was so badly preserved that it was not possible to see if there had been a liripipe. Lying together with the hood was the one half of a 100 mm long wooden cross (No. 164).

No. 82 The tip of a liripipe. The fragment was found in the National Museum's storage facility. Nørlund believes it to be from the Kielsen excavation in 1840. The fragment was later numbered D12790.

No. 84 'Pill-box' cap found together with the garment D10589 and with parts of one or several garments that are not described. The cap consisted of a circular crown made of two unequally large pieces sewn together and a 100 mm high border. The border had the same broad unstitched seam allowance that can be seen on two other caps.

In the description of the unpreserved garments, Poul Nørlund writes that the material is four-shaft twill and often with the addition: black warp and brown weft. That is, 2/2 twill with black warp and brown weft – a description that can be recognized from the preserved garments.

With regard to three garments he writes that two middle gussets (marked in quotation marks) are inserted in the back-pieces. He probably means a two-part middle gusset, as there are no back-pieces or front-pieces with two middle gussets in any of the preserved garments.

The Length of the Garments

Chronological Presentation of the Finds

Viborg shirt (Denmark)	950 mm	around year 1000
Kragelund gown (Denmark)	1140 mm	1045-1155
Moselund gown (Denmark)	1280 mm	1050-1155
Söderköping (Sweden)	1200-1250 mm	beg. of 1200s
Herjolfsnæs, type 1c		
(D2625), 'Rønbjerg' (Denmark)	1120 mm	around 1280
(D10585,1)	1160 mm	no carbon dating
(D10587)	1185-1200 mm	no carbon dating
Skjoldehamn, shirt (Norway)	900 mm	12-1300s
Skjoldenhamn, gown (Norway)	1060-1080 mm	12-1300s
Bocksten, gown (Sweden)	1150 mm	1300s
Herjolfsnæs, type 1a		
(D5674)	1090 mm	no carbon dating
(D10579)	1220 mm	no carbon dating
Herjolfsnæs, type II		
(D10594)	1050 mm	1305-1375
(D10595)	1250 mm	no carbon dating
Herjolfsnæs, type 1b		
(D10580)	1230 mm	no carbon dating
(D10581)	1210-1230	around 1434
(D10582)	1195 mm	no carbon dating
(D10583)	1280 mm	no carbon dating
(D10584)	1190-1265 mm	no carbon dating
Guddal shirt (Norway)	short	medieval
Guddal gown (Norway)	mid-thigh	medieval
Uvdal (Norway)	?	?

Chronological Presentation of the Finds

Herjolfsnæs (D5674)	found in 1839	**Herjolfsnæs**	
Moselund gown	found in 1884	(all other numbers)	found in 1921
Kragelund gown	found in 1898	'Rønbjerg' (D2625)	found in 1921
Herjolfsnæs (D8080-8081)	found in 1900	Skjoldehamn	found in 1936
Herjolfsnæs (No. 75)	found in 1900	Bocksten	found in 1936
Herjolfsnæs (D6473)	found in 1906	Guddal	found in 1970
		Magnificent Leksand cape	found in 1971
		Uvdal	found in 1978
		Söderköping gown	found in 1984
		Viborg shirt	found in 1984

Analytical Tables of all Textile Finds

UJARASSUIT (Anavik Churchyard)

THE MUNICIPALITY OF NUUK, RUIN GROUP V7, ANTIQUITY NUMBER 64V2-IV-515.

Inv. No. D12556 Serial No.	Measure-ments in mm	Spin	Angle of spin/ply of threads	C. diameter of threads in mm	Thread count per. cm	Weave	Remarks (Colour description giving the present-day colour)
1.	250x240 180x120 140x100 150x70 30x40	Z/S	40°/35°	1.0/1.0	8/12	2/2	Brownish, grooved on back, false seam and remains of tablet-woven piped edging(?) by a seam.
2.	105x220	Z/S 2Z1S	40°/35° 35°	1.2/1.5-2.0 1.2	6/4	Tabby	Greyish, 30 mm wide stripe with plied threads in the warp, 15 mm long grey stitch sewn in cross.
3.	230x90	Z/S	45°/35°	1.0/1.0	7/10	2/2	Brownish, 11 mm wide seam allowance, tablet/stitching
4.	150x70 50x50	Z/S	45°/35°	1.2/0.8	8/9	2/2	Reddish
5.	155x100	Z/S	45°/30°	0.9/1.0	9/10	2/2	Brownish, few stitches
6.	130x95	Z/S	45°/30°	1.0/1.2	7/8	2/2	Brownish, 8 mm wide seam allowance, stab stitching, overcast stitching
7.	245x160	Z/S	45°-50°/30°	0.9/0.9	9/14	2/2	Reddish, 'grey' border
8.	450x180 120x55	Z/S	40°/30°	1.2/0.7	7/14	2/2	Brownish, false seam, 9 mm wide seam allowance
D12557	100x530	Z/S	45°/30°	1.0/1.1	9/12	2/2	Brownish, selvedge with two crossing wefts, 14 mm wide seam allowance, 10 mm wide seam allowance, overcast stitching over light thread
D12557	120x120	Z/S	45°/40°	1.0/1.2	8/8	2/2	Dark brown
D12560	110x80 40x65 and several smaller	Z/S	45°/30°-20°	1.0/0.8-0.4	8/16	2/2	Red-brown, very bad state of preservation
D12560	100x120 and several smaller	Z/S	45°/35°	1.0/1.0	8/10	2/2	Dark brown, very bad state of preservation

The textiles were transferred to the Greenland National Museum and Archives in February 2001

NIAQUUSAT

THE MUNICIPALITY OF NUUK, RUIN GROUP V48, ANTIQUITY NUMBER 64V2-III-507

Inv. No. KNK 985 Serial No.	Measure-ments in mm	Spin	Angle of spin/ply of threads	C. diameter of threads in mm	Thread count per. cm	Weave	Remarks (Colour description giving the present-day colour)
x79	30x40	Z/S				2/2	Brownish, the one thread system has almost disappeared
x80	60x30	Z/S	50°/40°	0.7-1.0/1.0	21/11	2/1	Reddish, diamond twill
x97	20x15	Z/S	35°/35°	0.1/0.1	12/9	2/2	Dark brown
x177	12x18	Z/S	55°/45°	1.0/1.5			Red-brown, only a few threads in the warp
x1019	20x50	Z/S	40°/40°	1.0/1.5	6/5	Tabby	Red-brown
x1020	25x25	Z/S	35°/40°	0.7-1.0/1.5		2/2	Brown
x1023	70x100	Z/S	?/45°	?/0.8-1.5	?/9	2/2	x79 and x1023 are from the same textile, the warp threads are probably of flax
x1024	40x50	Z/S	50°/35°	1.0/1.0-2.0	12/7	2/2	Light brown, 8 mm wide seam allowance, overcast stitching
x1114	70	Z	25°	2.0-2.5			Two single threads

SANDNÆS (Kilaarsarfik)

THE MUNICIPALITY OF NUUK, RUIN GROUP V51. ANTIQUITY NUMBER 64V2-III-511

Inv. No. D11920.353 Serial No.	Measurements in mm	Spin	Angle of spin/ply of threads	C. diameter of threads in mm	Thread count per. cm	Weave	Remarks (Colour description giving the present-day colour)
a	305x165	Z/S	45°/30°	1.0/1.5	11/10	2/2	Brownish, three pieces sewn together, 15 mm wide seam spread out to each side and sewn down with overcast stitching
b	240x180	Z/S	40°/30°	1.0/1.2	9/9	2/2	Light brown, opened hem
c	230x250 80x60	Z/S	45°/35°	1.2/1.2	8/8	2/2	Dark brown, 10 mm wide seam allowance, stab stitching
d	220x120	Z/S	40°/25°	0.8/1.2	12/8	2/2	Light
e	garment part	Z/S	45°-50°/30°	1.0/1.2	8-9/9	2/2	Brownish, neck or shoulder section(?)of child's garment, consisting of three pieces, 10 mm wide seam spread out to each side and sewn down with overcast stitching, stab stitching
f	100x175	Z/S	45°/30°	0.9/1.0	10/10	2/2	Light brown with stripes in weft, four dark, two light and five reddish threads, false seam that crosses the textile diagonally
g	80x130 140x200	Z/S	40°/30°	1.2/1.5-2.0	6/5	Tabby	Light, very bad, 150 mm long starting border
h	120x220	Z/S	45°/30°	1.0/1.2	9/10	2/2	Brown

The fragments are mentioned in Roussell, Aa. 1936, p. 130 and p. 189

SANDNÆS (Kilaarsarfik)

THE MUNICIPALITY OF NUUK, RUIN GROUP V51. ANTIQUITY NUMBER 64V2-III-511

Inv. No. KNK 4 Serial No.	Measurements in mm	Spin	Angle of spin/ply of threads	C. diameter of threads in mm	Thread count per. cm	Weave	Remarks (Colour description giving the present-day colour)
x398	80	S		5.0			Brown thread
x801	40x20	Z/S			13/9	2/2	Dark brown
x808	60x80	2Z1S/2Z1S				Tabby	Grey-brown, two seamed fragments with selvedge, laid over each other during seaming, overcast stitches
	50	S		5.0		Cord	A double seam
	80x30						
	40x50	Z/S			14/6	2/2	Light brown, blue-black
x819	15x80 and several smaller	Z/S			8/6	2/2	Golden brown, shreds, cut on the diagonal of the weave
	50x30	Z/S			12/9	2/2	Dark brown
x830	20x90	Z/S			10/8	2/2	Brown-black, folded, overcast stitching at the ends, stab stitching
x842	40	S, 2Z1S					Light brown, S-spun thread wound around an S-twisted thread
x849	40x190	Z/S			6/5	2/2	Brown
x851	40x60	Z/S			7/4(x2)	Tabby (Panama)	Brown, woven with two parallel threads in the weft, 11 mm wide seam allowance, overcast stitching
	80x60 and more	Z/S			12/7	2/2	Brown
x855	80	2Z1S					Brown threads and raw wool
x861	30x35	Z/S			14/11	2/2	Light brown
x907	40x20	Z/S			12/5	2/2	Brown
x920	145	4S1Z		4.0			Brown cord
x925	40x40 and more	Z/S			9/9	2/2	Grey-brown
	50x50	Z/S			6/5	Tabby	Brown
x932	45x45 and more	Z/S			6/6	2/2	Brown
	160	3S1Z		4.0			Light brown cord
	90x40	Z/S			12/9	2/2	Several fragments, sewn together, consist of a dark and a light
	and several smaller	Z/S			11/11	2/2	weave, selvedge with overcast stitching
x944	100	3S1Z		10.0			Brown cord
x946	160x120	Z/S			11/7	2/2	Brown-black, made up of several pieces,
	and several smaller	Z/S			15/10	2/2	which also include a reddish piece

Inv. No. KNK 4 Serial No.	Measure-ments in mm	Spin	Angle of spin/ply of threads	C. diameter of threads in mm	Thread count per. cm	Weave	Remarks (Colour description giving the present-day colour)
x950							Raw wool
x1007	30	S					Brown threads
x1011	60x80				10/9	2/2	Brown, 'embroidery'(?)
	10x105	Z/S					
x1029	40x55	Z/S			10/7	2/2	Brown
x1033	30x70	Z/S			13/14	2/2	Red-brown
	65x70	Z/S			15/11	2/2	Grey-brown
	20x30	Z/S			14/18	2/2	Dark brown
x1035	45x45	Z/S			10/8	2/2	Brown, 15 mm wide seam allowance with three-ply S-twisted
		3Z1S					threads over a frayed edge, overcast stitching
x1038	70x80	Z/S			10/6	2/2	Light grey-brown
x1055	30x30	Z/S			7/5	Tabby	Light grey brown
x1058	270x120	Z/S			11/5	Tabby (repp)	Greyish, consisting of two pieces sewn together, false seam
x1064	50x60	Z/S			13/12	2/2	Brown
	and several smaller						
x1064	30x40	Z/S			8/6	2/2	Dark brown
		2Z1S					four threads knotted together, and raw wool
x1071	30x40	Z/S			9/6	Tabby	Grey-brown
x1114	50x50	Z/S			7/7	2/2	Dark brown
x1118	100	2Z1S					Brown thread
x1182	50						Brown hair or raw wool
x1211	30x70	Z/S					Dark brown,
	250	3Z1S					Nine twists per cm
x1228							Raw wool/hair
x1244							Light brown, raw wool
x1245	70x70	Z/S			11/8	2/2	Dark brown
	40x90						
x1275	60x40	Z/S			9/7	2/2	Dark brown
	60x50	Z/S			8/5	2/2	Golden and light brown
x1279	70	2Z1S		0.9			Light brown thread
x1292	50x60	Z/S			9/8	2/2	Dark brown
x1308	50x50	Z/S			16/8	2/2	Dark brown, grey-brown, 10 mm wide seam allowance,
	40x60	Z/S			10/10	2/2	overcast stitches, raw wool and single thick threads

On one of the fragments under KNKx808 the presence of the blue dye, indigotin, has been detected
On the fragment x1011 there is an 'embroidery', consisting of 4-5 threads, which together are sewn down with an S-twisted thread at a distance of 7 mm.
The stitching is situated 25 mm from the cut-off edge. Perhaps the remains of an opened hem?

UMIIVIARSUK (Austmannadalen)
THE MUNICIPALITY OF NUUK, RUIN GROUP V52a. ANTIQUITY NUMBER 64V2-III-513

Inv. No.	Measure-ments in mm	Spin	Angle of spin/ply of threads	C. diameter of threads in mm	Thread count per. cm	Weave	Remarks (Colour description giving the present-day colour)
D12407	25x70	Z/S	40°/35°	0.9/1.0-1.2	9/8	2/2	Dark brown
D12407	160x70	Z/S	45°/35°	1.0/0.8	8/14	2/2	Dark brown, stitching
	110x95						
D12408	120	2Z1S	20°	2.0-5.0			Two-plied thread: a light and a dark
D12408	100x35	Z/S	50°-45°/35°	1.0/0.5-0.9	9/12	2/2	Red-brown, selvedge with crossing weft, stitching
	double in the one side						
D12409	190x55	Z/S	45°/35°	1.0/1.0	9/9	2/2	Greyish, stitching
D12409	185x45	Z/S	45°/35°	1.0/1.0	8/8	2/2	Brown
D12410	200x200	Z/S	45°-50°/40°	1.0/0.5-1.0	7/5	Tabby	Greyish, the threads are unevenly spun
D12410	210x225	Z/S	35°-45°/35°	0.7/2.0	6/6	2/2	Brown with light weft
		S	30°	1.0			stitching
		2Z1S	25°	2.0			and light button-hole loops
No number	30x30	Z/S	45°/35°	1.0/1.0	8/8	2/2	Reddish
	35x30	Z/S	45°/35°	1.0/1.0	8/8	2/2	Brownish
No number	65x185	Z/S	45°/35°	1.0/0.3-0.8	10/18	2/2	Red-brown, stitching and 'museum stitching'

Inv. No.	Measure-ments in mm	Spin	Angle of spin/ply of threads	C. diameter of threads in mm	Thread count per. cm	Weave	Remarks (Colour description giving the present-day colour)
D12411 1	230x155 180x133 90x90	Z/S	35°/30°	1.0/1.0	9/7	2/1	Checked fragments in light and dark brown, 20 mm wide seam
2	275	2S1Z	20°	4.0			Brownish, goat-hair? Cord
3	90x300	Z/S	40°/30°	1.1/1.3	7/7	2/2	Brown, stitching
4	160x155	Z/S	50°/35°	1.0/1.0	9/9	2/2	Light brown, stitching
5	110x120	Z/S	45°/30°	1.2/1.0	5/8	Tabby	Brown, stitching
6	130x90	Z/S	40°/30°	1.2/1.0	7/11	2/2	Brown, grooved back
7	50x70	Z/S	40°/25°	1.0/1.0	8/10	2/2	Brown, hide or skin on the fragment
8	160x40 250x15	Z/S	40°/35°	1.0/1.2	9/9	2/2	Brownish, stitching, starting border
		2S1Z	25°	2.0			Sewing thread
No number	60-70x185	Z/S	45°/30°	1.0/0.3-0.8	9/20	2/2	15 mm wide seam allowance, seam
No number	30x30	Z/S	45°/35°	1.0/1.0	8/8	2/2	Reddish weft, almost black warp

D12407.354, D12408.355, D12409.356 and D12410.357 are mentioned in Roussell, Aa., 1936, p. 130, 189-90
The greyish fragment D12409 represents the best preserved of all the Norse footwoven edges

UMIIVIARSUK (Austmannadalen 4)

THE MUNICIPALITY OF NUUK, RUIN GROUP V53c. ANTIQUITY NUMBER 64V2-III-518

Inv. No. D12787.226 Serial No.	Measure-ments in mm	Spin	Angle of spin/ply of threads	C. diameter of threads in mm	Thread count per. cm	Weave	Remarks (Colour description giving the present-day colour)
0,1	60x75	Z/S	40°/25°	1.0/0.8	9/13	2/2	Red-brown, folded together
0,2	70x55	Z/S	40°/25°	1.0/1.0	6/7	2/2	Dark brown
0,3	165x50	Z/S	40°/30°	1.0/0.8	9/12-15	2/2	Brown, stitching
0,4	150x150	Z/S	45°/40°	1.2/1.5-2.0	5/5	Tabby	Red-brown
0,5	115x40	Z/S	40°/25°	1.0/1.0	7/12	2/2	Red-brown
0,6	110x50	Z/S	45°/30°	1.0/1.0	8/9	2/2	Grey-brown

The textile fragments are mentioned in Roussell, Aa., 1941, p. 265. Textiles were transferred to Greenland's National Museum and Archive in February 2001

UMIIVIARSUK (Austmannadalen 5)

NUUK KOMMUNE, RUINGRUPPE V53d, FORTIDSMINDENUMMER 64V2-III-519

Inv. No. D12807.456 Serial No.	Measure-ments in mm	Spin	Angle of spin/ply of threads	C. diameter of threads in mm	Thread count per. cm	Weave	Remarks (Colour description giving the present-day colour)
	170	Z	40°	0.9-1.2			Brown, eight parallel threads, attached by means of a knot at each end
	450	2Z1S	20°	3.0-5.0			Brown, several threads knotted to each other to form a 'ring', goat-hair

The textile fragments are mentioned in Roussell, Aa., 1941, p. 287. Cords are made of wool and hair

NIPAATSOQ

THE MUNICIPALITY OF NUUK, RUIN GROUP V54. ANTIQUITY NUMBER 64V2-III-502.

Inv. No. KNK991	Measure-ments in mm	Spin	Angle of spin/ply of threads	C. diameter of threads in mm	Thread count per. cm	Weave	Remarks (Colour description giving the present-day colour)
x122	50x45	Z/S			12/16	2/2	
x188	140x50	Z/S			7/7	2/2	
x198	110x30	Z/S			12/16	2/2	
x261	80x25	Z/S			9/9	2/2	
x274	60x30	Z/S			8/11	2/2	The same as x301
x287	130x40	Z/S			8/12	2/2	
x298	70x20	Z/S					Badly preserved

Inv. No. KNK991	Measure-ments in mm	Spin	Angle of spin/ply of threads	C. diameter of threads in mm	Thread count per. cm	Weave	Remarks (Colour description giving the present-day colour)
x301	110x90	Z/S			8/11	2/2	The same as x274
x393	160	Z					One thread
x448	160x260	Z/S	50°/45°	1.5/1.5-2.0			Reddish, part of a garment
		Z	40°	1.2	7/7	2/1	4 mm thick, braided cord along a 10 mm wide hem
x577		Z/Z	15°/15°	1.3/1.3	20/18	Tabby	Charred clump
x653b	80x10	Z/S	50°/35°-40°	1.0/1.0	9/12	2/2	Dark brown, double

Measurements have not been taken of the angle of spin and thread thickness of the first ten fragments mentioned

A braided cord consisting of six two-ply Z-spun threads (2Z1S) is sewn down to one of the fragments from x448

THE FARM BENEATH THE SAND

THE MUNICIPALITY OF NUUK. ARTIQUITY NUMBER 64V2-III-55

Inv. No. 1950 x Room 1	Measure-ments in mm	Spin	Angle of spin/ply of threads	C. diameter of threads in mm	Thread count per. cm	Weave	Remarks (Colour description giving the present-day colour)
528	100x170 100x125 70x90	Z/S	50°/35°	1.0/1.0-1.5	7/13	2/2	An almost black warp and brown weft, sewing
529	150x150		50°/30°-40°	1.0-1.5/1.5	5/4	Tabby	Light brown, 70 mm long selvedge with crossing weft
531	30x25	Z/S	45°/30°	1.2/1.5	7/9	2/2	Brown
543	10						c. 20 hairs
545	50x60	Z/S	40°-45°/25°	0.9/0.9	8/10	2/2	Brown, burnt edges
546	30x30	Z/S	45°/35°	1.0/1.5	7/9	2/2	Brown with dark warp, sewing
566	100x160 90x80 70x80	Z/S	45°/35°	1.2/1.5	5/6	Tabby	Red-brown, 7 mm wide seam allowance with stab stitching
567	20-30						Raw wool
568	80x200	Z/S	45°/30°-40°	1.0/1.5	8/8	2/2	Brown, sewing over parallel threads
568	70x90	Z/S	30°-40°/45°	1.5/1.0-1.5	5/8-9	2/1	Patch
569	20						Raw wool 0,027 g
570	20-30						Raw wool 0,056 g
602	40x50 30x20	2Z1S/S	35°/30°	2.0-3.0/1.5-2.0	3/18	Tabby (repp)	Brown, selvedge(?)
602	40x50 30x25	Z/S	45°/30°-35°	1.5/1.5-2.0	7/9	2/2	Dark brown
604	70x40 and more	Z/S	45°/40°-45°	1.5/1.5-2.0	7/6	2/2	Brown
606							Hair 0,250 g
608	350x255	2Z1S/ 2Z1S	25°-45°/25°-45°	2.0-4.0/2.0-4.0	4/3 pr 2 cm	Tabby	Threads vary in dark/light combination, selvedge, goat-hair
608	250x225	Z/S	50°/20°-30°	1.0/2.5	5/4	Tabby	12 mm wide seam allowance, goat-hair textile, sewing
608	170	4S2Z1S	30°	2.0-3.0			Dark brown cord
608	30-155	Z	40°-45°	1.0-2.0			c.15 threads bound together, two or more in continuation
613a	130x130	Z/S	40°/35°-40°	1.0/1.0	8/9	2/2	Brown
613b	135x120						Fragment consisting of two brown seamed pieces:
-	130x60	Z/S	40°/35-40°	1.0/1.5	10/10	2/2	a compact weave and
-	70x40	Z/S	55°/25°-30°	1.2/1.5	6/8	Tabby	a more open weave, to which a lighter weave was sewn on the three sides, now preserved only as an border
613	10x80 10x60 50x17	Z/S	45°/30°	1.5/1.0-1.5	9/10	2/2	Borders of a lighter weave, sewn to the above-mentioned brown weaves
633 detached find	300	2Z1S	20°	4.0			Black, four cords drawn through a hole in an antler
634	40x70	Z/S	45°/30°	1.0-2.0/2.0	6/6	2/2	Dark brown, fibre emanating from a plant is visible in the threads
635	260x110	Z/S	45°/25°	1.5/2.0	7/8	2/2	Dark brown warp and lighter weft, 12 mm seam allowance, remains of seam
655	30x355	2Z1S	30°-40°	2.0-3.0			Goat-hair threads

Inv. No. 1950 x Room 1	Measure-ments in mm	Spin	Angle of spin/ply of threads	C. diameter of threads in mm	Thread count per. cm	Weave	Remarks (Colour description giving the present-day colour)
767	195x80	Z/S	45°/35°	1.0/1.3	8/8	2/2	Dark brown, sewing
769	Uneven lengths	2Z1S Z	35°-60°	0.5-2.5			Brown, thrums(?), many knots, 33,996 g
776	140x140 and several smaller	Z/S	35°/25°	1.0/1.5	8/10	2/2	6 mm wide stripe of white hare fur, in brown textile of goat-hair
790	73x40 50x30	2Z1S/ 2Z1S	25°-45°/ 25°-45°	2.0-4.0/ 2.0-4.0	4/3 pr 2 cm	Tabby	The same weave as 608, in goat-hair
791	475	4S1Z	30°	3.0-4.0			Cord, tied with a 70 mm long loop
814	160	2Z1S	25°	3.0			Goat-hair cord in loomweight; loomweight weighs 680 g
819	160	10Z5S1Z	20°	3,0			Wool cord in loomweight; loomweight weighs 590 g
846	125x110						Fur fragment 7.966 g
394 (Room 3)							Dark brown raw wool 2.188 g
431							Completely light-coloured raw wool 1.257 g
434	145x80 200x50	Z/S	45°/35°	1.3/1.0	9/11	2/2	Almost black warp and brown weft, 9 mm wide seam allowance, stitching
447	115x60	Z/S	50°/40°	1.0-2.0/ 2.0-4.0	3/5	Tabby	One light warp thread, The others dark brown
464	50						Grey-brown hair 0.5 g
464	50-75	S	25°	2.0-5.0			Threads of wool (?)
465	50-100						Hair, four black and one light
469	60						Hair and raw wool 0.09 g
473	40-435	Z	40°-50°	1.0-2.0			14 dark and light threads
479	80-100						Brownish raw wool 0.3 g
482							Light raw wool 1.837 g
492	120x30	Z/S	40°/25°-35°	1.2-2.0/3.0	8-10/5	Tabby	Almost black and red-brown, 100 mm long selvedge, stitching
492	135x80	Z/S	45°/35°-50°	1.5/1.5	6/5	Tabby	8 mm wide seam allowance, stitching
496	175x70	Z/S	45°/30°-35°	1.3/1.0	9/10	2/2	The same as No. 434
497	50						Reindeer hair 0.3 g
500	185	2Z1S	25°	1.0-3.0			Two light brown threads tied together
502							'regurgitated matter', wool fibre 0.7 g
507	115x70	Z/S	45°/30°-35°	1.5/1.0	6/12	2/2	Red-brown, compact weave
509	100-140	2Z1S	25°-35°	2.0-4.0			Greyish threads of goat-hair
514	130x130	Z/S	45°/35°-50°	1.3/2.0	6/5	Tabby	Brown
521	100x170	Z/S	40°/35°	1.3/1.5	8/8	2/2	Dark brown
523							Hair(?), 0.7 g
679							Brown raw wool 0.7 g
698	150-500	Z	40°-50°	0.7-1.0			Light and dark yarn ends (?), many knots, 1.010 g
698	105	2Z1S	25°-30°	1.5-2.0			Goat-hair thread
706	130-1100	2Z1S	10°-30°	1.0-4.0			Five dark brown threads tied together
740	90x90	Z/S	55°/35°	0.5-1.0/ 0.5-2.0	6/ 4-5	Tabby	Dark brown, very open weave
742	60x50	Z/S	35°/30°	1.3/1.3	7/7	2/2	Sewn with dark thread to the fragment named below
742	130x130	Z/S	50°/40°-45°	1.0/1.0-3.0	12/4	Tabby	Brown unevenly woven, 70 mm long selvedge
885							Raw wool 0.1 g
923	45x20	Z/S	55°/45°-40°	1.5/1.5	7/7	2/2	Light with dark threads, part of a seam, 10 mm seam allowance, stitching
924	60x60	Z/S	45°/40°	1.0-1.5/1.5	4/4	Tabby	Red brown
954							Raw wool 0.2 g
970	220x110 40x170	Z/S	50°/40°	1.2/1.5	5/7	Tabby	Brown, open weave, 7 mm seam allowance Frayed edge covered by Z-twisted filler thread, fragment (40x170 mm) sewn at the top
977		Z/S	50°-30°/30°	1.2/1.5	?	?	Red-brown, badly preserved
981	150x95	Z/S	45°/35°	1.0/1.0	9/13	2/2	Dark brown
981							Light raw wool with dark top hair 1.083 g
1014							Light raw wool with dark top hair 0.5 g
1014	110 og 70	6S1Z	35°	5.0			Two brown cords
1018	70x115	Z/S	45°/30°-35°	1.0/0.9	8/10	2/2	Dark brown, 10 mm seam allowance, stitching
1020	125x140	Z/S	45°/50°	1.0/1.0	9/11	2/2	Brown, compact weave, gusset from a hood (?), 7 mm seam allowance, stab stitching, seam
1024	Several	Z	30°-40°	1.0-3.0			Reddish and brown threads
1024	125	2S1Z	20°	4.0			Red-brown thread

Inv. No. 1950 x Room 1	Measurements in mm	Spin	Angle of spin/ply of threads	C. diameter of threads in mm	Thread count per. cm	Weave	Remarks (Colour description giving the present-day colour)
1035	90x45	Z/S	50°/35°	1.0/0.8	7/11	2/2	Brown, 7 mm seam allowance
1041	Several	Z	40°-50°	0.8-2.0			Brown threads
1041	Several	S	30°	2.5			Brown threads
1041	90x95	Z/S	45°/30°	1.0/1.0	7/11	2/2	Light and dark brown threads in weft in stripes, 11 mm seam allowance stitching
1053	110x80	Z/S	50°/30°	1.2/0.9	8/11	2/2	Brown, burnt edges
1063	120	2S1Z	25°	2.0			Light thread
1063	73	8Z4S1Z	30°	2.0			Light cord of wool
1084	80x105	Z/S	45°/30°	1.0/1.0	8/8	2/2	Brown
1084	70x90	Z/S	50°/20°	0.9/0.5	10/18	2/2	Reddish, very compact weave, stitching triangular fragment
1107	200	Z	40°	1.0			Dark brown thread
1107	215	2S1Z	40°	1.5			Goat-hair thread
1107	170 og 55	2Z1S	30°	2.5-5.0			Goat-hair thread
1107	230	Z	40°	0.8			Very fine thread of goat-hair
1109	400	3S1Z	15°	4.0			Wool cord in loomweight, tied in a bow, loomweight weighs 411.2 g
1114	130 og 125	2Z1S	40°	1.5-2.0			Light goat-hair threads
1114	Uneven lengths	Z	40°-50°	0.8-2.5			Dark wool threads, warp remains, of which six threads are tied together in a knot, 2.703 g
1239	115x110	Z/S	45°-50°/35°	1.0/1.2	8/9	2/2	Dark warp, light red-brown weft
1239	45x50 30x115	Z/S	40°/30°	1.2/1.2-1.5	6/6	2/2	Dark warp, light weft
1275	Uneven lengths	Z	40°-45°	1.0-3.0			Wool threads 0.241 g
1288	80x115	Z/S	45°/30°	1.0-2.0/ 1.5-2.5	9/7	2/2	Brown
1298	150x70	Z/S	45°/40°	1.0/0.8	10/15	2/2	Dark brown, very compact weave
1330	200	Z	40°	1.0-1.5			Light threads of goat-hair
1337	110x110 70x70 25x50	Z/S	45°/35°	1.0/1.0	9/11	2/2	Reddish fragments from, in total, eight pieces sewn together
1337	30x55 20x40	Z/S	45°/45°	1.0/1.0	8/10	2/2	Brownish fragments belonging to the above-named Stitching
1337	100x100 155x120 120x20	Z/S	50°/25°-35°	1.0/1.5	6/5	Tabby	Brownish fragments, belonging to the above named, the eight fragments make a sleeve-like piece.
1341	195x220 40x4	Z/S	50°/35°	1.2/1.0	8/9	2/2	Garment fragment, dark warp and light weft, 10 mm seam allowance, stitching, seam, braided cord along the border
1341		2Z1S	30°	1.0			Dark threads, which are part of the braided cord, altogether six threads
1341	20x20	Z/S	45°/35°	1.2/1.0	8/13	2/2	Reddish fragment
1349	Uneven lengths	Z	40°-50°	1.0-2.5			Light and dark warp remains (?), 0.550g
1350	Uneven lengths	Z	40°-50°	0.8-2.0			Light and dark warp remains (?) 0.241 g
1361	Uneven lengths	2Z1S	20°-35°	2.0-5.0			Goat-hair threads, two are tied together
1361	140	2Z1S	20°	2.0-4.5			Brown thread
1361	Uneven lengths	Z	45°	1.2			Brown threads
1361	35x60 50x50	Z/S	45°/35°	1.0/1.0	9/12	2/2	Brown
1386							Light raw wool with dark top hair 5.952 g
1415	130	2Z1S	30°	2.0-3.0			Dark goat-hair thread
1416	300 og 250	2Z1S	20°	1.5			Two dark brown threads tied together in a bow
1416							Light raw wool 0.823 g
1426	165x90	Z/S	45°/40°	0.9/1.0	11/11	2/2	Dark brown, 160 mm long selvedge with sewn-on braided cord
1426	110x105	Z/S	40°/30°	1.2/1.2	8/9	2/2	Dark brown, very beautiful
1426	160	2Z1S	30°	0.6			Six(?) dark brown threads in the braided cord
1430	85x100 50x70 and several smaller	Z/S	35°-40°/25°	1.0/1.5	6/6	2/2	Red brown
1435	240x125	Z/S	50°/40°-45°	1.0/0.8	9/11	2/2	Red-brown, two pieces sewn together, 9 mm wide seam
1439	225x380	Z/S	40°/30°	0.9/0.9	8/9	2/2	Dark warp and light weft
1439	235x130	2Z1S/ 2Z1S	25°-45°/ 25°/45°	2.0-4.0 2.0-4.0/	4/3-4 pr. 2 cm	Tabby	Goat-hair weave Same as No. 608 (1992 excavation)

Inv. No. 1950 x Room 1	Measure- ments in mm	Spin	Angle of spin/ply of threads	C. diameter of threads in mm	Thread count per. cm	Weave	Remarks (Colour description giving the present-day colour)
1439							Hair from ? 0.23 g
1447	120x70	Z/S	50°/30°	1.2/1.0	7/11	2/2	Light brown, 10 mm seam allowance, stitching
1447	120x145	Z/S	40°/25°	1.2/1.5	6/5	2/2	Brown
1458	70x55						
	and several smaller	Z/S	50°/30°	1.2/0.6-8	7/18	2/2	Dark brown, very compact weave, 10 mm seam allowance, stitching
1477	325	Z	35°	1.0-1.5			Wool thread
1481	170	2Z1S	25°	1.0-1.5			Goat-hair thread
1482							Red brown raw wool 4.317 g
1529	135x60	S/S	40°/30°	1.2/1.2	7/7	2/2	Brown
	50x40						
1543	70x85	Z/S	35°/30°	1.0/1.5	8/6	2/2	Brown
1543	120x105	Z/S	45°/35°	1.0/1.0	9/9	2/2	Dark brown warp and light weft
	80x70 and more						
1543	30x40	Z/S	40°/30°	1.2/1.2-1.5	6/5	2/2	Brown
1543	95	Z	45°	1.0			Brown thread and hair from (?) 0.131 g
1543	160x155	Z/S	45°/30°	1.2/1.5	7/8	2/2	Dark warp light weft
1545	575x9	2Z1S	50°-30°	1.0-1.2			Light brown circlet of intertwined human hair, see drawing p. 108
1548	ca.120	S	25°	3.4-4.0			Red-brown thread wound around a wooden stick
1567	70x50	Z/S	40°/30°	1.0/1.2	7/8	2/2	Light brown goat-hair weave
	50x55 and more						
1567	80x75	Z/S	45°/40°	1.0/1.0	8/9	2/2	Red brown
1567	100x250	Z/S	45°/35°	1.2/1.2	8/8	2/2	Dark brown, stitching
	140x45 and more						
1567	125 og 60	2Z1S	30°	1.0-3.0			Light and brown goat-hair threads
1567	235 and more	S	25°-30°	2.0-4.5			Brown, knots on several threads
1567	75 and more	Z	30°-45°	0.8-1.0			Brown threads
1569	165	Z	30°	1.0			Black thread
1569	215	2S1Z	25°	2.0-4.0			Light and black goat-hair threads tied together
1569	170	Z	35°	2.0			Almost black thread
1573	180x40	Z/S	40°/30°	1.0/1.0	10/11	2/2	Reddish, tablet/stitching
1573	160 and more	Z	35°	1.0-1.5			Reddish threads
1600	110x25	Z/S	40°/30°	1.0/1.3	8/8	2/2	Light brown, 110 mm long selvedge
1606	30x54						Skin
1606	540, 265	3S1Z	20°-25°	4.0-5.0			Light threads
	og 135						
1606	50x65	Z/S	45°/35°	0.7/1.0	10/11	2/2	Brown
1606	50x85	Z/S	45°/35°	1.5/1.9	5/6	Tabby	Light brown
1606	50x60 and more	Z/S	40°-30°	1.5/2.0-2.5	4/4	Tabby	Dark brown, seam and 10 mm wide seam allowance
1607	190	Z	35°	1.5			Black threads
1607	120	S	20°	1.5			Brown threads
1607	80 (loops)	2Z1S	35°	2.0-4.5			Red-brown thread tied as a loop and with a knot,
	40 and 35 ends						through which another thread runs
1607	110x30	Z/S	40°/30°	1.5/1.5	7/7	2/2	Brown
	40x50						
1607	80x100	Z/S	40°/35°	1.0/1.0	9/10	2/2	Brown
1607	45x30	Z/S	40°/30°	1.5/2.0	5/5	Tabby	Dark warp and light weft
1611	70	4S2Z1S	20°	4.0			Dark brown cord
1615	90	Z	50°	1.0-1.5			Brown thread
1651	300	2Z1S	30°	3.0			Brown goat-hair thread
1653	280	Z	35°-40°	1.0-2.0			Brown thread
1653							Light raw wool 0.265 g
1654	180	2Z1S	45°	1.0-1.5			Light thread
1654	160	2Z1S	30°	3.0			Goat-hair thread
1664	100 og 90	2Z1S	25°	4.0			Very light cord
1674	740	2Z1S	25°	2.0			Brown thread with knots
1685	1100	Z	45°-50°	0.8-1.2			Brown thread, fine spinning
1704	240x80	Z/S	45°/35°	1.0/1.0	10/14	2/2	Reddish, compact weave
1736	120x80	Z/S	40°/30°	1.0/1.2	9/10	2/2	Brown, 10 mm long seam allowance along the three sides, stitching
1737	100x110	Z/S	45°/30°	0.8/1.5	7/7	2/1	Dark, reddish
1779	90x40	Z/S	40°/35°	1.0/1.0	9/10	2/2	Brown

Inv. No. 1950 x Room 1	Measure-ments in mm	Spin	Angle of spin/ply of threads	C. diameter of threads in mm	Thread count per. cm	Weave	Remarks (Colour description giving the present-day colour)
1779	110x50 80x60 70x50 70x35	Z/S	40°-45°/30°	1.0/0.5	10/20	2/2	Brown, very compact weave, 'withered' edges on some fragments
1785	105x45 and more	Z/S	40°/35°	0.9/1.5	9/9	2/2	Brown, 95 mm long selvedge with crossing weft
1796	340	2Z1S	30°	3.5-4.0			Light brown thread of top hair with knots in each end
1796	75 og 70	Z	35°	1.0			Two brown threads knotted into one of the above named knots
1822	125 og 275	2Z1S	25°-30°				Goat-hair threads 0.317g
1822	30-70	Z, S, 2S1Z and 2Z1S	30°-50°	0,7-4,0			Brown, dark brown threads together with goat-hair threads
1846	180 and 140	Z	40°-45°	1.0-1.5			Light brown threads
1846	90	4S2Z1S	20°	2.0			Brown cord
1846	110	2Z1S	30°	4.0			Goat-hair thread
1846	130 og 70	4S2Z1S	25°	4.0-5.0			Brown cord
1857	110x100	Z/S	40°/35°	0.9/1.2	11/11	2/2	Brown, compact weave with false seam or notch, 9 mm wide seam allowance
1872	20x30	Z/S	40°/30°	1.0/1.5	11/12	2/2	Brown, compact weave
1872	85x95	S/S	35°/25°	0.9/1.5	9/5	Tabby	Lighter patch sewn on the following compact vaðmál, 85 mm long selvedge, on two sides 8 mm wide seam allowance, stitching
1872	100x90	Z/S	45°-50°/25°	0.8/0.5	14/15	2/2	Brown vaðmál, on which the patch is sewn with a dark thread
1872	40x20	Z/S	40°/25°	0.8/1.0	12/12	Tabby	Completely light
1873	180x160	Z/S	40°/35°	1.0/1.0	8/9	2/2	Dark warp and light weft
1889	35 og 110	2Z1S	25°	3.0-4.0			Dark goat-hair threads
1889	70 og 35	Z	40°	2.0			Brown threads
1998	80x90	Z/S	40°/35°	0.9/1.2	11/11	2/2	Dark brown, 8 mm wide seam allowance, false seam
1902	35x35	Z/S	45°/35°	1.0/1.2	8/9	2/1	Light warp and dark weft
1902	80x35	Z/S	40°/25°	1.0/1.5	7/8	lærred	Dark brown warp and lighter weft
1902	100x60	Z	45°/30°	1.0/0.5	10/20	2/2	Red brown
1902	100x30	Z/S	40°/30°	1.0/1.0	8/10	2/2	Brown, 8 mm wide seam allowance
1902	60x35	Z/S	45°/35°	1.0/0.8	9/13	2/2	Brown
1902							Hair from a seal 0.102 g
1902	70	2Z1S	30°	3.0			Goat-hair thread
1902	45	2Z1S	20°	4.0			Brown cord
1902	100	2Z1S	20°	2.0			Brown thread
1902	200, 130 and more	Z og S	15°-45°	0.2-3.0			Brown threads
1902	290	2Z1S	25°	4.0			Brown thread
1906	135	Z	45°	1.0-1.5			Brown thread
1906	70						Brown thread and wool hair 0.014 g
1921	70x15 120x115	Z/S	45°/30°	1.2/1.2	9/10	2/2	Brown, 10 mm wide seam allowance, a few stitches can be seen
1921	100x80 60x70 60x50	Z/S	45°/30°	1.0/1.2	8/10	2/2	Dark brown, l0 mm wide seam allowance
1925	115						Hair 0.047 g
1959	300	Z	40°	1.0			Dark brown thread
1959	160	2Z1S	25°	4.0			Goat-hair thread
1959	90	2Z1S	20°	4.0-5.0			Thread of light and dark top hair
1977	110x20	Z/S	40°/25°	2.0/2.5	4/4	Tabby	Brown
1980	340 plus knot and a loop on 100	2Z1S	30°	3.0-5.0			The long thread is tied to yet another thread in the knot and hereby the loop is secured
1980	40	2Z1S	25°	3.0			Light goat-hair thread
2000	100x95 90x110	Z/S	35°/30°	1.2/1.5	11/10	2/2	Brown, 10 mm wide seam allowance
2107	55x60	Z/S	40°/35°	1.0/0.9	9/11	2/2	Red-brown
2110	80x70	Z/S	40°/35°	0.8/1.0	13/13	2/2	7 mm wide seam allowance
2110							Raw wool

Inv. No. 1950 x Room 1	Measurements in mm	Spin	Angle of spin/ply of threads	C. diameter of threads in mm	Thread count per. cm	Weave	Remarks (Colour description giving the present-day colour)
2119	65	6S1Z	25°	5.0			Brown cord
2204	55x45	Z/S	45°/30°	1.5/1.5	5/6	Tabby	Warp threads are almost black, weft threads are brown
2204	75x30	Z/S	45°/30°	1.5/2.0	4/8	Tabby	Dark brown, lighter thread in tablet/stitching
2204	70	2Z1S	35°-25°	2.0			Light thread
2204	170x55	Z/S	50°/45°	1.0/1.5	7/9	2/2	Brown, selvedge with crossing weft
2216	60x70 120x100	Z/S	45°/25°	1.0/1.7	7/13	2/1	Light brown, 60 mm long selvedge, the compact weft gives an S-twill grain
2217	180x170	Z/S	40°/35°	1.0/1.0	9/11	2/2	Light red-brown, sewn together with the following dark, Tabby weave vaðmál
2217	30x130	Z/S	45°/30°	1.0/1.5	6/5	Tabby	Dark brown, several stitches
2224	25x10	2Z1S/S	15°/20°	3.0/3.0	?/4	Tabby	Goat-hair/wool
2224	135x85 and more	Z/S	35°/30°	1.0/1.5	8/6	2/2	Red-brown, badly preserved
2224	70	2Z1S	30°	4.0			Goat-hair thread
2225	25x55	Z/S	40°/30°	1.0/1.3	9/10	2/2	Brown, compact weave
2225	100x80	Z/S	45°/30°	0.9/1.2	10/10	2/2	Red brown
2225	80x10	Z/S	40°/?	1.5/?	?	?	Very badly preserved
2225	30x30	Z/S	45°/35°	1.0/1.2	8/9	2/2	Brown
2225	60x50	Z/S	40°/30°	1.0/1.0	9/10	2/2	Dark brown, 10 mm wide seam allowance, sewing
2288	10x40 50x30	Z/S	40°/30°	1.2/1.5	6/6	2/2	Light brown 8 mm wide seam allowance, a few stitches
2288	180x120	Z/S	45°/35°	1.0/1.0	8/10	2/2	Dark brown, notch or pleat on the diagonal of the weave, single stitches
2288	80x100	Z/S	45°/30°	1.2/1.0	10/12	2/2	Dark brown 8 mm wide seam allowance
2288							Light and dark raw wool 1.454 g
2288	255x270	Z/S	35°/30°	1.5-1.5	7/5	2/1	Light brown, several pieces sewn together, 9 mm seam allowance
2291	220x110	Z/S	45°/35°	1.2/1.5	9/10	2/2	Brown, 10 mm wide seam allowance, stab stitching
2336	95x65	Z/S	40°/35°	1.0/1.0	10/11	2/2	Light brown
2336	20x60	Z/S	40°/30°	1.0/1.0	8/9	2/2	Brown
2349	60x20						Brown caulking
2445	140	2Z1S	25°	3.0			Goat-hair thread
2446							Raw wool 0.301 g
2488	230x30	2Z1S/2Z1S	40°/25°	4.0/3.0	4/3-4 pr. 2 cm	2/2	Brown, weave in goat-hair, 80 mm long selvedge
2506	40,30, og 25	6S1Z	35°-40°	5.0-6.0			Brown cord
2519	65x20	Z/S	40°/30°	1.2/1.5	?	?	Light brown, fragment is doubled and sewn through with many stitches
2519	35x20	Z/S	40°	1.2/1.2	4/10	2/1	Dark brown, 10 mm wide seam allowance, a few stitches can be seen
2519	100	2Z1S	20°	1.2			Knot on the one Z-spun thread
2519	55x120	Z/S	40°/30°	1.2/3.0	6/3	Tabby	Dark warp and light weft, selvedge with crossing weft
2519	50x40	Z/S	40°/30°	1.2/1.5	4/5	Tabby	Light brown
2519	35	2Z1S	30°	3.0-4.5			Thread of goat-hair
2519	100						Brown, hair from a bear 0.315 g
2519	145	Z	45°	1.0			Light brown thread
2553	180x150	Z/S	45°/35°	1.0/1.3	8/9	2/2	Dark/light, seam
2554	80x170	Z/S	40°/30°	1.0/1.3	5/6	Tabby	Light brown, compact weave
2554	90x160	Z/S	35°/25°	1.0/1.3	4/6	2/1	Light brown, unevenly woven
2554	390x100	Z/S	40°-45°/35°	0.9/1.2	10/9	2/2	Narrow pleats lengthwise in warp direction, sewing
2592	200x80 40x50 and 30x30	Z/S	45°/30°	0.5/1.0	14/12	2/2	Several seamed pieces, in three layers in some places
2655	250	S	20°	1.0-1.2			Brown thread
2675							Pollen glass with single fibres
2726	390	3S1Z	30°	4.0-5.0			Brown thread
2734	240x100	Z/S	40°/30°	0.7/1.0	11/11	2/2	Dark warp, light weft, lovely weave
2752	170						Raw wool 1.620 g and hair
2769	85	Z	45°	1.0			Dark brown thread
2815	70x70	Z/S	45°/30°	1.0/1.5	8/6	2/2	Brown, the warp is darkest
2825	85 og 125	2Z1S	30°	4.0			Brown threads of goat-hair
2860	190	S	15°	1.4-4.5			Brown thread

Inv. No. 1950 x Room 1	Measurements in mm	Spin	Angle of spin/ply of threads	C. diameter of threads in mm	Thread count per. cm	Weave	Remarks (Colour description giving the present-day colour)
2862	160x135	Z/S	50°/30°	0.5-1.5/ 1.0	12/6	Tabby (repp)	Brown, several places two-three warp threads can be seen in the same reed
2891	150x20 (db.)	Z/S	45°/35°	1.0/1.0	10/8	2/2	Dark brown seam allowance with close sewing over two parallel threads
2916	20x15 and more	Z/S	45°/40°	1.0/1.0-2.0	11/6	2/2	Light brown
2992							Raw wool 1.030 g
3048	130x60 160x60 220x100	Z/S	45°/25°	0.5/1.5	16/5	Tabby (repp)	Light brown, unevenly woven, thickness of thread varies a lot
3056	20x270	Z/S	40°/25°	1.0/1.5	9/8	2/2	Light brown with stripe effect in the weft, 12 mm seam allowance, sewing
3058	150x150 100x100 and more	Z/S	45°/35°	1.0/1.0	9/9	2/2	Light brown, very badly preserved, sewing
3058	50x70	2S1Z/2Z1S	40°/40°	1.2/1.5	5/4	Tabby	Snow hare, completely light
3058	60x50	Z/S	35°/20°	1.2/1.5	8/6	2/2	Light brown
3058	20x15(db)	Z/S	45°/30°	0.8/1.0	12/10	2/2	Light brown, fragment is a seam allowance parallel with warp threads, few stitches
3091	70x270	S/2S1Z	30°/40°	1.0/2.0	5-6/5-7	Tabby	Brown, 40 mm wide stripe in the direction of the weft, consisting of twisted threads
3095	130x140	Z/S	35°-40°/20°	1.0/2.0-3.0	10/4	2/2	Red-brown, shag pile weave, sewing
3095	?	Z	35°	1.5			The pile is woven with two parallel threads
3103	260x55 140x55	Z/Z	40°/50°	0.4/1.0	16/8	Tabby	Black, two bands, each 27 mm wide, sewn together along the one side, carbonised
3103	150x90 180x90 and more	Z/Z	40°-45°/ 30°-45°	0.5-1.0/ 0.5-1.0	8/8	Tabby	Black, varying thicknesses of thread and unevenly woven, carbonised
3103	120x5 130x5	Z/Z			16/14	Tabby	Black, binding band/rouleau, material is rollen lengthwise together and sewn, carbonised
3103	280x2						Black, outermost edge of a tablet weaving, carbonised
3192	35	3Z1S	30°	1.0			Red, new thread
3391							Black raw wool 0.305 g
3457	175	3S1Z	35°	4.0			Brown cord
3457	140	8S1Z	35°	5.0-7.0			Brown cord

NUNATAQ
MUNICIPALITY OF NARSAQ, RUIN GROUP Ø1. ANTIQUITY NUMBER 61V3-III-545

Inv. No.	Measure-ments in mm	Spin	Angle of spin/ply of threads	C. diameter of threads in mm	Thread count per. cm	Weave	Remarks (Colour description giving the present-day colour)
No Number	30x22 and several smaller pieces	Z/S				2/2	

NARSAQ BY (Landnáma Farm)
MUNICIPALITY OF NARSAQ, RUIN GROUP Ø17a. ANTIQUITY NUMBER 60V1-00I-518

Inv. No. D5/1992	Measure-ments in mm	Spin	Angle of spin/ply of threads	C. diameter of threads in mm	Thread count per. cm	Weave	Remarks (Colour description giving the present-day colour)
7	100x100	Z/S	45°/20°	1.0/1.5	9/7	2/2	Dark brown, seam allowance 10 mm, overcast stitches
8	140x115	Z/S 2Z1S	45°/30° 20°	0.5/0.9 1.5	18/11	2/2	Brownish, seamed, 5 mm seam allowance, 'couched needlework', Thread
9	310x160	Z/Z	30° -45°/ 30°- 45°	1.0/1.0	14/6-10/5	Tabby (repp)	Dark brown, selvedged starting border, 5 mm seam allowance, seam.
10	340x140	Z/S	45°-50°/25°	1.0/2.0	5x2/4	Tabby	Black, warp threads that run two and two
11	60x120	Z/S	40°/25°	0.9/1.2	8/7	2/2	Black
12	65x90 85x80	Z/S	45°/25°	0.9/1.2	9/7	2/2	Black, 7 mm seam allowance
13	200x180	Z/S	40°/25°	1.0/1.5	13/6	2/2	Dark brown
14	130x210	Z/S	40°/20°	1.0/1.2	10/5	2/2	Brown
15	160x100	Z/S	50°/20°	1.2/1.6	7/6	2/2	Black, seamed, frayed seam allowance, long stitches, doubled.
16	150x30	Z/S	40°-50°/20°	1.2/2.5	9/4	2/2	Dark brown, fragment is a seam allowance.
17	170x320	Z/S Z	45°/10° 10°	1.2/2.5 2.5-3.0	7/4	2/2	Red-brown, shag pile weave Pile
18	60x80	Z/S	45°/25°	1.0/1.5	10/8	2/2	Dark
19	80x45	Z/S	45°-50°/25°	1.0/1.0	12/11	2/2	Light brown
20	85x95	Z/S	45°/25°	0.8/1.0	15/9	2/2	Brown, false seam
21	80x130	Z/S	45°/30°	1.0/2.0	10/6	2/2	Black
22	170x40	Z/S	45°/25°	0.7/ 1.0	14/12	2/2	Dark
23	40x100	Z/S	45°/25°	1.0/1.2	7/7	2/2	Black
24	50x120	Z/S	45°/25°	1.0/1.5	8/7	2/2	Black, seamed
25	70x150	Z/S	40°/25°	1.5/1.5-2.0	7/6	2/2	Black, selvedge, seamed
26	100x55	Z/S	40°/30°	0.8/1.0	11/9	2/2	Brown, seamed, frayed seam allowance
27	130x170	Z/S	45°-50°/25°	1.0/1.0	13/11	2/2	Selvedge med crossing weft, 15 mm seam allowance, overcast stitching, seamed
28	70x70	Z/S	45°/20°	1.0/2.0	9/4	2/2	Black
29	70x70	Z/S	45°/20°	1.2/2.0	8/6	2/2	Brownish
30	50x220	Z/S	40°/20°	1.0/1.3	12/7	2/2	Black
31	20 - 40	S	20°-30°	1.0-2.0			A bundle of thread

TUNUARMIUT, TUNUGDLIARFIK
THE MUNICIPALITY OF NARSAQ, RUIN GROUP Ø20, ANTIQUITY NUMBER 60V2-0IV-661

Inv. No. D5/1992	Measure-ments in mm	Spin	Angle of spin/ply of threads	C. diameter of threads in mm	Thread count per. cm	Weave	Remarks (Colour description giving the present-day colour)
D7499.4	20x80						
	25x40	Z/S	45°/40°	1.5/1.5	6/6	2/2	Red-brown, fragments sent into the National Museum in 1894

QASSIARSUK (Brattahlid)
THE MUNICIPALITY OF NARSAQ, RUIN GROUP Ø29a. ANTIQUITY NUMBER 61V3-III-539

Inv. No. D12210 A Serial No.	Measure-ments in mm	Spin	Angle of spin/ply of threads	C. diameter of threads in mm	Thread count per. cm	Weave	Remarks (Colour description giving the present-day colour)
A,1	80x125	Z/S	45°/25°	1.0/0.9	8/10	2/2	Brownish
A,2	170x85	Z/S	45°/20°	1.2/0.5	8/22	2/2	Red-brown, stab stitching, overcast stitching.
A,3	80x65	Z/S	45°/25°	1.0/0.5	9/18	2/2	Dark brown
A,4	65x85	Z/S	45°/30°	1.0/1.0	8/14	2/2	Dark brown
A,5	70x95	Z/S	40°/25°	1.0/1.0	8/11	2/2	Brown
A,6	120x95 110x120	Z/S	45°-55°/30 °	1.2/0.9	9/12	2/2	Brown, tablet/stitching
A,7	50x50 60x100	Z/S	40 °/30 °	1.0/0.7	8/15	2/2	Light brown, seamed.
A,8	70x30	Z/2Z1S 2Z1S	35°/20° 20 °	1.0/1.2 1.2	7/12-14 ?	Tabby	Light brown, poor state of preservation, therefore analyses are a little doubtful, some loose threads
A,9	170x110	Z/S	50°/30°	1.2/0.8	8/12	2/2	Red-brown

QORLORTUP ITINNERA
THE MUNICIPALITY OF NARSAQ, RUINGRUPPE Ø34. ANTIQUITY NUMBER 61V3-III-525

Inv. No. No. Ø34	Measure-ments in mm	Spin	Angle of spin/ply of threads	C. diameter of threads in mm	Thread count per. cm	Weave	Remarks (Colour description giving the present-day colour)
x38	14x10 55x14 10x14	Z/S	45°/30°	1.0/1.0	11/11	2/2	Brown
x38	20x15	Z/S	45°/40°	1.0/0.6	11/18	2/2	Brown, very compact weft.
x104	55x20 45x15	Z/S	40°/30°	1.0/1.0	10/13	2/2	Brown
x105	50x45	Z/S	40°/30°	1.0/1.0	7/8	2/2	Reddish
x106	105x70 50x50 55x45	Z/S	45 °/35 °	1.0/0.9	9/12	2/2	Red-brown, on one of the fragments - a gusset(?) - the remains of stitching can be seen, plant remains.
x362	50x40	Z/S	45°/25°	1.0/1.0	7/8	2/2	Mistake, three threads in same shed
x398	90x125	Z/S	40°/25°	1.0/0.5	8/16	2/2	Light brown, single stitch, 7 mm seam allowance
x640	285 140	S 2Z1S	20°-30°	1.2-2.0 3.0			Brownish, from one 'skein' garn, 20 threads, plant remains. Braided cord
x775	30x45	Z/S	40°/35°	1.0/1.0	9/9	2/2	Almost black
x779	190x90	Z/S	45°/30°	1.0/0.8	7/14	2/2	Brown
x1702	18x90	Z/S	45°/25°	0.9/0.7	11/15	2/2	Dark brown
x1703	130x120	Z/S	40°/30°	0.9/0.8	10/11	2/2	Brown
x1705	110x100	Z/S	45°/30°-40°	1.2/1.5-2.0	7/7	2/2	Red-brown, thick and compact weave.
x1709	55x40	Z/S	45°/35°	1.0/1.0	10/10	2/2	Brownish
x1713	185x130	Z/S	40°/30°	1.0/1.0	12/14	2/2	Brownish
x1714	80x70	Z/S	45°-40°/30°	0.9/0.8	10/12	2/2	Brown shades, striped in direction of the warp threads with a dye change in every second thread
x1715	136x80	Z/S	40°-50°/40°	1.0/0.6-0.8	8/14	2/2	Brown
x1716	250x28-30 (double)	Z/S 2Z1S	45°/30° 25°-30°	1.0-0.9 0.7-1.0	8/12	2/2	Brown, part of a liripipe, sewing and seam sewing thread
No number	170x130	Z/S	40°-45°/25°	0.9/0.8	10/16	2/2	Dark brown, very compact weft

Among the textile fragments from Ø34 there are exceptionally many weaves with a high number of weft threads per cm in relation to the number of warp threads. The braided cord (x640) consists of six two-plied S-spun threads. Holes from sewing are visible in the cord

GARDAR (Igaliku)

THE MUNICIPALITY OF NARSAQ, RUIN GROUP Ø47, ANTIQUITY NUMBER 60V2.IV.621

Inv. No.	Measure-ments in mm	Spin	Angle of spin/ply of threads	C. diameter of threads in mm	Thread count per. cm	Weave	Remarks (Colour description giving the present-day colour)
D1451/	270x140	Z/S	30°-50°/30°	1.0-2.0/	10/7	2/2	Brownish, number of threads is measured at 20 mm,
1977	45x105			3.0-5.0			selvedge with crossing weft threads
No number	More pieces	Z/Z	20°/20°	0.4/0.4	16/16	Tabby	Black, organic material, carbonised

D1451/1977, both fragments are from the same weave - a weave that has very thin warp threads in relation to the weft threads.
No number, fragments of organic material, carbonised. There are two 'clumps' of flax(?), compressed. Measurement: c. 100x80 mm and 100x60 mm,
together with other smaller pieces. In a piece of 4-5 mm in the smallest clump, narrow pleats can be seen which lie staggered to each other.
The depth of the pleats cannot be measured. There is a selvedge preserved in 30-40 mm's length.

RUSSIP KUUA, VATNAHVERFI

THE MUNICIPALITY OF QAQORTOQ, RUIN GROUP Ø71. ANTIQUITY NUMBER 60V2-0IV-602.

Inv. No. D23/1991	Measure-ments in mm	Spin	Angle of spin/ply of threads	C. diameter of threads in mm	Thread count per. cm	Weave	Remarks (Colour description giving the present-day colour)
nr. 8	220	3S1Z					A three-threaded cord in several pieces, 3-4 mm thick
nr. 13	27x21 og flere mindre stykker	Z/S	45°/25°	0.8/1.2	10/8	2/2	Brown

Textile fragments are named in C.L. Vebæk 1992, p. 112

QAQORTOQ (Hvalsø Fjord Church)

THE MUNICIPALITY OF QAQORTOQ, RUIN GROUP Ø83. ANTIQUITY NUMBER 60V2-0IV-646

Inv. No.	Measure-ments in mm	Spin	Angle of spin/ply of threads	C. diameter of threads in mm	Thread count per. cm	Weave	Remarks (Colour description giving the present-day colour)
D8079	25x80 and several smaller pieces	Z/S	50°-45°/35°	1.2/1.0	7/8	2/2	Brownish, excavated on 2nd July 1902
D12685	60x45	Z/S		0.8/1.0	9/12	2/2	Red-brown, stab stitching, 10-12 mm seam allowance
-	35x03	2Z1S	30°	3.0			Greyish braided cord
D12690	120x120	Z/S	40°/25°	1.0/1.0	10/10	2/2	Red-brown

D12685: On this fragment, along a narrow turned edge, a very fine braided cord can be seen, sewn down with flax thread.
D12690.83 is mentioned in Rousell, Aa., 1941, p. 259

HERJOLFSNÆS (Ikigaat)

THE MUNICIPALITY OF NANORTALIK, RUIN GROUP Ø111. ANTIQUITY NUMBER 59V1-0IV-502

Inv. No.	Measure-ments in mm	Spin	Angle of spin/ply of threads	C. diameter of threads in mm	Thread count per. cm	Weave	Remarks (Colour description giving the present-day colour)
D5674	Garment	Z/S	40°/35°	1.0/1.5	10/11	2/2	Brown, stitching
D5674	Fragment	Z/S	40°/30°	1.0/0.7	11/15	2/2	Red-brown (the half of a sleeve)
D5674	Fragments	Z/S	40°/25°	1.0/0.9	12/18	2/2	Black/reddish (the half of a sleeve) and gusset?
D5677	Fragment	Z/S	50°/25°	1.2/0.7	8/18	2/2	Brown
D6473	'Hip-piece'	Z/S	45°/30°	1.2/1.2	9/9	2/2	Dark brown, sewn narrow pleats
D7649	Fragment	Z/S	45°/?	1.2/?	8/?	2/2	Dark brown, stitching
D8080	Garment parts	Z/S	45°/35°	1.0/1.0	9/11	2/2	Black, charred clumps of clothing
D8081	Garment parts	Z/S	45°/30°	1.0/0.9	11/15	2/2	Red-brown, altogether 20 fragments
D10577	Garment part	Z/S	45°-40°/40°	1.2/1.0	6/7	2/2	Red-brown, side panels, grooved on the back, stitching
D10577	Fragment	Z/S	40°/30°	1.0/0.7	8/15	2/2	Red-brown
D10577	Fragments	Z/S	40°-50°/35°	1.0/1.0	8/9	2/2	Red-brown with many black fibres
D10578	Garment part	Z/S	45°-40°/40°	1.2/1.0	7/7	2/2	Red-brown, side panels

Inv. No.	Measure-ments in mm	Spin	Angle of spin/ply of threads	C. diameter of threads in mm	Thread count per. cm	Weave	Remarks (Colour description giving the present-day colour)
D10579	Garment parts	Z/S	40°/35°-40°	1.0/1.0	9/10	2/2	Dark brown, stitching
D10580	Garment	Z/S	35°/45°	1.0/1.0	9/11	2/2	Dark brown, stitching, braided cord
D10581	Garment and	Z/S	45°-40°/35°	0.9/0.8	10/14-16	2/2	Red-brown, stitching
	Fragment	Z/S	40°/30°	1.0/1.2	7/9	2/2	Brown
D10582	Garment and	Z/S	40°/35°	1.0/1.1	10/10	2/2	Red-brown, two selvedges with crossing weft, stitching red-brown,
	Fragment	Z/S	40°/35°	1.0/1.1	10/10	2/2	stitching
D10583	Garment	Z/S	45°-50°/35°	1.0/0.9	9/12	2/2	Dark brown, stitching, buttonholes
D10583	Buttons						Dark brown, seven buttons
D10584	Garment	Z/S	40°/30°	1.2/1.0	8/9	2/2	Dark brown, stitching, braided cord
D10585.1	Garment	Z/S	45°/35°	1.0/0.9	10/13	2/2	Dark brown, two selvedges with crossing weft, stitches
		Z/S	45°/30°	1.2/0.4	7/24	2/2	Light brown patch
		Z/S	50°/35°	1.0/0.5	8/22	2/2	Light brown patch
		Z/S	45°/25°	1.0/0.9	8/13	2/2	Greyish patch
D10585.2	Hood	Z/S	45°/35°	1.2/1.2	7/8	2/2	Dark brown, stitching
D10586	Child's garment	Z/S	45°/35°	1.0/1.2	8/9	2/2	Brown
D10587	Garment	Z/S	40°/35°	1.0/1.2	9/8	2/2	Dark brown, stitching, braided cord
D10588	Garment part	Z/S	45°/30°	0.8/1.0	8/10	2/2	Light brown, four panels
D10589	Fragment	Z/S	45°/35°	1.0/1.0	9/10	2/2	Dark brown, part of child's garment (½ yoke)
D10590	Fragments	Z/S	50°/30°	1.0/0.9	9/12	2/2	Brown, stitching
D10590	Garment part,	Z/S	40°/30°	1.0/1.0	10/10	2/2	Black, sewn pleat
	Fragment	Z/S	40°/30°	1.0/1.0	10/10	2/2	Fragment with pleat
D10590	Fragments	Z/S	40°/30°	1.0/1.0	10/10	2/2	Almost black
D10591	Garment part	Z/S	40°/30°	1.0/1.0	8/9	2/2	Brown, top and five panels, stitching
D10592	Child's garment	Z/S	35°-40°/30°	0.9/1.2	10/15	2/2	Light red-brown
D10593	Child's garment	Z/S	40°/30°	1.2/2.0-1.0	7/9	2/2	Red-brown, false seam
D10594	Garment	Z/S	45°/35°	1.0/1.0	8/10	2/2	Dark brown, stitching, buttonholes,
	Border	Z/Z	40°/40°	0.9/0.9	11/11	2/1	Lighter brown
D10595	Garment	Z/S	45°/25°	1.0/0.8	10/16	2/2	Light brown, stitching
D10596	Hood	Z/S	40°/30°	1.0-1.2/1.0	8/8-9/10	2/2	Brown-black, stitching
D10597	Hood	Z/S	45°/30°	1.0/0.9	8/11	2/2	Red-brown
D10598	Hood	Z/S	45°/25°	1.0/0.8	8/11-18	2/2	Red-brown, selvedge
D10599	Hood	Z/S	45°/35°	1.2/0.8	5/13-16	Tabby	Red-brown
						(repp)	Red-brown
D10600	Hood	Z/S	45°/35°	1.0/1.0	9/10	2/2	Dark brown
D10601	Hood	Z/S	45°/35°	1.0/1.0	8/9	2/2	Dark brown, stitching
D10602	Hood	Z/S	45°/35°	1.2/0.7	8/14	2/2	Dark brown
D10603	Hood	Z/S	35°/25°	1.0/0.5	8/20-22	2/2	Brownish, selvedge,
	Gussets	Z/S	45°/30°	1.0/0.8	8/12	2/2	Brownish
D10604	Hood	Z/S	45°/35°	1.2/0.9	9/10	2/2	Dark brown
D10605	Hood	Z/S	45°/30°	0.9/1.0	9/12	2/2	Grey-brown, stitching
D10606	Hood	Z/S	40°/30°	1.2/0.9	9/12	2/2	Red-brown, stitching
D10607	Hood	Z/S	45°/35°	1.0/0.8	9/12	2/2	Dark brown, stitching
D10608	Hood	Z/S	45°/35°	1.0/1.0	10/12	2/2	Dark red-brown, stitching
D10608	Cap crown	Z/S	40°/25°	1.0/0.5	9/21	2/2	Dark brown, dense weft,
	Side pieces	Z/S	45°/35°	1.1/1.0	8/9	2/2	Dark brown
		Z/S	45°/35°	1.0/1.0	9/10	2/2	Dark brown
D10609	Hood	Z/S	50°/30°	0.9/0.9	6/8	2/2	Brownish with 40 mm wide light stripes in warp direction, stitching
D10610	Crown	Z/S	55°/40°	1.0/0.8	10/14	2/2	Dark brown
	patch	Z/S	50°/45°	0.8/0.5	18/24	2/2	Dark brown, dense weft,
	border	Z/S	50°/30°	1.0/0.7	12/19	2/2	Dark brown
D10611	'Pill-box' cap	Z/S	40°/30°	1.2/1.0	7/10	2/2	Brown, stitching
10612	'Pill-box' cap	Z/S	35°-45°/ 30°-40°	1.0-2.0/ 1.0-1.5	6/9-13	Tabby	Light brown, sewing, very poor state of preservation
		Z/S	40°/35°	1.2/1.2	8/9	2/2	
D10613	Stocking	Z/S	45°/35°	1.2/1.2	7/8	2/2	Dark brown, selvedge, stitching
D10614	Stocking	Z/S	45°-50°/ 30°-35°	1.0/1.0-2.0	6/8	2/2	Brownish, selvedge with crossing weft
D10615	Stocking	Z/S	40°-45°/30°	1.0/1.5	5/6	Tabby	Red-brown

Inv. No.	Measure-ments in mm	Spin	Angle of spin/ply of threads	C. diameter of threads in mm	Thread count per. cm	Weave	Remarks (Colour description giving the present-day colour)
D10616	Stocking	Z/S,	40°/30°	1.0/1.0	8/9-10	2/2	Brown, starting border,
		2Z1S	30°	1.5-2.0			Threads in starting border
		2Z1S	30°	1.5-2.0			Threads in selvedge
D10617	Stocking	Z/S	35°-40°/35°	1.2/1.2-2.0	6-7/7	Tabby and	Red-brown, selvedge
					7/9	Diamond-twill	
D10618	Stocking	Z/S	40°-50°/30°	1.0/1.0-0.6	8/12	2/2	Red-brown
D10619							Leather fragment
D10620	Fragment	Z/S	45°-55°/25°	0.7/0.5	14/20	2/2	Red-brown, 'withered' edges
D10621	Fragment	Z/S	45°/35°	0.5/0.5	12/15	Tabby	Reddish, sewn to below named
		S/S	40°/40°	0.5/0.5	10/10	Tabby	Brownish
D10622	Cord	12S1Z	35°/40°	5-7			Light brown
D10623	Felt?						Has disappeared
D10624	Four pieces of a braid	2S1Z	30°	1.5			Red-brown with black fibres, braid consists of three times three threads.
No.75	Hood	Z/S	45°/35°	1.0/1.0-0.8	8/9	2/2	Reddish
D25-26/ 2001	235x210 sewing thread	Z/S 2Z1S	45°-50°/30° 30°	1.0-1.5/1.5 9,0	7/8	2/2	Brownish, remains of seam allowance along a corner, stab stitches and overcast stitches (filler threads) along the frayed edge

The fragment D25-26/2001 was delivered to the National Museum in a chocolate box in 1987.
Written on the box was: 'From Igigat Churchyard', and a note written later: 'Cloth from garments of Norse settlers in Greenland.
Valuable, must not be destroyed …found by Father' Probably Gustav Holm (1849–1940). With the textile fragment there was a piece of a wooden cross.

HERJOLFSNÆS (Ikigaat)
THE MUNICIPALITY OF NANORTALIK, RUIN GROUP Ø111. ANTIQUITY NUMBER 59V1.1V.502

Inv. No. D2625	Measure-ments in mm	Spin	Angle of spin/ply of threads	C. diameter of threads in mm	Thread count per. cm	Weave	Remarks (Colour description giving the present-day colour)
a-e	Garment	Z/S	45°-40°/30°	1.0/0.9	8-9/10	2/2	20 mm wide hem along the bottom edge, tablet /stitching
f							Not Norse textile
g							Not found
h							Not Norse textile
i	190x165	Z/S	45°-50°/40°	0.8/2.0	5-6/7-8	Tabby	Red-brown, singling and tablet/stitching
	530x130	Z/S	45°-50°/40°				
j	180x160	Z/S	45°/30°-40°	1.5/2.0	7/6	Tabby	Red-brown, singling
	240x10-15	Z/S	45°/30°-40°	1.5/2.0	7/6	Tabby	Red-brown, singling
	535x115-130	Z/S	45°/3o°-40°	1.5/2.0	7/6	Tabby	Red-brown, light edges on all three fragments
No number	195x100 190x50 230x110	Z/S	45°/30°	1.0/1.0	9/11	2/2	Brown, 10-15 mm seam allowance
No number	150x130	Z/S	40°/25°	1.0/1.0	9/10	2/2	Dark brown, singling

Textile fragments (D2625a-j) are wrongly registered under RØNBJERG, see Hald, M., 1950, pp. 58-61, fig. 44-45. 1980, pp. 62-64 fig. 44-45

HERJOLFSNÆS (Ikigaat)
THE MUNICIPALITY OF NANORTALIK, RUIN GROUP Ø111. ANTIQUITY NUMBER 59V1.1V.502

No. Number Serial No.	Measure-ments in mm	Spin	Angle of spin/ply of threads	C. diameter of threads in mm	Thread count per. cm	Weave	Remarks (Colour description giving the present-day colour)
A	260x220 185x100 115x110 60x100	Z/S	40°-50°/20°	1.2/0.5	7/24	2/2	Brownish
B	340x190 310x280 255x95 190x85 80x180	Z/S	45°-50°/25°	1.0/0.8	8/14	2/2	Brownish

Inventory No.	Measure-ments in mm	Spin	Angle of spin/ply of threads	C. diameter of threads in mm	Thread count per. cm	Weave	Remarks (Colour description giving the present-day colour)
C	180x205 170x100	Z/S	45°/35°	1.2/0.7	8/16	2/2	Dark brown, 10 mm seam allowance
D	140x55	Z/S	45°/35°	1.0/1.0	13/13	2/2	Reddish
E	170x260	Z/S	50°/30°	1.2/0.6	8/14	2/2	Brownish, 7 mm seam allowance, 7 mm wide seam
F	120x230	Z/S	45°/30°	1.0/0.8	9/13	2/2	Black/reddish, 7 mm seam allowance , overcastting
G	65x115	Z/S	40°/25°	1.0/0.7	9/18	2/2	Reddish, 7 mm seam allowance
H	120x140	Z/S	50°/30°	1.0/0.9	8/11	2/2	Black/reddish
I	280x285-	Z/S	50°/30°	1.1/0.9	9/12	2/2	Brownish, sleeve fragment, vents: 85 mm long in the one side, 75 mm in the other. Two selvedges with crossing weft sewn together as a sleeve seam under the arm. As an extension of the vent there is also a seam. 'Museum seam'. Patches of shirting on the back.
J	160x300-240 150x120 190x170	Z/S	45°-40°/35°	1.2/2.0	6/6	Tabby	Brownish, sleeve fragment(?), 12 mm seam allowance and original sewing with black thread. 10 mm wide seam. Overcast stitches. Lined with brown shirting. Fragmentary
K	40x50	Z/S	35°/35°	1.2/0.8	5/15	Repp	Reddish
L	110x70 215x110	Z/S	50°/30	1.0/1.0	7/9	2/2	Brownish, grooved back. Selvedge with two crossing wefts.
M	115x90	Z/S	45°/30°	1.0/1.0	8/10	2/2	Brownish, 10 mm seam allowance
N	120x230	Z/S	45°/30°	1.0/0.8	7/16	2/2	Black/reddish, 10 mm wide seam. At the cut off edge stitches from a singling can be seen. Weft effect, 30 mm wide with black threads. Seen in the direction of the warp, three reddish threads that alternate with one black warp thread
O	185x240	Z/S	40°/30°	1.0/1.0	10/10	2/2	Brownish, 15 mm seam allowance. Stripe effect with black threads in warp direction
P	110x190 210X210	Z/S 2S1Z	45°/35° 25°	1.0/1.0 2.0	6/10	2/2	Brownish, 7 mm seam allowance, dense stab stitching with 3 mm long stitches, many twisted threads in warp direction have the effect that the weave is uneven and slightly striped
Q	120x170 110x130 120x65	Z/S	45°/25°	1.0/0.7	8/16	2/2	Reddish, 6 mm wide seam with overcast stitching over thick thread
R	30x110	Z/S	50°/30°	1.0/0.8	10/15	2/2	Dark brown, 5-7 mm seam allowance, triangular
S	180x140	Z/S	45°/25°	1.0/0.5	9/22	2/2	Reddish
T	60x120 55x115	Z/S	50°/35°	1.2/1.0	8/9	2/2	Brownish, 5 mm seam allowance, triangular gussets
U	290x160	Z/S	45°/25°	0.9/0.9	10/12	2/2	Reddish
V	240x200 130x90	Z/S	35°/30°	1.0/1.0	9/12	2/2	Brownish, seam allowance 9 mm wide, dense overcast stitching over thick thread
X	120x185 130x90	Z/S	45°/35°	1.0/0.9	9/18	2/2	Dark brown, 9 mm seam allowance, tablet/stitching, singling
Y	580x460 120x110	Z/S	45°/35°	1.2/1.0	7/10	2/2	Brownish, weaving mistake, two warp threads in the same 'heddle'

A large collection of fragments in Greenlandic vaðmál in different sizes
Of 24 registered fragments there are 22 woven in 2/2 twill. The remaining two are in tabby weave.

HERJOLFSNÆS (Ikigaat)
THE MUNICIPALITY OF NANORTALIK, RUIN GROUP Ø111. ANTIQUITY NUMBER 59V1.IV.502

Inventory No. 106 Serial No.	Measure-ments in mm	Spin	Angle of spin/ply of threads	C. diameter of threads in mm	Thread count per. cm	Weave	Remarks (Colour description giving the present-day colour)
a	195x165	Z/S	40°/30°	1.5/2.0	6/5	2/2	Black/brown, selvedge
b	100x140	Z/S	40°/40°	1.0/1.0	7/10	2/2	Black/brown, selvedge, on the other three sides a 15 mm seam allowance can be seen
c	82x80	Z/S	45°/30°	1.0/0.9	9/12	2/2	Dark brown, 7-20 mm seam allowance on all four sides
d	80x145	Z/S	45°/30°	1.0/0.9	9/12	2/2	Brownish, on four sides 7-12 mm seam allowance, on two sides overcast stitching
e	200x150	Z/S	50°/35°	1.0/1.0	9/11	2/2	Brownish, 8-20 mm seam allowance, overcast stitching as well as two rows of stab stitching

Inventory No. 106 Serial No.	Measurements in mm	Spin	Angle of spin/ply of threads	C. diameter of threads in mm	Thread count per. cm	Weave	Remarks (Colour description giving the present-day colour)
f	170x100 370x270 470x210	Z/S	45°/30°	1.0/1.0	10/13	2/2	Brownish, 8-10 mm seam allowance and tablet/stitching along seam
g	100x150	Z/S	50°/35°	1.0/0.8	10/15	2/2	Dark brown, 10 mm seam allowance with tablet/stitching
h	100x60	Z/S	50°/30°	1.0/1.0	10/10	2/2	Brownish, seam allowance 5-12 mm wide
i	130x80	Z/S	50°/30°	1.0/0.8	8/15	2/2	Red-brown, 'grooved' back, 15 mm seam allowance
j	55x110	Z/S	45°-50°/30°	1.0/1.0	10/14	2/2	Red-brown, 70 mm selvedge, 15 mm seam allowance
k	135x80	Z/S	45°/30°	1.0/0.8	8/13	2/2	Dark brown, remains of seam along two sides and stab stitching
l	110x60	Z/S	45°/35°	1.0/1.0	9/12	2/2	Black/red-brown, 7 mm wide seam with overcasting and stab stitching
m	90x150	Z/S	50°/25°	1.0/0.8	8/12	2/2	Brownish, 7 mm seam allowance with two rows of stab stitching and compact overcast stitching
n	210x70	Z/S	45°/30°	1.0/0.8	8/14	2/2	Red-brown, 9-22 mm seam allowance, remains of organic sewing thread
o	190x100	Z/S	45°/25°	1.2/1.0	7/9	2/2	Dark brown, 5-10 mm seam allowance
p	100x105	Z/S	50°/30°	1.0/0.8	8/14	2/2	Brownish, selvedge with crossing weft, remains of organic sewing thread of plant fibres
No number	115x180	Z/S	45°/35°	1.0/1.2	8/9	2/2	Red-brown (dark/light) animal hair

Textile fragments with the number 106 are probably all from Herjolfsnæs. See main text, page 230.

NORSE TEXTILES – GARMENT PARTS

No. Number Serial No.	Measurements in mm	Spin	Angle of spin/ply of threads	C. diameter of threads in mm	Thread count per. cm	Weave	Remarks (Colour description giving the present-day colour)
0,1	Panels	Z/S	45°/30°	1.0/0.8	8/12	2/2	Light brown, rather decayed. Five panels, stitching
0,2	830x175	Z/S	40°/30°	1.0/0.7	9/16	2/2	Brownish, stitching
0,3	470x490	Z/S 6S3Z1S	50°/25°	1.0-1.5/1.0 3.0-5.0	5/10	Tabby	Reddish, 10 mm wide starting border, stitching The starting border has three thick black threads
0,4	360x440 235x80 More smaller	Z/S	45°/30°	1.0/1.0	7/9	2/2	Dark brown, stitching
0,5	700x140 540x290 490x150 380x110 270x250 195x160 150x400 60x70	Z/S	50°/35°	1.0/0.8	9/12	2/2	Red-brown, stitching, selvedge with crossing weft
0,6	450x510 450x170 Sleeves: 470x340-170	Z og 2Z1S/S	50°-35°/35°	1.0-2.0/0.1	8-9/11	2/2	Red-brown, stitching. New seams in the sleeves
0,7	150x120	Z/S	45°/30°	1.1/0.5	7/18	2/2	Red-brown, warp threads completely hidden
0,8	330x90	Z/S	40°/30°	1.0/0.8	10/12	2/2	Dark/light brownish
No number	30x30 30x40	Z/S	45°/30°	1.0/1.0	8/8	2/2	Brown-black warp and red-brown weft
No number	60-70x185	Z/S	45°/30°	1.0/0.3-0.8	9/20	2/2	Red-brown 14-15 mm seam allowance, seam
No number (603)	100x95	Z/S	45°/30°	1.0/0.9	8/10	2/2	Red-brown
No number (603)	75x50	Z/S	35°-45°/35°	0.8/0.8	13/13	2/2	Coloured black, fulled, sewn on sewing machine. Not a Norse textile
No number	60x70	Z/S	40°/30°	1.0/0.9	8/12	2/2	Red-brown
No number	60x165	Z/S	45°/35°	1.0/0.9	9/13	2/2	Red-brown, found in 1839

A collection of fragments without number. One fragment is from a later date, as it is seamed using a sewing machine.

NARSARSSUAQ (Uunartoq fjord)

THE MUNICIPALITY OF NANORTALIK, RUIN GROUP Ø149. ANTIQUITY NUMBER 60V2.IV.504

Inv. No. D1/1991 Serial No.	Measure-ments in mm	Spin	Angle of spin/ply of threads	C. diameter of threads in mm	Thread count per. cm	Weave	Remarks (Colour description giving the present-day colour)
11	150x200 60x40 and more smaller pieces	Z/S	45°/30°	1.0/1.0	8/10	2/2	Light brown, flat, compressed textile pieces together with smaller pieces. Written on a slip of paper is: 'Little rag for shoe soles'
12	200x170 200x190 190x150 190x130 160x350 160x105 and several smaller	Z/S	45°/35°	1.0/0.9	9/12	2/2	The largest fragment is made up of two different pieces in two shades of brown that are sewn together, while another fragment has alternately a light and a dark weft thread, selvedge, false seam, and a seam
14	410x200	Z/S	40°/30°	1.0/1.2-1.5	8/7	2/2	Black with a reddish tinge, probably coloured with korkje (lichen)
15	170x115	Z/S 2S1Z	40°/25° 20°	1.0/1.5-2.0 2.0 - 2.5	11/5-6	2/2	Dark brown on one side, reddish on the other, shag pile weave. Pile

ABELS FARM (Vatnahverfi)

THE MUNICIPALITY OF QAQORTOQ, RUIN GROUP Ø167. ANTIQUITY NUMBER 60V2-0IV-603

Inv. No. D24/1991 Serial No.	Measure-ments in mm	Spin	Angle of spin/ply of threads	C. diameter of threads in mm	Thread count per. cm	Weave	Remarks (Colour description giving the present-day colour)
52	250x210 and more	Z/S	45°/30°	1.2/1.0	8/10	2/2	Reddish
53	80x235	Z/S	45°/35°	1.0/3.0	8/4	2/2	Light brown
54	120x80	Z/S	40°/25°	1.0/1.0-1.5	10/8	2/2	Light brown
55a	130x50	Z/S	40°/40°	1.1/1.3	9/7	2/2	Brownish, felted, fulled(?), selvedge with crossing weft. Fragment is a thick seam, after being sewn to another piece.
55b	130x30	Z/S	50°/30°	1.1/1.5	8/7	2/2	Brownish, stitching
56	80x55	Z/S	40°/25°	1.0/1.0-1.5	10/8	2/2	Light brown, the same as Serial No. 54. There are many reindeer hairs in the textile
56b	185x60	Z/S	45°/30°	0.6/1.0	15/12	2/1	Dark brown
56c	50x40	Z/S 2Z1S	40°/40° 25°	1.0/3.0 1.5	6/4	Tabby	Brownish, 15 mm long stitch

Textile fragments are discussed in Vebæk, C.L., 1992, p. 123.
The fragments differ from most other Norse textiles in that they have more threads pr. cm. in the warp than in the weft.

KIRKESPIRDALEN

THE MUNICIPALITY OF NANORTALIK. ANTIQUITY NUMBER 60V2-0II-574

Inventory No. NKA	Measure-ments in mm	Spin	Angle of spin/ply of threads	C. diameter of threads in mm	Thread count per. cm	Weave	Remarks (Colour description giving the present-day colour)
136X4	60x65	Z/S	45°/25°	0.9/0.6-1.0	8/12	2/2	Brownish, 7 mm wide seam allowance along one side

The fragment was found in a rock cleft in connection with the exploration of gold in the Greenland sub-surface.

INUSSUK (Inuit Settlement)

THE MUNICIPALITY OF UPERNAVIK. ANTIQUITY NUMBER 72V1-0IV-022.

L4.4892	Measure-ments in mm	Spin	Angle of spin/ply of threads	C. diameter of threads in mm	Thread count per. cm	Weave	Remarks (Colour description giving the present-day colour)
	70x65	Z/S	40°/35°	1.0/0.8	8/7	2/2	Dark brown, a couple of stitches on a seam allowance.

TUTTUTUUP ISUA (Inuit Settlement)
THE MUNICIPALITY OF NARSAQ. ANTIQUITY NUMBER 60V1-00I-060.

L15.187	Measure-ments in mm	Spin	Angle of spin/ply of threads	C. diameter of threads in mm	Thread count per. cm	Weave	Remarks (Colour description giving the present-day colour)
	40x150					2/2 (?)	Fragment has been lost

INGLEFIELD LAND (Inuit Settlement)
RUIN Ø, NORTH WEST GREENLAND. ANTIQUITY NUMBER 78V2-000-002.

L3.2591	Measure-ments in mm	Spin	Angle of spin/ply of threads	C. diameter of threads in mm	Thread count per. cm	Weave	Remarks (Colour description giving the present-day colour)
	520x360	Z/S	40°/25°-30°	1.0/1.8	8/6	2/1	Dog hair mingled with wool, weight 120 g

ELLESMERE ISLAND, (Ruins of a House)
SKRAELING ISLAND, BUCHANAN BAY, N.W.T. CANADA.

Site SfFk 4-1234	Measure-ments in mm	Spin	Angle of spin/ply of threads	C. diameter of threads in mm	Thread count per. cm	Weave	Remarks (Colour description giving the present-day colour)
	40x150	Z/S	40°-50°/35°	1.0/1.2-3.0	9/7	2/2	Brownish
	160x680						

Radiocarbon Dating of Norse Textiles

The fundamental principle for radiocarbon dating is based on the fact that all living organisms absorb carbon from their surroundings, thus the amount of radioactive carbon present at any particular point in time in humans, animals and plants is identical everywhere in the world. The absorption of carbon atoms stops when organisms die.

Half of the radioactive carbon decays in 5,730 years. By measuring the remaining amount of radiocarbon in the archaeological specimen the age can be calculated: the lower the content, the older the specimen. Before the specimen can be dated, it is subjected to a chemical process by which possible contamination with modern or old carbon is removed. After this process, the specimen is transformed into CO_2 by combustion.

The introduction of the so-called AMS-technique (Accelerator Mass Spectrometry) in the 1980s made it possible to carry out radiocarbon dating of archaeological textile finds. With this technique one can date very small specimens, c. 1 mg pure carbon. An element of uncertainty will be present, though, of approximately plus/minus 35 years for medieval specimens.[1]

When Poul Nørlund dated the garments from Herjolfsnæs, his dating was based on some few individual examples. The same garment pieces have now been dated with the AMS method, and with one exception there is complete compliance with Nørlund's cultural-historical dating. (In the following one must compare the information in the above chart with the numbers of the objects).

The exception was the so-called *'Burgundian cap'* (D10612), which Nørlund dated to the end of the 1400s: radiocarbon dating, however, moved the age of the cap back by at least 100 years.

Interesting also is the new dating of the short-sleeved woman's garment (D10581) and the hoods (D10605) and (D10606), which are all from graves which lay directly on top of each other in the northeastern corner of the churchyard. The hood from the bottom-most grave can be dated to almost the same time as the woman's garment from the middle-most grave. The liripipe hood (D10606) lay in the youngest, top-most grave. It was dated to some decades earlier. Along with the radiocarbon dating of the textiles, the buried skeletons were also dated.[2]

The oldest dated textile from the churchyard is, however, the newly found garment, which mistakenly was registered under Rønbjerg (2625 a-e). The dating is 1180-1310. The two pleated garment pieces from the burials must also be named: they are now dated respectively to 1300-1370 (D6473) and 1300-1410 (D10590). It appears from the datings, therefore, that the textile fragment from the long house at GUS (The Farm Beneath the Sand) is, until now, the oldest piece of textile from the Norse settlements in Greenland. The dating is AD 990-1190.[3]

The following textile fragments are AMS-dated, indicated with plus or minus 1σ calibrated according to 1998 curves:

Analysis Nos.	Textile Nos.	Radiocarbon Nos.	Datings
AAR-3682	GUS x3048	965±45BP	AD 990-1190
K-1489	L3.2591	680±100BP	AD1150-1450
Ka-6982	D2625a-e	755±45BP	AD1180-1310
GSC3038	Site SfKk-4-1234	700±50BP	AD1220-1330
AAR-2201	D10612	685±50BP	AD1250-1410
AAR-2200	D10594	650±40BP	AD1280-1400
AAR-1290	D10606	553±45BP	AD1300-1370
AAR-4960	D6473	575±30BP	AD1300-1370
AAR-4959	D10590	605±30BP	AD1300-1410
AAR-1288	D10581	480±60BP	AD1380-1530
AAR-1289	D10605	480±43BP	AD1390-1490
AAR-3896	60V2-II-574	510±30BP	AD1390-1450

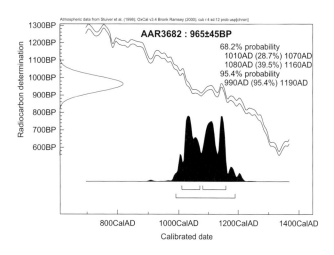

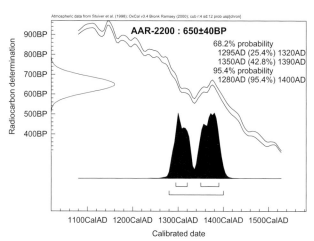

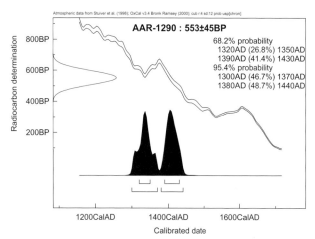

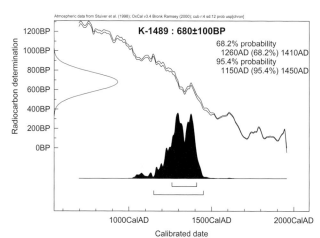

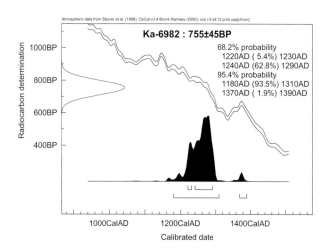

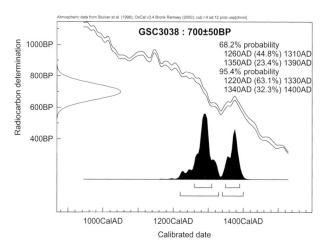

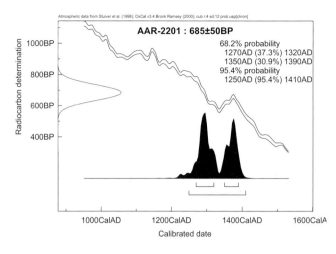

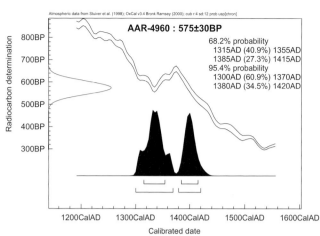

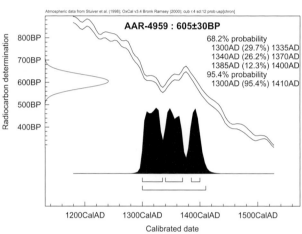

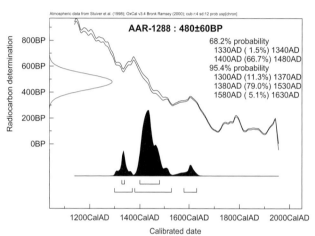

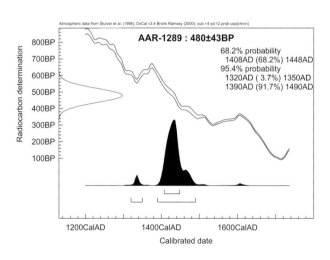

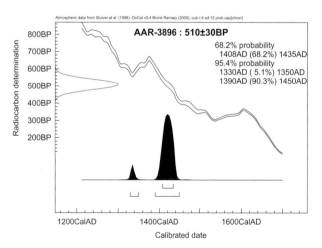

255

Notes

INTRODUCTION

1. Nørlund 1924, p. 239.
2. Krogh 1982, pp. 11-26.
3. Excavation numbers Ø = Eastern settlement. V = Western settlement.
4. Gad 1978, p. 30.
5. *Kongespejlet*, p. 51. (The King's Mirror).
6. Nørlund 1925, p. 36.

FINDS OF NORSE TEXTILES IN GREENLAND

1. Nørlund 1924, p. 17.
2. By word of mouth tradition, the Herjolfsnæs garments were found under the following conditions: Work was going according to plan and was nearly finished when the excavation team was caught by bad weather and forced to remain in the tents. The rain continued, however, and some helpers were sent out to dig ditches around the tents so that the water could run away. The weather changed. The sun began to shine, thawing the topmost permafrost layers so much that one garment after the other could be dug up out of the mire. Thus began what was to be the 20th century's greatest textile event. Left lying in the Herjolfsnæs Churchyard were ten garments and two hoods which could be described, but not saved.
3. Berglund 1998, p. 11.
4. Arneborg 1998, p. 41.
5. Nørlund 1925, p. 42.
6. Hald 1950, pp. 33-35 fig. 23-24, pp. 56-59 fig. 42-45, pp. 350-354 fig. 399-401. 1980, pp. 39-41 fig. 23-24, pp. 60-64 fig. 42-45 pp. 340-343 fig. 408-411. Sandklef 1943. Gjessing 1938.

THE EXCAVATIONS

1. *KLNM 5*, 1960, sp. 243.
2. Meldorf 1912, p. 1.
3. Meldorf 1912, p. 3.
4. Nørlund 1924, pp. 100, 105, 119, 123.
5. Nørlund 1924, pp. 87 note 2, 153-154.
6. Nørlund 1924, pp. 87 note 2, 165-167.
7. Nørlund 1924, pp. 119-120.
8. Nørlund 1924, pp. 165-167.
9. Nørlund 1924, pp. 90.
10. see note 2.
11. Römpp 1966. Beticol, a glue which is used in the carton and shoe industries.
12. Nørlund 1924, p. 39.
13. Østergård 1980.
14. Penelope Walton Roger's pers. comm., 28. August 1999.
15. Nørlund & Stenberger 1934, p. 40.
16. Krogh 1982, pp. 42-47.
17. Andreasen 1982, pp. 177-188, Arneborg 1999, pp. 353-373, Roussell 1936.
18. Vebæk 1993.

19. Walton Rogers 1993, pp. 56-58. Østergård 1993, pp. 52-56.
20. Berglund 1998, pp. 7-13.
21. Albrethsen & Ólafsson 1998, pp. 19-26.

THE SOURCE OF RAW MATERIALS

1. *KLNM* 5, 1960, p. 243.
2. Halldórsson 1996, pp. 155-157. KLNM 5, 1960, p. 290.
3. See Note 1.
4. *Kongespejlet,* p. 52 (The King's Mirror).
5, 6. Hatting 1993. Andersson 1995, pp. 7-79.
7. Tarnovius 1950. Reference on page 34, note 1, to theories from the 15- and 1600s regarding the name of *Færøerne* (the Færoe Islands). One of the theories is that it could not be the word *får* (sheep) that has given the Islands their name as this word is Danish. The Færøe Islands were populated by Norwegians. In Norwegian sheep are called *saud,* thus the Islands ought to have been called *Saudøi.* The name *Færøerne* comes instead from the feathers of the many birds that are to be found on the Islands. Correctly: *Fierøerne.*
8. Thorsteinsson 1985, p. 19.
9. Møhl 1982, pp. 290-293.
10. Forthcoming publication.
11. Adalsteinsson 1991, p. 285.
12. Hinnerson Berglund 1998, p. 169.
13. Ryder 1983, pp. 712-757.
14-16. Adalsteinsson 1991, pp. 287-289.
17. Grierson 1985, p. 4. Ryder 1983, p. 508.
18. Buckland, Buckland, Skidmore 1998, pp. 76-77.
19. Thorsteinsson 1985, p. 31.
20. Hoffmann 1964, p. 77.
21. Hoffmann 1991, pp. 19, 63.
22. Bojsen Christensen 1989, pp. 7-26.

PROCESSING OF THE RAW WOOL

1. Lise Warburg, 1974, p. 38.
2. Roussell 1936, p. 110 fig. 88, p. 177. KLNM 14, 1969, p. 674.
3. Vebæk 1992, p. 83 fig. 116, p. 127.
4. Øye 1988, p. 109 fig. V. 4.
5. Roesdahl 1977, p. 100 fig. 135, p. 120 fig. 189, p. 122 fig. 94, p. 136.
6. Hald 1941, p. 122.
7. Roussell 1936, p. 131 fig. 117, p. 188.
8. Guðjónsson 1979 (a), pp. 207-210, fig. 1. 1992, pp. 21-23, fig. 15.
9. Ryder 1983, p. 539.
10. Thanks to Nicolina Beder, Thorshavn, for this information.

THE PRODUCTION OF THE THREAD

1. Munksgaard 1974, p. 27 fig. 9.
2. Ingstad 1992, pp. 185, 190. Øye 1988, p. 36 fig. II.5.2.
3. Warburg 1974, pp. 90-96.
4. Andersson 1995, p. 8.
5. Vallinheimo 1956, pp. 130-131.
6. Grenander Nyberg 1990, pp. 78-79.

7. Vallinheimo 1956, pp. 137-138.

8. Nordland 1961, pp. 124-128 fig. 73-75.

9. Broholm & Hald 1935, p. 296 fig. 79. 1940, pp. 108-109 fig. 154.

10. Grenander Nyberg 1990, pp. 74-75.

11. Bender Jørgensen 1991. pp. 66-67 fig. 9.

12. Olaus Magnus, 1951, vol. 1, p. 103.

13. Thanks to Arne Thorsteinsson, Thorshavn, who drew my attention to this record.

14. Roussell 1936 pp. 131-134 fig. 118, 119 pp. 188-189.

15. Roussell 1941, pp. 275-277 fig. 170-171.

16. Vallinheimo 1956, pp. 137-138, note 18.

17. Roussell 1941, pp. 275-277 fig. 170.

18. Øye 1988, p. 36 fig. II. 6.

19. Broholm & Hald 1935, p. 296 fig. 76. 1940, p. 108 fig. 152.

20. Stoklund 1992, pp. 90-93 fig. 133.

21. Vebæk 1992, pp. 80-81 fig. 109 a, b, pp.122-123.

22. Nørlund 1924, p. 223 fig. 155.

23. Petersen 1951, pp. 235-37. Molaug 1991, p. 94. Øye 1988, p. 38.

24. Øye 1988, p. 52.

25. Vebæk 1943, (Ø64a, pp. 97-98, 103), (Ø64c, pp. 97, 103).
    Vebæk 1992, (Ø70, p. 80 fig. 108, p. 110) (Ø71, p. 112).

26. Roussell 1936, pp. 133-134, 188-189.

27. Nørlund & Stenberger 1934, pp. 128-129.

28. Nørlund 1930, pp. 163-165, pp. 147, 164.

29. Stoklund 1982, p. 202 fig. 5.

30. Hoffmann 1991, pp. 84-85. Hald 1950, p. 132, the fixation of thread.

THE WARP WEIGHTED LOOM

1. Guðjónsson 1985, pp. 116-128. 1989, pp. 185-197. 1990 (a), pp. 165-179. 1994, pp. 178-195. In the four articles the author carefully documents the Icelandic loom. The correct Icelandic designations for the individual parts of the loom are also given. See also Hoffmann 1964, pp. 114-140.

2. Broholm & Hald 1935, p. 301. *Kliggjavevur:* To *kliggja* means to hang a weight on something. 1940, pp. 112-113. Thanks to Nicolina Beder in Thorshavn for the information regarding *Kliggjavevur.*

3. *KLNM* 2, 1957, pp. 667-668.

4. Guðjónsson 1985, pp. 123-124. 1989, pp. 185-187.

5. Guðjónsson 1994, p. 184, note 34.

6. Broholm & Hald 1935, pp. 302-303 fig. 85-86. 1940, p. 113 fig. 162.

7. Broholm & Hald 1939, pp. 70-73.

8. Hoffmann 1964, pp. 126-127. Guðjónsson 1990 (a), pp. 173-174.

9. Nørlund 1930, p. 165.

10 Hoffmann 1964, p. 146.

11. Andreasen 1982, p. 182 fig. 9.

12. Rui 1991, p. 118.

13. Stoklund 1982, pp. 197-206 fig. 9. 1993, p. 52 fig. 85. 1998, pp. 55-57.

14. Resi & Schjølberg 1998, pp. 129-154.

15. Nørlund 1924, pp. 68, 224.

16. Nørlund 1924, p. 68.

17. Nørlund & Stenberger 1934, p. 126.

18. Roussell 1936, p. 131 fig. 116, p. 188.

19. Roussell 1941, pp. 275-276 fig. 171.
20. Vebæk 1943, p. 85 fig. 58, p. 102. 1993, 35-36 fig. 46-47, p. 75.
21. Hoffmann 1964, pp. 279-283 fig. 112-116. Øye 1988, pp. 70-71.
22. Ólafsson 1987, pp. 347-350.
23. Kjellberg & Hoffmann 1991, p. 61.
24. Arneborg & Østergård 1994, p. 170. Guðjónsson 1994, p. 188.
25. Roussell 1941, pp. 173-175, 183-184, 202.
26. Andersson 1996, p. 72. Rui 1991, pp. 127-128.
27. Stærmose Nielsen 1999, pp. 81-88 fig. 45 A-B.
28. Arneborg & Østergård 1994, p. 170.
29. Guðjónsson 1994, p. 188, note b.
30. See Note 27.
31. Roussell 1936, pp. 130, 187.
32. Roussell 1941, p. 183.

TECHNIQUES
1. Guðjónsson 1985, pp. 123-124. 1990 (a), p. 173.
2. Falk 1919, p. 17, note 1.

GREENLANDIC TEXTILES
1. Gudmundsson 1997, p. 63.
2. Thorsteinsson 1985, p. 35.
3. Andersen 1995, pp. 251-253. Hoffmann 1964, p. 194.
4. Østergård 1998, pp. 58-65.
5. Hoffmann 1964, p. 146, note 8.
6. Arneborg & Østergård 1994, pp. 167, 170 (1950x598). Guðjónsson 1994, pp. 188-189.
7. *KLNM* 19, 1975, pp. 409-410. Hoffmann 1964, p. 195.
8. Guðjónsson 1985, pp. 118-120. 1990 (a), pp. 166-169 fig. 1-4.
9. Hoffmann 1964, p. 152 fig. 70, p. 155.
10. Lindström 1976, pp. 282-292 fig. 249 a-b, fig. 250 a.
11. Franzén & Nockert 1992, pp. 23-26 fig. 10-11.
12. Hoffmann 1964, p. 149 fig. 68, pp. 171-183 fig. 82-87. Kjellberg 1979, p. 87 fig. 2-3.
    Stærmose Nielsen 1999, pp. 100-103, fig. 56 A-B, fig. 57, fig. 58 A-B, fig. 59 A-B.
13. Guðjónsson 1983, p. 138 fig. 3. Mus. No. CLII, 1819. 1997, p. 89 fig. 5.
14. Hoffmann 1964, p. 148 fig. 67.
15. Hoffmann 1964, p. 146, note 12. Broholm & Hald 1939 p. 70.
16. Guðjónsson 1985, p. 116.
17. Nørgård 1999, p. 2.
18. Walton 1989, p. 320 fig. 127d.
19. Hald 1950, pp. 33-35 fig. 23-24, pp. 56-59 fig. 42-43, pp. 350-354 fig. 399. 1980, pp. 39-41 fig. 23-24, pp. 60-61 fig. 42-43, pp. 340-343 fig. 409. Lindström 1976, p. 283 fig. 250 a.
20. Nockert 1997, pp. 56, 68.
21. See note 13.
22. Kjellberg 1997, pp. 91-92 fig. 3.
23. Kjellberg & Hoffmann 1991, p. 22 fig. 6.
24. Østergård 1992, pp. 52-53 fig. 86.
25. Hoffmann 1964, p. 199, note 14 p. 360.
26. Kjellberg & Hoffmann 1991, p. 24.
27. Bender Jørgensen 1986 (b), pp. 76, 172-179. 1992, p. 24 (type 5), pp. 26-27.
28. Kjellberg & Hoffmann 1991, pp. 46-48 fig. 27-31.

29. Hoffmann 1964, pp. 149, note 18.
30. Bender Jørgensen 1986 (b) pp. 84, 172-173.
31. Maik 1988, p. 201.
32 The two-beam vertical loom, the occurrence of 2/1 twill, and the Tavistock Abbey textile, all appear in: P. Walton Rogers 2001, pp. 158-171. 'The re-appearance of an old Roman loom in medieval England', in P. Walton Rogers, L. Bender Jørgensen and A. Rast-Eicher, *The Roman Textile Industry and its Influence: a Birthday Tribute to John Peter Wild*, Oxford: Oxbow.
33. Kjellberg & Hoffmann 1991, p. 34.
34. Hald 1950, pp. 100-107 fig. 92-96. 1980, pp. 102-105. Østergård 1991, pp. 123-138.
35. Østergård 1987, p. 97.
36. Geijer 1938, pp. 22-29.
37. Walton Rogers 2001, pp. 166-171.
38. Walton Rogers 1998, pp. 1-7. Thanks to Penelope Walton Rogers for this information. (Diamond twill 2/1, 22/12 thr./½ cm, Z/Z).
39. Nockert 1982, pp. 149-150 fig. 14-16. Diamond twill 2/2 (22/11 thr./cm, Z/S).
40. Andreasen 1982, p. 185 fig. 12.
41. Østergård 2002, Greenlandic Vadmál. *NESAT* forthcoming publication.
42. Munksgaard 1974, pp. 25, 142-143. Munksgaard & Østergård 1988, pp. 53-64.
43. Pritchard 1990, pp. 156-157 fig. 182.
44. Gjessing 1938, pp. 51-52.
45. Guðjónsson 1980, pp. 41-45 fig. 1-4.
46. Pritchard 1992, pp. 95-98 fig. 3
47. Lindström 1982, pp. 182-190 fig. 6.
48. Heckett 1992, pp. 158-168 fig. 2-4.
49. Broholm & Hald 1935, pp. 232-234 fig. 17-18. 1940, 27-29 fig. 25-26.
50. *KLNM* 14, 1969 pp. 513-518. Geijer 1972, pp. 211-215.
51. Kjellmo 1996, pp. 16, 79.
52. Gjøl Hagen 1994, pp. 178-180, 337. Lindström 1976, p. 284. Kjellberg & Hoffmann 1991, p. 21. Tidow 1982, p. 169.
53. Crowfoot 1992, p. 79 fig. 53.
54. Kjellberg 1943, p. 65.
55. Thanks to Penelope Walton Rogers for this information.

FLAX AND LINEN
1. Sørensen 1982, pp. 296-302.
2. Fredskild & Humle 1991, pp. 77-80.
3. Andersson 1996, p. 12.
4. See note 1.
5. Grenander Nyberg 1967, pp. 35-47.
6. Vebæk 1993, p. 34, fig. 45, p. 75.
7. Hoffmann 1991, pp. 57-58, fig. 62. Thanks to Penelope Walton Rogers for drawing my attention to this implement.
8. Øye 1988.
9. *KLNM* 10, 1965, p. 581.
10. *KLNM* 10, 1965, p. 580.
11. Nockert 1997, p. 110. Thanks to Maj Ringgaard for this information.
12. Fentz 1998, pp. 249-266 fig. 1-25.
13. *KLNM* 5, 1960, p. 580.

THE PRODUCTION OF GARMENTS

1. Thanks to Julie Ross, Alberta, who drew my attention to this similarity.
2. Stefánsson 1997, p. 27 fig. 2.
3. Roussell 1941, pp. 273, 335 fig. 169.
4. Roussell 1936, pp. 43-44, 163 fig. 31, 178.
5. Staniland 1993, pp. 7, 49 fig. 4, 54.
6. Nockert 1997.
7. Kjellberg & Hoffmann 1991, p. 16.
8. Gjessing 1938, p. 449.
9. Hald 1950, pp. 393-395. 1980, pp. 387-389.
10. Fentz 1998, pp. 249-266 fig. 5.
11. Newton 1981, pp. 342-348.
12. Geijer, Franzén, Nockert, 1985, pp. 13-20.
13. *KLNM* 15, 1970, p. 714.
14. De Alcega 1979, pp. 9-12.
15. Arnold 1985, p. 4.
16. Nørlund 1924, p. 109.
17. Gjøl Hagen 1992, pp. 26-28, 88-89 fig. 15, 16. Vedeler Nilsen 1998, pp. 74-76 fig. 4.
18. Shee & O'Kelly 1966, pp. 81-91 Plate II, III.
19. Kjellberg & Hoffmann 1991, pp. 50-53 fig. 33-36. Lindström 1976, p. 281 fig. 245.
20. Geijer 1938, pp. 14-17 Table. 1-2.
21. Hägg 1974, pp. 30-38 fig. 21-26. Nockert 1984, pp. 191-196.
22. Mygdal 1930, p. 86.
23. Seen by the author in the Museo Della Basilica, Bergamo, Italy.
24. Walton Rogers 1993, pp. 56-58. Østergård 1993, pp. 55-56 fig. 89-91.
25. Guðjónsson 1983, pp. 129, 138-39 fig. 3, NM, CLII, 1819, fig. 4, NM, CXCVIII, 1820, pp. 142-43 fig. 8, NM, CLV, 1819, pp. 146-48 fig. 11, 12, 13, Pjms. 3924, NM, 15379, 1856, Pjms. 4380 b.
26. Guðjónsson 1972, pp. 133, 144-47 fig. 2, Pjms. 4797.
27. Ingstad 1992, pp. 206-208.
28. Kjellberg 1997, p. 92 fig. 4.
29. Rud 1974 p. 9.
30. Nørlund 1930, p. 163.
31. Andreasen 1982, p. 184 fig. 11.
32. Crowfoot 1992, pp. 164-172 fig. 141, 143-44, 147-48.
33 Pritchard 1990, p. 17.
34. Nørlund 1924, p. 95. Falk 1919, p. 151.
35. Möller-Wiering 1998, pp. 32-34 fig. 1-2.

DECORATION OF THE GARMENTS

1. Thanks to Sigrídur Halldórsdóttir, Heimilisiðnaðarskálinn in Rykjavik, who explained in a letter in 1987 how a slynging is produced. Haldórsdottir 1973.
2. Guðjónsson 1983, pp. 133, 139 fig. 4. *KLNM* 8, 1963, p. 164. 2003, pp. 50-51 fig. 52 (Inven. No 11008).
3. *KLMN* 18, 1974, p. 14.
4. Mitchell 1978, pp. 43-45.
5. Wild 1970, pp. 57, 99.
6. Thanks to textile expert the late Dr.phil. Marta Hoffmann, who on a visit to Brede drew my attention to foot-woven borders, and in a subsequent letter mentioned that this technique was also known in the Caucasus.

7.	Crowfoot 1992, pp. 135, 161 fig. 134.
8.	Andreasen 1982, p. 184 fig. 11.
9.	Hald 1975, pp. 34-39 fig. 67-81.
10.	Guðjónsson 1979 (b), pp. 65-68 fig. 1-2.
11.	Strömberg 1950, pp. 64-69.
12.	Sorber 1988, pp. 93, 169-225.
13.	Ingstad 1992, p. 199. Holm-Olsen 1976, pp. 197-198.
	Geijer 1938, p. 128.
14.	Roussell 1936, p. 122 fig. 105.
15.	Gjessing 1938, p. 43 fig. 2.

ACCESSORIES
1.	Andersen 1984, pp. 16-24.
2.	John Donne:
	THE RELIQUE
	When my grave is broke up againe
	Some second ghest to entertaine,
	(For graves have learn'd that woman-head,
	To be to more than one a Bed)
	And he that digs it, spies
	A bracelet of bright hair about the bone,
	Will he not let'us alone,
	And thinke that there a loving couple lies,
	Who thought that this device might be some way
	To make their soules, at the last busie day,
	Meet at this grave, and make a little stay?
3.	Nørlund 1924, pp. 68, 192 fig. 136.
4.	Vebæk 1993, p. 33 fig. 419, p. 75. Nørlund 1924, p. 192 fig. 137.
5.	Nørlund & Stenberger 1934, pp. 136-137.
6.	Roussell 1936, pp. 117, 122 fig. 105, 181 fig. 194.
7.	Hald 1950, p. 44. 1980, p. 52. Munksgaard 1974, p. 143.
8.	Hoffmann 1964, p. 146, note 8.
9.	Roesdahl 1995, pp. 10-12.
10.	Roussell 1936, pp. 117-122, 184.
11.	Andreasen 1982, pp. 183-184.
12.	Nørlund 1924, p. 191 fig. 133, p. 192.

IMPLEMENTS
1.	Østergård 1982, pp. 303-313 fig. 11.
2.	Andersson 1996, p. 17.
3.	Øye 1988, pp. 85-112 fig. IV. 3, 1-2.
4.	Nordland 1961, pp. 45-52, 67, 78-83, 85-87.
5.	Holtved 1945, p. 82.
6.	Petersen 1951, pp. 324-325.
7.	Riismøller 1960, pp. 117-131.
8.	Behr 2000, pp. 121-122.
9.	Nørlund & Stenberger 1934, pp. 134-135 fig. 100 E.
10.	Roussell 1936, pp. 135, 189 fig. 199.
11.	Vebæk 1992, pp. 80, 116, fig. 106-107.
12.	Pritchard 1990, pp. 15-17.

13,14. Ræder Knudsen 1991, pp. 149-150 fig. 2. 1996, pp. 106-108.

15.   Walton 1989, pp. 381-382 fig. 160. Walton Rogers 1997, pp. 1786-1788 fig. 835.

16.   Schmidt & Østergård 1973, pp. 135-144.

17.   Hald 1950, pp. 227-242. 1980, pp. 225-239.

18.   See note 1, p. 304.

19.   Petersen 1951, p. 329.

20.   Noss 1965, pp. 1-3 fig. 1-4.

21, 22. Petersen 1951 pp. 329-337.

23.   Roussell 1941, p. 245 fig.154, p. 284. Behr 2000, p. 100.

OTHER USES OF TEXTILES

1.   Vinner 1993, pp. 67-76.

2.   *Kongespejlet,* p. 10. (The Kings Mirror).

3.   Andersen & Malmros 1993, pp. 118-122.

4.   Meldgaard 1995, p. 203.

5.   Christensen 1992, pp. 138-153. Ingstad 1992, pp. 19-98.

6.   Nørgård 1999, pp. 8-9. Andersen 1995, pp. 249-270.

7.   Schledermann 1982, pp. 218-225 fig. 2. 1993, pp. 54-66.

8.   Holtved 1945, p. 80. Meldgaard 1995, pp. 210-213.

9.   Mathiassen 1931, pp. 286, 333, Plate 22. no. 2.

10.   Mathiassen 1936-37, pp. 78-80.

11.   Walton Rogers 1999, pp. 194-202.

12.   Sutherland 2000, p. 239.

13.   Thanks to Penelope Walton Rogers for this information.

14.   Hallström 1909, p. 97.

15.   Christensen 1992, p. 129.

16.   Thorsteinsson 1985, p. 26.

17.   Engelstad 1952, pp. 13-18, notes 35, 36, 38.

FURS AND SKINS

1.   Magnusen & Rafn 1838-1845, vol. I, p. 375.

1a.   According to Elsa E. Guðjónsson, double-sided fur is an incorrect translation. Röggvarfeldur (a shaggy-pile woven cloak for a man) is actually meant. Guðjónsson 1962, pp. 12-71.

2.   Arneborg 1993, pp. 17-18.

3.   *KLNM* 15, 1970, p. 519.

4.   *KLNM* 15, 1970, p. 531.

5.   *KLNM* 14, 1969, p. 13.

6.   Nørlund 1924, pp. 87, 203.

7.   *KLNM* 11, 1966, p. 504.

8.   *KLNM* 1, 1956, p. 663.

9.   *KLNM* 13, 1968, p. 554.

10.   Falk 1919, p. 185. The full meaning of the designations can change over time.

11.   Hägg 1984, p. 220.

12.   Not published.

13.   Nørlund 1924, p. 190 fig. 132.

14.   Østergård 1993, p. 56 fig. 92.

15.   Nørlund & Stenberger 1934, p. 140.

16.   Roussell 1936, pp. 116-19 fig. 97, 98, 99, 190 Shoemaking.

17.   Andersson 1995, pp. 7-19.

18.   Roussell 1936, pp. 108-10 fig. 83, 84, 85, 87, 175-176 (D11713.163, D11709.167, D11710.168, D11755.162, D11711.159, D11712.160).

TEXTILE FRAGMENTS FROM GREENLAND

1.   See under list of Garments Types where each individual find is described.
2.   Geijer 1938. Hägg 1984. Holm-Olsen 1976, pp. 197-205.
3.   Hägg 1974. Bender Jørgensen 1986 (a), pp. 20-22. Demant 2000, pp. 1-9.
4.   Hägg 1991, pp. 155-162. Østergård 1991, pp. 123-138.
5.   Hägg 1984, pp. 176-180.
6.   Fentz 1998, pp. 249-266.
7.   Munksgaard 1974, pp. 131-134. Bender Jørgensen 1986 (b), pp. 146-155 fig. 222-224.
8.   Hald 1950, p. 33. 1980, p. 39.
9.   Bau 1983, pp. 16-17. Mannering 1999, pp. 20-27.
10. Nancke-Krogh 1995.
11. Franzén & Nockert 1992. Hougen 1940, pp. 85-124 Pl. V. Ingstad 1992, pp. 176-223. Engelstad 1952, pp. 53-57.
12. Thanks to my colleague Irene Skals, who drew my attention to this garment.
13. Falk 1919, p. 81.
14. Nørlund 1924, p. 122 fig. 74 below, p. 124 fig. 75.
15. Shee & O'Kelly 1966.
16. Gjøl Hagen 1992. fig. 15-16. Vedeler Nilsen 1998, p. 75 fig. 4.
17. Gjessing 1938, pp. 27-83. Vedeler Nilsen 1997, pp. 20-22.
18. Thanks to Patrik Djurfeldt, Västerås in Sweden, for drawing my attention to this painting.
19. Mathiassen 1931, pp. 287-288 pl. 22. 3a-b. Gulløv 1982, pp. 226-234. Meldgaard 1995, pp. 208-209 fig. 7 C.
20. Nørlund 1934, p. 115.
21   Possnert 1997, pp. 125-136.
22. Falk 1919, p. 95.
23. Noss 1976, pp. 57-92.
24. Roussell 1936, pp. 123-124 fig. 108, p. 184.
25. Guðjónsson 1990 (b), pp. 27-37.
26. Nørlund 1924, p. 174 fig. 114.
27. Nørlund 1934, pp. 118-121. Arneborg 1996 (a), pp. 75-83.
28. Meldgaard 1995, pp. 208-209 fig. 8-9. Mathiassen 1931, pp. 290-291 pl. 22. 5a-b.
29. Hald 1950, pp. 56-58 fig. 42-43. 1980, pp. 60-61 fig. 42-43.
30. Nockert 1992, pp. 5-11.
31. Nockert 1982, pp. 146-150 fig. 7-16.
32. Vedeler Nilsen 1997, pp. 20-22.
33. Gjessing 1938.
34. Nockert & Possnert, 2002, pp. 59-62, 111.
35. Holck 1991, pp. 109-115.
36. Sandklef 1943. Nockert 1996, pp. 205-206. Nockert 1997.
37. Nørlund & Stenberger 1934, pp. 39-46. Krogh 1982, pp. 29-52.
38. Nørlund 1924, p. 258.

CARBON DATING

1.   Rasmussen 1994.
2.   Arneborg, 1996 (b), pp. 75-83. Arneborg, et al. 1998, pp. 27-30.
3.   Rud & Heinemeier 1999, pp. 34-40.

Bibliography

Adalsteinsson, S.: Importance of Sheep in Early Icelandic Agriculture. The Norse of the North
   Atlantic. *Acta Archaeologica* Vol. 61-1990. København 1991 pp. 285-291.
Albrethsen, S.E. & Ólafsson, G.: A viking age hall. J. Arneborg & H.C. Gulløv (eds.), *Man,
   Culture and Environment in Ancient Greenland. Report on a Research Programme.*
   The Danish National Museum & Danish Polar Center. Viborg 1998 pp. 19-26.
Andersen, E.: Square Sails of Wool. Olaf Olsen et al. (eds.), *Shipshape. Essays for Ole
   Crumlin-Pedersen.* The Viking Ship Museum. Roskilde 1995 pp. 249-270.
Andersen, E. & Malmros, C.: Ship's parts found in the Viking Settlements in Greenland.
   Preliminary assessments and wood-diagnoses. B.L. Clausen (ed.), *Viking Voyages to
   North America.* The Viking Ship Museum in Roskilde 1993 pp. 118-122.
Andersen, K.: *Hårkullorna fra Våmhus.* Bangsbomuseet. Frederikshavn 1984 p. 20.
Andersson, E.: Invisible Handicrafts. The General Picture of Textile and Skin Crafts in
   Scandinavian Surveys. *Lund Archaeological Review* I. Lund 1995 pp. 7-20.
Andersson, E.: *Textilproduktion i arkæologisk kontext.* (University of Lund. Institute of
   Archaeology. Report Series No. 58). Lund 1996.
Andreasen, C.: Nipaitsoq og Vesterbygden. *Tidsskriftet Grønland* Nr. 5-7. Tema: Nordboerne
   1. del. Det grønlandske Selskab. Skjern 1982 pp. 177-188.
Appleyard, H.M.: *Guide to the Identification of Animal Fibres WIRA.* Leeds 1978.
Arneborg, J.: Greenland, the starting-point for the voyages to North America. B.L. Clausen
   (ed.), *Viking Voyages to North America.* The Viking Ship Museum in Roskilde 1993 pp.
   13-20.
Arneborg, J. & Østergård, E.: Notes on Archaeological finds of textiles and textile equipment
   from the Norse Western Settlement in Greenland (a preliminary report). G. Jaacks &
   K. Tidow (eds.), *Textilsymposium Neumünster 1993, archäologische Textilfunde,
   archaeological textiles* (NESAT V). Neumünster 1994 pp. 162-177.
Arneborg, J.: Grønland, de nordiske kolonier ved verdens ende. K. Grinder Hansen (red.),
   Margrete I. Nordens Frue og Husbond. Kalmarunionen 600 år. Essays og udstillings-
   katalog. Danmarks Nationalmuseum. København 1996 (a) pp. 196-199.
Arneborg, J.: Burgunderhuer, baskere og døde nordboer i Herjolfsnæs, Grønland.
   Nationalmuseets Arbejdsmark. København 1996 (b) pp. 75-83.
Arneborg, J.: Artefacts from rooms XVII (the hall), XIII, XXVII & XIX (Stratigraphical ana-
   lysis). J. Arneborg & H.C. Gulløv (eds.), *Man, Culture and Environment in Ancient
   Greenland. Report on a Research Programme.* The Danish National Museum &
   Danish Polar Center. Viborg 1998 pp. 37-44.
Arneborg, J., Heinemeier, J., Rud, N., Sveinbjörnsdottir, A.: AMS from the hall (XVII). J.
   Arneborg & H.C. Gulløv (eds.), *Man, Culture and Environment in Ancient Greenland.
   Report on a Research Programme.* The Danish National Museum & Danish Polar
   Center. Viborg 1998 pp. 27-30.
Arneborg, J.: Nordboliv i Grønland. Else Roesdahl (red.), *Dagligliv i Danmarks middelalder.
   En arkæologisk kulturhistorie.* København 1999 pp. 353-373.
Arnold, J.: *Patterns of Fashion. The Cut and Construction of Clothes for Men and Women c.
   1560-1620.* New York 1985.
Bau, F.: Seler og slæb. *Tidsskriftet SKALK* Nr. 4, Århus 1983 pp. 16-17.
Behr, G.: *Tekstilredskaber i det middelalderlige Danmark.* Afdelingen for Middelalderarkæo-
   logi, Aarhus Universitet 2000.

Bender Jørgensen, L.: Oldtidens metervarer. *Lolland-Falsters Stiftsmuseums Årbog* 1986 (a)
pp. 5-29.

Bender Jørgensen, L.: *Forhistoriske Textiler i Skandinavien.* Det Kongelige Nordiske
Oldskriftselskab. København 1986 (b).

Bender Jørgensen, L.: Hørvævninger og oldtidsvæve. *KUML* 1990. Årbog for Jysk
Arkæologisk Selskab. Aarhus Universitetsforlag, Århus 1990 pp. 77-84.

Bender Jørgensen, L.: Textiles and Textile Implements. *Ribe Excavations 1970-76,* Volume 3.
Sydjysk Universitetsforlag, Esbjerg 1991 pp. 59-78.

Bender Jørgensen, L.: *North European Textiles until AD 1000.* Aarhus University Press,
Aarhus 1992.

Berglund, J.: The Excavations at The Farm beneath the Sand introduction. J. Arneborg & H.C.
Gulløv (eds.), *Man, Culture and Environment in Ancient Greenland. Report on a
Research Programme.* The Danish National Museum & Danish Polar Center. Viborg
1998 pp. 7-13.

Bojsen Christensen, K.M.: En undersøgelse af den grønlandske norrøne areal- og ressourceudnyttelse i Vesterbygden i Grønland. *hikuin* 15, 1989.

Bolton, E.M.: *Lichens for Vegetable Dyeing.* McMinnville Oregon 1960, revideret udgave 1982.

Broholm, H.C. & Hald, M.: *Danske Bronzealders Dragter. Nordiske Fortidsminder* bind II,
5-6, udgivet af Det Kgl. Nordiske Oldskriftselskab. København 1935.

Broholm, P.C. & Hald, M.: Skrydstrupfundet. En sønderjydsk Kvindegrav fra den ældre
Bronzealder. *Nordiske Fortidsminder III,* 2. Hefte. København 1939.

Broholm, H.C. & Hald, M.: *Costumes of the Bronze Age in Denmark.* København 1940.

Buckland, P.C., Buckland, P.I, Skidmore, P.: Insect remains from GUS, an interim report. J.
Arneborg & H.C. Gulløv (eds.), *Man, Culture and Environment in Ancient Greenland.
Report on a Research Programme.* The Danish National Museum & Danish Polar
Center. Viborg 1998 pp. 74-79.

Christensen, A.E.: Kongsgårdens håndverkere. *Oseberg Dronningens Grav. Vår arkeologiske
nasjonalskatt i nytt lys.* Oslo 1992 pp. 85-137.

Crowfoot, E., Pritchard, F. & Staniland, K.: *Textiles and Clothing c.1150-c.1450.* (Medieval
Finds from Excavations in London, 4.) London 1992.

De Alcega, J.: *Tailor's Pattern Book 1589.* Facsimile. Introduction and notes by J.L. Nevinson.
Bedford 1979.

Degerbøl, M.: Animal remains from the West Settlement in Greenland, with special reference
to livestock. *Meddelelser om Grønland,* 88/3, København 1936 pp. 1-54.

Deggim, C. & Möller-Wiering, S.: Die Gugel – Eine Mittelalterliche Seemannskleidung? Über-
legungen zu ihrer Herkunft, ihrer Funktion im Hanseraum und zu den Interpretationen
der Lübecker Schiffssiegel. *Hansische Geschichtsblätter,* 119. Jahrgang. Köln Weimar
Wein 2001 pp. 163-187.

Demant, I.: Mikrostratigrafisk analyse af tekstilpræparaterne fra Lerdal grav 101. *Arkæologi i
Schleswig* 28-29/1, 2000 pp. 1-9, fig. 1, 2 a-b.

Engelstad, H.: Det bevarte materiale. Refil Bunad Tjeld. *Fortids Kunst i Norges Bygder.* Oslo
1952 pp. 53-57.

Falk, H.: *Altwestnordische Kleiderkunde.* Kristiania 1919.

Fentz, M.: En hørskjorte fra 1000-årene. *Viborg Søndersø 1000-1300.* Byarkæologiske undersøgelser 1981 og 1984-85. Aarhus Universitetsforlag 1998 pp. 249-266.

Fentz, M.: Dragter. Else Roesdahl (red.), *Dagligliv i Danmarks middelalder.* En arkæologisk
kulturhistorie. København 1999 pp. 150-171.

Franzén, A.M. & Nockert, M.: *Bonaderna från Skog och Överhogdal, och andra medeltidavägg-
beklädnader.* Kungl. Vitterhets Historie och Antikvitets Akademien. Stockholm 1992.

Fredskild, B. & Humle, L.: Plant remains from the Norse farm Sandnes in the Western

Settlement, Greenland. *Acta Borealia* 1-1991 pp. 65-81

Gabra-Sanders, T.: The Orkney Hood Re-dated and Re-considered. *The Roman Textile Industry and its Influence. A Birthday Tribute to John Peter Wild.* Walton Rogers, P., Bender Jørgensen, L. & Rast-Eicher, A. (eds.). Oxford 2001 pp. 98-104.

Gad, F.: *Grønlands historie indtil 1700.* 2. oplag. København 1978.

Geijer, A.: *Birka* III. *Die Textilfunde aus den Gräbern.* Kungl. Vitterhets Historie och Antikvitets Akademien Stockholm 1938.

Geijer, A.: *Ur textilkonstens historia.* Lund 1972.

Geijer, A., Franzén, A.M. & Nockert, M.: *Drottning Margaretas gyllene kjortel i Uppsala Domkyrka.* Kungl. Vitterhets Historie och Antikvitets Akademien. Stockholm 1985.

Gjessing, G.: Skjoldehamndrakten. En senmiddelaldersk nordnorsk mannsdrakt. *Viking. Tidsskrift for norrøn arkeologi,* 2. 1938 pp. 27-81.

Gjøl Hagen, K.: *Solplissé – En reminisens av middelalderens draktutvikling? En komparativ studie i plisserte stoffer fra Birka, Vangsnes, middelalderens Trondheim, Uvdal og Setesdal.* Oslo 1992.

Gjøl Hagen, K.: *Profesjonalisme og urbanisering. Profesjonalismeproblemet i håndverket belyst ved et tekstil- og vevloddsmateriale fra middelalderens Trondheim fra 1000-tallet frem til slutten av 1300-tallet* (Universitetets Oldsaksamlings Skrifter. Ny rekke Nr.16). 1994.

Grenander, G.N.: *Linodling och Linnevävning i Själevad och dess grannsocknar 1750-1900.* (Själevads Hembygdsförenings Skriftserie Nr. 4), Ågrens Boktryckeri AB, Örnsköldsvik 1967.

Grenander, G.N.: Spinning implements of the Viking Age from Elisenhof in the light of ethnological studies. P. Walton, & J.P. Wild (eds.), *Textiles in Northern Archaeology. Textile Symposium in York 1987.* (NESAT III). Archetype Publications. London 1990 pp. 73-84.

Grierson, S.: *Whorl and Wheel. The Story of Handspinning in Scotland.* 1985.

Grierson, S.: *The Colour Cauldron: The History and Use of Natural Dyes in Scotland.* Perth 1986.

Guðjónsson, E.E.: Íslenzk útsaumsheiti og útsaumsgerdir á midöldum. *Islandske broderitermer og broderiteknikker i middelalderen. Árbók Hins Islenzka Fornleifafélags. Sérprent* 1972 pp. 130-151.

Guðjónsson, E.E.: Togcombs in the National Museum of Iceland. With some Notes on Icelandic Wool-Comb in General. *Textile History,* 10, London 1979 (a) pp. 207-210.

Guðjónsson, E.E.: Icelandic loop-braided bands: Krílud Bönd. *Bulletin de liaison du centre international d'etude des textiles anciens* 1979 (b), pp. 65-68.

Guðjónsson, E.E.: A Note on Medieval Icelandic Shaggy Pile Weaving. *Bulletin de liaison du centre international d'etude des textiles anciens* 1980 pp. 41-45.

Guðjónsson, E.E.: Islandske broderier og broderersker i middelalderen. Förändringar i kvinnors villkor under medeltiden. *Rit Sagnfrædistofnunar* 9. Reykjavik 1983 pp. 127-158. Eng. udg.: Icelandic Embroidery. Domestic Embroideries in the National Museum of Iceland. Reykjavik, 1983. 9 bls.

Guðjónsson, E.E.: Nogle bemærkninger om den islandske vægtvæv, vefstadur. *By og Bygd årbok 1985.* Oslo, pp. 116-128.

Guðjónsson, E.E.: Járnvarðr Yllir. A Fourth Weapon of the Valkyries in Darradarljóð? *Textile History,* 2 (2), London 1989 pp. 185-197.

Guðjónsson, E.E.: Some Aspects of the Icelandic Warp-Weighted Loom, Vefstaður. *Textile History,* 21 (2), London 1990 (a) pp. 165-179.

Guðjónsson, E.E.: Om de traditionelle islandske hvide kvindehovedsæt med tilbehør. *Rapport fra Nordisk hovudbunadseminar på Valdres Folkehøgskule. Fagernes,* 1990 (b) pp. 27-37.

Guðjónsson, E.E.: Fágæti úr fylgsnum jardar. Fornleifar í págu textíl- og búningarannsókna. *Skírnir* 1992 pp. 7-40.

Guðjónsson, E.E.: Warp-Weighted Looms in Iceland and Greenland, Comparison of Mediaeval Loom Parts excavated in Greenland in 1934 and 1990-1992 to Loom Parts from Eighteenth and Nineteenthe Century Warp-Weighted Looms in Iceland. Preliminary Remarks. *Textilsymposium Neumünster* 1993. (NESAT V). Neumünster 1994 pp. 178-195.

Guðjónsson, E.E.: Islandske kirketekstiler i middelalderen. Lilja Árnadóttir, Ketil Kiran (ed.) *Kirkja ok Kirkjuskrud. Kirker og Kirkekunst på Island og i Norge i Middelalderen.* Norsk Institutt for Kulturminneforskning NIKU. Islands Nasjonalmuseum, Reykjavik 1997 pp. 85-90.

Guðjónsson, E.E.: Traditional Icelandic Embroidery. Kópavogur 2003 pp. 50-51.

Guðmundsson, G.F.: Islandske måldager. Lilja Árnadóttir, Ketil Kiran (ed.) *Kirkja ok Kirkjuskrud. Kirker og Kirkekunst på Island og i Norge i Middelalderen.* Norsk Institutt for Kulturminneforskning NIKU. Islands Nasjonalmuseum, Reykjavik 1997 pp. 61-64.

Gulløv, H.C.: Eskimoens syn på europæeren. *Tidsskriftet Grønland.* Nr. 5-6-7. Tema: Nordboerne 1. del. Det grønlandske Selskab. Skjern 1982 pp. 226-234.

Hald, M.: *For lud og koldt vand.* (Kulturminder). København 1941.

Hald, M.: *Olddanske Tekstiler.* (Nordiske Fortidsminder V). København 1950.

Hald, M.: *Flettede Baand og Snore.* København 1975 pp. 34-39.

Hald, M.: *Ancient Danish Textiles From Bogs and Burials. A Comparative Study of Costume and Iron Age Textiles.* (Publications of the National Museum. Archaeological-Historical Series Vol. XXI). Copenhagen 1980.

Halldórsson, Ó.: Bogproduktion. P. Grinder Hansen (red.), *Margrete I. Nordens Frue og Husbond.* Kalmarunionen 600 år. Essays og Udstillingskatalog. Nordisk Ministerråd. Nationalmuseet, København 1996 pp. 155-157.

Hallström, G.: Båtar och båtbyggnad i Ryska Lappmarken. *Fataburen.* Stockholm 1909 pp. 85-100.

Hatting, T.: *Fåret i oldtid og nutid.* Historisk-Arkæologisk Forsøgscenter, Lejre 1993.

Heckett, E.W.: An Irish »Shaggy Pile« Fabric of the 16th Century – An Insular Survival? *Tidens Tand* Nr.5, Archaeological Textiles in Northern Europe. Konservatorskolen, Det Kongelige Danske Kunstakademi, København 1992 pp. 158-168.

Hinnerson Berglund, M.: Red sandstone and Greenlandic wool. Two diagnostic artefacts in the interpretation of a newly discovered saeter in southern Greenland. *Acta Borealia* 2, 1998 pp. 153-174.

Hoffmann, M.:. The Warp-Weighted Loom. *Studia Norvegica* No. 14, Universitetsforlaget. Oslo 1964.

Hoffmann, M.: *Fra fiber til tøj.* Landbruksforlaget, Oslo 1991.

Holck, P.: Myrfunnet fra Skjoldehamn – mannlig same eller norrøn kvinde? *Viking 1988. Tidsskrift for norrøn arkeologi.* Oslo 1991.

Holm-Olsen, I.M.:. Noen gravfunn fra Vestlandet som kaster lys over vikingetidens kvinnedrakt. *Viking. Tidsskrift for norrøn arkeologi* Bd. XXXIX. Oslo 1976 pp. 197-205.

Holtved, E.: Har Nordboerne været i Thule Distriktet? *Nationalmuseets Arbejdsmark.* København 1945 pp. 79-84.

Hougen, B.: Osebergfunnets billedvev. *Viking. Tidsskrift for norrøn arkeologi* Bd. IV. Oslo 1940.

Hägg, I.: *Kvinnodräkten i Birka. Livplaggens rekonstruktion på grundval av det arkeologiska materialet.* Uppsala 1974.

Hägg, I.: *Die Textilfunde aus dem Hafen. Berichte über die Ausgrabungen in Haithabu. Bericht 20.* Neumünster 1984.

Hägg, I.: Rangsymboliska element i vikingatida gravar. Hedeby-Birka-Mammen. M. Iversen (red.), *Mammen. Grav, kunst og samfund i vikingetid.* Jysk Arkæologisk Selskab.

Aarhus 1991 pp. 155-162.

Ingstad, A.S.: Tekstilene i Osebergskipet. *Oseberg Dronningens Grav. Vår arkeologiske nasjonalskatt.* Oslo 1992 pp. 176-223.

Jónasson, K.: Ad kemba i togkömbum. *Arbók hins Islenzka Fornleifafélags.* Reykjavik 1974 pp. 135-142.

Jørgensen Bender, L.: se Bender Jørgensen, L.

Kjellberg, A.: I. Tekstilmaterialet fra »Oslogate 7«. Erik Schia (red.), *De arkeologiske utgravninger i Gamlebyen, Oslo,* Bd. 2. Feltene »*Oslogate 3 og 7«:* Bebyggelsesrester og funngrupper. Universitetsforlaget, Oslo 1979 pp. 83-104.

Kjellberg, A. & Hoffmann, M.: Tekstiler. *De arkeologiske utgravninger i Gamlebyen, Oslo, Bd. 8. Dagliglivets gjenstander Del II.* Universitetsforlaget, Oslo 1991. pp. 13-80.

Kjellberg, A.: Norske tekstiler. *Kirkja ok kirkjuskrud. Kirke og kirkekunst på Island og i Norge i Middelalderen.* Norsk Institutt for Kulturminneforskning NIKU. Islands Nasjonalmuseum, Reykjavik 1997 pp. 91-92.

Kjellberg, S.T.: *Ull och Ylle.* Lund 1943.

Kjellmo, E.: *Båtrya i gammel og ny tid.* Orkano Forlag, Stamsund 1996.

KLNM, se *Kulturhistorisk leksikon for nordisk middelalder.*

Kongespejlet. Konungs Skuggsjá, i dansk oversættelse ved F. Jónsson. København 1926.

Krogh, K.J.: *Erik den Rødes Grønland.* Nationalmuseet. København 1982.

Kulturhistorisk leksikon for nordisk middelalder m.m 1956-78 (genoptrykt 1980-82): Björn, Darradarljód, Get, Geiteal, Guldsmeder, Kalkkläder, Lin, Oppstadvev, Prästdräkt, Reip, Rya, Saks, Skinnare, Skinnhandel, Skrædder, Sömnad og Vadmål.

Lindström, M.: Textilier. *Uppgrävt förflutet för PKbanken i Lund* 1976 pp. 279-292.

Lindström, M.: Medieval Textile Finds in Lund. L. Bender Jørgensen & K. Tidow (eds.), *Textilsymposium Neumünster* 1981. Neumünster 1982 pp. 179-191.

Lunde, D.: Forsøk med Korkje, Rød Tråd: Drakt og Tekstil. *Kunstindustrimuseet Årbok* 1972-75. Oslo 1975 pp. 119-130.

Magnus, O.: *Historia om de nordiska folken.* Stockholm 1951.

Magnusen, F. & Rafn, C.C.: *Grønlands historiske Mindesmærker* I –III. København 1838-45. Bd. II, pp. 331.

Maik, J.: *Wyroby Wlókiennicze na Pomorzu z Okresu Rzymskiego i ze Sredniowiecza.* Ossolineum 1988.

Mannering, U.: Sidste skrig. *Tidsskriftet SKALK* Nr. 4. Århus 1999 pp. 20-27.

Mathiassen, T.: Inugsuk. A mediaeval Eskimo settlement in Upernavik district, West Greenland. *Meddelelser om Grønland,* bd. 77. København 1931 pp. 284-303, pl. 22.

Mathiassen, T.: The Eskimo Archaeology of Julianehaab District. *Meddelelser om Grønland,* bd. 118. København 1936-37 pp. 78-83.

McGovern, T.: Bones, buildings and boundaries: palaeoeconomic approaches to Norse Greenland. C.D.Morris & D.J.Rackham (eds), *Norse Settlement and Subsistence in the North Atlantic.* Glasgow 1992 pp. 193-230.

Meldgaard, J.: Eskimoer og Nordboer i Det yderste Nord. *Nationalmuseets Arbejdsmark.* København 1995 pp. 199-214.

Meldorf, G.: *Fund af Ligklæder paa Kirkegaarden ved Ikigait og Bidrag til Oplysning om Nordbodragten i Grønland i Middelalderen.* Nationalmuseet, Antikvarisk Topografisk Arkiv, ad 326/12. 1912.

Mitchell, L.: In Living Memory Traditions, Aran Islands. *Irish Spinning, Dyeing and Weaving.* Dundalgan Press, Dundalk 1978 pp. 43-45.

Molaug, P.B.: C. Sneller til håndtein. Erik Schia & Petter B. Molaug (red.), *De arkeologiske utgravninger i Gamlebyen, Oslo,* Bd. 8. Dagliglivets gjenstander Del II. Universitetsforlaget, Oslo 1991 pp. 81-112.

Munksgaard, E.: *Oldtidsdragter.* Nationalmuseet. København 1974.

Munksgaard, E. & Østergård, E.: Textiles and Costume from Lønne Hede. An Early Roman
Iron Age Burial. *Archaeological Textiles.* Arkæologisk Institut, Københavns Universitet.
København 1988 pp. 53-64.

Mygdal, E.: Amagerdragter. *Vævninger og Syninger.* Første Halvbind. Det Schønbergske Forlag,
København 1930.

Møhl, J.: Ressourceudnyttelse fra norrøne og eskimoiske affaldslag belyst gennem knoglemateri-
alet. *Tidsskriftet Grønland.* Nr. 8-9. Tema: Nordboerne 2. del. Det grønlandske Selskab.
Skjern 1982 pp. 286-295.

Möller-Wiering, S.: Tekstiler fra Trondenes kirke – dele af et uldsejl? *Marinarkæologisk
Nyhedsbrev* nr. 11, Roskilde 1998.

Nancke-Krogh, S.: *Stenbilleder i danske kirker.* København 1995.

NESAT = North European Symposium for Archaeological Textiles

Newton, S.M.: 1981. Queen Philippa's Squirrel Suit. *Documenta Textilia. Festschrift für Sigrid
Müller-Christensen.* Deutscher Kunstverlag 1981 pp. 342-348.

Nockert, M.: Textilfynden. *Tusen år på Kyrkudden. Leksands kyrka, arkeologi och byggnads-
historia.* Falun 1982 pp. 143-157.

Nockert, M.: Medeltida dräkt i bild och verklighet. *Den Ljusa Medeltiden. Studier tillägnade
Aron Andersson.* (The Museum of National Antiquities. Stockholm Studies 4). 1984
pp. 191-196.

Nockert, M.: Unam Tunicam Halwskipftan. *S:t Ragnhilds Gille Årsbok.* Söderköping 1992
pp. 5-11.

Nockert, M.: *Bockstensmannen och hans dräkt.* Borås 1997.

Nockert, M. & G. Posnert 2002: *Att datera textilier.* Södertälje.

Nordland, O.: *Primitive Scandinavian Textiles in Knotless Netting.* Oslo 1961.

Noss, Aa.: Før strykejernet. Slikjekjake og Mangletre. *By og Bygd,* bd. 18. Oslo 1965. pp. 1-18.

Noss, Aa.: Draktfunn og Drakttradisjon i det Vestnordiske Området frå Vikingtid til
Högmellomalderen. *Viking* 38. Oslo 1974 pp. 39-67.

Noss, Aa.: *Eit Mellomalderplagg i Levande Tradisjon.* Norsk Folkemuseum. Oslo 1976
pp. 57-92.

Nørgård, A.: *Vævning af sejldugsprøver på opstadvæv.* Udført på Vikingeskibsmuseet 1999
pp. 1-12, 6 plancher. Roskilde 2000.

Nørlund, P.: Buried Norsemen at Herjolfsnes. *Meddelelser om Grønland,* Bd. 67. København
1924.

Nørlund, P.: Herjolfsnes Fundet og de sidste Nordboer paa Grønland. *Nationalmuseets Bog om
sjældne Fund fra de seneste Aar.* København 1925 pp. 35-50.

Nørlund, P.: Norse Ruins at Gardar. *Meddelelser om Grønland,* Bd. 76. København 1930.

Nørlund, P. & Stenberger, M.: Brattahlid. *Meddelelser om Grønland,* bd. 88/1. København 1934.

Nørlund, P.: *De gamle Nordbobygder ved Verdens Ende.* Nationalmuseet 1934. Sidste genud-
givelse fra 1967.

Nørlund, P.: Klædedragt i Oldtid og Middelalder. Dragt. *Nordisk Kultur XV:* B. København
1941 pp. 1-88.

Ólafsson, G.: Ljósfæri og lýsing. *Íslensk þjóðmenning I.* Frosti F. Jóhannsson (red.) Uppruni og
umhverfi. Reykjavik 1987 pp. 347-369.

Olaus Magnus, se Magnus, O.

Petersen, J.: *Vikingetidens redskaper.* Oslo 1951.

Possnert, G.: *Radiometrisk* [14]*C-datering av Bockstensfyndet. Bockstensmannen och hans dräkt.*
Borås 1997 pp. 125-136.

Pritchard, F.: Missing threads from Medieval textiles in North Europe. *Archaeological Textiles,*
No.10 UKIC 1990 pp. 15-17.

Pritchard, F.: *Patterned cloth from 14th-century London. Textiles in Northern Archaeology.* NESAT III: Textile Symposium in New York 1987. NESAT 1990 pp. 155-164.

Pritchard, F.: Aspects of the Wool from Viking Age Dublin. *Tidens Tand* Nr. 5. Archaeological Textiles in Northern Europe. Konservatorskolen. Det Kongelige Danske Kunstakademi, København 1992 pp. 93-104.

Rasmussen Lund, K.: *Kulstof–14 datering – Datering af arkæologiske fund.* København 1994.

Resi Gjøstein, H. & Schjølberg, E.: *IAKN, Universitetes Oldsaksamling og Botanisk Institutt.* Universitetet i Bergen 1998 pp. 129-154.

Riismøller, P.: *KUML.* Årbog for Jysk Arkæologisk Selskab. Universitetsforlaget i Aarhus, Århus 1960 pp. 117-131.

Roesdahl, E.: *Fyrkat. En jysk vikingeborg,* bd. 2. *Oldsagerne og gravpladsen.* (Nordiske Fortidsminder, bd.4). Det kgl. nordiske oldskriftselskab 1977.

Roesdahl, E.: *Hvalrostand elfenben og nordboerne i Grønland.* Odense Universitetsforlag, Odense 1995.

Roussell, Aa.: Sandnes and the Neighbouring Farms. *Meddelelser om Grønland,* bd. 88/2. København 1936.

Roussell, Aa.: *Farms and Churches in the Mediaeval Norse Settlements of Greenland.* København 1941.

Rud, M.: *Bayeux-Tapetet og slaget ved det grå æbletræ.* Politikens forlag, København 1974.

Rud, N. & Heinemeier, J.: Isotoperne fortæller om de grønlandske vikingers liv. *Carlsbergfondet. Årsskrift.* København 1999 pp. 34-40.

Rui, L.M.: Kljåsteiner – Vevlodd. Erik Schia & Petter B. Molaug (red.), *De arkeologiske utgravninger i Gamlebyen, Oslo,* bd. 8. *Dagliglivets gjenstander* Del II. Universitetsforlaget, Oslo 1991 pp. 113-130.

Ryder, M.L.: Fleece structure in some native and unimproved breeds of sheep. *Zeitschrift für Tierzüchtung und Züchtungsbiologie* 85/2, 1968 pp. 143-170.

Ryder, M.L.: Changes in the fleece of sheep following domestication. P.J.Ucko & G.E.Dimbleby (eds.), *The Domestication and Exploitation of Plants and Animals.* London 1969 pp. 495-521.

Ryder, M.L.: A survey of European primitive breeds of sheep. *Annales Génétiques Sélection Animale,* 13/4, 1981 pp. 381-418.

Ryder, M.L.: The primitive breeds of domestic sheep of Europe. Archaeozoology 1: *Proceedings of the 3rd International Archaeozoological Conference,* Poland 1978. 1983 pp. 533-558.

Ryder, M.L.: *Sheep and Man.* London 1983.

Ræder Knudsen, L.: Det uldne brikvævede bånd fra Mammengraven. M. Iversen (red.), *Mammen. Grav, kunst og samfund i vikingetid.* (Jysk Arkæologisk Selskabs Skrifter XXVIII). Aarhus Universitetsforlag, Århus 1991 pp. 149-150.

Ræder Knudsen, L.: *Analyse og rekonstruktion af brikvævning.* 2. dels opgave. Konservatorskolen. København 1996.

Römpp, H.: *Chemie Lexikon,* Stuttgart 1966.

Sandklef, A.: *Bockstensmannen.* Stockholm 1943.

Schledermann, P.: Ellesmere Island. Eskimo and Viking Finds in the High Arctic. *National Geographic,* Vol. 159/5. 1981 pp. 575-601.

Schledermann, P.: Nordbogenstande fra Arktisk Canada. *Tidsskriftet Grønland,* Nr. 5-6-7. Tema: Nordboerne 1. del. Det Grønlandske Selskab. Skjern 1982 pp. 218-225.

Schledermann, P.: Norsemen in the High Arctic. B.L. Clausen (ed.), *Viking Voyages to North America.* The Viking Ship Museum in Roskilde, Denmark 1993 pp. 54-66.

Schmidt, O. & Østergård, E.: Undersøgelser af tekstilfragmenter fra ærkebiskop Absalons grav i Sorø kirke. *Nationalmuseets Arbejdsmark.* København 1973 pp. 135-144.

Shee, E.A. & O'Kelly, M.: A Clothed Burial from Emlagh near Dingle, Co. Kerry. *Journal of the Cork Historical and Archaeological Society*, Vol. LXXI. 1966 pp. 81-91.

Sorber, F.: Randverschijnselen: Kwasten en koorden. *Tongeren Basiliek van O.-L.-Vrouw Geboorte*, vol. I. Textiel van de vroege middeleeuwen tot het Concilie van Trente. Leuven 1988 pp. 89-97.

Staniland, K.: *Medieval craftsmen. Embroiderers*. London 1993.

Stefánsson, H.: Islandske Middelalderkirker. Lilja Árnádottir, Ketil Kiran (ed.) *Kirkja ok Kirkjuskrud. Kirker og Kirkekunst på Island og i Norge i Middelalderen*. Norsk Institutt for Kulturminneforskning NIKU. Islands Nasjonalmuseum 1997 pp. 25-41.

Stoklund, M.: Nordboruner. *Tidsskriftet Grønland*, Nr. 8-9. Tema: Nordboerne 2. del. Det grønlandske selskab. Skjern 1982 pp. 197-206.

Stoklund, M.: Objects with runic inscriptions from Vatnahverfi. Vatnahverfi, An inland district of the Eastern Settlement in Greenland (C.L. Vebæk). *Man & Society*, 17. København 1992 pp. 90-93.

Stoklund, M.: Objects with runic inscriptions from Ø 17a. Narsaq – a Norse landnáma farm (C.L. Vebæk). *Man & Society* 18. København 1993 pp. 47-52.

Stoklund, M.: Runes. J. Arneborg & H.C. Gulløv (eds.), *Man, Culture and Environment in Ancient Greenland. Report on a Research Programme*. The Danish National Museum & Danish Polar Center. Viborg 1998 pp. 55-57.

Strömberg, E.: Fyrkantiga snodder. *Rig*. Stockholm 1950 pp. 65-69.

Stærmose Nielsen, K.H.: *Kirkes Væv. Forsøg med fortiden 6*. Historisk-Arkæologisk Forsøgscenter Lejre 1999.

Sutherland, P.D.: The Norse and Native North Americans. The Vikings. *The Norse Atlantic Saga*. The Smithsonian Institution 2000 pp. 238-247.

Sørensen, I.: Pollenundersøgelser i møddingen på Niaqussat. *Tidsskriftet Grønland*. Nr. 8-9. Tema: Nordboerne 2. del. Det grønlandske Selskab. Skjern 1982 pp. 296-302.

Tarnovius, T.: *Ferøers Beskrifvelser*. Utgitt av Håkon Hamre. København 1950.

Tidow, K.: Untersuchungen an Wollgeweben aus Schleswig und Lübeck. L. Bender Jørgensen & K. Tidow (eds.), *Textilsymposium Neumünster 1981, Archäologische Textilfunde*. Neumünster 1982 pp. 163-178.

Thorsteinsson, B.: *Island. Politikens Danmarks Historie*. København 1985.

Thorfinn Karlsefnes Saga. Grønlandske Historiske Mindesmærker. Rosenkilde og Bagger. København 1976.

Vallinheimo, V.: *Das Spinnen in Finnland. Unter besonderer Berücksichtigung schwedischer Tradition*. Helsinki 1956.

Vebæk, C.L.: Inland Farms in the Norse East Settlement. *Meddelelser om Grønland*, Bd. 90/1. København 1943.

Vebæk, C.L.: Vatnahverfi. An inland district of the Eastern Settlement in Greenland. *Man & Society* 17. København 1992 p. 17.

Vebæk, C.L.: Narsaq – a Norse landnáma farm. *Man & Society*, 18. København 1993 p. 18.

Vedeler Nilsen, M.: Gravdrakt i østnorsk middelalder. Et eksempel fra Uvdal. *Collegium Medievale*, vol. 11, 1988 pp. 69-85.

Vedeler Nilsen, M.: Middelalderdrakt i lys av kirkekunst og arkeologisk materiale. *Spor – fortidsnytt fra midt-norge*, Nr. 2, 12. Årgang, 24. Hefte, 1997 pp. 20-22.

Vinner, M.: Vinland the Good – or the lost. B.L. Clausen (ed.), *Viking Voyages to North America*. The Viking Ship Museum in Roskilde, Denmark 1993 pp. 67-76.

Walton, P.: Dyes of the Viking Age: a summary of recent work. *Dyes in History and Archaeology* (formerly Dyes on Historical and Archaeological Textiles) 7, 1988 pp. 14-20.

Walton, P.: *Textiles, Cordage and Raw Fibre from 16-22 Coppergate* (Archaeology of York, 17, The small Finds, fasc. 5). London 1989.

Walton, P., & Taylor, G.: The characterisation of dyes in textiles from archaeological excavations. *Chromatography and Analysis,* 17. 1991 pp. 5-7.

Walton Rogers, P.: Dyes and wools in Norse textiles from Ø 17a. Narsaq – a Norse landnáma farm (C.L. Vebæk). *Man & Society,* 18. København 1993 pp. 56-58.

Walton Rogers, P.: *Textile Production at 16-22 Coppergate.* (The Archaeology of York, 17: The small Finds, fasc. 11). York 1997.

Walton Rogers, P.: The raw materials of the textiles from GUS, with a note on fragments of fleece and animal pelts (identification of animal pelts by H.M. Appleyard). J. Arneborg & H.C. Gulløv (eds.), *Man, Culture and Environment in Ancient Greenland, Report on a Research Programme.* The Danish National Museum & Danish Polar Center, Viborg 1998 pp. 66-73.

Walton Rogers, P.: Textile, Yarn and Fibre from the Biggings. B.E. Crawford & B.B. Smith (eds.) *The Biggings Papa Stour Shetland.* The History and Excavation of a Royal Norwegian Farm. Society of Antiquaries of Scotland and Det Norske Videnskaps-Akademi. Edinburgh 1999 pp. 194-202.

Walton Rogers, P.: The Re-Appearance of the old Roman Loom in Medieval England. P. Walton Rogers, L. Bender Jørgensen & A. Rast-Eicher (eds.), *The Roman Textile Industry and its Influence. A Birthday Tribute to John Peter Wild.* Oxford 2001 pp. 158-171.

Warburg, L.: *Spindebog.* København 1974.

Wild, J.P.: *Textile Manufacture in the Northern Roman Provinces.* Cambridge University Press 1970 pp. 57.

Øye, I.: Textile Equipment and its Working Environment, Bryggen i Bergen. *The Bryggen Papers.* Main Ser. 1988.

Østergård, E.: Rapport vedrørende konserveringen af nordbodragterne i 1921 og 1980. *Bevaringsafdelingens arkiv i Brede.* 1980.

Østergård, E.: Nordbosyninger og -kantninger. *Tidsskriftet Grønland,* Nr. 8-9. Tema: Nordboerne 2. del. Det Grønlandske Selskab. Skjern 1982 pp. 303-313.

Østergård, E.: Nordboernes tøj - dagligdragten i middelalderen. *Textila Tekniker i Nordisk Tradition* (ETNOLORE 6. Skrifter från Etnologiska institutionen vid Uppsala Universitet). Uppsala 1987 pp. 95-104.

Østergård, E.: Textilfragmenterne fra Mammengraven. M. Iversen (red.), *Mammen. Grav, kunst og samfund i vikingetid.* Jysk Arkæologisk Selskabs Skrifter XXVIII. Aarhus Universitetsforlag 1991 pp. 123-138.

Østergård, E.: Tøj til nordbobørn. C. Hinsch (red.), *Lille Margrete og andre børn i middelalderen.* Århus 1997 pp. 12-13.

Østergård, E.: The textiles – a preliminary report. J. Arneborg & H.C. Gulløv (eds.), *Man, Culture and Environment in Ancient Greenland. Report on a Research Programme.* The Danish National Museum & Danish Polar Center. Viborg 1998 pp. 58-65.

Østergård, E.: Greenlandic Vadmel. *NESAT VII,* Edinburgh 2002 (forthcoming).

Østergård, E.: *The Remarkable Clothing of the Medieval Norse Greenlanders,* British Museum Press 2004 (forthcoming).

DRESS- AND TEXTILE NAMES IN THE MIDDLE AGES

Deggim & Möller-Wiering 2001 pp. 163-187.

Falk 1919.

Fentz 1999 pp. 150-171.

Gabra-Sanders 2001 pp. 98-104.

Hägg 1984.

Nockert 1997.

Nørlund 1941 pp. 1-88.

Explanation of Specific Words

Broge. Trousers with feet.

Búalög. An Icelandic Peasant Law.

Dyngja. Icelandic designation for a weaving room, a "women's room".

Fell wool. Wool from dead animals.

Einskefta. Icelandic designation for a tabby (plain) weave.

Eskimo. Inuit. Any of a group of peoples from Greenland, Northern Canada, Alaska, and the
eastern tip of Siberia.

Fjolgeirungr. Icelandic term for garments containing many widths and gussets.

Grágás. The oldest collection of laws in Iceland.

Grene. The Saami designation for striped blankets woven by Saamis.

Guldgubber. Gold-leaf pieces, the size of a fingernail, and impressed.

Guterlov. Collection of laws from the 1200s concerning Gotland.

GUS. Abbreviation for Gården under Sandet (the Farm Beneath the Sand) (64V2-III-555). A farm
in the Western Settlement.

Haberget. Medieval designation for a weave known at that time.

Hairy. International wool classification.

Hairy Medium. International wool classification.

Histogram. Graphical presentation of the number and occurrences of a continuous variable in the
form of rectangles, the height and area of which are decisive.

Hringaváðmál. Icelandic designation for the goose-eye weaving pattern.

Hræll. Icelandic designation for a pin beater made of bone, used – among other things - to push the
weft into place after changing the shed, and to 'play' on the warp threads (to even them out).

Haircloth. Old designation for clothes woven from goat and cattle hair.

Kliggjavevurin. Faroese designation for a warp-weighted loom.

Kljåstein. Norwegian designation for soapstone.

Kobberem. Strips of sealskin.

King's Mirror, The (Kongespejlet). A Norwegian scholarly script from 1200s.

Korkje. Norwegian designation for a product made of lichen for dying textiles.

'Hags' Spinning Wheel'. Norwegian designation for the weights for flywheels in drills.

Måldag. Old Norse designation for any collective bargaining or agreement – oral or written. In a
more restricted sense, a catalogue covering the property (including inventory) of churches and
other holy places, and their rights and duties.

Norse Greenlanders. Description of the Norse settlers who lived in Greenland from the end of the
900s to the middle of the 1400s.

Nøste. Norwegian word for a ball of yarn and for winding wool.

Pile weaving. Cut threads or wool staples – rising above the surface of a fabric like a long-haired
nap – can also be described as shaggy pile weaving.

þriskeft Vaðmál. Weaving in 2/2 twill.

Refil, Refill. Norwegian word for a wallhanging.

Refilsaumur. Icelandic designation for couched work.

Repp. A plain weave, where the number of threads and/or quality of threads decide the type of
repp. In warp repp there are many closely placed warp threads with few, often rough, weft thre-

ads that more or less cover the warp threads. The weaving in this way is given some characteristic grooves in the direction of the weft. In the weft repp the opposite applies: few warp threads with considerable distance between them and a close weft with thin threads that cover the warp, resulting in a grooved weaving in the direction of the warp threads.

Ringvend. Norwegian designation for a twill weaving. Danish: *Goose-eye*. Islandic: *Hringaváðmál*.

Shirting. Cheap and strong plainly woven cotton. Originally the English designation for a shirt of cotton.

Slikisteinn, slikjekjake. Icelandic and Norwegian designation for seam smoothers.

Snáldr. Spindle whorl.

Spinning or twining hooks. Wooden implements for the production of thread (see figs. 17 and 18).

Spjaldvefnadur. Icelandic designation for tablet weaving.

Tigler. Strong pins that, together with string, function as a type of spreader.

Tjald, tjeld. Old Norwegian designation for a tent.

Tvistur. Twist. Icelandic and Norwegian designation for a Panama weave.

Tvujskefta. Weaving in 2/1 twill(?) Hoffmann 1964, p. 351, note 17 and 18.

Ullkambr. Wool combs for combing the long hairs from the undercoat. Used in pairs.

Váð. Cloth.

Váðmál. Cloth measure.

Valkyrie. The feminine creatures in Nordic mythology who decided who should fall in battle.

Vefstaður. Icelandic designation for a warp-weighted loom.

Vinda, snakkur, vindur. Icelandic and Faroese designations for the weft that is found in wedge formed balls of yarn.

Vørpur. Icelandic designation for wooden sticks that are used when setting up the warp.

List of Illustrations

Logo drawings: Irene Skals.

LIST OF OBJECTS

Herjolfsnæs: Single wooden cross and some few garments were transferred to Greenland
National Museum and Archive in Nuuk. The other objects are found at the National Museum in Copenhagen.

Sandnæs: All material excavated before 1982 is to be found at the National Museum in
Copenhagen. Everything excavated after 1982 is at the Greenland National Museum and
Archive in Nuuk.

Most of the textile fragments and other objects from the Landnáma Farm (Ø17a) in Narsaq
are to be found at the Greenland National Museum and Archive in Nuuk.

All finds from GUS (The Farm Beneath the Sand) are at the Greenland National Museum and
Archive in Nuuk.

OBJECT NUMBERS AND OTHER INFORMATION ON FIG. 17

Disc formed whorl (D11164), dia. 58-64, h. 12 mm, weight 92 g. Semi-rounded (D11942), dia. 38 mm, h. 20 mm, weight 35 g. Disc formed (D11164) dia. 37 mm, h. 11 mm, weight 26 g. Semi-rounded (D11985), dia. 30 mm, h. 10 mm, weight 12 g. Cone formed (D11164), dia. 34 mm, h. 12 mm, weight 16 g. Disc formed (D11985), dia. 31-34 mm, h. 6 mm, weight 15 g. Semi-rounded (D11164), dia. 35 mm, h. 19 mm, weight 23 g. Semi-rounded (D11988), dia. 30 mm, h. 17 mm, weight 21 g. Semi-rounded (D11985), dia. 30 mm, h. 27 mm, weight 15 g. Cone formed dia. 40 mm, h. 20 mm, weight 50 g. The half weight (D11164), dia. c. 35 mm, h. 19 mm. The "hags spinning wheel" (D24/1991.51) 455 g. Information concerning the spindles can be found in the text.

OBJECT NUMBERS AND OTHER INFORMATION PERTAINING TO FIG. 24

Two narrow wooden swords (D12809.341 and –344) together with two of whalebone (D5/1992.66 and D12809.343). Four soapstone loom weights from Landnáms Farm (Ø17a). The weight with a double cross (D5/1992.403) weighs 400 g, the weight with two holes (–377) weighs 420 g, the 58 mm high pearl-like weight (–205) weighs 155 g. and the chipped-rim weight (–395) weighs 270 g.

OBJECT NUMBERS TO FIG. 83

A needle case made of bone D11715.348. Scissors D12811.303. A seam smoother of bone D12783.205. Needle case without lid D12404.350. Two grinding stones D12785.202 and –203. Decorated needle of bone D12207. Stiletto D12351.243 and curved weaving pin *(bræll)* of bone D12348.

CATALOGUE

John Lee: Fig. 1, 2, 7, 8, 9, 11, 16, 17, 18, 19, 20, 21, 24, 25, 26, 27, 28, 29, 30, 31, 32, 33, 34, 35, 36, 37, 38, 40, 41, 43, 44, 45, 49, 50, 51, 52, 57, 58, 59, 60, 62, 63, 64, 65, 66, 67, 68, 69, 70, 71, 72, 73, 74, 75, 78, 79, 85, 86, 87, 88, 89, 90, 91, 92, 93, 94.
Peter Danstrøm: Figs. 3, 5, 12, 13, 14, 15, 39, 46, 47, 56.
Niels Erik Jehrbo: Figs. 53, 54, 55, 77, 80, 81, 82, 84, 95
Harry Foster, Canada: Figs. 76.
Birgitte Krag: Figs. 96.
The National Museum: Figs. 42, 49.
Irene Skals: Figs. 4, 6, 10, 22, 23, 48, 60, 61a+b.
Henrik Wichmann: Figs. 83.

NAALISAANEQ

Qallunaatsiaat, tassa vikingit Islandimeersut, ukiut 900-t ingerlaneranni Grøn-
landimik tassamik (Kalaallit Nunaat) kitaata kujataani nunassipput. Taakku naaso-
rissaasuupput pisuut, inussiaateqarlutillu uumasuutillit, pisuungaaramimmi umi-
arsualiortitseriarlutik sunik atortussanik tamanik usilersortarpaat, nunassaminnillu
ujarlertarput nunani inoqanngitsuni, naak aqqutaa ulorianartaraluartoq. Nuunni
isikkivigilluartuni kangimullu ivigarilluartunik narsaamanertalinni illuliorlutillu
oqaluffiliortarput. Nunasisut ilaasa qanoq ateqarneri Islandimiut oqaluttuatoqaan-
nit ilisimavagut.

Siulleq tassaavoq Erik Aappalaartoq, taassuma nunaqarfittaani atserpaa Brattahlid (Qassiarsuk). Kingorna Herjolf Bårdson tikippoq nunaqarfittaanilu atserpaa
Herjolfsnæs – Herjolf-ip nuua – (Ikigaat). Taakku erneri Leif Iluanaarajooq (Leifr
inn heppni Eiríksson) aamma Bjarni Herjólfsson kimmut kujammut umiartortillutik
siullermik nalaatsornikkut Vinland tikissimavaat, kingusinnerusukkullu orneqqillu-
gu. Taamani Vinland-mik taasaat tassaavoq Newfoundland-ip ilaa ateqartoq L'Anse
aux Meadows.

Qallunaatsiaat qanoq ateqarsimaneri ilerrit sanningasortaanni sakkukuinilu
takuneqarsinnaapput. Qallunaatsiaat ilisimaneqanngitsut qanoq ateqarsimaneri
atuarlugit pingaartumillu atisarisimasaat takullugit soorlu uaneralannguamiilersart-
ut. Ukiut vikingeqarfiusut naalerneranni Islandimiut Norgemiullu kristumiunngor-
put. Tamannali sioqqullugu kelterit kristumiut Islandimiissimapput, isumaqartoqar-
porlu oqaluffiit siullersaat ukiut 800-kkut ingerlanneranni sananeqarsimasoq,
qisuillu oqaluffiliornermut atorneqartut qeqertanit Hebriderne-nit aaneqarsimaso-
rineqarput. Nunani Atlantikup avannaanniittuni oqaluffiliortuusarsimapput høvd-
dingit imaluunniit naasorissaasorsuit. Grønlandimi aamma inuit taamaattut oqaluf-
filiortitsisarsimapput. Norgemiu Arnald Grønlandimi biskoppit siullersaraat. Taanna Lund-imi ukioq 1124 biskoppinngortitaavoq, ukiullu marluk qaangiummata
Gardar-imi (Igaliku) biskoppinngorpoq. Taamanikkut Grønland, Island, Norge,
Savalimmiut aamma Qeqertat Orkney Norgemi Nidaros-imi biskoppiuneqarfimmut
atapput, biskoppiuneqarfillu taanna 1152-53-mi pilersinneqarsimavoq.

Kristumiut katuullit taamani nunarsuaq tamaat siammarsimalereerput. Ukiuni
akullerni Islandimi Norgemilu oqaluffinni pequtit kusanartut suliarilluakkat pigine-
qarput, tamakkulu ilarpassui Europap avannaani nunanit pingaartumik Englan-
dimit tikisitaasimapput. Oqaluffinni pequtit atortullu naalagiartitsinermi ileqqunut
naleqqussagaapput oqaatsinullu naalagiarnerni atorneqartartunut assiliartaallutillu
oqaluffimmi kusassaataapput. Inuit ulluinnarni tamakkuninnga misigisaqarneq
ajortut oqaluffimmi kusanartulianik assilianillu qalipaatilinnik isigisaqartarput erin-
nanillu tusarnaartarlutik. Annoraamerngit kusanartorsuit atortunut ilaapput altari-
mi oqaluffimmilu pinnersaatitut palasillu atisaattut.

Ukiuni akullerni mattuttoqarfinni biskoppeqarfinnilu suliffiit assassornermut
tunngasut ingerlanneqarluarput, sorpassuillu kusanartorsuit suliarineqartarsimallu-

tik. Assassortartut Islandimiut Norgemiullu nunanut allanut pikkorissariartortar-
put, nunat allamiullu assassortartui taakkununnga tikeraartarlutik. Atuakkanik kristumiut naalagiarnerini atorneqartartunik kusanartunik assilialersukkanillu naqite-
risarneq Islandimiut immikkut pikkoriffigaat. Qallunaatsiaat Grønlandimiilersut
tamakkuninnga kultureqartunut ilaagamik atuakkanik tamakkuninnga ilisimas-
aqarsimapput. Sanningasuaqqap Nuup Kangerluani Sandnæs-mi (Kilaarsarfik) nas-
saarineqartup ilusaata tamanna ersersippaa. Maaria Iluartoq atuakkamik tigummi-
artoq sanningasuaqqami assiliartaavoq. Assiliaq qaqutigoorluinnarpoq, sanninga-
summi taamaattut assiliartallit ikittuinnaat ilisimaneqarput.

Arnat allapalaarinermut ikaartiterinermullu qanoq pikkoritsigineri Islandimiut
oqaluttuatoqaanni allaaserineqarput. Taakkua ilagaat Skálholt-imi palasip nulia
Margrét hin haga (assassullaqqissoq), taama taaneqartarsimavoq Islandimi qisun-
nik kigartuilluni assilialiortartut akornanni pikkorinnersaanini pissutigalugu. Arnaq
alla ilisimatooq Ingun ukiut 1100-kkut ingerlaneranni Hólar-ip biskoppeqarfiani
ilinniartuunermi nalaani saniatigut oqaasilerinermik ilinniartitsisarlunilu latineritut
atuakkianik kukkunersiuisarlunilu allapalaarillaqqissuusimavoq allanillu assassornermut tunngasunik suliaqartarsimalluni. Qallunaatsiaat arnartaat Grønlandimut
nunasisut arnanit taamaattunit ilinniartinneqartarsimanerat ilimanarsinnaavoq.

Oqaluffik qallunaatsiaat Grønlandimiittut inuunerannut pingaaruteqarluarsima-
voq. Naapiffiusarpoq, ulluinnarnilu ingerlaqqinnissaminnut nukissanik pissarsiffigi-
sarpaat. Nalliuttorsuarni oqaluffik pingaartumik Gardar-imiittoq (Igaliku) aamma
takornartanit ornigarneqartarsimassaaq. Taamatut naapeqatigiinnerni niiveqatigiit-
toqartarsimassaaq nunat allaniillu nutaarsiassat ingerlateqqinneqartarsimassallutik.
Takornartat qallunaatsiaanit savat meqquinit ikaartitikkanik atisalinnit naapin-
neqartarsimassapput, ilaallumi akimarpalaarnerusut tungujortunik, aappalaartu-
nik, kajortunik qernertunillu qalipaatilinnik atisaqartarsimassapput. Qalipaat qarsu-
jasoq issuatsiaanit pissarsiarineqartartoq tunguusaq aappaluaartoq (korkje) piffis-
sami sivikitsumi qalipaatigissaartorsuit akornanni takussaasarsimassaaq.

Qallunaatsiaat naasorissaasut illussaminnik nappaaniariarlutik ikaartiterussuaq
nassatartik inimut ikaartiterisarfimmut (dyngja) iikkamut tunorlermut uingatilaar-
lugu inissittarpaat inip qeqqani ikumatitsiviup qaamarnganit qaammaqquserneqar-
sinnaasumi. Itsarnitsanik assaanermi takuneqarsinnaapput init ikaartiterisarfiit
naqqi init allat natiinit itinerusartut ikaartiterutip portussusaa pissutigalugu. Ikaartiterutit qanoq silitsigisimaneri ikaartiterutit ilamernganik nassaat ersersippaat,
qanorli portutigisimaneri takuneqarsinnaanngilaq.

Uumasuutimik nassarsimasamik savat savaasallu meqqui atisassiornerminni
atortarpaat, ukiulli ingerlanerini aamma ukallit meqqui ikaartitikkaminnut allalers-
uutitut atortalerpaat immikkullu atisassiassatut ikaartitertalerlugit.

Ukiut 1200-kkunni sila nillernerulermat qallunaatsiaat Grønlandimiittut ikaarti-
tereriaasertik Islandimi ilikkarsimasartik allanngortippaat. Ikaartitigaat ussinneru-
lerlutillu oqornerulerput. Annoraamineq Grønlandimi suliarineqartartoq immikku-
ullaarissoq ussissoq pilersinneqarpoq. Annoraamerngit taamaattut amerlanersaanni
ikaartitikkat ammukaartortai ersinneq ajorput.

Ikaartitikkat issusuut meqqualuallit Grønlandimeersut taaneqartartut "vadmel"
ima pitsaatigilerput allaat avammut nioqqutissatut piukkunnarsillutik. Ikaartitereriaaseq ikaartiterivissuarmut naleqqunnerpaaq "2/2 kiper" atorlugu ikaartiteris-
oqartalerpoq. Aammali ikaartitereriaaseq "2/1 kiper" atorneqartarpoq. Ikaartitikkat ammukaartortai taartunik qalipaatillit qaamanerusunik sanimukaartulerlugit
2/1-kiper atorlugu ussissumik ikaartitikkat atisassianngortarput issusuut illua'tun-

gaa taarnerusoq illua'tungaalu qaamanerusoq. Taamanikkullu Grønlandimi nuna-
nilumi allani ammukaartunik igalaasanillu allalersuinerit atorneqalereersimapput.
Aammattaaq misileraallunilu ikartiterisoqartarpoq.

Meqquluanik ikaartiterinermi pilersitaq annoraamineq "vadmel" oqortoq atis-
assiarineqartarpoq Europamiut ilissereriaasaat nutaanerpaat ilaarlugit. Atisat nasal-
lu ninngunerusumik sinaakkuserneqartalerput ikaartiterineq mersornerlu ataatsi-
moortillugit suleriaaseq atorlugu.

Kalaallit Nunaanni atisassianik ikaartiterisartut ima pikkoritsigilersimapput
allaat ikaartiterisartut assigiinngitsunik immikkut pikkoriffigisaminnik suliaqarta-
lersimanerat ilimagineqarsinnaalluni. Arnat ikaartiterillaqqissut meeqqatik kiffatil-
lu piginnaaneqaraangata ilinniartittarsimagunarpaat, imaalluarsinnaavorlu naasorissaasut illorsuisa ilaanni aaqqissuussaasumik ilinniartitsisoqartarsimasoq.

Ukiut akulliit aallartinneranni Tuluit Nunaat Norgillu kitaa imminnut attaveqatigi-
illuarput, tamannalu aamma Grønlandimut sunniuteqarsimavoq. Ikaartitereriaatsit
assigiinngitsut, soorlu "den rødlige diamantkiper" Tuluit Nunaannit aallartif-
feqartoq, "flosvævning" (ikaartitikkat akornisigut meqquluanik ikkussuineq rya-
tæppiliornermut assingusoq) – aamma aappaluaartumik qalipaateqartoq – Irlandi-
mut attuumasssuteqartoq kiisalu mersorneq ikaartiterinerlu atorlugit suleriaaseq
"slynging" qallunaatsiaat atisassiornerminni atortarsimasaat ulloq manna tikillugu
Islandimi qeqertanilu Aranøerne Irlandillu kitaani suli ilisimaneqarput. Ikaartiteri-
nermili sakkut Kalaallit Nunaanni nassaarineqarsimasut amerlanersaat Norgep kitaani atorneqartarsimasunut assingupput.

Qallunaatsiaat Grønlandimiittut Herjolfsnæs-imi (Ikigaat) iliveqarfimmi nassaarin-
eqartunit allaanerusunik aamma atisaqarsimassapput, atisammi tassani nassaat tas-
saapput illerfinnut taarsiullugit aammisitut atukkat. Qaatiguunik oqortunik suli
nassaartoqanngilaq naak Grønland ukiukkut issillunilu anorlertarmat pinngitsoor-
natik oqortunik qaatigooqartarsimanissaat ilimanaraluartoq. Nuup eqqaani kan-
gerluup Amerallap qinnguani Nipaatsup Narsaamarngani qallunaatsiaat naasorissaasut "sioqqat ataanni illorsuannik" nassaarfimmi 1990-imi ukiukkut issip minus
45 gradit angusarpai. Qallunaatsiaat nalaanni ukiut akulliit aallartinneranni sila
taama nillertigisimanngikkaluarpoq, kisianni atisat Herjolfsnæs-imi (Ikigaat) nass-
arineqartut taamanikkut ukiumi qaatigoorissallugit naleqqussimassanngillat. Meq-
quluat ikaartitikkat issup ataani asiusimanngillat ammilli asiusimapput. Kisianni
Grønlandimi uumasuunngitsut meqquinik nassaartoqarpoq, ammillu tamakku eski-
moonik eqqilinnilluunniit Amerika Avannarlermiunik niiveqateqartarnikkut pis-
sarsiarineqartarsimassapput. Ammit oqortuliarineqartartut nassaarineqanngitsut
qularnanngitsumik tassanngaanneersimassapput.

Iliveqarfimmik assaasoq Poul Nørlund isumaqarpoq nasat ikaartitikkat tikkuju-
kuut pamiuusartallit "strudhætte" angutit nasarigaat. Tamannali qularnarpoq.
Ukiuni akulleri arnat assigiinngitsunik ilusilersukkanik nasaqartarput. Assaanermi
annoraaminialuit nassaat ilaat aamma nasartaatit ilaminerissagaat ilimanarpoq,
nasartaammi itsarsuarli arnat atortaraat ilisimaneqarpoq.

Atisat Herjolfsnæsimi (Ikigaat) iliveqarfimmi nassaarineqartut saniatigut Narsap
eqqaani illukumi aamma Nuup Kangerluani illukuni atisat ilamernginik nassa-
artoqarnerisigut annoraamerngit periaatsit assigiinngitsut atorlugit ikaartitikkat
mersoriaatsillu kusanartut nassaarineqarput. Tamakku siunissami atisatut nassa-
arineqarsimasutut ilisimaneqartigilissapput.

Qallunaatsiaat Grønlandimi naasorissaasutut inuuniarnerat ajornarsigaluttuinnaraluartoq atisassiassanik ikaartiterisarneq ingerlatiinnarneqarsimavoq, atisanillu ilissereriaaseq Europamiut atisaannut assingusoq atuinnarneqarsimalluni.

Annoraamerngit qanoq nutaanngitsiginerat paasiniarlugu kulstof 14 atorlugu savat meqqui qanga piiarneqarsimanersut paasineqartarpoq, imaanngilarli meqqui-aasoqaraangat meqqut ingerlaannaq ikaartiterinerni atorneqartarsimasut. Atisat toqusut aammisaattut atorneqarsimasut ilaat nutaanngitsuullutillu ilaartugaapput ilaallu nutarpasillutik. Ikaartitereriaatsit mersorneqarnerisalu ersersippaat inuit taamak suliaqartut nukissaqangaatsiarsimasut. Inuit isumalluutaaruttut imaluunniit qimaasut taamak pitsaassusilinnik atisassiorneq ajorput. Inuuneq pissusissamisut ingerlasoq atisat ersersippaat. Soorlumi Islandimiut 1408-mi Hvalsø-mi (Qaqor-tukulooq) katittunut tikeraartut uteramik qallunaatsiaat Grønlandimiittut pillugit ima oqaluttuarsimasut: "Suut tamarmik ajunngillat".

Subject Index

Place and Name Index

Measurements

The measuring of garments carried out by Else Østergård.
Drawings by Joy Boutrup.

Garment D 10587

Stocking 10613

Hood D 10600

D10587
Front piece and
two-part
middle gusset

10 cm

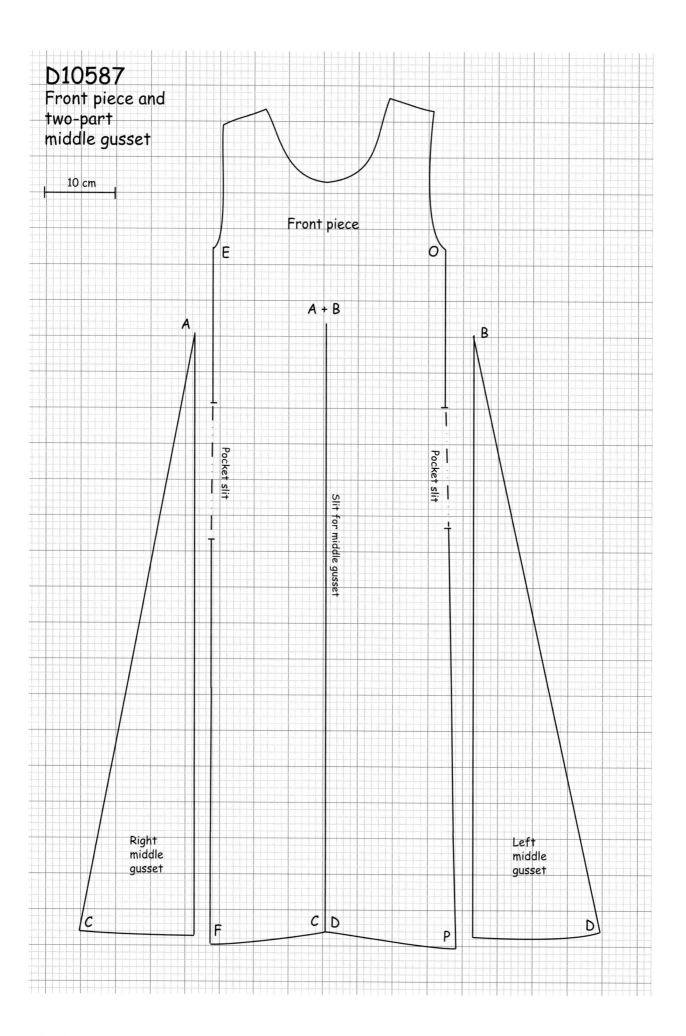

Front piece

E

O

A

A + B

B

Pocket slit

Slit for middle gusset

Pocket slit

Right
middle
gusset

Left
middle
gusset

C

F

C D

P

D

D10587
Back and two-part middle gusset

10 cm

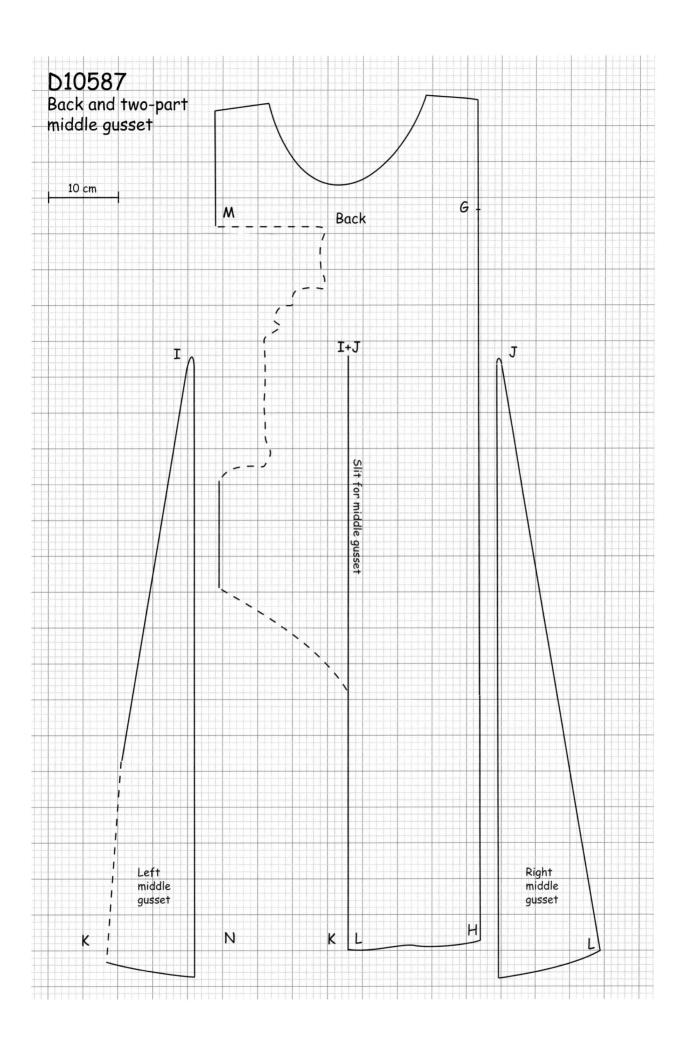

M   Back   G

I   I+J   J

Slit for middle gusset

Left middle gusset   Right middle gusset

K   N   K L   H   L

D10587
Left side-panels

10 cm

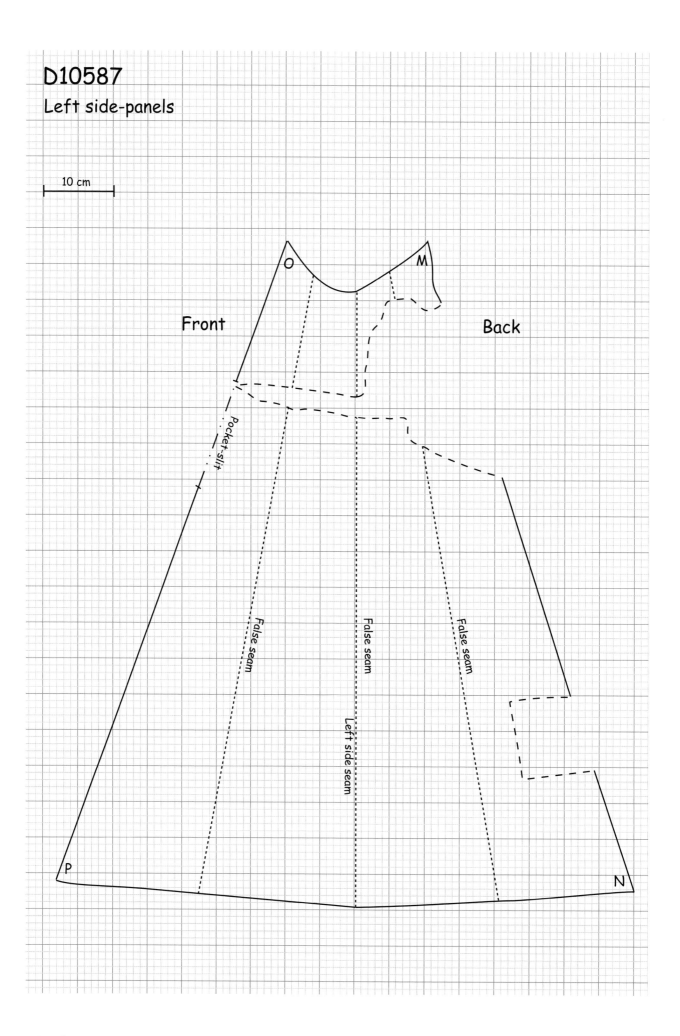

Front

Back

O

M

Pocket-slit

False seam

False seam

False seam

Left side seam

P

N

D10587
Right side-panels

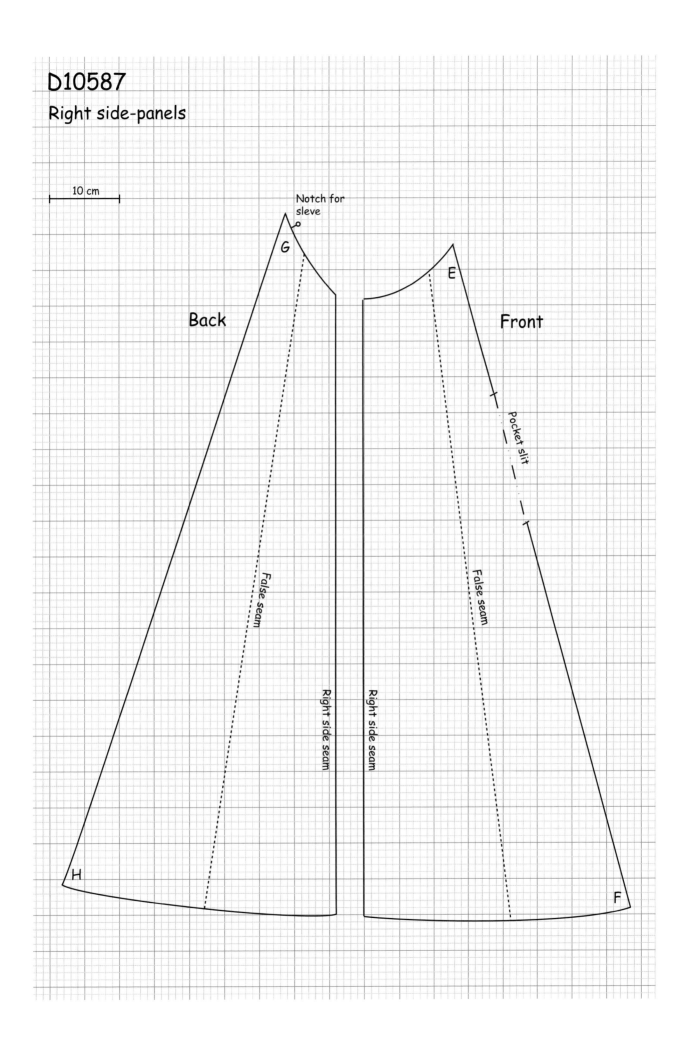

10 cm

Notch for
sleve

G

Back

E

Front

Pocket slit

False seam

False seam

Right side seam

Right side seam

H

F

D10587

Right sleeve

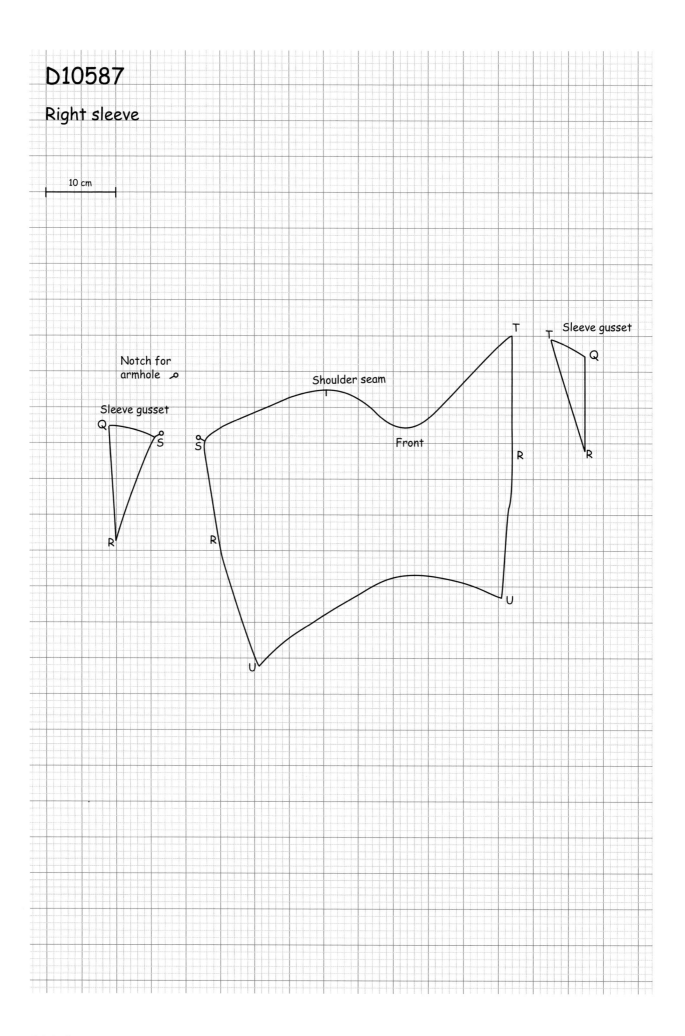

10 cm

Notch for
armhole

Sleeve gusset

Shoulder seam

Sleeve gusset

Front

D10613
Stocking

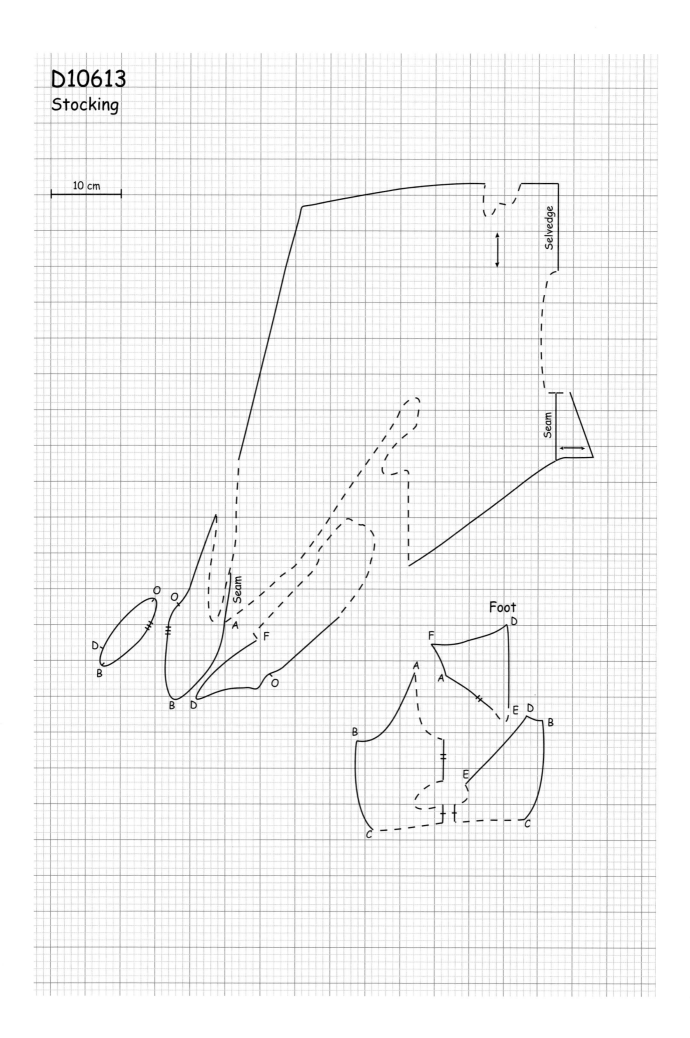

10 cm

Selvedge

Seam

Seam

O

O

A

F

D

B

B

D

O

Foot

F

D

A

A

E

D

B

B

E

C

C

D 10600

Liripipe Hood

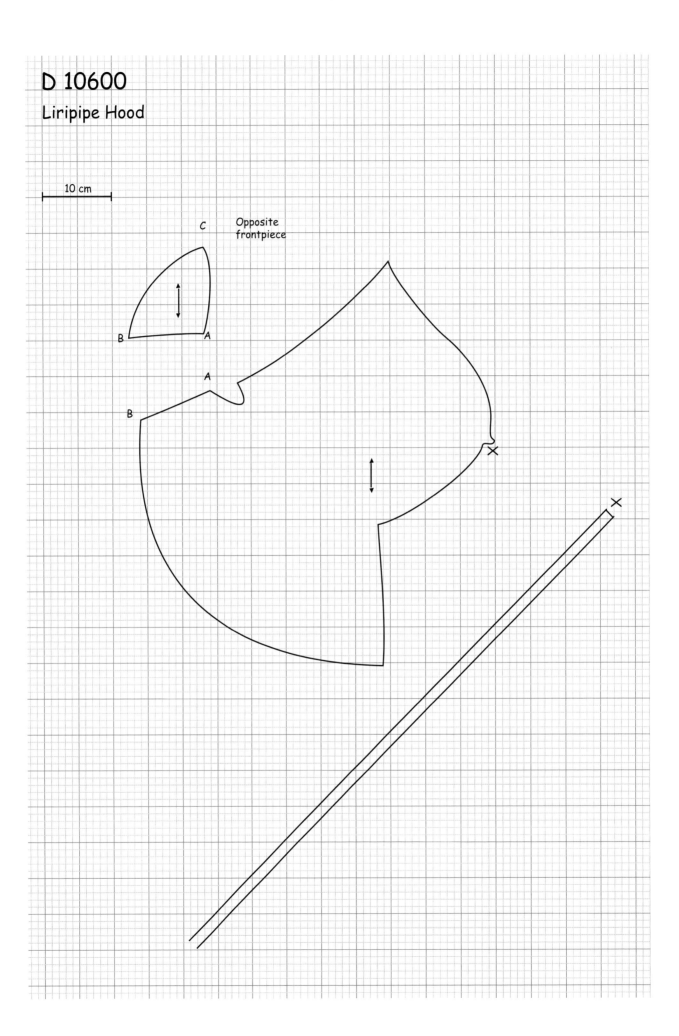

10 cm

C

Opposite
frontpiece

B   A

A

B

×

×